UBICOMM 2018

The Twelfth International Conference on Mobile Ubiquitous Computing, Systems, Services and Technologies

November 18 - 22, 2018

Athens, Greece

UBICOMM 2018 Editors

Claudio de Castro Monteiro, IFTO - Palmas Brazil

Konstantinos Chatzikokolakis, MarineTraffic, United Kingdom

Carlos Henrique Corrêa Tolentino, IFTO - Palmas, Brazil

Printed from e-media with permission by:

Curran Associates, Inc.
57 Morehouse Lane
Red Hook, NY 12571

CURRAN ASSOCIATES INC.
proceedings
.com

Some format issues inherent in the e-media version may also appear in this print version.

Printed by Curran Associates, Inc. (2019)

International Academy, Research, and Industry Association (IARIA)
412 Derby Way
Wilmington, DE 19810

Phone: (408) 893-6407
Fax: (408) 527-6351

petre@iaria.org

Additional copies of this publication are available from:

Curran Associates, Inc.
57 Morehouse Lane
Red Hook, NY 12571 USA
Phone: 845-758-0400
Fax: 845-758-2633
Email: curran@proceedings.com
Web: www.proceedings.com

Table of Contents

UBICOMM 2018

Forward

The Twelfth International Conference on Mobile Ubiquitous Computing, Systems, Services and Technologies (UBICOMM 2018), held between November 18, 2018 and November 22, 2018 in Athens, Greece, continued a series of evens meant to bring together researchers from the academia and practitioners from the industry in order to address fundamentals of ubiquitous systems and the new applications related to them.

The rapid advances in ubiquitous technologies make fruition of more than 35 years of research in distributed computing systems, and more than two decades of mobile computing. The ubiquity vision is becoming a reality. Hardware and software components evolved to deliver functionality under failure-prone environments with limited resources. The advent of web services and the progress on wearable devices, ambient components, user-generated content, mobile communications, and new business models generated new applications and services. The conference makes a bridge between issues with software and hardware challenges through mobile communications.

Advances in web services technologies along with their integration into mobility, online and new business models provide a technical infrastructure that enables the progress of mobile services and applications. These include dynamic and on-demand service, context-aware services, and mobile web services. While driving new business models and new online services, particular techniques must be developed for web service composition, web service-driven system design methodology, creation of web services, and on-demand web services.

As mobile and ubiquitous computing becomes a reality, more formal and informal learning will take pace out of the confines of the traditional classroom. Two trends converge to make this possible; increasingly powerful cell phones and PDAs, and improved access to wireless broadband. At the same time, due to the increasing complexity, modern learners will need tools that operate in an intuitive manner and are flexibly integrated in the surrounding learning environment.

Educational services will become more customized and personalized, and more frequently subjected to changes. Learning and teaching are now becoming less tied to physical locations, co-located members of a group, and co-presence in time. Learning and teaching increasingly take place in fluid combinations of virtual and "real" contexts, and fluid combinations of presence in time, space and participation in community. To the learner full access and abundance in communicative opportunities and information retrieval represents new challenges and affordances. Consequently, the educational challenges are numerous in the intersection of technology development, curriculum development, content development and educational infrastructure.

The conference had the following tracks:

- Ubiquitous software and security
- Ubiquitous networks
- Fundamentals

- Users, applications, and business models
- Ubiquity trends and challenges
- Telematics Applied

We take here the opportunity to warmly thank all the members of the UBICOMM 2018 technical program committee, as well as all the reviewers. The creation of such a high quality conference program would not have been possible without their involvement. We also kindly thank all the authors that dedicated much of their time and effort to contribute to UBICOMM 2018. We truly believe that, thanks to all these efforts, the final conference program consisted of top quality contributions.

We also gratefully thank the members of the UBICOMM 2018 organizing committee for their help in handling the logistics and for their work that made this professional meeting a success.

We hope that UBICOMM 2018 was a successful international forum for the exchange of ideas and results between academia and industry and to promote further progress in the field of mobile ubiquitous computing, systems, services and technologies. We also hope that Athens, Greece, provided a pleasant environment during the conference and everyone saved some time to enjoy the historic charm of the city.

UBICOMM 2018 Chairs

UBICOMM Steering Committee

Sathiamoorthy Manoharan, University of Auckland, New Zealand
Ann Gordon-Ross, University of Florida, USA
Jaime Lloret Mauri, Polytechnic University of Valencia, Spain
Radosveta Sokullu, Ege University, Izmir, Turkey
Michele Ruta, Technical University of Bari, Italy
Wladyslaw Homenda, Warsaw University of Technology, Poland
Hiroaki Higaki, Tokyo Denki University, Japan

UBICOMM Industry/Research Advisory Committee

Miroslav Velev, Aries Design Automation, USA
Cornel Klein, Siemens AG/Corporate Research and Technologies - Münich, Germany
Dmitry Korzun, Petrozavodsk State University, Russia
Carla-Fabiana Chiasserini, Politecnico di Torino, Italy
Volkan Gezer, German Research Center for Artificial Intelligence (DFKI), Germany
Shaohan Hu, IBM Research, USA
Elmano Ramalho Cavalcanti, Federal Institute of Education Science and Technology of Pernambuco, Brazil
Lars Braubach, Complex Software Systems | Bremen City University, Germany
Jon M. Hjelmervik, SINTEF Digital, Norway
Ming Jin, Lawrence Berkeley National Laboratory (LBNL) and UC Berkeley, USA

UBICOMM 2018
Committee

UBICOMM Steering Committee

Sathiamoorthy Manoharan, University of Auckland, New Zealand
Ann Gordon-Ross, University of Florida, USA
Jaime Lloret Mauri, Polytechnic University of Valencia, Spain
Radosveta Sokullu, Ege University, Izmir, Turkey
Michele Ruta, Technical University of Bari, Italy
Wladyslaw Homenda, Warsaw University of Technology, Poland
Hiroaki Higaki, Tokyo Denki University, Japan

UBICOMM Industry/Research Advisory Committee

Miroslav Velev, Aries Design Automation, USA
Cornel Klein, Siemens AG/Corporate Research and Technologies - Münich, Germany
Dmitry Korzun, Petrozavodsk State University, Russia
Carla-Fabiana Chiasserini, Politecnico di Torino, Italy
Volkan Gezer, German Research Center for Artificial Intelligence (DFKI), Germany
Shaohan Hu, IBM Research, USA
Elmano Ramalho Cavalcanti, Federal Institute of Education Science and Technology of Pernambuco, Brazil
Lars Braubach, Complex Software Systems | Bremen City University, Germany
Jon M. Hjelmervik, SINTEF Digital, Norway
Ming Jin, Lawrence Berkeley National Laboratory (LBNL) and UC Berkeley, USA

UBICOMM 2018 Technical Program Committee

Emad Abd-Elrahman, National Telecommunication Institute, Cairo, Egypt
Afrand Agah, West Chester University of Pennsylvania, USA
Taleb Alashkar, Northeastern University, Boston, USA
Mehran Asadi, Lincoln University, USA
Fredrick Awuor, Kisii University, Kenya / Academia Sinica, Taiwan
Liz Bacon, University of Greenwich, UK
Ali Balador, RISE SICS Västerås, Sweden
Matthias Baldauf, FHS St.Gallen, Switzerland
Felipe Becker Nunes, Federal University of Rio Grande do Sul (UFRGS), Brazil
Neil Bergmann, The University of Queensland, Brisbane, Australia
Simon Bergweiler, DFKI GmbH, German Research Center for Artificial Intelligence, Germany
Aurelio Bermúdez, Universidad de Castilla-La Mancha, Spain

Qiang (Nathan) He, Swinburne University of Technology, Australia
Hiroaki Higaki, Tokyo Denki University, Japan
Jon M. Hjelmervik, SINTEF Digital, Norway
Dong Ho Cho, KAIST, Republic of Korea
Wladyslaw Homenda, Warsaw University of Technology, Poland
Tzung-Pei Hong, National University of Kaohsiung, Taiwan
Sun-Yuan Hsieh, National Cheng Kung University, Taiwan
Shaohan Hu, IBM Research, USA
Yu-Chen Hu, Providence University, Taiwan
Edward Y. Hua, Janus Research Group, Inc., USA
Malinka Ivanova, Technical University of Sofia, Bulgaria
Nafaa Jabeur, German University of Technology in Oman (GUtech), Oman
Fang-Zhou Jiang, Data61 | CSIRO & UNSW, Australia
Ming Jin, Lawrence Berkeley National Laboratory (LBNL), USA
Charalampos Kalalas, Centre Tecnològic de Telecomunicacions de Catalunya (CTTC) /
Universitat Politècnica de Catalunya (UPC - BarcelonaTECH), Spain
Mehmet Karakoç, Independent Consultant, Antalya, Turkey
Fazal Wahab Karam, COMSATS Institute of Information Technology, Pakistan
Sye Loong Keoh, University of Glasgow, UK
Cornel Klein, Siemens AG/Corporate Research and Technologies - Münich, Germany
Reinhard Klemm, Avaya, USA
Vitaly Klyuev, University of Aizu, Japan
Sönke Knoch, German Research Center for Artificial Intelligence - DFKI GmbH, Germany
Thomas Kopinski, University of South Westphalia, Germany
Dmitry Korzun, Petrozavodsk State University, Russia
Konstantinos Kotis, University of Piraeus, Greece
Abderrafiaa Koukam, Université de Technologie de Belfort-Montbéliard, France
Jarosław Koźlak, AGH University of Science and Technology, Poland
Michal Kvet, University of Zilina, Slovakia
Soo Kyun Kim, Paichai University, South Korea
Philippe Lalanda, Université Grenoble Alpes, France
Frédéric Le Mouël, INSA Lyon, France
Dongman Lee, KAIST, Korea
Gyu Myoung Lee, Liverpool John Moores University, UK
Pierre Leone, University of Geneva, Switzerland
Wenjuan Li, City University of Hong Kong, Hong Kong
Xiuhua Li, University of British Columbia, Canada
Ruilin Liu, Rutgers - The State University of New Jersey, USA
Xiaodong Liu, Edinburgh Napier University, UK
Jaime Lloret Mauri, Polytechnic University of Valencia, Spain
Aliane Loureiro Krassmann, Federal Institute Farroupilha, Brazil
Derdour Makhlouf, University of Tebessa, Algeria
Elsa Maria Macias Lopez, University of Las Palmas De Gran Canaria, Spain
Elleuchi Manel, National Engineering School of Sfax (ENIS), Tunisia

Ganapathy Mani, Purdue University, USA
Sathiamoorthy Manoharan, University of Auckland, New Zealand
Luis Marcelino, Polytechnic Institute of Leiria / Instituto de Telecomunicações, Portugal
Hector Marco Gisbert, University of the West of Scotland, UK
Francesca Martelli, Institute for Informatics and Telematics (IIT) - Italian National Research Council (CNR), Italy
Sergio Martin, Universidad Nacional de Educación a Distancia, Spain
Nils Masuch, Competence Center Agent Core Technologies | DAI-Lab | TU Berlin, Germany
Natarajan Meghanathan, Jackson State University, USA
Weizhi Meng, Technical University of Denmark, Denmark
Philippe Merle, Inria, France
Daniela Micucci, University of Milano Bicocca, Milan, Italy
Reona Minoda, Basisconsulting Inc., Tokyo, Japan
Moeiz Miraoui, University of Gafsa, Tunisia
Jin Nakazawa, Keio University, Japan
Ryo Nishide, Kobe University, Japan
Andrea Giovanni Nuzzolese, STLab | ISTC-CNR, Rome, Italy
Kouzou Ohara, Aoyama Gakuin University, Japan
Satoru Ohta, Toyama Prefectural University, Japan
Carlos Enrique Palau Salvador, University Polytechnic of Valencia, Spain
Kwangjin Park, Wonkwang University, South Korea
K. K. Pattanaik, ABV-Indian Institute of Information Technology and Management Gwalior, India
Evangelos Pournaras, ETH Zurich, Switzerland
Elmano Ramalho Cavalcanti, Federal Institute of Education Science and Technology of Pernambuco, Brazil
Maurizio Rebaudengo, Politecnico di Torino, Italy
Valderi Reis Quietinho Leithardt, University of Vale do Itajai - Univali, Brazil
Elena Renda, IIT - CNR, Italy
Abdallah Rhattoy, Moulay Ismail University | Higher School of Technology, Morocco
Marcos Rodrigues, Sheffield Hallam University, UK
Michele Ruta, Technical University of Bari, Italy
Prasan Kumar Sahoo, Chang Gung University / Chang Gung Memorial Hospital, Taiwan
Antonio José Sánchez Salmerón, Instituto de Automática e Informática Industrial | Universitat Politècnica de València, Spain
Ana Lucila Sandoval Orozco, Universidad Complutense de Madrid (UCM), Spain
José Santa, University of Murcia, Spain
Floriano Scioscia, Technical University of Bari, Italy
Zary Segall, UMBC, USA
Hamed Shah-Mansouri, University of British Columbia, Vancouver, Canada
Alireza Shahrabi, Glasgow Caledonian University, UK
Vishakha Sharma, Georgetown University, Washington D.C., USA
Shih-Lung Shaw, University of Tennessee, Knoxville, USA
Haichen Shen, University of Washington, USA

Copyright Information

Dummy-Based Anonymization for Voice-Controlled IoT Devices

Katrin Winkler and Erik Buchmann

Hochschule für Telekommunikation Leipzig, Germany
Email: {s111132|buchmann}@hft-leipzig.de

***Abstract*—Voice assistants like Amazon Alexa, Google Assistant or Siri are becoming increasingly popular. Such assistants allow for complex interactions with smart Internet-of-Things (IoT) devices that do not have a traditional user interface, such as monitor and keyboard. However, while voice assistants foster the proliferation of numerous convenient services from smart homes to connected cars, they are problematic from the perspective of user privacy. In many cases, IoT devices are permanently listening for keywords in sensitive areas such as living rooms or bed rooms. Once such a word is recognized, voice samples are sent to the voice-assistant provider into the cloud for further analyses. We explore how the users of IoT devices can anonymize the voice recordings sent to the voice-assistant provider. To this end, we identify categories of information sent to the provider, we describe an anonymization approach based on dummy voice commands, and we describe a prototypical anonymization device based on a Raspberry PI. Our device confirms that it is possible to anonymize some information sent to Alexa with limited inconveniences for the user.**

Keywords–User Privacy; Internet of Things; Voice Control.

I. Introduction

A major success factor for the Internet of Things (IoT) is the availability of reliable, user-friendly voice assistants. Without assistants like Alexa, Siri, Bixby or Cortana, it would be difficult to integrate IoT services with everyday appliances that do not possess graphical user interfaces. Today, a large number of voice-controlled services exist. Such services manage light bulbs, radio and video receivers, heating systems or alarm equipments, provide access to emails, text messages and calendar information, and activate vacuum cleaner robots.

A voice-controlled IoT device consists of one or more microphones, a small voice processor and an Internet link to a cloud service. The microphone records environmental sounds, which are locally processed. When the IoT device recognizes a preconfigured wake-up word ("'Alexa, ...'", "'Ok Google, ...'"), it sends a few seconds of sound records to a cloud service. This cloud service does a more complex voice processing in order to extract spoken commands. Finally, the cloud service sends – depending on the IoT service invoked – control commands and/or information back to the IoT device (cf. Figure 1).

While this approach works very well from a technical point of view, and supports a plethora of useful and user-friendly IoT services, it is problematic from a privacy perspective. Typically, voice assistants are permanently listening, and placed in highly private areas, such as living rooms, kitchens or bed rooms. Experience has shown that the IoT devices react not only on the owner saying the wake word [15]. Thus, the service provider might overhear deeply private conversations.

Many voice-controlled IoT devices integrate third-party services. For example, Amazon Alexa allows to control components of the Philips Hue lighting system. Thus, the processing of voice commands depends on a complex interaction of services from various parties. In consequence, the privacy policies of the service providers are also complex. Data breaches might occur at any place in this service architecture, revealing deeply sensitive personality profiles. Finally, guests of the device's owner might not be aware that their conversation can be transferred to a cloud service for further processing.

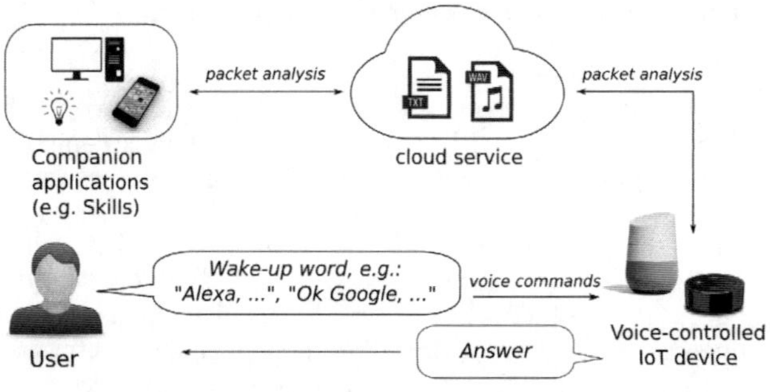

Figure 1. Ecosystem of voice-controlled IoT devices [26]

The purpose of this paper is to fuel the ongoing discussion about options on the user's side to mitigate the impact of voice assistants on privacy. To this end, we explore technical options to anonymize IoT devices using voice assistants from the user perspective. That is, we systematically analyze in which way a user of an IoT device can control or influence voice records sent to an IoT service in order to have certain sensitive information anonymized. As a prominent example, we focus on Amazon Echo. We explicitly leave aside legal questions, and we assume that the IoT service provider handles any user data as described in it's privacy policy. We also do not discuss the responsibility of the users, say, not to use voice assistants in public spaces [40]. In particular, we make the following contributions:

- We identify which private information can be potentially observed by the service provider.
- We analyze options for the user to control the voice records sent to the provider.
- We explore a dummy-based approach to anonymize the information sent to the provider.
- Finally, we describe what we have learned from implementing a prototypical anonymization device.

Our anonymization device demonstrates that it is possible to anonymize a part of the information sent to Amazon Echo, with little inconvenience for the user. We point out that some information cannot be anonymized without making the service useless. However, it is challenging to infer what the service provider might learn from the voice records sent to the cloud.

The rest of the paper is structured as follows. Section II reviews related work. Sections III and IV introduce Amazon Alexa and Amazon Echo. Section V outlines options to anonymize voice assistants. Section VI describes our anonymization device. The paper concludes with Section VII.

II. Related Work

In this section, we review related work on (a) voice assistants for IoT services, (b) data privacy in IoT and (c) dummy-based anonymization techniques.

A. Voice Assistants

The IoT is evolving rapidly. The worldwide IoT market is expected grow to $1.1 trillion in 2021 with a compound annual growth rate of 14.4% [16]. Similarly, the worldwide market for virtual personal assistant-enabled wireless speakers will reach $2.1 billion by 2020 [12]. Currently, the U.S. market is dominated by Amazon Echo with 73% and Google Home with 27% [13]. Thus, voice assistants like Amazon Echo, Google Home or Apple HomePod are popular devices for users to control their smart home appliances, adjust thermostats, activate home security systems, purchase items online, initiate phone calls, and many other tasks in their daily life. Voice assistants and smart speakers exist in many different types with varying level of capabilities. Some of them can be integrated into party products, such as connected cars [46]. For example, BMW customers can enable different vehicle functions via voice assistants like Google Home or Amazon Alexa since November 2017 [7]. Other examples are smart fridges like Samsung Family Hub 3.0, which communicates with its users via Bixby [14]. There are even voice-controlled toys for children (Mattels Hello Barbie [39]) or toilets with integrated voice assistants [9].

B. Privacy in the Internet of Things

As soon as appliances interact with their users in a natural way, such as per voice, humans tend to see them as partners instead of machines [30]. Thus, users are tempted to assign attributes regarding morale, attitude or responsibility to voice assistants [31]. This is problematic, as voice assistants often have access to data with a high impact on privacy and security [23]. This allows for numerous new threats and attacker models [27]. A large share of cell phone users face similar privacy risks as the users of voice-controlled IoT devices. However, in direct comparison cell phone users adjust their system settings in much more restrictive way [24] than users of voice-controlled IoT devices.

Since voice assistants typically do not distinguish different speakers – a feature that is helpful for anonymization – adversaries in microphone range might issue commands to the voice assistant. This has been already demonstrated in multiple ways [34], e.g., via television, via ultrasonic frequencies that are too high for the human ear to hear, or through closed windows. Furthermore, manipulated voice commands can lead to financial losses because the user's payment data is often accessed directly [34]. Currently, the best approach for consumer privacy is to unplug any IoT device when not in use. In addition, the user should frequently review the voice assistants history for unauthorized actions [34]. Typically, this history is accessible via the Web page of the service provider.

C. Anonymization Techniques

Anonymization means to protect the privacy of an individual regarding certain features, e.g., the presence of the individual in a data set, if the individual shares similar characteristics with a control group or if the individual can be assigned with certain attributes. There is a broad variety of anonymization approaches available (see [21] for an overview). State of the art is Differential Privacy [29], which ensures that the presence or absence of an individual record in a database has a very small impact on the result of a specific analysis. However, such privacy measures need data from multiple users as an input for the anonymization. From the perspective of a single user who wants to protect himself against a curious service provider, such approaches cannot be applied.

Dummy-based annonymization [35][36] has been extensively studied in the context of location based systems. Dummy-based anonymization means that a user does not only send its real position to a location-based system, but a number of made-up positions as well. From the set of answers provided by the system, the user considers only information regarding his real position. This approach has numerous benefits: (i) Anonymity can be obtained without the help of a trusted third party or other users. (ii) Each user can decide individually which properties to be hidden in the dummy requests. (iii) Finally, the approach scales linearly with the number of dummies sent. However, it is difficult to create a realistic set of dummies where the real information cannot be singled out by statistical means or other properties [32][33]. Dummy-based anonymization has been already studied in other contexts, e.g., social networks [25] or database tables [22].

III. Amazon Alexa

Without loss of generality, we will use Amazon Alexa as a prominent example of a voice assistant. Amazon operates the cloud service that extracts commands from voice records and provides an adequate reaction to this commands. Devices that allow to access Alexa are offered either by Amazon (e.g. Echo Family, Dash Wand, Fire Tablet, Fire TV), or by third-party-providers that provide devices based on a recent Android, iOS or Windows operating system. Other assistants operate in a similar way, e.g., Siri (Apple), Bixby (Samsung) or Cortana (Microsoft).

In this section, we will briefly describe Alexa's IT ecosystem. As Figure 2 shows, the cloud service plays the most prominent role. It allows Alexa to continually adapt to the speech patterns, vocabulary and personal preferences of the users [10]. Furthermore, it allows Alexa to integrate new functionality and to connect to other services by using the Alexa Skills Kit (ASK) and the Alexa Voice Service (AVS).

A. Alexa Skills Kit (ASK)

The Alexa Skills Kit is a collection of APIs, tools, documentations and source code samples. Initially, ASK has been designed for internal Amazon developers to build new features of Alexa's Automatic Speech Recognition (ASR) and Natural Language Understanding (NLU) systems. Right now, ASK is available for any third-party developer [37], and more than 25,000 skills have been built and deployed [1].

Figure 3 shows how ASK processes a request. In a first step, the IoT device waits the wake-up word from the user

Figure 2. The Alexa Ecosystem [19]

Figure 3. Request and response with the Alexa Skills Kit [19]

and sends a voice recording to the Amazon cloud service that provides Alexa. Alexa identifies the skill and recognizes the user's intent via ASR and NLU. This intent is sent to the service identified by the skill. This service responds to the intent. Depending on the user's device, the response can be a textual message, a verbal answer through Alexa's Text-to-Speech Synthesis (Figure 4) or a graphical response [19]. Any information flow is encrypted.

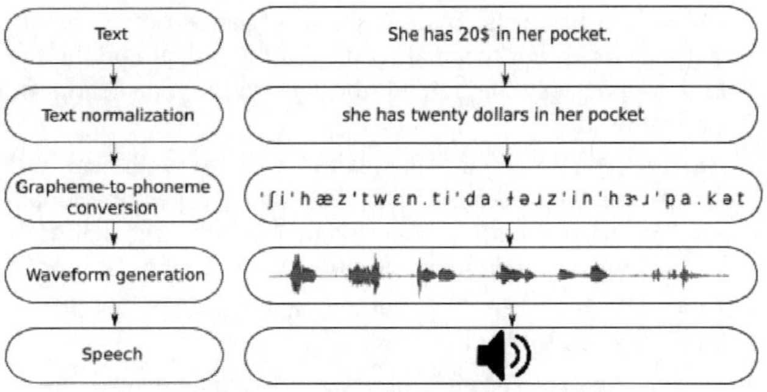

Figure 4. Text-to-Speech Synthesis [4]

B. Alexa Voice Service (AVS)

The Alexa Voice Service allows to connect Alexa skills with third-party services and -products. Similarly to ASK, the AVS consists of a set of development tools and resources, e.g., technical documentation and development kits. While ASK is intended to build skills that reside in the Amazon cloud, AVS allows third-party vendors of IoT devices to connect their products to Alexa [2]. Typical examples of such devices are mobile phones, connected cars and smart home appliances.

C. Amazon Web Service (AWS) Lambda

Skill developers are able to use other services from the Amazon cloud [6]. A prominent example is AWS Lambda, a scalable, cloud-based data processing service that executes code in the backend, based on customer-specified events. Such events could be calendar entries, conditions in a stream database, push-services from external sources on the Internet, etc. To use AWS Lamda with Alexa, a developer creates an Alexa skill, uploads it to AWS Lambda and connects it with an event source that triggers its execution. Thus, Alexa is open to big-data management.

IV. Amazon Echo

One of the most prominent IoT devices accessing Alexa is the Amazon Echo and its smaller version, the Echo Dot. These devices are hands-free, voice-controlled speakers which connect to the Alexa Voice Service to play music, control smart home devices, make phone calls, etc. In this section, we will describe the hardware and the user interface of the Echo Dot, together with the respective privacy policy.

A. Hardware and User Interface

Figures 5 and 6 show the structure and internals of an Echo Dot. It comes with seven far-field microphones with beamforming technology and noise cancellation. Thus, verbal commands can be perceived from every direction in a noisy environment [10]. When the Dot recognizes the wake-up word, the light ring turns blue. This allows the user to see when a sound recording is sent into the Amazon cloud. The light also indicates the direction of the voice received. The mute button on the upper side allows to deactivate the microphones, indicated by a red light. Two other buttons adjust the speaker volume.

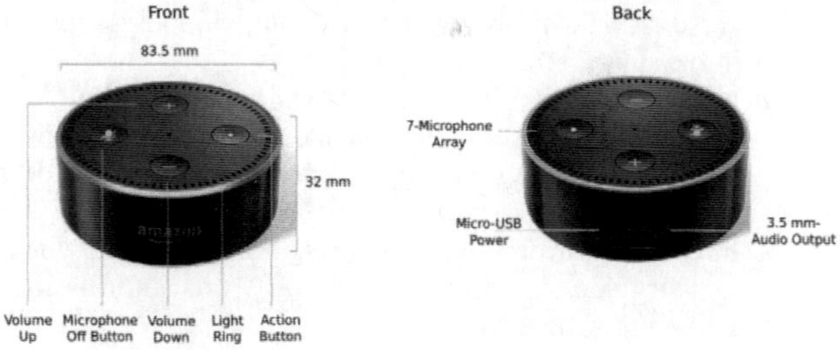

Figure 5. Basic structure of the Amazon Echo Dot [30]

To use the Dot, each user must create an Amazon account. This account is used to configure the Dot, either via the Alexa app or website [3]. The configuration includes network settings, the wake-up word and individual preferences, such as alarms, music, shopping lists and active skills. If the user registers multiple Dots, Alexa always responds from the closest Dot using Echo Spatial Perception (ESP) [20]. Many configuration options can be accessed via voice interface. For example, the default wake-up word can be modified by saying "Alexa, change the wake-up word to Echo". Similarly, the user can instruct Alexa to install a new skill by using the voice command "Alexa, activate <skill name>". Few information is stored locally at the Dot. In particular, this is the network configuration, and preferences, such as the volume and the wake-up word. Any other information is sent to and stored at

Figure 6. Teardown of the Echo Dot [5]

the Amazon cloud and linked with the user's personal Amazon account. This is important, as the voice recordings transport much personal information (cf. Section V).

B. Alexa's Privacy Policy

To register an account, the user must consent to Amazon's privacy policy (In our case, it is the privacy policy of Amazon Europe S.a.r.l., Luxembourg and its subsidiaries). Thus, Amazon does not provide a separate privacy policy for Alexa services that is different from the policy of other Amazon services. Amazon provides a detailed list of personal data, as follows:

- Any information that is sent directly to Amazon, e.g., personal data from the user account, shipping and order information, etc.
- Any information that is obtained automatically when interacting with one of the Amazon services, e.g., browser type, operating systems, time zones or location data of the device used.
- Information from other sources. For example, when a logistics service confirms a delivery, this information is sent back to Amazon.

Furthermore, Amazon's privacy policy contains a section that explains the stored information with its purposes in detail. This section states that modes of usage, voice recordings and interactions from the past are essential to let Alexa provide meaningful recommendations and reasonable answers. This means that Amazon will not delete any information on its own accord, unless the user issues a request for deletion based on the EU-General Data Protection Regulation or decides to unregister and delete the personal Amazon account. Furthermore, the user might use the Amazon website to delete particular information, e.g., certain voice recordings or orders from the online shop that might result in misleading recommendations. In total, the user has to agree to the following documents [18]:

- Alexa Terms of Use
- Amazon Conditions of Use
- Amazon Privacy Notice
- Cookies & Internet advertising
- Amazon Prime Terms & Conditions
- Amazon Music Terms of Use
- Kindle Store Terms of Use
- Audible Service Conditions of Use
- Amazon Device Terms of Use

V. PRIVACY AND VOICE CONTROL

In this section, we identify categories of private information a voice assistant might obtain or infer. Furthermore, we explore alternatives to anonymize such classes of information for voice-controlled IoT devices.

A. Categories of Private Information

To the best of our knowledge, there is no survey about the impact of voice assistants on the privacy of its users. However, we can learn from the ongoing discussion on the privacy aspects of smart cellphones [43]. Furthermore, some details can be inferred from the technical setup of voice assistants. We have identified three categories of information that can be obtained from the service provider in the cloud-based backend of a voice assistant:

1. Application Data: This category of data refers to any information a skill must access to perform a certain service. Application data can be information stored in a database at the site of the service provider. It can be also external information fetched via HTTP-request over the Internet. For cell phones, this kind of information corresponds to *content data* [45].

Example: Assume a user wants to manage calendar entries via commands like "'Alexa, when is my next event?"' or "'Alexa, add an event to my calendar"'. In this case, the service provider needs access to the user's personal calendar. Additional information, such as event priorities or alert times, emphasize the significance of calendar entries.

Privacy Issues: The impact of application data on the privacy of the user depends heavily on the service and the context the service is used. With our example, it makes a difference if the calendar is used personally to manage birthdays of friends, if it is used in a business environment to organize office meetings, or if it is used in a medical facility to fix patient appointments in an aseptic way. In general, the service provider learns from application data:

- The content of an interaction with the voice-controlled device, i.e., user interests, attitudes and personal data.
- The modes of use of a certain service, e.g., habits like asking for a certain stock price every day in the morning.

If the service is offered by an external provider, this information also goes to third parties.

If the voice assistant is used by individual persons, application data is a promising subject for anonymization techniques that aim for*hiding personal interests, attitudes and modes of use*. However, as application data are inherently needed to provide a service, there is a conflict between anonymity and user experience.

2. Technical Data: Data from this category is necessary to provide the service or stem from the domain of the service provider. It is needed or generated automatically when a service is executed and messages flow between the IoT device and the service provider. With cellphones, this is known as *call detail record* [45].

Example: With our personal calendar, the voice-assistant provider needs the user login to identify the personal calendar.

If the calendar is provided by third parties, say, on a Microsoft Exchange server, external login data is also needed. Furthermore, the service provider learns meta-data, such as date and time of use, IP addresses, time-zones etc.

Privacy Issues: Technical data allow to infer personal information that are related to the interaction with the voice assistant. For example, times of use correspond to the daily routine of the users. Furthermore, the IP address can be a user pseudonym and reveals the location of the user. However, any technical information is routed through the cloud of the voice-assistant provider. Thus, if the voice assistant accesses a service provided by a third party, the external provider might only "‘see"' that a server from the cloud of the voice-assistant provider is communicating – the IP address or the time zone of the user's IoT device can be hidden by network address translation.

Privacy-Enhancing Technologies, such as the TOR onion routing [28], I2P [44] or the JonDo Web Proxy [42] focus on technical data. Since voice-controlled IoT devices are required to send login information to the service provider anyway, it does not make sense to apply such technologies. However, technical data can be considered for anonymization techniques that *hide usage patterns, habits or activity periods*.

3. Adjunct Data: This category contains information that is neither needed to provide the service nor to communicate with the IoT device, but it is interwoven with other data. It corresponds to issues similar to location tracking [41] or activity recognition [38] of modern cellphones.

Example: The voice recordings sent to the service provider for speech recognition do not only transfer commands to the voice assistant. Instead, features like linguistic stress patterns, regional accents, the number of different speakers using the voice assistant or environmental sounds are part of the recording. Such information is independent from the service used, i.e., it is not bound to our ongoing example of using a personal calendar.

Privacy Issues: It is straightforward to infer sensible personal details from adjunct data. For example, a provider might be able to learn from environmental noises (perhaps accompanied by commands to the voice assistant) that the user performs a certain action, e.g., watching TV or making breakfast.

Information from this class *can be removed without loss of user experience* from the data sent to the service provider. However, this information comes as a byproduct of the sensory equipment or the information technology used to provide the service. Thus, it might be prohibitively expensive in terms of computational costs to filter adjunct data. Basically, this means to perform speech recognition locally instead of using a powerful cloud service. This calls for other options to anonymize voice assistants.

B. Options to Anonymize Voice-Controlled IoT Devices

From the perspective of the individual user, only a few options exist to anonymize a voice-controlled IoT device to some extent without abandoning the use of the device and without sacrificing user experience to a large extent. Firstly, recall that the data flow to and from the IoT device is encrypted. Thus, it is not an option to manipulate the data packets. Secondly, the IoT device is bound to a service provider hosting (a) the voice assistant and (b) the service infrastructure that allows to access a huge number of convenient services, such as calendar management, radio stations, etc. As a result, in many cases it is not an option to simply switch to a more privacy-friendly voice-assistant provider (if there were any). Third, for technical reasons it is not an option to do all voice processing locally at the IoT device and only send commands to the service provider that have been stripped from adjunct data.

However, is is possible to use a variant of the dummy-based anonymization (cf. Section II), i.e., to control what the IoT device is allowed to hear and to hide sensitive personal information in a number of dummy requests that are sent through the IoT device to the voice assistant.

Example: Assume a user wants to anonymize its personal calendar by using dummy requests. In the first step, the user identifies the information to be obscured. With our example, assume the user wants to conceal (i) which are the most sensitive calendar entries, (ii) how many people use the voice assistant and (iii) what are the typical daily activity times. For this purpose, the user asks a number of friends to provide voice samples, such as "‘Alexa, when is my next event?"', "‘Alexa, add an event to my calendar."', "‘Alexa, delete an event from my calendar"' together with times and dates. A reasonable set of dummy requests would order Alexa to read, add and remove calendar entries at different times, by different voices, without having an impact on the correctness of the service. Similar dummy requests can be defined for other services, say, playing radio stations. We see three different options to realize such an anonymization:

External anonymization via speakers: This is the most simple option. An anonymization device with a speaker, e.g., a Raspberry Pi, is placed nearby the IoT device. Whenever the user is in the room, he or she uses the IoT device normally. When the user leaves the room, the anonymization device starts to play voice samples from an internal database containing dummy requests through its speaker to the IoT device. Our anonymization device implements this approach (cf. Section VI).

User Experience: Since the user does not have to manipulate the IoT device, this approach can be easily implemented. Furthermore, as long as the dummy requests are played only as long as the user is not in the room, user experience is high.

Anonymity: Assuming a good set of dummy requests for anonymization, and assuming further that the voice-assistant provider does the speech recognition automatically, it is possible to obscure private application data and adjunct data among dummy requests. Furthermore, it is possible to hide habits and activity times. However, a suspicious voice-assistant provider may sort out dummy requests that follow a different data distribution than the real requests, that are heard always from the same direction at the same sound volume or that are issued with the same accentuation. Furthermore, this approach assumes that the IoT device is listening only when the user deliberately says the wake-up word.

External anonymization via relay: A second option is to disassemble the IoT device and to connect the built-in microphones and the speaker to a relay that is controlled by the anonymization device. Thus, the anonymization device can protect against cases where the voice assistent is activated without intention of the user. Furthermore, the input and the output of the IoT device can be muted at any time with certainty. Thus, it is possible to, say, let the IoT device read dummy calendar entries or play dummy radio stations while the user is in the room.

User Experience: In comparison to the first variant, the implementation efforts of this approach are significantly increased. Because the input and the output of the IoT device can be externally controlled, the user experience is slightly higher.

Anonymity: The fact, that it is possible to mute the output while the user is in the room, allows for more options to issue dummy commands to the voice assistant. Ensuring that the IoT device is only listening when allowed increases the privacy of the user. This means that the anonymization device also needs to listen to the wake-up word. However, this can be realized locally, without having to send voice recordings into the cloud [17].

Re-wiring the IoT device: From the perspective of the IoT device, the most impacting approach is to re-wire the speakers and microphones directly to the anonymization device. Thus, any input or output is supervised. Verbal commands to the voice assistant are synthesized at the anonymization device and sent directly, without using speakers and microphones, to the IoT device. A similar approach would be to install the voice-assistant application on a standard Windows PC and to re-route the audio-drivers to a program that handles anonymization.

User Experience: In comparison to the other approaches, it is possible to control the input and output of the IoT device in a fine-grained way. However, the implementation effort of this variant is high. It requires expert knowledge to set up an anonymization device that sends synthesized voice commands to the voice assistant without loss of user experience.

Anonymity: This approach ensures that no information is sent unfiltered to the voice-assistant provider. It would be possible even to let the anonymization device synthesize verbal requests from the user and a database of dummy commands with the same artificial voice, i.e., the provider does not have an option to distinguish various speakers according to certain verbal characteristics. However, as with the other approaches, a fraction of the requests sent is still the real interest of the user. Thus, it remains challenging to create a set of dummy requests with exactly the same statistical characteristics as the real requests.

VI. Dummmy Requests for the Echo Dot

In this section, we describe our prototypical anonymization device. It is based on a Raspberry Pi-based that sends dummy requests via speaker to Alexa. Furthermore, we discuss what we have learned during its implementation.

To create a setting that is easily reproducible, we have decided to play various radio stations. In this setting, we have to consider only two voice commands: "‘Alexa, play <radio station> on Tune In"’ and "‘Alexa, stop"’. The skill "‘Tune in"’ provides 41 different genres of music. Every genre is associated with multiple radio stations. A typical voice command is "‘Alexa, play Radio Bob on Tune In"’. Our objective is to anonymize our (a) taste for music and our (b) activity times. Thus, we focus on anonymizing information from our category "‘Application Data"’.

A. Hardware Setup

Our anonymization device is shown in Figure 7. It consists of three components:

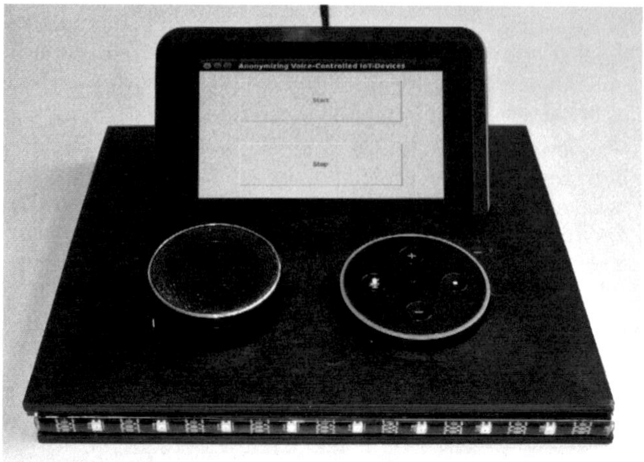

Figure 7. Our anonymization device

1) *Amazon Echo Dot 2nd generation:* This is the lower right device in Figure 7. The Echo hardware complement includes a 64-bit quad-core MEDIATEK ARM MT8163V 1636-KBCAH CCMKYRHS processor, 512 MB of LPDDR3 SDRAM and 4GB of storage space. It connects to the Internet via WiFi 802.11a/b/g/n.
2) *Raspberry Pi 3 Model B Rev 1.2 with 7 inch touch display:* This is the upper device in Figure 7. The Raspberrys operating systems is Raspbian GNU/Linux 8 (Jessie). For this project, we've used a Raspberry Pi 3 Model B, which uses a Broadcom BCM2837 SoC with a 1.2 GHz 64-bit quad-core ARM Cortex-A53 processor, 1 GB of LPDDR2-SDRAM and can be connected to the WiFi through 802.11a/b/g/n.
3) *Nubwo Wireless Speaker:* This is the device in the lower left position in Figure 7. This is a wireless bluetooth speaker with integrated microphone. It is compatible with different devices, such as tablets, laptops or smartphones.

B. Software Setup

The Raspbian Linux already comes with all the tools needed to play dummy commands that follow a certain distribution: With the scripting language Python and its toolkits, we have realized a graphical user interface to control the order and the distribution of the dummy voice commands. Python allows to start linux commands to play voice samples in various audio file formats that have been recorded in advance and stored on the local SD card of the Raspberry Pi. Alternatively, we have tested Google's text-to-speech synthesis "‘Simple Google TTS"’ to generate voice commands from text, that is, without having to record voice samples beforehand. This synthesis can be accessed via Python library "‘gTTS"’.

C. Dummy-based Anonymization

Figure 8 shows our process to generate dummy commands. We have written a Python script for the Raspberry Pi, which plays dummy voice commands. When the user is about to leave the room, he starts this script via command line or a graphical user interface. Subsequently, the script randomly selects a radio station, plays "‘Alexa, play <radio station> on Tune In"’ via speaker to the Dot, waits a random time interval ranging from

10 seconds to 60 minutes, and plays "'Alexa, stop"'. This procedure recurs, until it is terminated by the user.

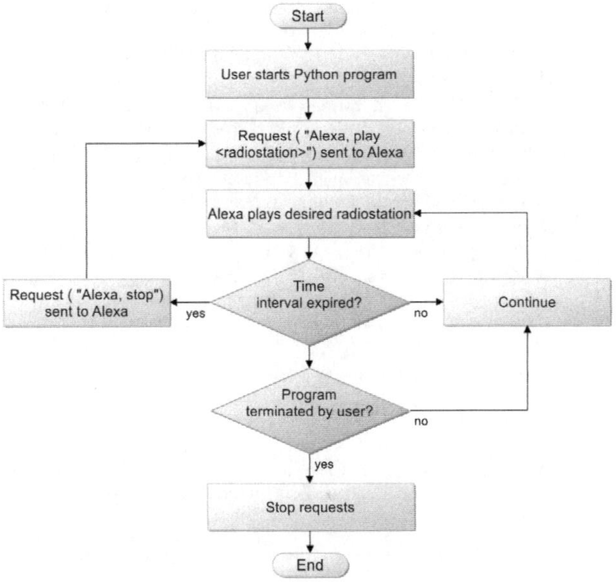

Figure 8. Flowchart of the dummy-based anonymization

Switching radio stations after a few seconds corresponds to a user browsing for a station that fits to his mood at the moment. Switching stations randomly with a frequency between some seconds and 60 minutes corresponds to a user having heard songs he dislikes. After 60 minutes, the user might have lost interest in listening to the station. We assume, that this procedure creates realistic dummy commands, which cannot be distinguished from user commands with the algorithms currently used by the service provider.

D. Discussion

We have implemented a scenario that is understandable yet realistic. By anonymizing music taste and activity times when listening radio stations via Amazon's Echo Dot, we have made a number of observations.

It was surprisingly simple to issue dummy voice commands with a certain frequency and distribution by using off-the-shelf hardware and software components. With some experience in Linux, it did not took long to realize our anonymization device. It was not necessary to open the IoT device. Except for the touch-sensitive display used for debugging purposes, we have spent less than 50 EUR for hardware components. However, it needs a profound technical understanding to configure the generation of dummies according to a person's individual privacy requirements.

Alexa's Automatic Speech Recognition technology works very well, even with voice commands that are synthesized from text. For our tests, we have used Simple Google TTS, which is an online service of Google. However, we assume that offline text-to-speech engines like Cepstral [8] or eSpeak [11] would be applicable as well. This way, no external party might learn which dummy commands are synthesized and sent to Alexa.

We have observed that Amazon's recommendations for radio stations follow our dummy commands. This indicates that our anonymization approach is working as intended at the moment. On the other hand, a voice assistant that is based on garbled recommendations might reduce the user experience. Furthermore, it is impossible for the user to find out what the service provider learns indeed. If the provider implements machine-learning algorithms that distinguish different voices, only the rewiring approach from Section V might be able to provide some degree of privacy. Amazon says that voice samples are used to improve speech recognition. However, we did not observe that the the real user's voice was recognized less accurately due to learning from a synthesized voice.

In conclusion, at this moment, even a simple dummy-based anonymization approach allows for some more privacy regarding application data, than the voice-assistant provider is offering the user. We have focused on the user's activity times and his taste for music. In the same way, many other aspects and many other services could be anonymized. For example, it would be possible to anonymize the places of interest that are sent to a service for local weather reports. Similarly, events and holidays could be anonymized with calendar services. However, some services do not allow for this approach. For example, it would not make sense to turn on and off smart home components, such as cleaner robots, or to anonymize the wake-up alarm. Finally, it is impossible for the user to find out or influence which algorithms are implemented by the provider. In the worst case, the provider might implement machine learning to distinguish different personality profiles from voices and statistical properties of the commands, without telling in the privacy policy. Thus, it is impossible to give anonymity guarantees like differential privacy [29].

VII. Conclusion

Currently, voice assistants are integrated into a plethora of different IoT devices and used every day in numerous situations. Voice assistants on IoT devices make users' life more comfortable. On the other hand, such assistants send voice samples into the cloud, which contain private information from private places. Even more, the voice samples do not only transport the verbal commands required, but also adjunct information, such as verbal stress patterns or background noises indicating certain activities. Thus, the service provider is in a position to create deeply impacting personality profiles.

We have identified three categories of information that can be observed by the service provider. Furthermore, we have analyzed from the user perspective at which points it is possible to realize anonymization. We have described a dummy-based anonymization approach, and we have explored it's properties by implementing a prototypical anonymization device based on a Raspberry Pi that feeds dummy commands to an Amazon Echo Dot. Our device confirms that it is possible to anonymize a part of the information sent to Alexa with limited inconvenience for the user.

References

[1] Alexa Skills Kit. https://developer.amazon.com/de/alexa-skills-kit, retrieved: Aug. 2018.

[2] Alexa Voice Service. https://developer.amazon.com/de/alexa-voice-service, retrieved: Aug. 2018.

[3] Amazon Alexa. https://alexa.amazon.com, retrieved: Aug. 2018.

[4] Amazon Alexa Technologies, AWS Stockholm Summit 2017. https://de.slideshare.net/AmazonWebServices/amazon-alexa-technologies, retrieved: Aug. 2018.

[5] Amazon Echo Dot Teardown. https://de.ifixit.com/Teardown/Amazon+Echo+Dot+Teardown/61304, retrieved: Aug. 2018.

[6] AWS Lambda. https://aws.amazon.com/de/lambda/features/, retrieved: Aug. 2018.

[7] BMW is now integrated with the Google Assistant. http://www.bmwblog.com/2017/11/07/bmw-now-integrated-google-assistant/, retrieved: Aug. 2018.

[8] Cepstral. https://www.cepstral.com, retrieved: Aug. 2018.

[9] CES 2018: voice-controlled showers, non-compliant robots and smart toilets. https://www.theguardian.com/technology/2018/jan/12/ces-2018-voice-controlled-showers-robots-smart-toilets-ai, retrieved: Aug. 2018.

[10] Echo Dot (2nd Generation) - Smart speaker with Alexa. https://www.amazon.com/Amazon-Echo-Dot-Portable-Bluetooth-Speaker-with-Alexa-Black/dp/B01DFKC2SO/ref=sr/_1/_1, retrieved: Aug. 2018.

[11] eSpeak. https://espeak.sourceforge.net, retrieved: Aug. 2018.

[12] Gartner Says Worldwide Spending on VPA-Enabled Wireless Speakers Will Top 2 Billion by 2020. https://www.gartner.com/newsroom/id/3464317, retrieved: Aug. 2018.

[13] Home Automation Device Market Grows Briskly, to 27 Million. https://www.voicebot.ai/wp-content/uploads/2017/11/cirp-news-release-2017-11-06-echo-home.pdf, retrieved: Aug. 2018.

[14] Home has a new hub. https://www.samsung.com/us/explore/family-hub-refrigerator/connected-hub/, retrieved: Aug. 2018.

[15] How to Keep Amazon Echo and Google Home From Responding to Your TV. https://www.wired.com/2017/02/keep-amazon-echo-google-home-responding-tv, retrieved: Aug. 2018.

[16] IDC Forecasts Worldwide Spending on the Internet of Things to Reach 772 Billion in 2018. https://www.idc.com/getdoc.jsp?containerId=prUS43295217, retrieved: Aug. 2018.

[17] Jasper. https://jasperproject.github.io, retrieved: Aug. 2018.

[18] Nutzungsbedingungen für Alexa und Alexa-Geräte. https://www.amazon.de/gp/help/customer/display.html?nodeId=201566380, retrieved: Aug. 2018.

[19] Please meet Amazon Alexa and the Alexa Skills Kit. https://de.slideshare.net/AmazonWebServices/please-meet-amazon-alexa-and-the-alexa-skills-kit, retrieved: Aug. 2018.

[20] Using Multiple Alexa Devices. https://www.amazon.com/gp/help/customer/display.html? nodeId=202013740, retrieved: Aug. 2018.

[21] C. C. Aggarwal and S. Y. Philip. A General Survey of Privacy-preserving Data Mining Models and Algorithms. In *Privacy-preserving data mining*, pages 11–52. Springer, 2008.

[22] G. Aggarwal, T. Feder, K. Kenthapadi, R. Motwani, R. Panigrahy, D. Thomas, and A. Zhu. Anonymizing Tables. In *International Conference on Database Theory*, pages 246–258. Springer, 2005.

[23] E. Alepis and C. Patsakis. Monkey Says, Monkey Does: Security and Privacy on Voice Assistants. *IEEE Access*, 5:17841–17851, 2017.

[24] J. L. Boyles, A. Smith, and M. Madden. Privacy and Data Management on Mobile Devices. *Pew Internet & American Life Project*, 4, 2012.

[25] S. Chester, B. Kapron, G. Ramesh, G. Srivastava, A. Thomo, and S. Venkatesh. Why Waldo befriended the Dummy? k-Anonymization of Social Networks with Pseudo-Nodes. *Social Network Analysis and Mining*, 3(3):381–399, 2013.

[26] H. Chung, M. Iorga, J. Voas, and S. Lee. Alexa, Can I Trust You? *IEEE COMPUTER SOCIETY*, 50(9):100–104, 2017.

[27] W. Diao, X. Liu, Z. Zhou, and K. Zhang. Your Voice Assistant is Mine: How to Abuse Speakers to Steal Information and Control Your Phone. In *Proceedings of the 4th ACM Workshop on Security and Privacy in Smartphones & Mobile Devices*, pages 63–74. ACM, 2014.

[28] R. Dingledine, N. Mathewson, and P. Syverson. Tor: The Second-Generation Onion Router. In *Usenix Security*, 2004.

[29] C. Dwork. Differential Privacy: A Survey of Results. In *International Conference on Theory and Applications of Models of Computation*, pages 1–19. Springer, 2008.

[30] M. Ebling. Can Cognitive Assistants Disappear? *IEEE Pervasive Computing*, 15(3):4–6, 2016.

[31] L. Gong and C. Nass. When a Talking-Face Computer Agent is Half-Human and Half-Humanoid: Human Identity and Consistency Preference. *Human Communication Research*, 33(2):163–193, 2007.

[32] Q. Han, H. Zhao, Z. Ma, K. Zhang, and H. Pan. Protecting Location Privacy Based on Historical Users over Road Networks. In *International Conference on Wireless Algorithms, Systems, and Applications*, pages 347–355. Springer, 2014.

[33] T. Hara, A. Suzuki, M. Iwata, Y. Arase, and X. Xie. Dummy-based User Location Anonymization Under Real-world Constraints. *IEEE Access*, 4:673–687, 2016.

[34] C. Jackson and A. Orebaugh. A study of Security and Privacy Issues Associated with the Amazon Echo. *International Journal of Internet of Things and Cyber-Assurance*, 1(1), 2018.

[35] R. Kato, M. Iwata, T. Hara, A. Suzuki, X. Xie, Y. Arase, and S. Nishio. A dummy-based Anonymization Method Based on User Trajectory with Pauses. In *Proceedings of the 20th International Conference on Advances in Geographic Information Systems*, pages 249–258. ACM, 2012.

[36] H. Kido, Y. Yanagisawa, and T. Satoh. An Anonymous Communication Technique Using Dummies for Location-based Services. In *Pervasive Services, 2005. ICPS'05. Proceedings. International Conference on*, pages 88–97. IEEE, 2005.

[37] A. Kumar, A. Gupta, J. Chan, S. Tucker, B. Hoffmeister, M. Dreyer, S. Peshterliev, A. Gandhe, D. Filiminov, A. Rastrow, C. Monson, and A. Kumar. Just ASK: Building an Architecture for Extensible Self-Service Spoken Language Understanding. *arXiv preprint arXiv:1711.00549*, 2017.

[38] J. Kwapisz, G. Weiss, and S. Moore. Activity Recognition Using Cell Phone Accelerometers. *ACM SigKDD Explorations Newsletter*, 12(2):74–82, 2011.

[39] T. Lackorzynski and S. Koepsell. Hello Barbie - Hacker Toys in a World of Linked Devices. *Broadband Coverage in Germany; 11. ITG-Symposium*, 2017.

[40] A. E. Moorthy and K. L. Vu. Voice Activated Personal Assistant: Acceptability of Use in the Public Space. In *International Conference on Human Interface and the Management of Information*, pages 324–334. Springer, 2014.

[41] C. Ratti, D. Frenchman, R. M. Pulselli, and S. Williams. Mobile Landscapes: Using Location Data from Cell Phones for Urban Analysis. *Environment and Planning B: Planning and Design*, 33(5):727–748, 2006.

[42] S. Shakila and G. Ganapathy. Privacy for Interactive Web Browsing: A Study on Anonymous Communication Protocols. *International Journal*, 2(5), 2014.

[43] C. Spensky, J. Stewart, A. Yerukhimovich, R. Shay, A. Trachtenberg, R. Housley, and R. Cunningham. SoK: Privacy on Mobile Devices - Its Complicated. *Proceedings on Privacy Enhancing Technologies*, 2016(3):96–116, 2016.

[44] J. P. Timpanaro, T. Cholez, I. Chrisment, and O. Festor. Evaluation of the Anonymous I2P Network's Design Choices Against Performance and Security. In *Information Systems Security and Privacy (ICISSP), 2015 International Conference on*, pages 1–10. IEEE, 2015.

[45] H. Wang, F. Calabrese, G. Di Lorenzo, and C. Ratti. Transportation Mode Inference from Anonymized and Aggregated Mobile Phone Call Detail Records. In *Intelligent Transportation Systems (ITSC), 2010 13th International IEEE Conference on*, pages 318–323. IEEE, 2010.

[46] C. Wueest. A Guide to the Security of Voice-activated Smart Speakers - An ISTR Special Report (2017). https://www.symantec.com/content/dam/symantec/docs/security-center/white-papers/istr-security-voice-activated-smart-speakers-en.pdf, retrieved: Aug. 2018.

On the Effectiveness of Blockchain Against Cryptocurrency Attacks

Sarwar Sayeed, Hector Marco-Gisbert
School of Computing, Engineering and Physical Sciences
University of the West of Scotland
High St, Paisley PA1 2BE, UK
Email: {Sarwar.Sayeed,Hector.Marco}@uws.ac.uk

***Abstract*—Cryptocurrencies are being widely adopted to perform various online-based transactions; therefore, they are required to maintain a consensus to ensure a secured transaction. Blockchain comprises a distributed ledger, which holds digital records of individual crypto-transactions. Besides recording a particular activity, blockchain also ensures that the contents of the ledger are decided based on agreements of distinct participants. Various consensus mechanisms are followed by blockchain to ensure blocks are being summed up representing legitimate data on the network. However, the major consensus protocols comprise various limitations; and these are prone to different types of cyber attacks, such as Distributed denial-of-service, 51% attack, Double-spending, Long-range attack. In this paper, we analyze several attack vectors that can cause serious security threats due to the loopholes in the consensus mechanism. Our study involves examining 3 significant consensus mechanisms, which are followed by major cryptocurrencies. We also discuss the limitations of individual consensus mechanisms and demonstrate their robustness towards various attack vectors. We conclude that, although blockchain comprises proper consensus mechanisms to enhance secured crypto-transaction, unfortunately, it is not strong enough to defend against some cryptocurrency attacks which could discourage some users to adopt this technology.**

Keywords–Blockchain; Consensus; Cyber Attack.

I. INTRODUCTION

The blockchain is a medium of distributing digital information to users who are connected to the block. It uses a distributed system for verification and holds a record of every transaction that ever took place. Blockchain was first initiated in 2008 by a pseudonymous named Satoshi Nakamoto; however, it still remains a mystery about the founder of this technology. In the blockchain network, each block contains records of transactions and connected using cryptography. It is a secure and trustworthy platform, which can be used to produce applications, such as voting systems, games, online shops [1].

A cryptocurrency is a revolutionary growing technology that makes it possible for digital transactions to occur in just a few minutes. The transaction takes place in, an unidentified blockchain network; regardless of the network failure the transaction will still flow accordingly. In a blockchain network, every miner can keep their data and ensure that the chain is not corrupted. If an adversary tries to corrupt the block, then the whole system verifies every data for authenticity, and any corrupted finding gets restricted from the block.

Bitcoin is the first digital currency, which evolved in 2009 on blockchain platform. Data with several blocks in the chain cannot be altered without having every block changed; hence, making the whole process very secure and reliable. Beside Bitcoin, various other digital currencies, such as Ether, Litecoin, are currently being dominated in the crypto platform. Each cryptocurrency follows a consensus mechanism to make the transfer process secure and free from the attacks. However, recent attacks have questioned the reliability of the digital transactions and showed there is a loophole to bypass the security. Bitfinex and Dao incident are some of the recent incidents, which resulted in stealing millions of cryptocurrencies [2] [3]. Hence, it is essential to have a secure consensus mechanism in place.

Our major contributions in this paper are:

- We discuss ten cryptocurrency attacks, which not only can corrupt the cryptocurrencies but also can exploit the consensus mechanism.
- We assess three widely used blockchain consensus protocols, including their limitations.
- We evaluate the effectiveness of individual consensus mechanism by classifying towards discrete exploitation type.

This paper is organized as follows: Section II is the background section, which discusses the major cryptocurrencies. Section III presents the attack vectors that can be catastrophic to the blockchain network. In addition to that, phishing and scams are also discussed. Section IV summarizes the security enhancements in brief. Section V includes the discussion of 3 consensus mechanisms and limitations associated with each of the mechanisms. In Section VI, the consensus mechanisms are analyzed, in the context of attack vectors, and represented in a table. To conclude the paper, we discuss the findings from our analysis and future work to be undertaken.

II. BACKGROUND

In this section, we discuss five significant cryptocurrencies. Table I presents some cryptocurrencies that are classified according to the consensus mechanism. Figure 1 shows the recent market capitalization of 10 cryptocurrencies [4] that are dominating at the moment.

A cryptocurrency is a form of digital cash, which uses cryptography to process a secure and reliable transactions over a peer-to-peer (P2P) network. The transaction process is based on consensus, which means disagreement from any of the peers on the network will cause an interruption in the act. About 1662 cryptocurrencies exist at the moment and Bitcoin is the most widely used cryptocurrencies among all. The cryptocurrencies have limited supply as cash currencies do and they can be controlled by an algorithm process.

TABLE I. CRYPTOCURRENCIES BASED ON CONSENSUS MECHANISM

Consensus Mechanism	Cryptocurrencies
Proof of work	Bitcoin, Ether, Nimiq, Litecoin, Monero
Proof of stake	Linda, Neo, Pivx, Okcash, Stratis
Delegated proof of stake	Lisk, Ark, Rise, Oxycoin, BitShares

A. Bitcoin

Bitcoin was first proposed in 2008 and came into effect since 2009 [5]. It is an electronic based payment system where the authenticity is based on mathematical proof. The main concept of this cryptocurrency is to perform digital transactions and exchanges over a secured medium without having any central supremacy. Bitcoin is operated in a decentralized system, which can be considered as an alternative version of a bank. Once a transaction occurs, the sender is required to wait for the confirmations from the miners. The transactions get into the pool for authorizations. Mining computers then gather the unresolved transactions from the pool and switch them to a mathematical equation. Miners verify the transactions by solving the equation, and a new Bitcoin block gets added to the blockchain.

B. Ether

Ether is another popular cryptocurrency, which was launched in 2015. Ether, a crypto-fuel, is an important attribute to keep the Ethereum platform running [6]. Ether is used as an incentive for the application developers who develops efficient decentralized applications, a unique way of keeping the network active. Whenever a node validates a block on the Ethereum blockchain, 5 Ether is generated and rewarded as an incentive to the node. It normally takes 15-17 seconds for a new block to be publicized. Users wishing to utilize a decentralized application on the platform are required to pay in Ether as a service fee.

C. Ripple

Ripple came into effect in 2012. Ripple is a Real Time Gross Settlement system, which functions as a cryptocurrency and digital payment network [7]. Ripple relies on a common network, which is operated by a network autonomously validating server that can compare the transactions. The Ripple platform is decentralized and does not comprise proof of work (PoW) or proof of stake (PoS); instead, it relies on a shared public database. Since Ripple structure does not depend on mining; therefore, the cost of computing power and network latency is very low. A consensus protocol performs the validation of balances and transactions. The consensus process involves distinct nodes that determine the first transaction by going through a poll. The approval time from the poll is very fast and roughly takes 5 seconds.

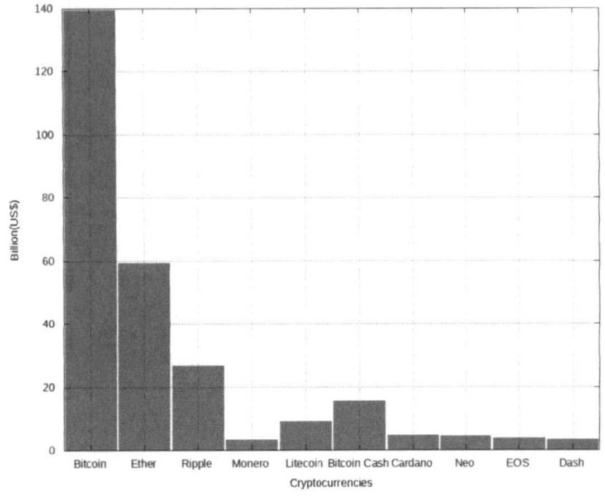

Figure 1. Market capitalization of cryptocurrencies (in billion) as of March 2018

D. Monero

Monero is a cryptocurrency, which was launched in 2014. It is privately based untraceable currency that focuses on decentralization [8]. The privacy is ensured by a special method called "ring signatures". The method works by having a group of signatures, which involves a minimum of one genuine participant. Monero is dynamically scalable and comprises isolated features comparing to Bitcoin or Ether. For instance, Monero includes cryptography that protects all the potential transaction information, such as sender, receiver, transaction amount, from the outside world and giving the sender the ability to decide who will be allowed to view a particular transaction.

E. Litecoin

Litecoin is another cryptocurrency, which was developed by Charlie Lee and came into effect since 2011 [9]. Litecoin is one of the oldest cryptocurrencies that came into effect after Bitcoin. It is able to manage a large volume of transactions than other cryptocurrencies, such as Bitcoin. Litecoin generates the blocks more frequently; hence, it supports more transactions at a faster pace. The transaction fees are relatively low and determined based on the size of the block. It comprises much shorter blocks comparing to Bitcoin; therefore, the fee is low.

III. Security Threats

In this section, we discuss some of the important attacking techniques that can be dangerous in corrupting the cryptocurrencies as well as exploiting the blockchain.

A. 51% Attack

The 51% attack can be very critical in the blockchain network if exploited successfully [10]. The vulnerability starts by creating a corrupt version of the blockchain, which is isolated from the real version. Since blockchain policy complies with the longest chain to demonstrate the accuracy of the transaction, if the adversary manages to drive the longest chain, the corrupt version of blockchain will be predicted as a genuine chain. Therefore, the transactions that are not listed in the corrupted chain will be reversed. In the context of Bitcoin, once a transaction is approved by the sender it gets into the pool. It is then picked by individual miners to develop a block of transactions. The miner who gets first to solve the problem produces it to other miners to check the authenticity. In a 51% attack, a group of adversaries tries to solve the problem and then generate child of the blockchain so that they can avoid showing the solution to other miners in the network. However, a large number of miners exist on the blockchain network, and it is nearly impossible to beat the hashing power of the network.

B. Sybil Attack

The Sybil attack comprises similar characteristics as 51% attack. This attacking method was first brought into attention by John Douceur, a researcher based on Microsoft [11]. In a Sybil attack, the adversary develops a vast amount of nodes in a sole network to cause disruptions over the network. This attack also involves corrupting a network to perform an unprivileged transaction or altering valid transactions. The network is unable to discover if multiple nodes are being controlled by a single attacker. In this attacking technique, the attacker may use several devices, virtual machines or Internet Protocol (IP) addresses. Normally in a centralized system, the monitoring process involves verifying if several requests are being made from the same device, but the blockchain does not possess such features. In blockchain technology, adversaries are restricted to the number of blocks they can produce. However, this attacking technique is very rare as the digital currency infrastructure was developed considering the restriction of the Sybil attack.

C. Distributed Denial-of-Service

Distributed denial-of-service (DDoS) is a type of cyber attack that exists from the past two decades to perform exploitation over various networks. DDoS is one of the most common attack vectors in the blockchain network, and the main objective of the adversary is to flood the network with a very high amount of traffic [12]. This attack is performed in the blockchain network so that authentic transactions could be stopped from being processed and invalid transactions could be accomplished. However, a DDoS attack over the blockchain network does not involve stealing the digital currency rather it just mitigates the network activity.

D. Mining Malware

In this attacking technique, the adversary takes advantage of cryptojacking malware to perform exploitation. It involves infecting miners system with malware to have the incentive directed to the attacker's wallet [13]. Regardless of the victim's location, mining malware can be exploited from any part of the world. Cryptojacking in mining malware comprises similar approach as ransomware. However, instead of having a good chunk of money within a short period, it focuses on achieving the targeted amount over a period. Cryptojacking works in stealth mode; hence, it is an attracting exploitation technique over ransomware. It may not require much effort to infect a system and can spread via corrupted websites or phishing campaigns.

E. P + Epsilon Attack

The PoW system is usually vulnerable to this type of attack [14]. It is a simple statical observation and based on the uncoordinated choice model. In an uncoordinated choice model, all the users are not inspired to engage with each other. Hence, they construct a group, which suddenly turns into big enough to dominate. Essentially when the network performs normal, the miners can never construct the miner group large enough to manipulate the network. It correctly assumes that the average miners will look after their interest.

F. Long-Range Attack

A long-range attack can occur due to the weak subjectivity model [15]. In the PoS chain, only a limited number of users participate at the beginning, and as the user increases, they form the chain as a pool of miners. Hence, users who staked at the chain, grow more prominent. Those limited number of users, from the beginning, can join together to maintain the previous chain back in action. In the following stages, they will be the one to dominate in mining blocks. PoS does not set a limit on the growth of the chain; hence, the chain can grow very long.

G. Eclipse Attack

In this attacking technique, an adversary manipulates the P2P network to control over the information that a node comprises. The exploitation may start when a peer communicates with other peers using gossip protocol [16]. An adversary can separate the target from the network chain so that the target could be diverted to misuse the computation power on invalid segment of the blockchain. In an eclipse attack, the adversary resides in between the nodes and the rest of the network by regulating the capacity of the node. It gives an attacker to perform a 51% attack with lot less mining power [17]. The attacker aims to manipulate the nodes to the attackers IP so that connections are made to their chosen destination. The attacking process goes through three phases. However, conducting this attack can be very expensive since the attacker is required to control the whole network system.

H. Border Gateway Protocol Hijacking

Border Gateway Protocol (BGP) hijacking is also known as routing attack. In this attacking technique, the Internet Service Provider makes false announcements over the routing system so that traffic could be diverted [18]. An investigation shows that the BGP attacks are increasing time to time over the Bitcoin network and a minimum of 100 BGP attacks are occurring on a monthly basis. The investigation also demonstrates that 447 nodes were hijacked in 2015. This attack vector can be performed to benefit from 2 attacking stages. Firstly, divide the network and secondly, obstruct the blocks by 20 minutes. Though the blockchain system is a decentralized network; however, when considering it from the routing perspective then it can be regarded as centralized as about 100 IP prefixes are managing about 20% of the Bitcoin hosts. Hence, this attacking technique can be proven fatal due to its centralization.

I. The Balance Attack

The Balance attack aims to focus on the nodes, which comprise balanced mining power. It mainly enforces double-spending on PoW consensus mechanism [19]. In this attacking technique, the adversary puts a delay between the legit subgroups of nodes. The next step involves the adversary mining as many blocks as possible in another subgroup confirming that other sub-tree puts importance on the transaction subgroups.

The adversary aims to exploit the ghost protocol by separating the blockchain branch from the other nodes in the network. At a later time, the separated branch will be furnished to other nodes to put an impact on the branch selection process.

J. Phishing and Scams

The number of scams occurs in the crypto-space is just remarkable, but not in a good sense. The main idea of the phishing and scams is to trick users to steal money from their wallet [20]. Phishing can spread from device to device, and technology-oriented people can easily fall for it without even noticing the influence. Scams can occur in many ways, for instance, an important email from the wallet asking to sync the account with a network which has just been hard-forked. Scams can also occur through social media by asking potential information from the user making it look like a legit request. Slack and forums attack can also occur by providing a corrupted link and asking the miners to log in through that link. Phishy wallets, fake ads are also some of the scam techniques being used to steal cryptocurrencies.

IV. Security Techniques

In this section, we summarize some of the security enhancements, which can be implemented to ensure a secured blockchain network.

A. SmartPool

SmartPool is a decentralized mining pool, which is based on Ethereum smart contracts [21]. SmartPool comprises various innovative data structures and design options, which have resulted in to be secure, efficient and reliable. SmartPool enhances probabilistic verification that helps to decrease the number of messages and cut down the expense for the miners. SmartPool provides a solution by ensuring a decentralized pool, mitigating transaction censorship threat, guaranteeing low variance.

B. Oyente

Oyente is a symbolic execution tool, which is used to find security bugs in smart contracts [22]. Oyente examines Ethereum smart contracts to figure out security loophole, which can cause potential threats. Oyente does not only detect unsafe bugs but also investigates every practical execution path. An experiment carried out by Oyente on 19,366 smart contracts, and it resulted in 8,833 of them are vulnerable.

C. Hawk

Hawk is a framework to develop privacy-preserving smart contracts [23]. Hawk does not require cryptography implementation, so it gives an opportunity to the non-programmers to write Hawk program. A Hawk compiler is in place to compile the Hawk program. One-chain privacy and contractual security are two security approaches guaranteed by Hawk to enhance security.

V. Blockchain Distributed Consensus Mechanisms

In this section, we analyze three blockchain consensus mechanisms, which are being utilized by the major cryptocurrencies such as Bitcoin, Litecoin, Ether and so on. We also put our focus on the limitations of each mechanism. Table II summarizes some of the main features of each consensus. The key point of the consensus mechanism is to ensure that the entire network agrees upon the contents of the ledger by following a set of rules. It also influences the security and economic guidelines of the blockchain network.

A. Proof of Work

Proof of work (PoW) is a consensus mechanism, which is based on solving a mathematical equation. PoW was first introduced by Bitcoin and currently implemented in many other cryptocurrencies [24]. The action involves mining where each node on the network is referred to as a miner. The process of rewarding miners ensures that it is running while establishing blocks. Miners are the foundation of PoW; hence, they are responsible for authorizing new transactions and recording them to the ledger. It usually takes 10 minutes to mine a Bitcoin block by solving strong mathematical equation based on a cryptographic hash algorithm. A successfully solved equation results in PoW; therefore, the transaction is considered as valid. Miners receive rewards for solving mathematical equation and transaction fees.

One of the major drawbacks of PoW is the cost of energy. The amount of energy the Bitcoin mining consumes per year is more than 159 countries individually. Research shows that Bitcoin to consume all the electricity of the world by February 2020 [25]. PoW for Bitcoin mining requires extensive hardware to make the mining process smooth and fast, which results in huge expenditures. Moreover, the effort in generating the blocks are useless as it can not be applied anywhere but takes a lot of time and energy to form the blocks.

B. Proof of Stake

Proof of stake (PoS) is another consensus mechanism, which has gained popularity in recent time. Peercoin was the first cryptocurrency to use this mechanism in 2012. In this consensus mechanism, a randomized system is applied to determine the creator of the following block [26]. The process involves giving information about the amount of cryptocurrency and the duration that cryptocurrency has been held for by a particular user. It does not need to meet any rigid hardware requirements and also abandons the high computation requirement. The possibility of obtaining the reward by developing a block entirely depends on the number of tokens possessed by potential users in the network. In PoS, each node is connected to an address and participants with a large number of coins likely to achieve the address, as well as involve in mining the

TABLE II. Main features of consensus mechanisms

Consensus	Energy Cost	Decentralization	Processing Speed
PoW	High	High	Low
PoS	Low	High	High
DPoS	Low	Low	High

next blocks. The advantage of PoS is that comparing to PoW; it is not energy intensive.

PoS suffers from weak subjectivity, and the implementation process is very complex and challenging. Another limitation of PoS system is that a large number of stakeholders have control over the network based on technical and economical aspects; therefore, making it a monopolized system.

C. Delegated Proof of Stake

Delegated proof of stake (DPoS) is another consensus mechanism that allows the shareholders to vote for witnesses [27]. One vote per share policy is performed giving the stakeholders the opportunity to have more votes if they own most coins. The witnesses get paid for building individual blocks, and failure to do so may result in being unpaid and voted out. They must obtain the largest number of votes from random stakeholders to perform the instructed task. The stakeholders also vote for the delegates to reform and make changes in the network which can be reviewed for an utmost decision. However, the rewards depend on the accomplishment of the DPoS mechanism. The voting power is endorsed by analyzing the number of tokens an account is holding. In a particular DPoS version, to prove dedication, the delegates may require to deposit funds in the time-locked security account and any corrupted behavior will result in money being seized. The version is called as deposit-based proof of stake [28].

Though DPoS enhances efficiency in the transactions; however, it comprises various limitations. The significant limitation of DPoS is that adequate decentralization cannot be obtained. An excessive amount of validators slow down the network. Moreover, delegates get penalized for not abiding with particular rules.

VI. Analysis

In this section, we evaluate the effectiveness of individual consensus mechanism. Our analysis does not involve discussing only the effectiveness rather it also classifies each mechanism towards distinct exploitation type and presents in a table. We assess three primary consensus mechanisms, and Table III shows that consensus mechanisms are vulnerable to various attack vectors.

The act of PoW method is too slow. Expensive hardware requirement and energy cost make it very costly. Some mining firms are dominating with enough mining power; hence, attacks to the mining firms can cause disruptions and also put massive impact over the cryptocurrency. PoW is vulnerable to the 51% attack, and a P + epsilon attack can also be carried out at no cost by having the required budget. Hence, the crypto-security level of the PoW based system towards P + epsilon attack can be considered as zero [29]. Our analysis indicates that the Sybil attack can exploit PoW as an adversary can interrupt the flow of the network by developing several malicious nodes. PoW is also vulnerable to the Balance attack. The Ethereum protocol and private blockchain are mainly vulnerable to this attacking technique. However, the adversary with much hashing power more likely to corrupt the Bitcoin blockchain network. In addition to that, our analysis also shows that the DDoS attack and BGP hijacking can corrupt the regular flow of this consensus mechanism.

Comparing to PoW, the significant advantage of PoS is the energy savings. However, in the context of security, it is not a fully secured mechanism. PoS is vulnerable to the 51% attack. To conduct a 51% attack, the adversary will have to achieve 51% of the cryptocurrency. Since it is quite tough to achieve 51% cryptocurrency; therefore, the threat of that attack can be very rare. However, PoS can be exploited by the long-range attack. PoS is not vulnerable to the P + epsilon attack since the adversary requires to produce a huge amount of budget to contribute as a security deposit for the participants when voting for the minority [29]. The Sybil attack can exploit PoS. A DDoS attack can also be carried out to disrupt the consensus mechanism. PoS can be an expensive option for novice attackers. It requires users to stake their own money first to validate transactions and produce blocks. Any corrupted activity in the network will confiscate the staked amount. Hence, the adversary will also lose their right to participate in future activities. This particular approach will demotivate potential attackers to carry out specific attack vectors; thus, it will enhance extra security.

Our analysis shows that comparing to PoS and PoW, DPoS comprises an entirely different consensus approach. Though the distinct approach holds advantages concerning energy cost, speed and processing time; however, in the context of security, DPoS is also not very secure. The adversary can convince the stakeholders to obtain 51% voting power and carry out a 51% attack [30]. It is also vulnerable to the other primary attack vectors, such as long-range attack, DDoS attack, P + epsilon attack, Sybil attack and the Balance attack. DPoS is not fully decentralized; therefore, it can always be the focal point of random attackers.

In the distributed network, a source entity can produce multiple entities from which some may not be reliable to perform particular tasks. Hence, a consensus algorithm is in place to ensure the reliability of the specific network. Cryptocurrencies in the blockchain network take advantage of the consensus algorithm to provide a secured transaction. Truechain is a blockchain platform, which comprises a hybrid consensus mechanism [31]. Proof of activity (PoA) is another hybrid consensus algorithm, which combines PoW with PoS [32]. Even though hybrid consensus ensures high security but PoA has been criticized due to the resources required for mining.

TABLE III. CONSENSUS MECHANISMS THAT ARE VULNERABLE TO VARIOUS ATTACKS

Consensus Mechanism	Long-Range Attack	51% Attack	DDoS	P + Epsilon Attack	Sybil Attack	The Balance Attack	BGP Hijacking
PoW	✗	✓	✓	✓	✓	✓	✓
PoS	✓	✓	✓	✗	✓	✗	✗
DPoS	✓	✓	✓	✓	✓	✓	✗

VII. Conclusion

The blockchain is a remarkable evaluation, and decentralization has made it a very reliable and secure medium for digital transactions. In this paper, we studied ten major attacking techniques. Our analysis indicated that some of the techniques could corrupt the consensus mechanism and also carry out crypto thefts. Major cryptocurrencies were discussed and presented in a table based on their consensus classification. We evaluated the effectiveness of 3 significant consensus mechanisms and pointed out that alongside various limitations, they are also vulnerable to different types of attack vectors.

Though blockchain consensus mechanism is a robust method conversely, it is visible that they are still vulnerable and can remarkably have an effect on particular cryptocurrency if successfully exploited. The vulnerability in the consensus mechanisms might discourage the miners to get involved in the mining process. Thus, we encourage the re-implementation of the mechanisms with robust security to mitigate the risks.

For our future work, we aim to analyze several other consensus mechanisms and develop a standard method, which can be used to relate various attack vectors and limitations to the consensus mechanisms. Our method will be used to determine particular exploitation class and constraints of individual consensus mechanism.

References

[1] "What is Blockchain," 2018, URL: https://lisk.io/academy/blockchain-basics/what-is-blockchain [retrieved: July, 2018].

[2] S. FalKon, The Story of the DAOŁŁIts History and Consequences, 2017 (accessed April, 2018), https://medium.com/swlh/the-story-of-the-dao-its-history-and-consequences-71e6a8a551ee.

[3] C. Baldwin, "Bitcoin worth 72 million stolen from Bitfinex exchange in Hong Kong," 2016, URL: https://www.reuters.com/article/us-bitfinex-hacked-hongkong/bitcoin-worth-72-million-stolen-from-bitfinex-exchange-in-hong-kong-idUSKCN10E0KP [retrieved: July, 2018].

[4] M. Frankel, "15 largest Cryptocurrencies by Market Cap," 2018, URL: https://www.fool.com/investing/2018/03/16/how-many-cryptocurrencies-are-there.aspx [retrieved: July, 2018].

[5] "What is Bitcoin," 2018, URL: https://www.coindesk.com/information/what-is-bitcoin/ [retrieved: July, 2018].

[6] "What is Ether," URL: https://bitcoinmagazine.com/guides/what-ether/ [retrieved: July, 2018].

[7] J. Martindale, "What is Ripple," 2018, URL: https://www.digitaltrends.com/computing/what-is-ripple/ [retrieved: June, 2018].

[8] P. Bajpai, "The 6 Most Important Cryptocurrencies Other Than Bitcoin," 2018, URL: https://www.investopedia.com/tech/most-important-cryptocurrencies-other-than-bitcoin/ [retrieved: July, 2018].

[9] J. Bushmaker, "What is Litecoin," 2018, URL: https://www.investinblockchain.com/what-is-litecoin/ [retrieved: July, 2018].

[10] J. S., "Blockchain: how a 51% attack works double spend attack," 2018, URL: https://medium.com/coinmonks/what-is-a-51-attack-or-double-spend-attack-aa108db63474 [retrieved: May, 2018].

[11] J. Risberg, "Yes, the Blockchain Can Be Hacked," 2018, URL: https://coincentral.com/blockchain-hacks/ [retrieved: June, 2018].

[12] S. Morgan, "Blockchain startup: 300,000 DDoS attacks will cause 150B in damages this year," 2017, URL: https://www.csoonline.com/article/3234775/security/blockchain-startup-300000-ddos-attacks-will-cause-150b-in-damages-this-year.html [retrieved: July, 2018].

[13] D. Palmer, "Cryptocurrency-mining malware: Why it is such a menace and where it's going next," 2018, URL: https://www.zdnet.com/article/cryptocurrency-mining-malware-why-it-is-such-a-menace-and-where-its-going-next/ [retrieved: June, 2018].

[14] V. Buterin, "The P + epsilon Attack," 2015, URL: https://blog.ethereum.org/2015/01/28/p-epsilon-attack/ [retrieved: June, 2018].

[15] A. Sharma, "Understanding Proof of Stake through its Flaws. Part 3 Long Range Attacks," 2018, URL: https://medium.com/@abhisharm/understanding-proof-of-stake-through-its-flaws-part-3-long-range-attacks-672a3d413501 [retrieved: June, 2018].

[16] F. Wang, "Eclipse Attacks on Bitcoins Peer-to-Peer Network," 2015, URL: https://medium.com/mit-security-seminar/eclipse-attacks-on-bitcoin-s-peer-to-peer-network-e0da797302c2 [retrieved: May, 2018].

[17] E. Heilman, A. Kendler, A. Zohar, and S. Goldberg, "Eclipse attacks on bitcoin's peer-to-peer network," in Proceedings of the 24th USENIX Conference on Security Symposium, ser. SEC'15. Berkeley, CA, USA: USENIX Association, 2015, pp. 129–144. [Online]. Available: http://dl.acm.org/citation.cfm?id=2831143.2831152

[18] P.-A. Vervier, "Why BGP Hijacking Remains a Security Scourge," 2018, URL: https://www.symantec.com/blogs/feature-stories/why-bgp-hijacking-remains-security-scourge [retrieved: July, 2018].

[19] C. Natoli and V. Gramoli, "The balance attack against proof-of-work blockchains: The R3 testbed as an example," CoRR, vol. abs/1612.09426, 2016.

[20] "Phishing in Cryptocurrency: How to Avoid Scams and Save Your Money," 2018, URL: https://medium.com/@Changelly/phishing-in-cryptocurrency-how-to-avoid-scams-and-save-your-money-d3d1b442a16a [retrieved: June, 2018].

[21] L. Luu, Y. Velner, J. Teutsch, and P. Saxena, "Smartpool: Practical decentralized pooled mining," in 26th USENIX Security Symposium (USENIX Security 17). Vancouver, BC: USENIX Association, 2017, pp. 1409–1426. [Online]. Available: https://www.usenix.org/conference/usenixsecurity17/technical-sessions/presentation/luu

[22] L. Luu, D.-H. Chu, H. Olickel, P. Saxena, and A. Hobor, "Making smart contracts smarter," in Proceedings of the 2016 ACM SIGSAC Conference on Computer and Communications Security, ser. CCS '16. New York, NY, USA: ACM, 2016, pp. 254–269. [Online]. Available: http://doi.acm.org/10.1145/2976749.2978309

[23] A. Kosba, A. Miller, E. Shi, Z. Wen, and C. Papamanthou, "Hawk: The blockchain model of cryptography and privacy-preserving smart contracts," Cryptology ePrint Archive, Report 2015/675, 2015, https://eprint.iacr.org/2015/675.

[24] A. Tar, "Proof-of-Work, Explained," 2018, URL: https://cointelegraph.com/explained/proof-of-work-explained [retrieved: June, 2018].

[25] "Bitcoin Mining," 2017, URL: https://powercompare.co.uk/bitcoin/ [retrieved: May, 2018].

[26] "Proof Of Stake," 2018, URL: https://lisk.io/academy/blockchain-basics/how-does-blockchain-work/proof-of-stake [retrieved: July, 2018].

[27] B. Asolo, "Delegated Proof of Stake (DPOS) Explained," 2018, URL: https://www.mycryptopedia.com/delegated-proof-stake-dpos-explained/ [retrieved: July, 2018].

[28] "Delegated Proof of Stake," 2018, URL: https://lisk.io/academy/blockchain-basics/how-does-blockchain-work/delegated-proof-of-stake [retrieved: June, 2018].

[29] K. Wang, "Cryptoeconomics: Paving the Future of Blockchain Technology," 2017, URL: https://hackernoon.com/cryptoeconomics-paving-the-future-of-blockchain-technology-13b04dab971 [retrieved: June, 2018].

[30] "Solving the Byzantine Generals Problem with Delegated Proof of Stake (DPoS)," 2018, URL: https://www.radixdlt.com/post/what-is-delegated-proof-of-stake-dpos [retrieved: August, 2018].

[31] "TRUE," 2018, URL: https://www.truechain.pro/ [retrieved: August, 2018].

[32] "Proof of Activity Explained: A hybrid Consensus Algorithm," 2018, URL: https://www.coinbureau.com/blockchain/proof-of-activity-explained-hybrid-consensus-algorithm/ [retrieved: August, 2018].

Slicedup: A Tenant-Aware Memory Deduplication for Cloud Computing

Fernando Vañó-García, Hector Marco-Gisbert

School of Computing, Engineering and Physical Sciences
University of the West of Scotland
High St, Paisley PA1 2BE, UK
Email: {Fernando.Vano-Garcia,Hector.Marco}@uws.ac.uk

Abstract—**Memory deduplication allows cloud infrastructure providers to increase the profit of memory resources by taking advantage of the redundant nature of virtual machines footprint. Although it is an important feature to manage the memory resources of a cloud system efficiently, unfortunately, it enables different types of side-channel attacks which, in practice, means disabling memory deduplication. In this paper, we present Slicedup, a tenant-aware memory deduplication mechanism that prevents side-channel attacks. Our proposal enables cloud providers to get the deduplication saving benefits while preventing side-channel attacks among tenants. Since Slicedup is a design-solution, it can be implemented in any operating system, regardless of its version, architecture or any other system dependence. Finally, we show how Slicedup prevents side-channel attacks while providing similar memory savings when the number of tenants per physical host is low.**

Keywords–Cloud; Memory Deduplication; Information Security; Memory Management; Virtualisation.

I. INTRODUCTION

Cloud computing has extraordinary importance in modern society. It is a computing paradigm that allows users to access external resources in an "on-demand" basis, without having to bear the costs of infrastructure maintenance (physical servers, electricity bills, etc.). Physical resources are owned and maintained by a third party (cloud infrastructure provider), and users can obtain the desired computing resources securely and flexibly [1]. It is commonly believed that the concept of cloud computing first appeared in the 90's [2]. Since then, its popularity has grown broadly. Nowadays, cloud computing has been widely adopted in many sectors (e.g., telecommunications, content providers, etc.), mainly because it reduces the cost of performing tasks in a scalable and reliable way.

Despite the effort of many researchers to provide protection mechanisms [3] [4], attackers always end up finding new techniques to achieve their goals. Cloud infrastructure providers desire efficient resource management as well as to provide adequate levels of security for their customers. Unfortunately, this is not always possible, and performance mechanisms can compromise the system security. Memory deduplication is an instance of this problem. On the one hand, it offers the possibility of saving memory by eliminating duplicate contents. On the other hand, memory deduplication in a multi-tenant cloud environment can lead to serious security issues, which could allow a malicious attacker to abuse it and compromise other customer's highly sensitive information. For this reason, operating systems recently decided to deactivate memory deduplication by default [5] [6].

The main contributions of this paper are the following:

- We provide a state-of-the-art review of the known side-channel techniques related to memory deduplication in cloud systems.
- We propose and discuss a suitable solution to enable memory deduplication, avoiding side-channel attacks in multi-tenant cloud systems.

In the following sections, we present the challenges of memory deduplication concerning security in cloud systems. Section III surveys the state-of-the-art of known problems that memory deduplication introduces in virtualised systems. Then, Section IV provides our proposed solution to solve the memory deduplication side-channels in multi-tenant cloud systems. Finally, in Section V, we discuss the advantages and disadvantages of this approach in contrast with other countermeasures, and Section VI concludes.

II. BACKGROUND

In this section, the memory deduplication saving mechanism and cache memories are summarised.

A. Memory Deduplication

Memory deduplication is a memory saving mechanism that consists in detecting identical pages in memory and unify them into one single copy, liberating the space occupied by the redundant copies. This technique allows a cloud infrastructure provider to reduce the consumption of physical memory. Given the exceptional importance of efficient memory resources utilisation on behalf of cloud computing providers, deduplication is an important feature. It can reduce the memory footprint across virtual machines, increasing the profit of existing memory resources and decreasing the total cost of managing and ownership.

When two pages are compared, and both contain identical contents, they are mapped into a single physical page frame in memory using `Copy-On-Write` (COW) semantics. The COW mechanism allows a memory manager to share an object among processes belonging to different virtual address spaces. It is an optimisation heavily used by operating systems for copy operations, for example when a new process is created. A *COWed* object is write-protected, and when any of the processes try to modify their own instance, a new copy is generated in such a way as to ensure the integrity of the contents.

In a virtualised environment, deduplication is commonly applied to the entire memory region corresponding to the virtual machine (often called guest physical memory). Hence, all those pages belonging to that memory region are candidates for being shared.

B. Cache Memory

Cache memory is a small and high-speed Static Random Access Memory (SRAM) located in the CPU, which stores recently accessed data from the main memory. The purpose is to speed up the access to program instructions and data, exploiting the principle of locality [7]. As a consequence, the processor can obtain the information directly from the cache rather than from main memory, which has more access latency. Modern processors contain different levels of cache in their memory hierarchy. Typically they consist of three cache levels, where the first and second are private for each execution core, and the last level is shared by all the cores. The lower levels in the memory hierarchy contain small and fast memories, while the higher levels consist of big and slow memories.

There are different ways of organising a cache. The simpler approach is a direct-mapped cache, where an address is always associated with a single entry in the cache. This is cheap and works fast, but it introduces problems of address collisions (conflict miss). Another approach is a fully-associative cache, where any address can be stored in any entry of the cache. It is more expensive because a comparator is used to check the existing tags in the cache for every access, along with the need for an eviction policy (e.g., Least Recently Used). The n-way set associative caches are a combination of both approaches. The cache is divided into cache sets, each consisting of several cache lines (or ways). Sets are indexed with addresses to map specific memory locations (directly mapped), and the lines of each set are fully associative.

III. Threats of Memory Deduplication

Memory deduplication is a significant mechanism to save considerable amounts of memory in a cloud environment. Nevertheless, it introduces weaknesses that can be exploited by a malicious attacker and compromise the security of the system. It allows guests to communicate through a covert channel, which can be used by attackers to perform cross-VM access driven attacks and leak sensitive information. In this section, we present the state-of-the-art of side-channel attacks where the attacker shares memory with the victim in a virtualised environment.

A. Shared Memory Side-Channels

In a virtualised environment, memory deduplication is applied to pages in the physical host. This includes the sharing of pages belonging to different virtual machines that are located in the same host. A covert channel can be made because of the timing difference of the write operation to a page that is being shared by deduplication. This operation can be distinguished from a standard write to a page which is not being shared because a private copy must be done, and it takes more time. Therefore, an attacker can craft a page in their own address space, and then check if it is deduplicated by the host. In the affirmative case, at least another virtual machine holds a page with those contents.

The first study that exploits memory deduplication to perform a side-channel was carried out by Suzaki et al. [8]. They were able to check/detect the existence of specific applications in a different virtual machine located in the same physical host. Later, the same authors improved their work, discussing more approaches and countermeasures, being able to detect a specific virtual machine previously marked in a multi-tenant cloud environment [9]. Concurrently, Owens and Wang [10] were able to fingerprint guest operating systems using the same technique.

Xiao et al. [11] [12] studied the security implications of memory deduplication from the perspectives of both attackers and defenders. They presented a method to detect virtualisation and another to detect rootkits that modify kernel read-only data, both using memory deduplication covert channels. Suzaki et al. [13] continued their research on this topic, presenting more memory disclosure attacks based on memory deduplication that are able to detect the security level of attacked operating systems, find vulnerable applications, and confirm the status of attacked applications.

Two years later, Barresi et al. [14] developed an attack using the same technique, leaking the address space layouts [15] of the victim virtual machines, while Gruss et al. [16] presented a memory-disclosure attack in sandboxed JavaScript, without the need for the victim to execute any program, merely visiting a remote website controlled by the attacker. Rong et al. [17] even proposed a practical protocol of Cloud Covert Channel based on Memory Deduplication (CCCMD).

B. Shared Memory + Cache Side-Channels

In addition to the techniques presented in the previous section, there is a rich literature of side-channel attacks that combine memory deduplication with cache covert channels. These techniques rely on memory sharing with the victim virtual machine. When an attacker accesses to one of these shared pages, she is accessing to the same physical page frame that the victim is using. As a consequence, that page is located in the same cache line for both attacker and victim, due to the physically-indexed Last-Level-Cache (LLC).

In 2014, Yarom et al. [18] [19] introduced the `Flush+Reload` technique as an extension of a previous study about cache side-channel attacks [20]. It consists in measuring the access time of a specific cache line in the LLC, instead of measuring the writing time to a COWed page. The attacker flushes the monitored cache line and waits for the victim to access the memory line. Given that the victim page is shared with the attacker, they share the cache set for that page, and the attacker can ensure that a specific memory line is evicted from the entire cache hierarchy. Then, if the victim accesses to the data while the attacker is waiting, the monitored cache line will be filled again. In the last phase, the attacker reloads the cache line and measures how much time it takes. If the victim has accessed the memory line, the time will be short. Otherwise, the cache line will be empty, and the operation will be longer. Given that this technique is using the LLC, the attacker and the victim can be running in a different execution core of the physical machine and the attack will still work. With this technique, the authors achieved a successful extraction of GnuPG private encryption keys from a victim, along with the exploitation of a vulnerability introduced to elliptic curve cryptographic protocols, recovering OpenSSL Elliptic Curve Digital Signature Algorithm (ECDSA) nonces.

This technique has been used by several studies since then. Irazoqui et al. [21] [22] retrieved an Advanced Encryption Standard (AES) cryptographic key and private keys from other cryptographic libraries in a cloud environment, using Flush+Reload. Later, they presented another paper where cryptographic libraries are detected across virtual machines, along with their IP addresses. Gülmezoğlu et al. [23] improved the technique and presented a *known-ciphertext only* cache side-channel attack against AES. Benger et al. [24] used Flush+Reload to attack OpenSSL ECDSA signatures.

The `Evict+Reload` technique, introduced by Gruss et al. [25], is a variation of Flush+Reload. It consists of two phases. First, in the profiling phase, the attacker crafts a model (a template [26] [27]) of signals and noise from the cache side-channel traces, which is a matrix with the cache-hit ratio of the address of a specific target event generated on a device that the attacker controls. Secondly, in the exploitation phase, the attacker uses the template matrix previously crafted to deduce events in the system cache, based on the differences of cache hits. After the attack is performed, a report is generated in the attacker machine to be manually analysed. Both phases use standard cache side-channel attack techniques (e.g., Flush+Reload) to obtain the cache hit ratio. Nevertheless, the authors noted that the technique can be adapted to evict a cache line without using the *flush cache line* instruction, thus invalidating a countermeasure proposed by other studies [18] [19] [28]. The method they used to evict a cache line indirectly is to access a physically congruent large array [25].

The `Flush+Flush` technique was presented by Gruss et al. [29]. With it, they achieved a stealthy method to perform cache side-channel attacks without access to the data. Consequently, Flush+Flush does not generate more cache misses than a benign program, avoiding some countermeasures that relied on hardware performance counters for detection [30]–[32]. Instead of measuring the access time of a memory location, they measured the time that the *flush cache line* instruction takes. If the data is cached, this instruction takes more time than if the data is not cached, enabling the side-channel. Furthermore, given that it can work at a higher frequency, Flush+Flush is more efficient than other cache side-channel techniques previously known, in terms of speed.

There is a study that introduces a different technique for victim-memory shared side-channel attacks, which avoids the measurement of time. Disselkoen et al. [33] proposed a method to abuse last level cache in a virtualised system using the Intel Transactional Synchronization Extensions (TSX) instruction set [34] [35]. Intel TSX allows the programmer to specify *transactions* of code, in a way that either all the code is successfully executed (transaction completed) or, if anything fails, all the changes made in memory during the transaction are cancelled (transaction aborted). The authors are able to determine if the cache state has been modified by the victim or not, by means of the hardware callbacks provided by Intel TSX. These callbacks are executed if the victim accesses to the target data. As a consequence, there is no need for timing measurement, given that the attacker gets a side-channel through the state of the transactions (completed or aborted).

C. Shared Memory + Rowhammer

Previous techniques exploit the fact that the attacker is sharing memory with the victim in a read-only fashion, to leak sensitive information of all kinds and bypass security mechanisms like Address Space Layout Randomisation [15]. On the other hand, some studies combine this condition with the `Rowhammer` technique [36] to not only read arbitrary data in the victim system but also to write. Rowhammer is a technique that exploits a hardware vulnerability present in many modern Dynamic Random-Access Memory (DRAM) modules. DRAM memory cells can leak their charges to nearby memory rows if they are repeatedly activated in a short period of time, modifying the contents of a row which was not intended to be accessed. As a consequence, an attacker is able to flip bits of arbitrary physical memory locations by repeatedly activating one or both adjacent rows.

Bosman et al. [37] built a "weird machine" that is able to perform a byte-by-byte disclosure of sensitive data of neighbour virtual machines. In this paper, they also disclose high-entropy randomised pointers, providing three different approaches: memory alignment probing, partial reuse, and birthday heap spray. After leaking and gathering all the needed information of the victim using the previous methods, the authors combine memory deduplication with Rowhammer to attack the browser, performing a write operation in a physical page belonging to the victim, without requiring any software vulnerability to perform the attack.

Similarly, Razavi et al. [38] introduced a novel exploitation technique called Flip Feng Shui (FFS). With it, an attacker is able to *exchange* the physical location of a page that is shared with the victim by using memory deduplication. Then, she can trigger a Rowhammer attack and modify their contents, inducing bit flips in a fully controlled way. As a consequence, this technique allows an attacker to write into a page of the victim virtual machine.

IV. Proposed Solution

In this section, we present Slicedup, a memory deduplication design for multi-tenant clouds, where each tenant is the administrator of a group of trust that consists of multiple virtual machines. The sharing is limited to a given group, and thus the sharing of pages belonging to different tenants is not allowed. This way, memory deduplication can be enabled,

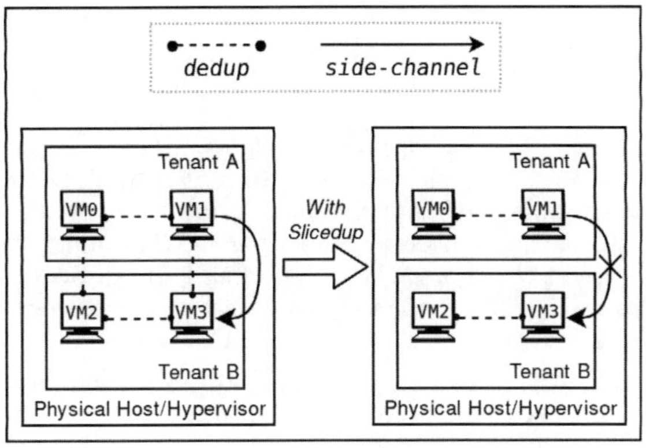

Figure 1. Tenant-aware memory deduplication scheme.

maintaining an equivalent level of security for each tenant, given that pages are never shared across security boundaries. In addition, the deduplication rates for the virtual machines of a specific tenant are not affected.

Our proposed solution is to add tenancy awareness to the deduplication algorithm, identifying every virtual machine based on a Tenant ID. Then, when a page is being processed before being shared with another one, the Tenant ID is combined with the page contents in a way that other pages with the same contents will only be shared with pages belonging to virtual machines of the same tenant. This solution provides a fair trade-off, where the isolation of virtual machines of a tenant is kept along with the sharing effectiveness of memory deduplication.

Figure 1 shows an example, where VM1 of the tenant A is attacking to VM3 of the tenant B. Memory deduplication is applied to all the virtual machines hosted in the same physical machine. Therefore, the attack that VM1 was performing to VM3 is prevented with Slicedup. As a trade-off, this action has a price because the sharing is being limited, and there will exist duplicates of pages from different tenants that would have been merged otherwise.

We have calculated an estimate of the sharing rate based on previous experiments [39] [40], fitting the points into the $log(x)$ function, using the *least-squares fit* technique. Figure 2 shows the resulting function, where the x-axis is the number of virtual machines running at the same time. We can get the amount of memory saved for a given number of virtual machines.

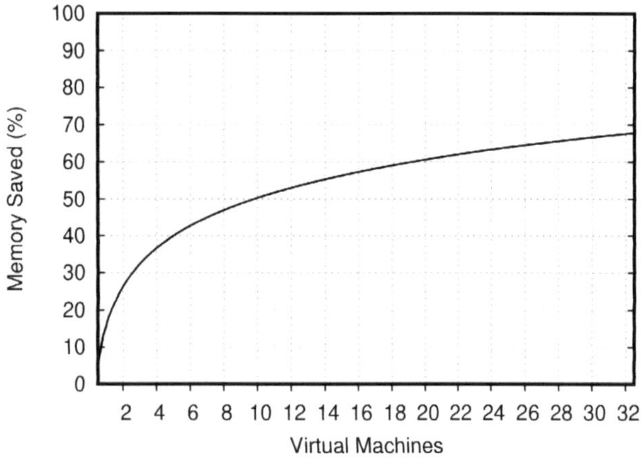

Figure 2. Estimated rate of memory saved by deduplication.

Table I shows the estimation of memory saved in a physical host, comparing two cases: with standard memory deduplication and with Slicedup. In the table, we are using the approximation showed by Red Hat [39] assuming that the virtual machines are Windows XP with 1 GiB of RAM. Then, the number of virtual machines in each case is the maximum we can run when memory deduplication is disabled.

Slicedup offers a compromise solution between performance and security, allowing memory sharing without compromising the system security. With it, customers of cloud infrastructure providers can run more virtual machines than if memory deduplication is disabled. For example, when the host has 32 GiB of RAM and 8 tenants, each tenant is allowed to run two more virtual machines.

TABLE I. MEMORY SAVED WITH STANDARD AND SLICEDUP.

Physical	Num. of	Memory Deduplication	
Memory	Tenants	Standard	Slicedup
8 GiB	2	3.76 GiB (47.00%)	2.94 GiB (36.75%)
	4	3.76 GiB (47.00%)	2.11 GiB (26.37%)
	8	3.76 GiB (47.00%)	1.29 GiB (16.12%)
16 GiB	2	9.17 GiB (57.31%)	7.52 GiB (47.00%)
	4	9.17 GiB (57.31%)	5.90 GiB (36.87%)
	8	9.17 GiB (57.31%)	4.20 GiB (26.25%)
32 GiB	2	21.6 GiB (67.50%)	18.30 GiB (57.18%)
	4	21.6 GiB (67.50%)	15.00 GiB (46.87%)
	8	21.6 GiB (67.50%)	11.70 GiB (36.56%)

V. SOLUTION DISCUSSION

Memory deduplication was designed as a performance technique to increase the memory savings of a system. It has been proved [41]–[44] that it offers an effective and efficient improvement of the physical memory resources management when it is enabled. However, the side-channel produced by memory deduplication is a security problem for the clients of cloud infrastructure providers. Although several studies proposed different possible countermeasures to avoid this issue, there is no consolidated solution which offers similar performance than the original implementations and provides a defence to all the possible attacks without adding complexity.

For example, Payer [32] proposed HexPADS as an anomaly detection system. It is a signature-based Attack Detection System that relies on performance counters. HexPADS analyses running processes, measuring their performance and checking a set of signatures. It is able to detect long running side-channel attacks with low overhead. Nevertheless, it is prone to false positives and false negatives. Besides, as a signature-based system, it doesn't detect new attacks (unknown signature). Furthermore, given that it is based on performance counters, other advanced and stealthy cache attacks can bypass the detection, such as Flush+Flush.

Oliverio et al. [45] proposed VUsion as a new design of memory deduplication that cuts information leaks and Rowhammer attacks based on memory deduplication. It hides the ability of the attackers to distinguish between shared pages and non-shared pages, thus reducing the attack surface. To achieve this, the authors follow a fundamental principle that they call Same Behavior (SB), which means that the attacker will obtain the same results whether the page being tested is merged or not. VUsion allows page sharing among different tenants with an acceptable memory sharing rate. On the other hand, the Same Behavior principle reduces the pages that can be candidates to be merged (only idle pages). Unfortunately, VUsion is intricate to implement. Author's *proof of concept* implementation relies on using reserved bits of the Page Table Entry (PTE) as an alternative to avoid the use of the `present` bit, which would need intrusive changes to the Linux kernel.

Other solutions were proposed, for example, to encrypt the memory of a given process to avoid deduplication [9] [18], software diversification to detect anomalies [18], to share only pages containing zeros [37], or to completely disable memory deduplication [28]. However, those ideas didn't get to consolidate a suitable solution that would provide secure memory sharing.

Slicedup achieves its purpose with a straightforward and simple but effective approach. It merges not only idle pages but also the active ones (as standard deduplication). There are also a few drawbacks to this approach. The memory sharing efficiency is tied to the number of tenants present in a physical host. Given that sharing pages among different tenants is not allowed, the set of pages that can be potentially shared decreases when more tenants are located in the same physical host. Besides, although Slicedup is providing protection among different tenants, it can not protect virtual machines residing in the same tenant. In that scenario, information disclosure and physical memory massaging [38] are still feasible. However, Slicedup offers strong protection on systems where all virtual machines in a particular tenant trust each other. Consequently, attacks from distrusting tenants are ineffective.

VI. Conclusions and Future Work

In this paper, we have presented Slicedup, a memory deduplication design for multi-tenant cloud systems. Slicedup offers a trade-off between sharing pages of all the virtual machines, which weakens the system, and disabling entirely memory deduplication, which means loss of memory savings.

With Slicedup, the virtual machines belonging to the same tenant are sharing their memory because they are part of a group of trust, but not among tenants. As we showed, this is preventing side-channel attacks among machines belonging to different tenants and, at the same time, it provides good memory savings. Our analysis showed that Slicedup prevents side-channels attacks while offering similar memory savings when the number of tenants per physical host is low, and around a 50% of memory savings when the number of tenants is higher.

In future work, a proper evaluation of this approach using benchmarks needs to be done, comparing it with existing solutions and measuring performance and memory saving rates.

References

[1] M. Armbrust et al., "A view of cloud computing," Communications of the ACM, vol. 53, no. 4, 2010, pp. 50–58.

[2] Compaq Computer Corporation. Internet solution division strategy for cloud computing. [Retrieved: Sep, 2018]. [Online]. Available: http://www.technologyreview.com/sites/default/files/legacy/compaq_cst_1996_0.pdf [retrieved: November, 1996]

[3] H. Marco-Gisbert and I. Ripoll, "Preventing brute force attacks against stack canary protection on networking servers," in Network Computing and Applications (NCA), 2013 12th IEEE International Symposium on. IEEE, 2013, pp. 243–250.

[4] K. Braden et al., "Leakage-resilient layout randomization for mobile devices." in NDSS, 2016.

[5] Red Hat. Disabling ksm service to avoid memory deduplication as an advanced exploitation vector. [Online]. Available: https://access.redhat.com/solutions/2356551 [retrieved: Sep, 2018]

[6] C. Huffman. Memory combining in windows 8 and windows server 2012. [Online]. Available: https://blogs.technet.microsoft.com/clinth/2012/11/29/memory-combining-in-windows-8-and-windows-server-2012/ [retrieved: Sep, 2018]

[7] P. J. Denning, "The locality principle," in Communication Networks And Computer Systems: A Tribute to Professor Erol Gelenbe. World Scientific, 2006, pp. 43–67.

[8] K. Suzaki, K. Iijima, T. Yagi, and C. Artho, "Memory deduplication as a threat to the guest os," in Proceedings of the Fourth European Workshop on System Security, ser. EUROSEC '11. New York, NY, USA: ACM, 2011, pp. 1:1–1:6. [Online]. Available: http://doi.acm.org/10.1145/1972551.1972552

[9] ——, "Software side channel attack on memory deduplication," in ACM Symposium on Operating Systems Principles (SOSP 2011), Poster session, 2011.

[10] R. Owens and W. Wang, "Non-interactive os fingerprinting through memory de-duplication technique in virtual machines," in Proceedings of the 30th IEEE IPCCC, ser. PCCC '11. Washington, DC, USA: IEEE Computer Society, 2011, pp. 1–8. [Online]. Available: http://dx.doi.org/10.1109/PCCC.2011.6108094

[11] J. Xiao, Z. Xu, H. Huang, and H. Wang, "A covert channel construction in a virtualized environment," in Proceedings of the 2012 ACM Conference on Computer and Communications Security, ser. CCS '12. New York, NY, USA: ACM, 2012, pp. 1040–1042. [Online]. Available: http://doi.acm.org/10.1145/2382196.2382318

[12] ——, "Security implications of memory deduplication in a virtualized environment," in Proceedings of the 2013 43rd Annual IEEE/IFIP International Conference on Dependable Systems and Networks (DSN), ser. DSN '13. Washington, DC, USA: IEEE Computer Society, 2013, pp. 1–12. [Online]. Available: http://dx.doi.org/10.1109/DSN.2013.6575349

[13] K. Suzaki, K. Iijima, T. Yagi, and C. Artho, "Implementation of a memory disclosure attack on memory deduplication of virtual machines," IEICE Transactions on Fundamentals of Electronics Communications and Computer Sciences, vol. E96-A, no. 1, 2013, pp. 215–224, qC 20170104.

[14] A. Barresi, K. Razavi, M. Payer, and T. R. Gross, "CAIN: Silently breaking ASLR in the cloud," in 9th USENIX Workshop on Offensive Technologies (WOOT 15). Washington, D.C.: USENIX Association, 2015. [Online]. Available: https://www.usenix.org/conference/woot15/workshop-program/presentation/barresi

[15] Pax address space layout randomization (aslr). [Retrieved: Sep, 2018]. [Online]. Available: https://pax.grsecurity.net/docs/aslr.txt

[16] D. Gruss, D. Bidner, and S. Mangard, "Practical memory deduplication attacks inźsandboxed javascript," in Proceedings, Part I, of the 20th European Symposium on Computer Security – ESORICS 2015 - Volume 9326. New York, NY, USA: Springer-Verlag New York, Inc., 2015, pp. 108–122. [Online]. Available: http://dx.doi.org/10.1007/978-3-319-24174-6_6

[17] H. Rong, H. Wang, J. Liu, X. Zhang, and M. Xian, "Windtalker: An efficient and robust protocol of cloud covert channel based on memory deduplication," in 2015 IEEE Fifth International Conference on Big Data and Cloud Computing, Aug 2015, pp. 68–75.

[18] Y. Yarom and K. Falkner, "Flush+reload: A high resolution, low noise, l3 cache side-channel attack," in Proceedings of the 23rd USENIX Conference on Security Symposium, ser. SEC'14. Berkeley, CA, USA: USENIX Association, 2014, pp. 719–732. [Online]. Available: http://dl.acm.org/citation.cfm?id=2671225.2671271

[19] Y. Yarom and N. Benger, "Recovering openssl ecdsa nonces using the flush+reload cache side-channel attack," IACR Cryptology ePrint Archive, vol. 2014, 2014, p. 140.

[20] D. Gullasch, E. Bangerter, and S. Krenn, "Cache games – bringing access-based cache attacks on aes to practice," in Proceedings of the 2011 IEEE Symposium on Security and Privacy, ser. SP '11. Washington, DC, USA: IEEE Computer Society, 2011, pp. 490–505. [Online]. Available: http://dx.doi.org/10.1109/SP.2011.22

[21] G. Irazoqui, M. S. Inci, T. Eisenbarth, and B. Sunar, Wait a Minute! A fast, Cross-VM Attack on AES. Cham: Springer International Publishing, 2014, pp. 299–319. [Online]. Available: https://doi.org/10.1007/978-3-319-11379-1_15

[22] ——, "Lucky 13 strikes back," in Proceedings of the 10th ACM Symposium on Information, Computer and Communications Security, ser. ASIA CCS '15. New York, NY, USA: ACM, 2015, pp. 85–96. [Online]. Available: http://doi.acm.org/10.1145/2714576.2714625

[23] B. Gülmezoğlu, M. S. İnci, G. Irazoqui, T. Eisenbarth, and B. Sunar, "A faster and more realistic flush+reload attack on aes," in Revised Selected Papers of the 6th International Workshop on Constructive Side-Channel Analysis and Secure Design - Volume 9064, ser. COSADE 2015. New

York, NY, USA: Springer-Verlag New York, Inc., 2015, pp. 111–126. [Online]. Available: http://dx.doi.org/10.1007/978-3-319-21476-4_8

[24] N. Benger, J. van de Pol, N. P. Smart, and Y. Yarom, ""ooh aah... just a little bit" : A small amount of side channel can go a long way," in Cryptographic Hardware and Embedded Systems – CHES 2014, L. Batina and M. Robshaw, Eds. Berlin, Heidelberg: Springer Berlin Heidelberg, 2014, pp. 75–92.

[25] D. Gruss, R. Spreitzer, and S. Mangard, "Cache template attacks: Automating attacks on inclusive last-level caches," in Proceedings of the 24th USENIX Conference on Security Symposium, ser. SEC'15. Berkeley, CA, USA: USENIX Association, 2015, pp. 897–912. [Online]. Available: http://dl.acm.org/citation.cfm?id=2831143.2831200

[26] S. Chari, J. R. Rao, and P. Rohatgi, "Template attacks," in Cryptographic Hardware and Embedded Systems - CHES 2002, B. S. Kaliski, ç. K. Koç, and C. Paar, Eds. Berlin, Heidelberg: Springer Berlin Heidelberg, 2003, pp. 13–28.

[27] B. B. Brumley and R. M. Hakala, "Cache-timing template attacks," in Advances in Cryptology – ASIACRYPT 2009, M. Matsui, Ed. Berlin, Heidelberg: Springer Berlin Heidelberg, 2009, pp. 667–684.

[28] Y. Zhang, A. Juels, M. K. Reiter, and T. Ristenpart, "Cross-tenant side-channel attacks in paas clouds," in Proceedings of the 2014 ACM SIGSAC Conference on Computer and Communications Security, ser. CCS '14. New York, NY, USA: ACM, 2014, pp. 990–1003. [Online]. Available: http://doi.acm.org/10.1145/2660267.2660356

[29] D. Gruss, C. Maurice, K. Wagner, and S. Mangard, "Flush+flush: A fast and stealthy cache attack," in Detection of Intrusions and Malware, and Vulnerability Assessment, J. Caballero, U. Zurutuza, and R. J. Rodríguez, Eds. Cham: Springer International Publishing, 2016, pp. 279–299.

[30] M. Chiappetta, E. Savas, and C. Yilmaz, "Real time detection of cache-based side-channel attacks using hardware performance counters," Cryptology ePrint Archive, Report 2015/1034, 2015, https://eprint.iacr.org/2015/1034.

[31] N. Herath and A. Fogh, "These are not your grand daddys cpu performance counters–cpu hardware performance counters for security," Black Hat Briefings, 2015.

[32] M. Payer, "Hexpads: A platform to detect "stealth" attacks," in Engineering Secure Software and Systems, J. Caballero, E. Bodden, and E. Athanasopoulos, Eds. Cham: Springer International Publishing, 2016, pp. 138–154.

[33] C. Disselkoen, D. Kohlbrenner, L. Porter, and D. Tullsen, "Prime+abort: A timer-free high-precision l3 cache attack using intel TSX," in 26th USENIX Security Symposium (USENIX Security 17). Vancouver, BC: USENIX Association, 2017, pp. 51–67. [Online]. Available: https://www.usenix.org/conference/usenixsecurity17/technical-sessions/presentation/disselkoen

[34] P. Hammarlund et al., "Haswell: The fourth-generation intel core processor," IEEE Micro, vol. 34, no. 2, 2014, pp. 6–20.

[35] P. Guide, "Intel® 64 and ia-32 architectures software developer's manual," Volume 3B: System programming Guide, Part, vol. 2, 2011.

[36] Kim et al., "Flipping bits in memory without accessing them: An experimental study of dram disturbance errors," SIGARCH Comput. Archit. News, vol. 42, no. 3, Jun. 2014, pp. 361–372. [Online]. Available: http://doi.acm.org/10.1145/2678373.2665726

[37] E. Bosman, K. Razavi, H. Bos, and C. Giuffrida, "Dedup est machina: Memory deduplication as an advanced exploitation vector," in IEEE Symposium on Security and Privacy, SP 2016, San Jose, CA, USA, May 22-26, 2016, 2016, pp. 987–1004. [Online]. Available: https://doi.org/10.1109/SP.2016.63

[38] K. Razavi et al., "Flip feng shui: Hammering a needle in the software stack," in 25th USENIX Security Symposium (USENIX Security 16). Austin, TX: USENIX Association, 2016, pp. 1–18. [Online]. Available: https://www.usenix.org/conference/usenixsecurity16/technical-sessions/presentation/razavi

[39] "Linux 2.6.32 release announcement," Dec 2009, [Retrieved: Sep, 2018]. [Online]. Available: https://kernelnewbies.org/Linux_2_6_32

[40] K. Suzaki, K. Iijima, T. Yagi, and C. Artho, "Effects of memory randomization, sanitization and page cache on memory deduplication," in Proc. European Workshop on System Security (EuroSec 2012) :, 2012, qC 20170104.

[41] D. Gupta et al., "Difference engine: Harnessing memory redundancy in virtual machines," in Proceedings of the 8th USENIX Conference on Operating Systems Design and Implementation, ser. OSDI'08. Berkeley, CA, USA: USENIX Association, 2008, pp. 309–322. [Online]. Available: http://dl.acm.org/citation.cfm?id=1855741.1855763

[42] A. Arcangeli, I. Eidus, and C. Wright, "Increasing memory density by using ksm," in In OLS, 2009.

[43] N. Rauschmayr and A. Streit, "Reducing the memory footprint of parallel applications with ksm," in Facing the Multicore-Challenge III. Springer, 2013, pp. 48–59.

[44] Y. Deng, X. Huang, L. Song, Y. Zhou, and F. Wang, "Memory deduplication: An effective approach to improve the memory system," Journal of Information Science and Engineering, vol. 33, no. 5, 2017, pp. 1103–1120.

[45] M. Oliverio, K. Razavi, H. Bos, and C. Giuffrida, "Secure page fusion with vusion," in Proceedings of the 26th Symposium on Operating Systems Principles, ser. SOSP '17. New York, NY, USA: ACM, 2017, pp. 531–545. [Online]. Available: http://doi.acm.org/10.1145/3132747.3132781

Wireless Multihop Networks with Network Coding Communication Using Collision Detection of Control Messages

Yusuke Aoi and Hiroaki Higaki

Department of Robotics and Mechatronics,
Tokyo Denki University, Japan
Email: {aoi,hig}@higlab.net

***Abstract*—In some wireless network applications using bidirectional wireless multihop transmissions of sequences of data messages, intermediate wireless nodes hold temporarily data messages in both directions with high probability. Network coding methods have been proposed for reduction of forwarding and end-to-end transmission delays and for increase of end-to-end data message throughput. However, for collision-free transmissions, 2-hop neighbor intermediate nodes are required to be suspended during a data message transmission. Some extended Request To Send/Clear To Send (RTS/CTS) controls have been proposed for network coding support; however, for avoidance of collisions between control messages, longer transmission delay is inevitable. This paper proposes a novel RTS/CTS control method for supporting network coding in bidirectional data message transmission. Here, the CTS and ACK control messages are transmitted with the usual Short Inter Frame Space ($SIFS$) interval and their correct simultaneous transmissions are detected by their collisions. In simulation experiments, 30.1% higher end-to-end throughput of data messages is achieved by the proposed RTS/CTS control in comparison with conventional methods.**

Keywords*–*Wireless Multihop Transmissions; Bidirectional Communications; Collision Avoidance; RTS/CTS Control.

I. INTRODUCTION

In wireless multihop networks, such as wireless ad-hoc networks, wireless mesh networks and wireless sensor networks consisting of numerous mobile and/or stationary wireless nodes with wireless transmission/reception devices, data messages are transmitted along a wireless multihop transmission route. It is a sequence of neighboring nodes, which forwards data messages from their previous-hop node to their next-hop node. Advantages of wireless multihop transmissions are reduction of end-to-end transmission delay by avoidance of collisions of wireless signals simultaneously transmitted by multiple nodes, reduction of required transmission power consumption in each node and improvement of data message reachability in wide-area and large-scale networks with a large number of nodes. Transmissions of data messages are realized by cooperation of all the intermediate nodes included in a route $||N_0 \dots N_n\rangle\rangle$ from a source node N_0 to a destination node N_n. Each intermediate node N_i $(1 \leq i \leq n-1)$ receives data messages from its previous-hop intermediate node N_{i-1} and forwards them to its next-hop intermediate node N_{i+1}.

In transmissions of a sequence of data messages, collisions between successively transmitted data messages might degrade their performance, i.e., such collisions cause longer end-to-end transmission delay and lower end-to-end throughput. Since most wireless LAN protocols, such as IEEE802.11, support Carrier Sense Multiple Access with Collision Avoidance (CSMA/CA) [7], neighbor intermediate nodes N_i and N_{i+1} do not transmit data messages simultaneously. However, N_{i-1} and N_{i+1} might transmit data messages simultaneously since N_{i-1} is out of the wireless signal transmission range of N_{i+1} and vice versa. Though their next-hop nodes N_i and N_{i+2} are different, a collision of data messages can occur at N_i since N_i is included in wireless signal transmission ranges of not only N_{i-1} but also N_{i+1}, as shown in Figure 1. Hence, data messages transmitted by not only N_{i-1} but also N_{i+1} reach N_i and the collision can occur at N_i. Retransmissions of data messages due to such collisions by the hidden-terminal problem at intermediate wireless nodes and transmission intervals for contentions, i.e., for avoidance of collisions caused by 1-hop and/or 2-hop neighbor intermediate nodes cause longer transmission delay for forwarding of data messages in each intermediate node. This makes end-to-end transmission delay of data messages longer. Hence, the source node should reduce its transmission rate of data messages. However, lower end-to-end throughput of data messages should be accepted.

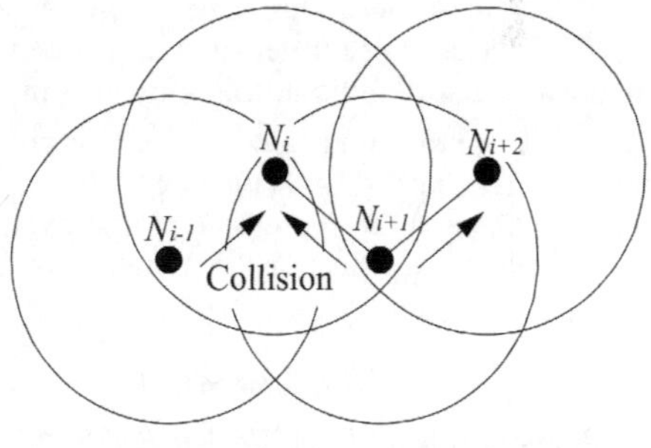

Figure 1. Collision of Successively Transmitted Data Messages due to the Hidden-Terminal Problem in Wireless Multihop Networks.

In Peer-to-Peer (P2P) type network applications in which multimedia data such as voice, picture and video data is transmitted bi-directionally, sequences of data messages are transmitted concurrently in both directions along a wireless multihop transmission route between two terminal wireless nodes, N_0 and N_n. Here, it is expected that collisions of data messages transmitted in the same and/or the opposite directions occur much more frequently than the cases of uni-directional transmissions of a sequence of data messages. For improvement of performance of bi-directional transmissions, the introduction of network coding communication has been proposed [2]. As shown in Figure 2, an intermediate node N_i broadcasts a network coded data message m_e for transmission of data messages m_f from N_{i-1} and m_b from N_{i+1}, e.g., $m_e := m_f \oplus m_b$. On receipt of m_e, N_{i-1} and N_{i+1} induce m_b and m_f by using m_e broadcasted by N_i and m_f and m_b buffered in N_{i-1} and N_{i+1}, respectively, e.g., $m_b = m_e \oplus m_f$ in N_{i-1} and $m_f = m_e \oplus m_b$ in N_{i+1}. By using this network coding communication, fewer messages are transmitted than the usual combination of two one-to-one data message transmissions from N_i to N_{i-1} and from N_i to N_{i+1}. In addition, by reducing the number of transmitted data messages, the opportunities of collisions among data messages and/or control messages, such as ACK control messages, are reduced. Hence, end-to-end performance such as transmission delay and throughput of data messages is expected to be improved.

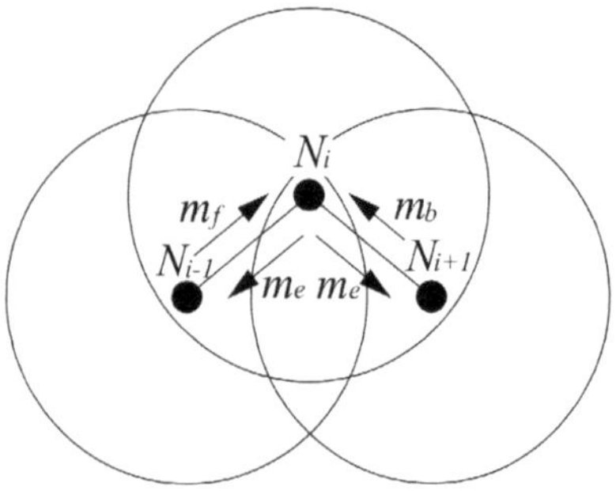

Figure 2. Network Coding Communication in Wireless Multihop Networks.

However, collisions between data and/or control messages caused by bi-directional transmissions of sequences of data messages might cause reduction of transmission performance. Hence, the RTS/CTS control should be introduced for collision avoidance, which should be modified for network coding communication since the original one is designed for ad-hoc communication and uni-directional wireless multihop transmission of data messages. This paper proposes a novel extended RTS/CTS control for network coding communication which improves end-to-end transmission performance.

In Section II, we explain related works. Our proposed novel RTS/CTS control method for network coding communication is proposed in Section III. Performance improvement by our proposal is evaluated in Section IV. Finally, we conclude in Section V.

II. RELATED WORK

This section explains conventional methods to exchange control messages such as RTS, CTS and ACK for collision avoidance in network coding communication in wireless multihop networks. Some of them are designed for wireless multihop networks and the others are designed for wireless ad-hoc networks, i.e., for supporting 1-hop data message exchanges between neighbor wireless nodes. However, for comparison with our proposal, they are explained as being used for data message transmissions along a wireless multihop transmissions. That is, as being network coding communication methods among successive intermediate nodes, N_{i-1}, N_i and N_{i+1}. Hence, N_i has two data messages, one is received from N_{i-1} and is about to be forwarded to N_{i+1} and the other is received from N_{i+1} and is about to be forwarded to N_{i-1}, configures a network encoded data message by using these data messages and then broadcasts the network encoded message to its wireless transmission area including both N_{i-1} and N_{i+1}.

COPE [2] and IFNCPA (Inter-Flow Network Coding with Passive ACK) [4] propose methods to exchange ACK control messages in network coding communication. If both N_{i-1} and N_{i+1} send back ACK control messages to N_i with a $SIFS$ interval after receipt of network coded data message broadcasted from N_i in accordance with a wireless LAN protocol IEEE 802.11, a collision between these two ACK control messages occurs at N_i and N_i fails to receive these ACK control messages. Hence, N_i cannot detect the correct receipts of the network coded data message in N_{i-1} and N_{i+1}. In order to avoid collisions between the ACK control messages transmitted simultaneously, COPE proposes a method in which an ACK control message for receipt of the network coded data message is piggybacked to the next data message transmitted by N_{i-1} and N_{i+1}, as shown in Figure 3. COPE was originally designed not for wireless multihop communication but for wireless ad-hoc communication. Since N_{i-1} and N_{i+1} independently require to transmit their next data message, collisions of the piggybacked ACK control messages are expected to be avoided; however, the intervals of the ACK control messages after receipt of the network coded data message depend on the applications in N_{i-1} and N_{i+1}. The network coded data message tends to be retransmitted frequently.

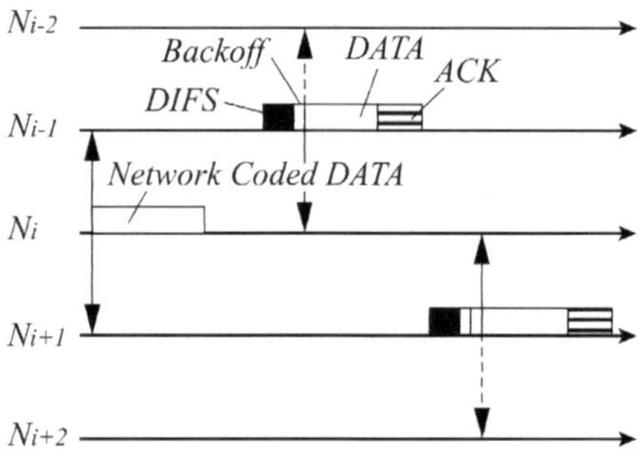

Figure 3. ACK Control Message Piggybacked to Data Message in COPE.

IFNCPA is based on the same idea in COPE but is designed for wireless multihop communication. On receipt of the network coded data message broadcasted from an intermediate node N_i, both of its neighbor intermediate nodes N_{i-1} and N_{i+1} extract the data messages to be received. Since all three wireless nodes are in a route, both N_{i-1} and N_{i+1} are required to forward data messages received from N_i. Thus, after a DCF Inter Frame Space ($DIFS$) interval and their random backoffs for collision avoidance, N_{i-1} and N_{i+1} forward the received data message to their neighbor intermediate nodes N_{i-2} and N_{i+2}, respectively. Since N_i is included in wireless transmission ranges of both N_{i-1} and N_{i+1}, it can overhear these data messages which play the role of passive ACK control messages for the network coded data message broadcasted by N_i. Different from the ACK control messages piggybacked to the next data messages in COPE, the passive ACK control messages in IFNCPA are surely transmitted after an estimated interval since the data messages are surely forwarded, as shown in Figure 4. This solves the retransmission problem in COPE. However, it is highly possible for N_{i-1} and N_{i+1} to forward the data messages simultaneously since N_{i-1} and N_{i+1} are hidden terminals for N_i. As a result, these forwarded data messages might collide at N_i. This means a failure of passive ACK control message transmissions to N_i. Hence, for network coding communication, the RTS/CTS control is mandatory for collision avoidance between the ACK control messages.

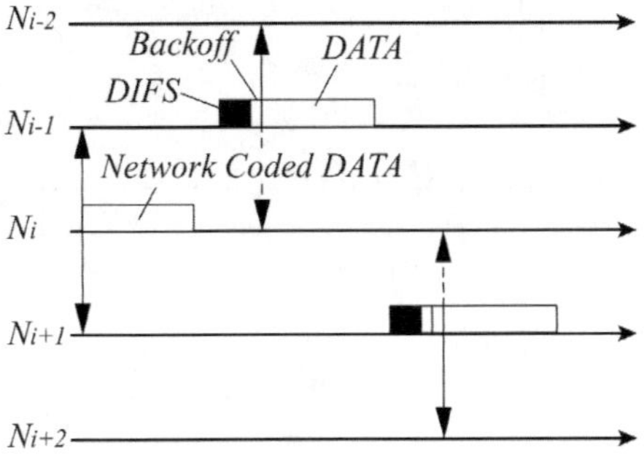

Figure 4. Pseudo ACK by Overhearing of Forwarded Data Message in IFNCPA.

In transmissions of data messages along a route, for avoidance of collisions caused between 1-hop neighbor intermediate nodes, i.e., between exposed ones, and between 2-hop neighbor intermediate nodes, i.e., between hidden ones, data and control message transmissions by 1-hop and 2-hop neighbor nodes, N_{i-2}, N_{i-1}, N_{i+1} and N_{i+2} should be suspended for data message transmissions by N_i. Thus, the introduction of the RTS/CTS control is inevitable. In the usual RTS/CTS control for a data message transmission from N_i to N_{i+1}, N_i broadcasts an RTS control message which reaches both N_{i-1} and N_{i+1} and then N_{i+1} broadcasts a CTS control message which reaches both N_i and N_{i+2}. Even if N_{i-1} receives an RTS control message from N_{i-2}, N_{i-1} never sends back a CTS control message. Therefore, a data message from N_i never collides with another data message transmitted along the route. However, in network coding communication, N_i transmits data messages to both N_{i-1} and N_{i+1} by broadcasting the network coded data message. So, the RTS control message transmission from N_{i-2} should also be avoided. This means that the transmission of the CTS control message is required not only for N_{i+1} but also for N_{i-1}. For collision-free transmissions of network coded data messages, it is required for N_i to receive the CTS control messages from both N_{i-1} and N_{i+1}. In the original RTS/CTS control in wireless LAN protocols such as IEEE 802.11, a CTS control message is broadcasted with the $SIFS$ interval after receipt of the broadcasted RTS control message. Hence, CTS control messages from N_{i-1} and N_{i+1} surely collide at N_i in network coding communication.

In CSMA with RTS/CTS [5] and NC-MAC [1], the order information of the transmissions of CTS control messages is included in an RTS control message. As shown in Figure 5, according to the order the information is piggybacked onto the RTS control message from N_i, one of N_{i-1} and N_{i+1} broadcasts a CTS control message with the $SIFS$ interval after receipt of the RTS control message and the other broadcasts a CTS control message with an interval enough for avoidance of a collision between the CTS control messages at N_i. This method is also applied to avoid collisions between the ACK control messages transmitted to N_i by N_{i-1} and N_{i+1} after receipt of a network coded data message from N_i. Though, different from the CTS control messages broadcasted by N_{i-1} and N_{i+1}, the ACK control messages are unicasted to N_i by N_{i-1} and N_{i+1}, these are transmitted simultaneously, which causes a collision at N_i. Hence, the order information of the ACK messages is included in the network coded data message. This method works well for avoidance of collisions of the CTS and ACK control messages at N_i; however, the required time duration for a transmission of a network coded data message causes a longer data message transmission delay and lower end-to-end throughput of data messages.

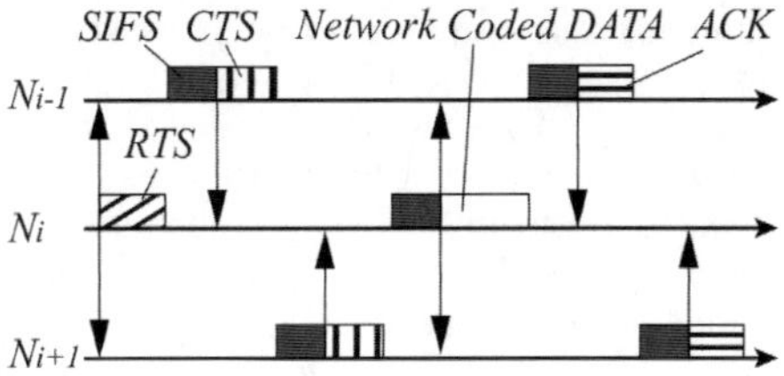

Figure 5. Collision Avoidance of CTS and ACK Control Messages in NC-MAC.

Adaptive Round-Robbin Acknowledge and Retransmit (ARAR) [3] is a method for a multicast data message transmission in a wireless ad-hoc network. A sender node N_s broadcasts an RTS control message to all its neighbor nodes in its wireless transmission range. After a $SIFS$ interval, all the receiver nodes which successfully receive the RTS control message send back a CTS control message to N_s. If multiple receiver nodes simultaneously send back the CTS control messages to N_s, these collide at N_s and N_s cannot receive these CTS control messages correctly, as shown in Figure 6. Hence, N_s cannot determine which receiver wireless nodes received the RTS control message correctly. However, N_s identifies the following three cases: (1) no receiver nodes correctly received the RTS control message if no CTS control message is sent back to N_s. (2) only 1 receiver node correctly received the RTS control message if only 1 CTS control message is transmitted and received by N_s correctly, i.e., without collisions. (3) multiple receiver nodes correctly received the RTS control message if multiple CTS control messages are transmitted and collide at N_s. Our proposal for performance improved network coding communication is based on this 3-cases identification in ARAR.

III. PROPOSAL

We suppose wireless multihop networks with bi-directional and concurrent transmissions of sequences of data messages along a wireless multihop transmission route between two

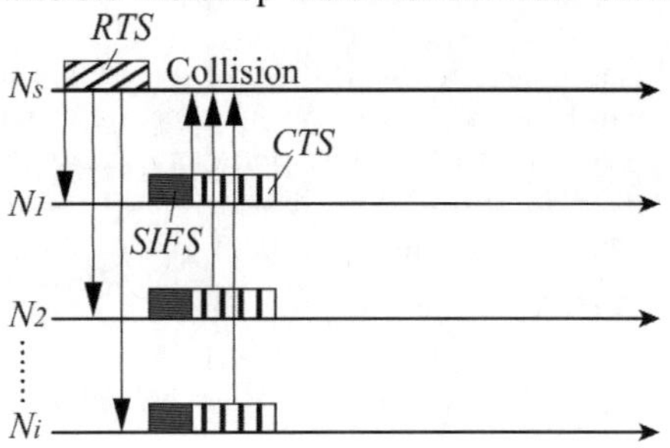

Figure 6. Collision of $CTSs$ in ARAR.

terminal wireless nodes. Here, most of the intermediate wireless nodes temporarily hold data messages in transmission for both directions in their buffer. This is because data message transmissions between two successive intermediate nodes are based on the half-duplex communication. Hence, there are so many opportunities to apply the network coding communication in which each intermediate node encodes data messages transmitted in different directions into one combined data message and broadcasts it to transmit it to its neighbor intermediate nodes in both directions that the end-to-end transmission performance such as end-to-end transmission delay and end-to-end throughput is expected to be improved. However, as discussed in the previous section, a sequence of data messages transmitted along a route tends to collide at intermediate nodes due to exposed and hidden node problems. Especially, it is more difficult to avoid and/or reduce collisions in bi-directional and concurrent transmissions of data messages along a route. Hence, collision avoidance methods such as the RTS/CTS control should be introduced. On the other hand, since an intermediate node broadcasts a network coded data messages to transmit original data messages to both directions to its two successive intermediate nodes in both directions different from the original one-way transmissions, an extended RTS/CTS control is required to be designed. Though some methods for the RTS/CTS control in network coding communication have been proposed as in the previous section; however, their additional overhead is unignorable. Thus, the advantage of the network coding communication is tremendously reduced.

In order to solve this problem, this paper proposes a novel extended RTS/CTS control and transmissions of ACK control messages for network coding wireless multihop transmissions based on ARAR supporting multicast transmissions of data messages in wireless ad-hoc networks. As shown in Figure 7, in order for an intermediate node N_i to broadcast a network coded data message m_e of data messages m_f and m_b received from N_{i-1} and N_{i+1}, respectively, N_i broadcasts an RTS control message destined to N_{i-1} and N_{i+1} to all its neighbor nodes within its wireless signal transmission range. On receipt of the RTS control message, N_{i-1} and/or N_{i+1} broadcast CTS control messages destined to N_i to all their neighbor wireless nodes within their wireless signal transmission ranges after a $SIFS$ interval if it is possible for N_{i-1} and/or N_{i+1} to receive a data message from N_i, i.e., N_{i-1} and/or N_{i+1} have not yet received RTS or CTS control messages from their neighbor wireless nodes. Neither N_{i-1} nor N_{i+1} is transmitting a data message since it is possible for N_i to transmit the RTS control message; this means that N_i has not received an RTS control message from N_{i-1} and/or N_{i+1}.

Among the neighbor nodes of N_i, which have received the RTS control message from N_i, it is possible only for N_{i-1} and N_{i+1} to broadcast CTS control messages. Hence, there are only the following 4 cases for N_i on receipts of CTS control messages (Figure 7):

- Both N_{i-1} and N_{i+1} broadcast CTS control messages and N_i detects a collision of them.
- Only N_{i-1} broadcasts a CTS control message and N_i receives it.
- Only N_{i+1} broadcasts a CTS control message and N_i receives it.
- Neither N_{i-1} nor N_{i+1} broadcasts a CTS control message and N_i receives no CTS control messages.

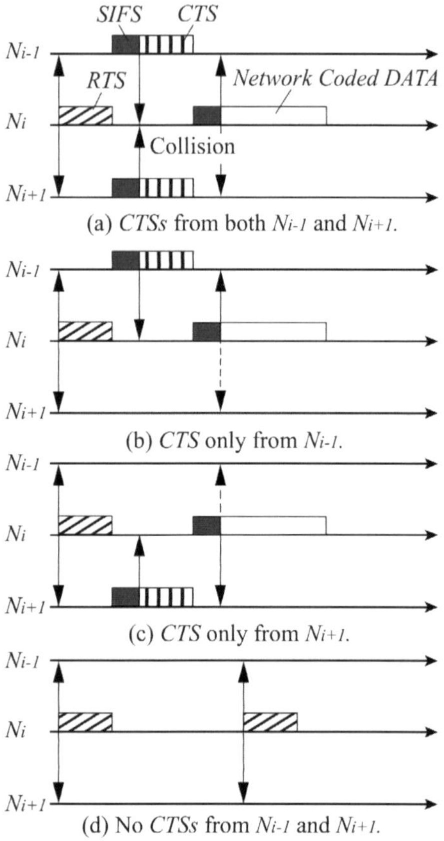

Figure 7. Acceptance of CTS by Collision Detection.

If both N_{i-1} and N_{i+1} broadcast CTS control messages, these CTS messages collide at N_i since both of them are transmitted with the same $SIFS$ interval after receipts of the RTS control message from N_i. However, since it is impossible for N_i to detect a collision in all the other 3 cases, by detection of a collision N_i determines that the collision is caused by the concurrently transmitted CTS control messages from N_{i-1} and N_{i+1}. That is, N_i finds that both N_{i-1} and N_{i+1} notify N_i of their possibility for receipt of a forthcoming data message by transmissions of their CTS control messages and broadcasts a network coded data message m_e of m_f and m_b.

If either N_{i-1} or N_{i+1} broadcasts a CTS control message in response to the RTS control message from N_i, N_i receives the CTS control message without a collision. Thus, N_i finds that only one of the successive intermediate nodes in a route broadcasts the CTS control message, which means that only the sender intermediate node is ready for receipt of a data message from N_i and the other is currently impossible to receive it. Then, N_i broadcasts the network coded data message or the original data message to the successive intermediate node broadcasting the CTS control message. The data message is expected to be received correctly by the receiver node. In addition, no collisions are caused at the successive intermediate node of N_i, which does not broadcast a CTS control message since it does not broadcast it due to not to be a sender or a receiver node but a receipt of an RTS or a CTS control message from its neighbor node other than N_i. Otherwise, both N_{i-1} and N_{i+1} has already been received RTS and/or CTS control messages from their neighbor nodes and are not possible to receive data messages from N_i. N_i tries to rebroadcast an RTS control message after a $DIFS$ interval.

Same as CTS control messages, ACK control messages for a network coded data message broadcasted by N_i are broadcasted by N_{i-1} and N_{i+1} and their collisions are treated. After detection of a collision between the CTS control messages from N_{i-1} and N_{i+1}, N_i broadcasts a network coded data message m destined to N_{i-1} and N_{i+1} with a $SIFS$ interval. On receipt of the network coded data message m, N_{i-1} and/or N_{i+1} transmit ACK control messages to N_i after a $SIFS$ interval if N_{i-1} and/or N_{i+1} receive the network coded data message correctly. Among the neighbor nodes of N_i, which have received the RTS control message from N_i, it is possible only for N_{i-1} and N_{i+1} to transmit ACK control messages. Hence, there are only the following 4 cases for N_i on receipts of ACK control messages (Figure 8):

- Both N_{i-1} and N_{i+1} transmit ACK control messages and N_i detects a collision of them.
- Only N_{i-1} transmits an ACK control message and N_i receives it.
- Only N_{i+1} transmits an ACK control message and N_i receives it.
- Neither N_{i-1} nor N_{i+1} transmits an ACK control message and N_i receives no ACK control messages.

If both N_{i-1} and N_{i+1} transmit ACK control messages, these ACK messages collide at N_i since both of them are transmitted with the same $SIFS$ interval after receipts of the network coded data message from N_i. However, since it is impossible for N_i to detect a collision in all the other 3 cases, by detection of a collision N_i determines that the collision is caused by the concurrently transmitted ACK control messages from N_{i-1} and N_{i+1}. That is, N_i finds that both N_{i-1} and N_{i+1} notify N_i of their receipt of the network coded data message by transmissions of their ACK control messages.

If either N_{i-1} or N_{i+1} transmits an ACK control message in response to the network coded data message from N_i, N_i receives the ACK control message without a collision. Thus, N_i finds that only one of the successive intermediate nodes in a route transmits the ACK control message, which means that only the sender intermediate node received the network coded data message from N_i and the other failed to receive it. Then, N_i tries to retransmit a data message destined to the successive intermediate node from which N_i does not receive an ACK control message. In this case, it is possible for N_i to transmit either only the original message failed to transmit to the node or another network coded data message for the original message failed to transmit to the node and another buffered data message destined to the other successive intermediate node of N_i. For performance improvement point of view, the latter, i.e., a network coded data message is desirable to be transmitted. Otherwise, both N_{i-1} and N_{i+1} has already been received RTS and/or CTS control messages from their neighbor nodes and are not possible to receive data messages from N_i. N_i tries to rebroadcast an RTS control message after a $DIFS$ interval.

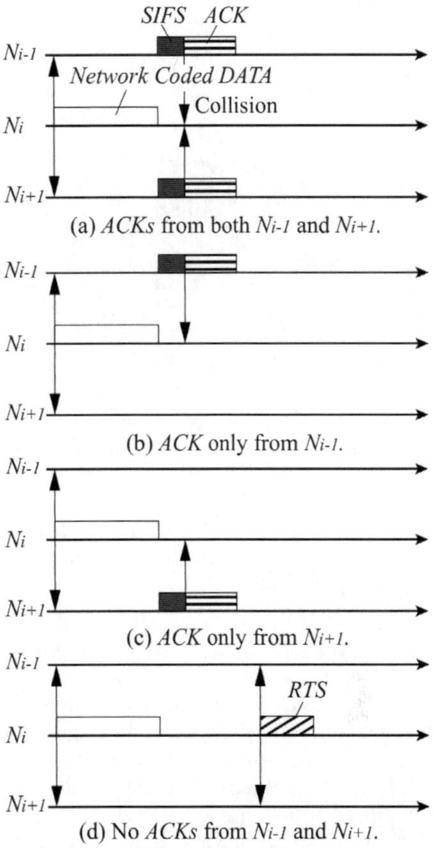

Figure 8. Acceptance of ACK by Collision Detection.

In the proposed method, the concurrent transmissions of CTS control messages transmitted by N_{i-1} and N_{i+1} are recognized by N_i by the collision of the messages at N_i. The collision is detected not only by N_i but also all the nodes included in both of the wireless signal transmission ranges of N_{i-1} and N_{i+1}. The nodes included in the wireless signal transmission range of N_i receive the RTS control message from N_i and is notified of the transmission request for a network coded data message by N_i and the NAV which represents the interval when the neighbor nodes suspend to initiate a data message transmission and keep silent. However, the nodes out of the wireless signal transmission range of N_i and detect the collision of the CTS control messages cannot achieve the NAV. Hence, it is possible for such nodes to broadcast an RTS or a CTS control message to initiate a transmission or a receipt of a data message though N_{i-1} and N_{i+1} are included in the wireless signal transmission range of the nodes as shown in Figure 9. The probability of occurrences of collisions at N_{i-1} and/or N_{i+1} caused by a data or a control message depends on the distances between successive intermediate nodes N_{i-1}, N_i and N_{i+1}, i.e., the lengths of communication links $\langle N_{i-1}N_i \rangle$ and $\langle N_i N_{i+1} \rangle$, their angle and transmission request ratio of data messages along the route.

IV. EVALUATION

This paper proposes a novel RTS/CTS control for collision avoidance in bi-directional wireless multihop transmissions of sequences of data messages supporting P2P type multimedia network applications. In order to evaluate the

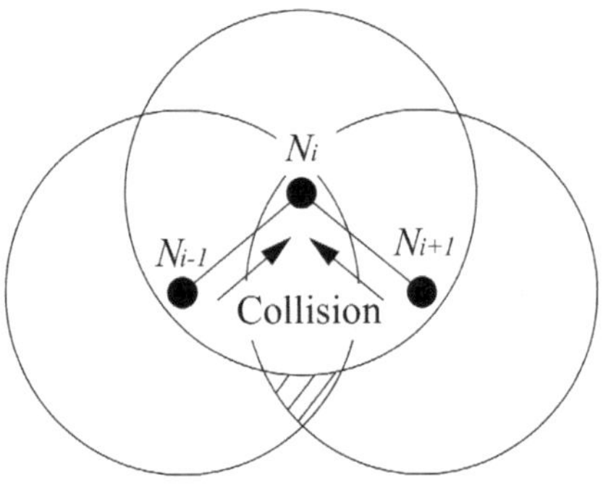

Figure 9. NAV Unacceptable Areas due to Collision of CTS Messages.

advantage of the proposed method, which allow two successive intermediate wireless nodes to broadcast CTS control messages and to transmit ACK control messages concurrently with the same $SIFS$ interval after receipts of a broadcasted RTS control message and a network coded data message from N_i, this section evaluates end-to-end throughput of data messages in simulation experiments.

Here, two terminal nodes and all the intermediate nodes are located with 100m spaces. All the nodes communicate with a 101m wireless signal transmission range by IEEE 802.11b wireless LAN protocol. Hence, in this simulation, only collisions of control and/or data messages along the route are considered. That is, there are no other routes. Appropriate routing tables are assumed to be set in advance in all the nodes. Length of routes are 2–19 hops, i.e., there are 1–18 intermediate nodes in a route and sequences of data messages are transmitted in both direction between the two terminal nodes. End-to-end throughput of data messages are evaluated in the proposed method in comparison with a naive wireless multihop transmission with the original RTS/CTS control and without network coding communication and NC-MAC where the transmission order of CTS and ACK control messages are indicated by the intermediate node broadcasting a network coded data message (See Section 2). All the related protocols are implemented on ns-3 simulator [6].

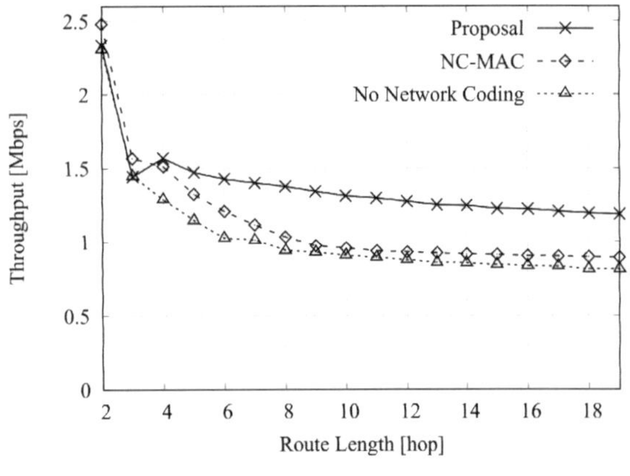

Figure 10. End-to-End Throughput of Data Message.

Figure 10 shows the results of the simulation experiments. The horizontal axis represents the length of routes and the vertical axis represents the average end-to-end throughput of data messages.

First, the end-to-end throughput of data messages in NC-MAC is averagely 11.5% higher than the naive transmissions with the usual RTS/CTS control and without network coding communication. In cases of more than 9-hop routes, the performance improvement is almost the same as 7.8%. Anyway, it is clear that the advantage of network coding communication and avoidance of collisions between data and control messages is reasonable. However, as mentioned in Section 2, 6-phase transmissions, i.e., RTS, CTS, CTS, network coded data message, ACK, ACK are required in NC-MAC and 8-phasetransmissions, i.e., RTS, CTS, original data message, ACK, RTS, CTS, original data message, ACK are required in the naive approach.

Next, in the comparison between our proposed method and NC-MAC, NC-MAC is superior to the proposed method in routes with less than 4 hops. However, in routes with more than 4 hops, the proposed method performs much better than NC-MAC. This is because the proposed method requires only 4-phase transmissions RTS, CTS, network coded data message, ACK by introduction of collision detection for receipt of concurrently transmitted CTS and ACK control messages. Totally, the proposed method achieves 30.1% and 42.2% higher end-to-end throughput of data messages than NC-MAC and the original RTS/CTS control without network coding communication, respectively.

V. Conclusion

This paper has proposed a novel RTS/CTS control for collision avoidance in network coding communication for bi-directional concurrent transmissions of sequences of data messages in wireless multihop networks. Here, receipt of CTS and ACK control messages from two successive intermediate nodes are recognized by an intermediate node transmitting a network coded data message by their collision. The results of simulation experiments show that the proposed method achieves more than 30% higher end-to-end throughput of data messages. For higher performance, the authors is designing a more cooperative protocol for network coding communication to have more opportunities to apply the network coding transmissions of both directional data messages.

References

[1] X. Deng and Y. Yang, "An Efficient MAC Multicast Protocol for Reliable Wireless Communications with Network Coding," Proceedings of IEEE Global Telecommunications Conference, 2011, pp. 1–6.

[2] S. Katti et al., "XORs in The Air: Practical Wireless Network Coding," Proceedings of the International Conference on Applications, Technologies, Architectures, and Protocols for Computer Communications, vol. 36, no. 4, 2006, pp. 243–254.

[3] J. Xie, A. Das, and S. Nandi, "An Improvement to The Reliability of IEEE 802.11 Broadcast Scheme for Multicasting in Mobile Ad Hoc Networks," Proceedings of the 1st International Conference on Sensor and Ad Hoc Communications and Networks, 2004, pp. 359–366.

[4] A. Makoto, T. Yumi, O. Chikara, and T. Hisashi, "A Study on Inter-flow Network Coding with Passive ACK for Efficient and Reliable Bidirectional Communication : Optimal Waiting Time for Encoding and Timing Control for Passive ACK," Technical Report in IEICE, vol. 115, no. 172, 2015, pp. 43–48.

[5] U. Daisuke, D. Satoshi, M. Masahiro, and S. Takatoshi, "RTS/CTS Effect on Two-Hop Wireless CSMA Network Coding," Technical Report in IEICE, vol. 109, no. 276, 2009, pp. 65–70.

[6] "NS-3," 2018, URL: https://www.nsnam.org/ [accessed: 2018-09-25].

[7] "Wireless LAN Medium Access Control (MAC) and Physical Layer (PHY) Specifications," Standard IEEE 802.11, 1997.

User-centric IoT: Challenges and Perspectives

Abdelghani Wafa*, Corinne Amel Zayani†, Ikram Amous† and Florence Sèdes*
*Paul Sabatier University, IRIT, Toulouse, France
Emails: {wafa.abdelghani, florence.sedes}@irit.fr
† Sfax University, MIRACL, Sfax, Tunisia
Emails: {corinne.zayani, ikram.amous}@isecs.rnu.tn

***Abstract*—The Internet of Things (IoT), this emerging technology connecting everyone, and everyones 'things', is not about objects, gadgets, databases, applications and profits to be made from it, but about people it enriches. Researchers, developers, industries, telecommunication companies, and scientific communities have been interested in this paradigm and have proposed different solutions from different perspectives. They are mainly focused on the technical level, like performance, interoperability, integration, etc. However, whenever use cases are targeting human users, the focus must not be merely on these sides, but on human factors as well. Thus, it is essential to apply a user-centric approach allowing identification of application-specific features and understanding users needs, motivations and beliefs. This survey aims at encouraging other IoT system developers and researchers to pay attention to the relationship between people and IoT systems. We emphasize the value of adopting a user-centric vision. The goal is not to provide solutions, but rather to raise the right issues.**

Keywords–Internet of Things; User-centric Internet of Things; Social Internet of Things; Social Cyberspace; Internet of People.

I. Introduction

The Internet of Things is a computing concept that describes the idea of everyday physical objects being connected to the Internet and being able to identify themselves to other devices. IoT is expected to be dominated by huge content-oriented traffic, intensive interactions between billions of persons often on the move and heterogeneous communications among hosts and smart objects [1]. It provisions millions of services, with strict real-time requirements and striking flexibility in connecting everyone and everything.

Interconnected things, such as sensors or mobile devices sense, monitor and collect all kinds of data about human social life. Those data can be further aggregated, fused, processed, analyzed and mined in order to extract useful information to enable intelligent and ubiquitous services [2].

This paradigm is the result of the evolution of a whole range of new trends following undeniable progress at different levels, such as the evolution of mobile and ubiquitous technologies, the evolution of sensors, wireless and cellular communication networks, as well as the evolution of data storage and processing technologies (Cloud Computing, Big Data, etc.).

Researchers, developers, industries, telecommunication companies, and scientific communities have been interested in this paradigm and have proposed different solutions from different perspectives. They have tried to deal with different problems, such as the heterogeneity of involved devices and communication protocols [3] [4], the security of communications and the minimization of energy consumption [5].

Nevertheless, consumption of IoT products and services remains above expectations [6]. It must be admitted that the user is somewhat excluded. The user is at the heart of IoT systems. It is both the source of data and the consumer. Adopting a user-centric vision is, therefore, a promising new trend. Advantages are numerous. Navigability and resources discovery are improved [7]. Scalability and heterogeneity problems are addressed [8]. The quantity and the variety of contextual data are increased [7] and the community is exploited to establish trustworthiness [9].

We wish through this survey to focus on the user-centric IoT. We emphasize the value of adopting such a vision, we study the user-centric IoT environments, the user in such a context, his needs, and barriers and obstacles to the acceptance of IoT products and services from users' point of view. The goal is not to provide solutions, but rather to raise the right issues.

The remainder of the paper is organized as follows. In Section 2, we introduce and compare different visions of the IoT paradigm and we underline and classify its main challenges. In Section 3, we focus on the user-centric IoT. We define the user in such a context, we report related paradigms and we underline highlights and advantages of adopting such vision. In Section 4, we report and analyze IoT challenges from a user vision. In Section 5, we compare researchers challenges with users challenge to give a glance at the open issues on which research should focus more. Conclusion and future research hints are given in Section 6.

II. Internet of Things

The IoT is emerging as one of the major trends shaping the development of technologies in the information and communication sector at large [5]. The shift from an Internet used for interconnecting end-user devices to an Internet used for interconnecting physical objects that communicate with each other and/or with humans in order to offer a given service, implies to rethink again about conventional approaches usually used in networking, computing and service provisioning.

The IoT is a technological phenomenon generated by innovative advancements in information and communication technologies related to: (i) Ubiquity, (ii) Pervasiveness and (iii) Ambient Intelligence [10].

A. *One Paradigm, Many Visions*

Manifold definitions of IoT are suggested from the research community which testifies to the complexity and to the multi-disciplinarity of this paradigm. The term IoT is broadly used to refer to:

- The global network connecting smart things through extended Internet technologies.
- The set of technologies supporting such a vision (e.g., Radio Frequency IDentification (RFIDs), sensors, actuators, machine-to-machine communication devices, etc.)
- The set of applications and services leveraging such technologies to give birth to new industrial opportunities [5].

From a *device-centric perspective*, the IoT is based on the concept of smart things, which are able to sense, detect or measure physical phenomena (e.g., temperature, light, etc.) or to perform actions having an effect on the real world [5]. This encompasses devices considered in RFID research [11], as well as those considered in Wireless Sensor Networks and Sensor/Actuator Networks [12] [13].

From a *network-centric perspective*, the IoT can be considered as a highly heterogeneous, dynamic and distributed networked system, composed of a great number of smart objects generating and consuming data [5].

From a *data-centric perspective*, IoT refers to entities processing as providers and/or consumers of data related to the physical world. This fact motivates the adoption of content-centric network architectures and principles [5].

In literature, many architectures are suggested for representing the IoT. However, the most common and basic adopted architecture is composed of three layers: (i) Physical layer also called perception layer, device layer or sensing layer; (ii) Network layer; and (ii) Application layer also called Service layer. (i) Physical layer concerns identifying, naming, addressing and managing IoT objects. (ii) Network layer encompasses networks and protocols used for allowing IoT objects to communicate and to interact. (iii) Application layer encompasses Data Management and Services Management modules and offers final IoT services to end-users.

B. *Underlined Challenges*

Although well known for a while, the IoT paradigm is still in its infancy and the road ahead is long. Researchers, projects, and industries are focusing on different issues. We cite in this section the main underlined challenges.

a) ***Heterogeneity and interoperability:*** IoT is characterized by a high heterogeneity at different levels. From *devices level*, IoT is a set of heterogeneous devices expected to present dissimilar capabilities from computational and communication standpoints. Identifying, addressing, naming and managing such devices in a standardized way is the first challenge [3] [14].

From a *network-centric perspective*, allowing those devices with various communication capabilities to communicate and interact through various networks and using different communication protocols is the second challenge [4]. It covers basic connectivity issues from the physical layer to the application layer without considering the content of information.

From a *data-centric vision*, IoT is about exchanging and analyzing massive amounts of data, to transform them into useful information and to guarantee interoperability among various applications and services. It is essential to provide data with standardized formats, models and semantic descriptions (meta-data), using well-defined languages. This will enable IoT applications to support automated reasoning, a key feature for enabling the proliferation of such a technology on a wide scale [15].

From a *service-oriented vision*, the main challenge relates to how to integrate and compose functionality provided by smart objects into services. This requires designing: (i) architectures and methods for creating a standardized representation of smart objects able to resolve the heterogeneity of devices/resources and (ii) methods for seamlessly integrating and composing resources/services of smart objects into value-added services for end users [5]. Table I shows the main protocols used for each IoT layer.

TABLE I. PROTOCOLS IN DIFFERENT IOT LAYERS

Application Layer	HyperText Transfer Protocol (HTTP), Constrained Application Protocol (CoAP), Embedded Binary HTTP (EBHTTP), Licklider Transmission Protocol (LTP), Simple Network Management Protocol (SNMP), IP Flow Information Export (IPfix), Domain Name System (DNS), Network Time Protocol (NTP), Secure SHell Protocol (SSH), Device Language Message Specification(DLMS), Distributed Network Protocol (DNP),
Network Layer	Internet Protocol Version 6 (IPv6), Routing Protocol for Low-power (RPL), User Datagram Protocol (UDP), Universal Logging Protocol˜(uIP), Serial Line Internet Protocol (SLIP), IPV6 LowPower wireless Area Network (6LoWPAN)
Physical Layer	IEEE 802.11, IEEE 802.15, IEEE 802.16, Z-Wave, Ultra˜WideBand protocol˜(UWB), Highway Addressable Remote Transducer protocol (WirelessHART), Infrared Data Association protocol(IrDA), Konnex protocol (KNX)

b) ***Scalability:*** As daily objects become connected to a global networked infrastructure, scalability issue arises at different levels, including: *(i) identifying, addressing and managing* due to the size of the resulting system and to the constrained nature of typical IoT devices which do not enable quite memory and computing capabilities; *(ii) data communication and networking* due to the high level of interactions, communications and data exchanges among involved entities; *(iii) information and knowledge management* due to the massive amount of data and information sensed, detected, generated and analyzed and (iv) *service provisioning and management* due to the high number of real-time services execution options that could be available and the need to handle heterogeneous resources [5].

c) ***Energy-optimized solutions:*** For a variety of IoT entities, minimizing the energy to be spent on communication/computing purposes will be a primary constraint [5]. While techniques related to energy harvesting (through piezo-electric materials or micro solar panels) will alleviate devices from constraints imposed by battery, energy remains a scarce resource which may not be wasted and which may be properly and reasonably consumed. Thereby, energy optimization concerns also the network level, because communication is recognized as the most energy-consuming task. It concerns also the application layer which justifies the need to design services, applications, and solutions that tend to optimize energy consumption even at the expense of performance.

*d) **Trust, security and privacy**:* Trust is a multidimensional, multidisciplinary and multifaceted concept. The concept of trust covers a bigger scope than security, thus it is more complicated and difficult to establish. It is also related to the concept of privacy that is the ability of an entity to determine whether, when, and to whom personal information could be disclosed. Trust, security and privacy are highly related crucial issues in emerging information technology areas, such as IoT [16].

A number of studies aim to improve identity trust and achieve privacy preservation in ubiquitous systems such as IoT. Fongen [17] propose a framework for authentication and integrity protection designed for IoT environment in order to ensure scalability and lightweight requirements. Gambs et al. [18] propose an implementation of a specific inference attack called the de-anonymization attack, based on Mobility Markov Chain (MMC). They suggest some distance metrics in order to measure the similitude among two MMCs and aggregate these metrics to create de-anonymizers able to recognize users in an Anonymized Geo-located Data-set. In [19], the authors propose an extended trust protocol to support secure mobility management in order to adapt the network to changes of location and infrastructure. This extension aims to improve fault tolerance capacity, connectivity, dependability and scalability in IP-based Wireless Sensor Networks.

Some other works, focus on data transmission and communication trust which is strongly related to security. A security protocol to support data exchange amongst objects was proposed by [20] and combined with a security framework for enhancing security, trust, and privacy for embedded systems. Lightweight symmetric encryption and asymmetric encryption in Trivial File Transfer Protocol (TFTP) were proposed to make the given protocol appropriate to the constrained nature of IoT devices. In [21], the authors propose mechanisms to ensure security at the network layer and at the application layer and perform an experimental study to identify the most appropriate secure communication mechanism for current sensing platforms. Raza et al. [22] introduce SVELTE, an intrusion detection system for the IoT, implemented and evaluated to permit resiliency face to routing attacks, such as spoofed or altered information, sinkhole, and selective-forwarding.

Some other works aim to establish trust management of a whole and propose various trust frameworks and architectures. In [23], the authors propose a system architecture that offers a solution to several challenges, such as general system security, network security, and application security with respect to basic information security requirements (confidentiality, integrity, availability, authority, non-repudiation, and privacy preservation). Quan et al. [24] propose a trusted architecture for a farmland wireless sensor network which includes four layers: (i) a perception logical layer, (ii) a mark recognition logical layer, (iii) a decision-control logical layer and (v) a trusted interface logical layer. This architecture aims to afford trusted and reliable data transmission in Wireless Sensor Networks. An IoT architecture investigated by EU FP7 IoT-A project [25] aims to consider both service privacy and IoT access security aspects for dealing with service accommodation, identification, and IoT-A platform realizations. Gessner et al. [26] propose a set of trust-enhancing security functional components which covers both basic IoT resources access control and essential functions, such as identity, trust and reputation management. This component composition provides mechanisms for securing communications between subjects to ensure data integrity and confidentiality, service trust and privacy of users.

III. User-Centric Internet of Things

The IoT is a vision of ubiquitous connectivity. With sensors, code, and infrastructure, any object can become networked. But the question we need to ask is: should they be? And if so, how? Public debate over the IoT is polarized. Commentators tend to voice either excessive optimism or total pessimism, with precious little in between.

Optimists describe IoT as a magical realm of “enchanted objects”, where our possessions gently anticipate our every need. The other camp paints a darker picture. They claim that, at best, the IoT is just another excuse for rampant consumerism, whose only contribution will be to clog basements with yet more unnecessary junk. They affirm that everyday household objects will be turned into enemy spies, placing us under constant surveillance. We will be nudged and manipulated at every moment. Our lives and possessions will be perpetually exposed to hackers.

The solution is intuitive: we need to forget about things. We need to stop obsessing over smart objects and start thinking smart about people. This is the true potential of the IoT. It could put our vast stores of tacit embodied knowledge to work online. It could unite the physical and digital worlds. It also could put us in control of our own information and contextual integrity, against a moral and political backdrop that is resolutely committed to human rights, the rule of law and social cohesion. It could become an Internet, not of smart things, but of smart empowered people.

A. The User in Intelligent Systems

The user is a human, defined by different characteristics: his name, his age, the country where he lives, his Job, his school level, but also his interests, his domains of expertise and his preferences. In computing systems, all these characteristics are classically represented by a profile. The user is also represented by the context where he evolves. A user context includes his location, his current activity, objects and other users in proximity but also his social context. The social context of a user is represented by a set of social relationships entertained with other users and forming the user social networks.

In intelligent systems, the user plays several roles. He is both the source of information, the provider of services and the consumer. The user is therefore in the heart of these processes. That is why some paradigms have appeared giving focus to the user. Several works focus on detecting user profile [27], user social characteristics [28] [29] and to adapting treatments and process to user context [30]. Those works can be reused to achieve a user-centric IoT.

B. Related Paradigms

In this section, we will address some new IoT paradigms aiming to give focus to the user.

1) Internet of People: Miranda et al. [31] define the Internet of People (IoP) as bringing the IoT closer to people in order to easily integrate into it and fully exploit its benefits. This new paradigm aims to put people at the center of innovation strategies and be able to make a profit from the power of collective intelligence. More than just smart applications and smart cities, the potential of IoP resides in smart people. IoP includes numerous topics, such as Biometric Sensors and Identification Technology, Wearable Technology, Brain Informatics Processing, Body Area Network technology, Social Computing, and Collective Intelligence, Technology for Biomedical and healthcare application etc.

In [31], the authors define a set of features they believe are essential foundations for any approach to the IoP: (i) IoP should be social and let devices interact with each other and with people more socially than does the IoT; (ii) IoP should be personalized which mean that interactions must be personalized to users sociological profiles and contexts; (iii) IoP should be proactive and not manually commanded by the user; (iv) IoP should be predictable which means that interactions must be triggered according to a predictable context that the user has previously identified, and for which a specific behavior has been defined.

2) Social Internet of Things: IoT embodies a large number of smart objects that, through standard communication protocols and unique addressing schemes, provide information and services to final users. Making objects smart was only the first step of an evolutionary process that affected modern communication devices and has been triggered by the advent of IoT in the telecommunication scenarios [1].

The second step consists of the evolution of objects with a certain degree of smartness to objects with an actual social consciousness. These objects can interact with the surrounding environment and feature a pseudo-social behavior with neighbors or within circles and communities. The third step consists of the birth of social objects that act in a social community of objects and devices giving birth to the Social Internet of Things (SIoT) [1].

SIoT objects are able to autonomously establish relationships with other objects, to join communities and to build their own social network which may be different from their owner's ones. SIoT has the potential to support novel applications and networking services for the IoT in more effective and efficient ways. Thus, within a given social network of objects, a key objective will be to publish information/services, find them, and discover novel resources to better implement services also through an environmental awareness. This can be achieved by navigating a social network of friend objects instead of relying on typical Internet discovery tools that cannot scale to trillions of future devices [1].

Short, SIoT permit to address some IoT challenges, such as scalability and heterogeneity, to allow trust-based social relationships among people and objects, to improve objects navigability and discovery by narrowing down its scope to a manageable social network of everything and to increases the quantity and the variety of contextual data

3) Physical Cyber Social Computing: [32] propose Physical-Cyber-Social (PCS) computing, that takes a human-centric and holistic view of computing by analyzing observations, knowledge, and experiences from physical, cyber, and social worlds. Some of the main challenges in healthcare, sustainability, crime prevention, and mitigation require a holistic approach to computing for providing actionable information. With the increased digitization of the physical world culminating in a massive data generated from sensors, mobile devices, and personal/social observations has led to a deeper view into our physical, cyber, and social worlds. The data generation rate has surpassed the ability to store all observations. PCS computing is envisioned to derive insights from these observations to provide actionable information to humans. Providing actionable information by taking a human-centric approach is the vision of PCS computing.

4) People as a Service: [33] People as a Service (PeaaS) is a mobile-centric computing model that allows a users sociological profile to be generated, kept, and securely provided as a service to third parties directly from a Smart-phone. PeaaS emphasizes smart-phones capabilities and relies on them for inferring and sharing sociological profiles. These profiles are not disclosed and are preserved on the device, making it easier for owners to keep their virtual identity under their own control and to preserve them privacy while still enabling third parties to make profit from users identities.

Serving individuals virtual sociological profiles through Smart-phones are different from other mobile-centric models that only provide data, such as GPS localization and temperature. PeaaS allows a variety of information to be collected, such as moods, tendency, preferences, social statuses, daily habits and health habits of a group of peoples in order to delimit their digital projection. However, filtering and analyzing this information to infer users characteristics and specificity or to generate relevant information is not a trivial task. Various techniques, including activity recognition approaches and affective computing, are used in PeaaS for building the richest sociological profile possible [33].

5) Social Devices: Social Devices is an IoT model, introduced by [34]. The motivation behind the model was that smart-phones have not only a lot of information about their owners, but also modalities that enable them to resemble humans. They can translate text into speech, for example. At present, Social Devices concept is supported by a middleware platform. This allows proactive triggering of interactions between devices of co-located people. Additionally, it offers a complete set of Web-based tools to define interactions and their triggering contexts.

6) Social Sensing: Social Sensing is an integral paradigm of the IoT when objects being tracked are associated with individual people. Mobile phones, smart watches, smart glasses, and wearable sensors are good examples of sensing objects. Such paradigms have tremendous value in enabling social networking paradigms in conjunction with sensing. The growing capability of basics hardware to track a wide variety of daily data, such as location, speed, and video leads to tremendous opportunity in enabling a connected and pervasive world of users that are ubiquitously connected to the Internet [35].

C. Highlights and Advantages

Adopting a user-centric vision is, therefore, a promising new trend. Advantages are numerous.

- Navigability and resources discovery are improved by narrowing down them scopes to a manageable social network of everything [7].
- Some IoT challenges, such as scalability and heterogeneity are addressed [7].
- The scalability is guaranteed like in human social networks [8] and the heterogeneity of devices, network

and communication protocols is resolved by the use of social networks.

- A larger data source becomes available as it comes from a set of users, a network of users, or a community rather than from a single user.
- The continuous feed of data from communities gives us big data team [9] and the quantity and the variety of contextual data is increased allowing improved services intelligence and adaptability to users' situational needs [7].
- A better user adaptation that will lead to the increased consumption of IoT products [9] and a better information filtering become possible, because communities of objects collaborate to provide a common view [36].
- Models designed to study social networks can be reused to address IoT related issues (intrinsically related to extensive networks of interconnected objects) [8].
- The focus and the consideration of user-side challenges will increase the acceptability of IoT products.
- The community is exploited to rate the trustworthiness of potential providers of information and services [36]. So, a level of trustworthiness can be established for leveraging the degree of interaction among things that are friends [8].

IV. IoT Challenges and Perspectives: A User Vision

The high cost of intelligent devices is one of the problems posed by users. According to statistics [37] drawn up in 2014 on a sample of 2000 French users, 59 % of users consider the price of IoT devices as one of the greatest constraints. High prices are not the only constraint. Indeed, the price constraint can disappear if these objects become useful and necessary. We expose in this section the main IoT challenge from the users point of view. We have relied on statistics and have chosen in this section the most cited users' problems, including the usefulness and usability of connected objects but also and above all, their ability to respect the users' privacy.

A. Utility

The majority of users find that these smart objects are not useful enough and that they do not bring much to their daily lives. The same statistic [37] show that 45 % of all users questioned and 52 % of users who are older than 50 years old do not see the usefulness of objects being conveyed, although the number of applications and IoT objects for the health and well-being of the elderly is quite high. Developers, designers, and creators of IoT objects and services are faced with a new challenge: developing more useful and interesting scenarios that can meet the specific need of users.

A study from LAPOSTE [38] carried out with a national sample of 1032 peoples classified areas of IoT applications according to users' expectations. This study revealed that proximity services are at the forefront, followed by home automation services and then health-care and wellness services. According to the same analysis, proximity services allow the rapid intervention of trusted personnel for isolated persons, the keep of elderly or dependents people at home or the safety of children. For home automation services, 77 % of users surveyed place an emphasis on security and protection against theft and intrusion. 74 % place more emphasis on fire risk services and energy-saving services. As for the field of health and well-being, 45 % of users give importance to services that make it possible to practice a sporting activity regularly. Another study [6], classifies health-care services on the first position, security management services on the second position and home automation and energy consumption management services in the third position.

The cited study [37] tried to clarify which prototype of users are most willing to use connected objects and which connected objects are most used. This study found that 23% of users interviewed have at least one intelligent object. For the most part, the latter are men, receiving a wage of more than 1500 euro and living for the most part in the Paris region. This study ranked the object "connected weather station" at the top of the list of most used intelligent objects. In the second position are connected gas, electricity and water meters, connected watches and bracelets, and connected alarm systems. In the third position, connected sphygmomanometers and scales, connected sockets and remotely controllable heating systems. Other objects are also used, such as connected refrigerators, but also connected baby monitors (which monitors babies quality of sleep) and connected baby scales (which monitor the growth curve of a baby).

Note that other areas are neglected and little known by users. Let us mention, for example, the field of transport and vehicular networks, although it is quite developed. We also note that applications and devices using the social environment of the user or the notion of collaboration are few.

B. Usability

The usability or the ease of use of connected objects and IoT services is also one of the brakes to the acceptability of these products by consumers. Indeed, a study [38] affirms that 74 % of users perceive the multiplication of applications to control each object as a brake on the purchase and use of the latter. Another study [39] shows that nearly 12 % of users who do not have connected objects say that it is useless to buy objects that are not compatible with all types of computers and Smart-phones. 15% say it is not easy to manage multiple connected objects at the same time. 9 % say they do not know how to operate these objects.

Establishing interoperability is a potential solution. It makes intelligent objects reconfigurable and autonomous, thus minimizing human intervention. It also allows easier control and management when it comes to a large number of objects. Integration of the social component and contextualization also present possible solutions to increase the quantity and variety of data in order to offer more intuitive, intelligent, personalized and adapted services.

C. Trust and Privacy

The mentioned study [39] tries to classify the brakes to the acceptance of IoT objects by users. 43% of users queried say they are afraid of the use that can be made of their personal data. 18 % find that the connected objects are not operational. 8 % believe they are unreliable. The second cited survey [6] joins the first one and states that: 33 % of the users questioned are afraid of what is done with the data collected by IoT objects; 19 % find that these objects quickly become obsolete and 17 % find they are not very efficient and very reliable.

The number increases when it comes to some more critical areas, especially the health field. Indeed, a barometer [40] was established in 2016 by the company VIDAL (company dedicated to information on health products), on a sample of 1402 doctors, revealed the following percentages: 33% of doctors surveyed say they have no confidence in healthcare applications and services in terms of securing personal data. 84 of the doctors questioned would not recommend connected health objects to their patients. However, there are a number of factors that could encourage them to advocate benefits, such as certification and labeling of the object (39%), its therapeutic area (37%) and the profile of its manufacturer or designer (8%). Doctors first trust their peers to make healt-related connected objects (scientists societies 67%, university doctors 53% and confreres developers 42%). In addition, certain promotional arrangements are more likely to convince doctors of the adoption of connected health objects. Recommendations made by scientists societies (67%), medical press (58%) and medical congresses (51%) are the most convincing.

Those apprehensions are not unjustified. Some past events confirm the fear of users. The first examples of dysfunctions observed date back to 2011. A pharmaceutical company had to warn its users that the rheumatology calculator application it had developed produced erroneous scores [41]. The following year, another laboratory had to recall its application of calculation of doses of insulin [42]. Then, Apple announced the removal of blood glucose monitoring from its health management application [42]. This has drawn attention to the fact that these solutions are not so simple to implement even for a technology champion.

According to these different statistics, we distinguish two major problems: trust and privacy. We also distinguish three levels of trust: trust in the object or IoT devices, trust in IoT services and applications, trust in the service provider or in the designer of the devices. We also distinguish a fourth level: trust in the recommender of the service or IoT object. We believe that trust management in IoT environments should necessarily consider these four levels in order to improve users' acceptability of IoT products and allow them to overcome their fears and apprehensions.

Several properties can allow measuring trust for each dimension. For example, reliability, connectivity, energy rates permit to measure trust in IoT devices and objects. Quality of Services (QoS), functional characteristics and non-functional characteristics (delay, availability, throughput, response time, etc.) permit to measure trust in IoT services and applications [43]. Expertise, past experiences, and QoS can be used to measure trust in service providers [44]. And centrality, honesty, and similarity of profile and interest can be used to measure trust in services and objects recommenders [45].

The problem of privacy concerns the protection of users' personal data. Indeed, the huge amounts of data that are collected by the connected objects with sensors, are usually stored on the Cloud and thus become exposed. The user must be able to control and choose whether or not to give access to his information. The de-anonymization techniques also make it possible to reduce this problem. Indeed, with these techniques, the majority of the data remains exposed, but the data which makes it possible to identify to whom they belong (name, address, age, etc.) are suppressed or hidden.

V. Synthesis

Some users' challenges are addressed by researchers, such as trust and privacy. However, the proposed solutions remain intangibles by users. Giving users the hand to participate in setting their own rules, the same way as proposed in social media, might be a potential solution. Reusing works and researches conducted in the context of usable security [46] [47] and usable privacy [48] [49] allows to resolve those challenges.

Ensuring interoperability and resolving heterogeneity can help to improve the usability of connected objects, but this is not a radical solution. We can have different solutions, such as applying HMI solutions [50] [51] which permit to have cognitive and adaptable users' interfaces, especially when use cases are targeting elderly and disabled persons.

Utility is a problem that is almost neglected, although it may be the key to improving the acceptability of connected objects by users. Researchers should focus on finding scenarios and use cases that can interest and motivate users.

VI. Conclusion

The IoT is emerging as one of the major trends shaping the development of the technologies sector at large. Researchers, developers and, industries have been interested in the IoT paradigm and have proposed different solutions for different issues, such as heterogeneity, scalability, and energy optimization.

Nevertheless, consumption of IoT products and services remains below expectations. Indeed, according to several studies and statistics, users claim other problems such as the cost of connected objects, but also and above all, their utility and usability. These problems are not addressed by researchers. Users also express their fears about the privacy of their personal data and do not trust connected objects. The problems of privacy and trust are addressed in the literature, however, the proposed solutions remain intangible by users.

We tried in this work to address these problems and to indicate some solution and some horizons of research.

Acknowledgment

This work was financially supported by the PHC Utique program of the French Ministry of Foreign Affairs and Ministry of higher education and research and the Tunisian Ministry of higher education and scientific research in the CMCU project number 18G1431.

References

[1] W. Abdelghani, C. Zayani, I. Amous, and F. Sèdes, "Trust management in social internet of things: a survey," in Conference on e-Business, e-Services and e-Society. Springer, 2016, pp. 430–441.

[2] M. Nitti, R. Girau, L. Atzori, A. Iera, and G. Morabito, "A subjective model for trustworthiness evaluation in the social internet of things," in Personal Indoor and Mobile Radio Communications (PIMRC), 2012 IEEE 23rd International Symposium on. IEEE, 2012, pp. 18–23.

[3] X. Jia, Q. Feng, T. Fan, and Q. Lei, "Rfid technology and its applications in internet of things (iot)," in Consumer Electronics, Communications and Networks (CECNet), 2012 2nd International Conference on. IEEE, 2012, pp. 1282–1285.

[4] C. Han, J. M. Jornet, E. Fadel, and I. F. Akyildiz, "A cross-layer communication module for the internet of things," Computer Networks, vol. 57, no. 3, 2013, pp. 622–633.

[5] D. Miorandi, S. Sicari, F. De Pellegrini, and I. Chlamtac, "Internet of things: Vision, applications and research challenges," Ad hoc networks, vol. 10, no. 7, 2012, pp. 1497–1516.

[6] OpinionWay, "Les franais et les objets connectés (french people and connected objects)," https://drive.google.com/file/d/0B6mEkutxBkwnXzlvQmpKLWZSNHc/view, 03 2016, accessed: 2018-02-09.

[7] D. H. Ali, "A social internet of things application architecture: applying semantic web technologies for achieving interoperability and automation between the cyber, physical and social worlds," Ph.D. dissertation, Institut National des Télécommunications, 2015.

[8] L. Atzori, A. Iera, G. Morabito, and M. Nitti, "The social internet of things (siot)–when social networks meet the internet of things: Concept, architecture and network characterization," Computer networks, vol. 56, no. 16, 2012, pp. 3594–3608.

[9] S. Geetha, "Social internet of things," World Scientific News, vol. 41, 2016, p. 76.

[10] A. Dohr, R. Modre-Opsrian, M. Drobics, D. Hayn, and G. Schreier, "The internet of things for ambient assisted living," in Seventh International Conference on Information Technology: New Generations (ITNG). IEEE, 2010, pp. 804–809.

[11] G. Roussos and V. Kostakos, "Rfid in pervasive computing: state-of-the-art and outlook," Pervasive and Mobile Computing, vol. 5, no. 1, 2009, pp. 110–131.

[12] I. F. Akyildiz, W. Su, Y. Sankarasubramaniam, and E. Cayirci, "Wireless sensor networks: a survey," Computer networks, vol. 38, no. 4, 2002, pp. 393–422.

[13] I. F. Akyildiz and I. H. Kasimoglu, "Wireless sensor and actor networks: research challenges," Ad hoc networks, vol. 2, no. 4, 2004, pp. 351–367.

[14] C. Sun, "Application of rfid technology for logistics on internet of things," AASRI Procedia, vol. 1, 2012, pp. 106–111.

[15] D. Singh, G. Tripathi, and A. J. Jara, "A survey of internet-of-things: Future vision, architecture, challenges and services," in Internet of things (WF-IoT), 2014 IEEE world forum on. IEEE, 2014, pp. 287–292.

[16] Z. Yan, P. Zhang, and A. V. Vasilakos, "A survey on trust management for internet of things," Journal of network and computer applications, vol. 42, 2014, pp. 120–134.

[17] A. Fongen, "Identity management and integrity protection in the internet of things," in 2012 third international conference on emerging security technologies. IEEE, 2012, pp. 111–114.

[18] S. Gambs, M.-O. Killijian, and M. N. del Prado Cortez, "De-anonymization attack on geolocated data," Journal of Computer and System Sciences, vol. 80, no. 8, 2014, pp. 1597–1614.

[19] A. J. Jara, L. Marin, A. F. Skarmeta, D. Singh, G. Bakul, and D. Kim, "Mobility modeling and security validation of a mobility management scheme based on ecc for ip-based wireless sensor networks (6lowpan)," in 2011 Fifth International Conference on Innovative Mobile and Internet Services in Ubiquitous Computing. IEEE, 2011, pp. 491–496.

[20] M. A. M. Isa, N. N. Mohamed, H. Hashim, S. F. S. Adnan, J. Manan, and R. Mahmod, "A lightweight and secure tftp protocol for smart environment," in Computer Applications and Industrial Electronics (ISCAIE), 2012 IEEE Symposium on. IEEE, 2012, pp. 302–306.

[21] J. Granjal, E. Monteiro, and J. S. Silva, "On the effectiveness of end-to-end security for internet-integrated sensing applications," in Green Computing and Communications (GreenCom), 2012 IEEE International Conference on. IEEE, 2012, pp. 87–93.

[22] S. Raza, L. Wallgren, and T. Voigt, "Svelte: Real-time intrusion detection in the internet of things," Ad hoc networks, vol. 11, no. 8, 2013, pp. 2661–2674.

[23] H. Ning, H. Liu, and L. Yang, "Cyber-entity security in the internet of things," Computer, 2013, p. 1.

[24] Z. Quan, F. Gui, D. Xiao, and Y. Tang, "Trusted architecture for farmland wireless sensor networks," in Cloud Computing Technology and Science (CloudCom), 2012 IEEE 4th International Conference on. IEEE, 2012, pp. 782–787.

[25] D. Seal, ARM architecture reference manual. Pearson Education, 2001.

[26] D. Gessner, A. Olivereau, A. S. Segura, and A. Serbanati, "Trustworthy infrastructure services for a secure and privacy-respecting internet of things," in Trust, Security and Privacy in Computing and Communications (TrustCom), 2012 IEEE 11th International Conference on. IEEE, 2012, pp. 998–1003.

[27] R. Z. Rebaï, L. Ghorbel, C. A. Zayani, and I. Amous, "An adaptive method for user profile learning," in East European Conference on Advances in Databases and Information Systems. Springer, 2013, pp. 126–134.

[28] M. Mezghani, A. Péninou, C. A. Zayani, I. Amous, and F. Sèdes, "Analyzing tagged resources for social interests detection," International Conference on Enterprise Information Systems, 04 2014, pp. 340 – 345.

[29] D. Tchuente, M.-F. Canut, N. Jessel, A. Péninou, and F. Sèdes, "Dérivation de profils utilisateurs à partir de réseaux sociaux: une approche par communautés de réseaux égocentriques (derivation of user profiles from social networks: a community approach of egocentric networks)," Ingénierie des systèmes d'information, vol. 18, no. 1, 2013, pp. 11–37.

[30] E. Khanfir, C. El Hog, R. B. Djmeaa, and I. A. B. Amor, "A web service selection framework based on user's context and qos," in Web Services (ICWS), 2014 IEEE International Conference on. IEEE, 2014, pp. 708–711.

[31] J. Miranda et al., "From the internet of things to the internet of people," IEEE Internet Computing, vol. 19, no. 2, 2015, pp. 40–47.

[32] A. Sheth and P. Anantharam, "Physical cyber social computing for human experience," in Proceedings of the 3rd International Conference on Web Intelligence, Mining and Semantics. ACM, 2013, p. 1.

[33] J. Guillen, J. Miranda, J. Berrocal, J. Garcia-Alonso, J. M. Murillo, and C. Canal, "People as a service: a mobile-centric model for providing collective sociological profiles," IEEE software, vol. 31, no. 2, 2014, pp. 48–53.

[34] N. Mäkitalo et al., "Social devices: collaborative co-located interactions in a mobile cloud," in Proceedings of the 11th International Conference on Mobile and Ubiquitous Multimedia. ACM, 2012, p. 10.

[35] C. C. Aggarwal, N. Ashish, and A. Sheth, "The internet of things: A survey from the data-centric perspective," in Managing and mining sensor data. Springer, 2013, pp. 383–428.

[36] L. Atzori, A. Iera, and G. Morabito, "From" smart objects" to" social objects": The next evolutionary step of the internet of things," IEEE Communications Magazine, vol. 52, no. 1, 2014, pp. 97–105.

[37] IFOP, "Les franais et la mobilité digitale (the french and digital mobility)," http://www.ifop.com/media/poll/2846-1-study_file.pdf, 04 2014, accessed: 2018-02-09.

[38] LaPoste, "Objets connectés: Ce qu'en attendent les franais (connected objects: What the french expect)," https://www.docapost.com/wp-content/uploads/2015/01/infographie-la-poste-generique.pdf, 12 2014, accessed: 2018-02-09.

[39] M. Nitti, R. Girau, and L. Atzori, "Trustworthiness management in the social internet of things," IEEE Transactions on knowledge and data engineering, vol. 26, no. 5, 2014, pp. 1253–1266.

[40] VIDAL, "L'utilisation de smartphones par les médecins (the use of smartphones by doctors)," http://www.vidalfrance.com/wp-content/download/info/Barometre_Mobile-VIDAL-CNOM-2016.pdf, 3 2016, accessed: 2018-02-09.

[41] A. Morris, Medical Research and Technology, ser. Cutting-Edge Science and Technology. ABDO Publishing Company, 2016. [Online]. Available: https://books.google.tn/books?id=N1kgCwAAQBAJ

[42] B. Patrick and L. Jacques, "Connected health: From e-health to connected health," CNOM, Tech. Rep., 06 2015.

[43] J. B. Bernabe, J. L. H. Ramos, and A. F. S. Gomez, "Taciot: multidimensional trust-aware access control system for the internet of things," Soft Computing, vol. 20, no. 5, 2016, pp. 1763–1779.

[44] N. B. Truong, T.-W. Um, B. Zhou, and G. M. Lee, "From personal experience to global reputation for trust evaluation in the social internet of things," in GLOBECOM 2017-2017 IEEE Global Communications Conference. IEEE, 2017, pp. 1–7.

[45] R. Chen, F. Bao, and J. Guo, "Trust-based service management for social internet of things systems," IEEE transactions on dependable and secure computing, vol. 13, no. 6, 2016, pp. 684–696.

[46] S. Lee, "A study on the need of the usable security in the corelation between it security and user experience," International Journal of Internet, Broadcasting and Communication, vol. 9, no. 4, 2017, pp. 14–18.

[47] P. Realpe-Muñoz, C. A. Collazos, T. Granollers, J. Muñoz-Arteaga, and E. B. Fernandez, "Design process for usable security and authentication

using a user-centered approach," in Proceedings of the XVIII International Conference on Human Computer Interaction. ACM, 2017, p. 42.

[48] H. Harkous, "Data-driven, personalized usable privacy," EPFL, Tech. Rep., 2017.

[49] J. Angulo, S. Fischer-Hübner, E. Wästlund, and T. Pulls, "Towards usable privacy policy display and management," Information Management & Computer Security, vol. 20, no. 1, 2012, pp. 4–17.

[50] U. E. Manawadu, M. Kamezaki, M. Ishikawa, T. Kawano, and S. Sugano, "A multimodal human-machine interface enabling situation-adaptive control inputs for highly automated vehicles," in Intelligent Vehicles Symposium (IV), 2017 IEEE. IEEE, 2017, pp. 1195–1200.

[51] J. D. Bauer, H. F. I. Kenneth, and R. N. Flores, "Intelligent human-machine interface," Jun. 21 2011.

SPACE: An Empirical Approach towards a User-Centric Smart Campus

Thammineni Prathyusha, Vipul Jindal, Saurabh Gangwar, Anand Konjengbam and Kotaro Kataoka

Indian Institute of Technology Hyderabad, India
Email: {ee14btech11034, es14btech11022, cs15mtech11019, cs14resch11004, kotaro}@iith.ac.in

***Abstract*—Making a campus smart involves a wide variety of devices, users, and other stakeholders. This gives rise to many issues including scalability, extensibility, user-centricity, and cost in terms of both deployment and maintenance. To overcome these issues, we propose a novel platform called SPACE that (1) enables end-to-end commanding and execution of tasks on a smart campus operation in a distributed and modulated manner, and (2) attempts to mitigate the above-mentioned issues. As an initial research testbed, the proposed SPACE has been deployed for different scenarios in a university campus including a classroom, a faculty office, and a lab. This paper empirically reports how the SPACE system enables a smart campus testbed and further lessons from the deployment.**

Keywords*–*Internet of Things (IoT); IoT Platform; Smart Building; Cloud-based IoT.

I. Introduction

While many research and development efforts were made under the concepts of ubiquitous computing, pervasive computing and Internet of Things (IoT), we have not seen dominating research in the area of IoT platforms that addresses the challenges affiliated with providing seamless user-experience and ease of maintaining the system [1]. Moreover, many of the papers on IoT platform assume that the devices (e.g., bulb, fan, Air Conditioner (AC), etc.) are already smart and have communication capabilities [2][3]. There are virtually unlimited number of "things" that can be connected to the Internet under the umbrella of IoT. Hence, an IoT platform that can connect and accommodate such "things" is needed.

A university campus is an interesting and challenging premises to apply the concept of IoT. A university campus involves many smart contexts [4][5]. Many stakeholders including students, professors, working staff, guests, and administrators are involved there and they have various needs to be satisfied. Professors and students need features such as user-centricity, universal access, and multi-purpose space sharing. Administrators would prefer an economically viable and easy to maintain IoT-enabled campus. A smart campus provides intelligent facilities like universal access, location awareness, user-centricity, and support for heterogeneous devices to the campus community, while the operational cost gets reduced.

This paper presents a platform called SPACE for making a university campus smart by connecting various types of things and facilities (e.g., AC, fan, and bulb) in one system. The proposed platform enables 1) integration of existing campus facilities into SPACE in a cost-effective manner, 2) end users with personalized access to the campus facilities, and 3) an extensible platform where end users can easily assemble new components such as new end devices, controllers, and new communication modules supporting different protocols and standards.

In this paper, we present the implementation and deployment of the proposed platform, and a reference model of end-user oriented and ad-hoc deployment of a smart campus that has not been originally designed and constructed to be smart and user-centric. We introduce the concept of Device Interfacing Gateway (DIGW) and used it to connect any campus facility to the system.

The rest of the paper is organized as follows. Section II provides an overview of related works. Then, we discuss the problems of modelling the system design in Section III, and present the implementation details in Section IV. We evaluate and validate the system in Section V and finally, we conclude the paper and discuss the future works in Section VI.

II. Related Work

Zhang et al. [6] addressed the problem of lack of a versatile and cost-effective software platform for smart buildings. They developed an open source software called Building Energy Management Open Source Software (BEMOSS) that works on a single board computer for monitoring and controlling energy consumption of a building. The system included features like plug and plays using device discovery, and interoperability of different communication protocols. However, the supported devices were limited to already smart ones.

Sánchez et al. [7] implemented IoT applications and services in the city of Santander, Spain, with a physical deployment of more than 2000 sensors. They presented a high-level architectural model supporting real-world IoT experimentation facilities on different devices. In order to address the problem of scale and heterogeneity of devices and application domains, they divided their architecture into three tiers; IoT device, gateway, and server. Georgakopoulos et al. [8] presented an IoT architecture with the concept of service discovery and on-demand integration of devices, storage and computing resources over the cloud. They incorporated data analytics and visualization to create an on-demand IoT application. Although progress has been made on implementation of large-scale IoT, the implementations are generic and personalization of the system is not considered.

The following works addressed the lack of standards for IoT and discussed frameworks for integrating various smart devices. Puatru et al. [9] presented a solution for connecting different types of home appliances to one platform. They focused on how different platforms like Google Nest and Philips Hue can be operated via a mobile device with a Web browser for easy accessibility and better user experience. Nati et al. [10] worked on user-centric IoT for integrating embedded heterogeneous smart devices in a real-life office environment. The solution offered modular implementation of an open source smart home system using Intel Edison board [11] as a gateway. Mozzami et al. [12] proposed a smart phone based platform to handle heterogeneous devices and multi-vendor smart home appliances in home environment without the need for painstaking configuration and custom programming. They developed an Android application with an open specification for XML driver support. Hernandez et al. [13] proposed a framework for the development of IoT applications where smart objects exhibit autonomy in regards to platforms and human users through management functions. These works assumed that such smart devices can be IP-proxied and capable of sensing and actuating, and device-specific applications are already available.

Hentschel et al. [14] proposed a campus-wide sensor network using Raspberry Pi. They defined supersensors as sensors (light, temperature, motion, sound, and Wi-Fi) attached to Raspberry Pi that are capable of local computer operations and data transmission to a centralized database. The use of Raspberry Pi reduced the cost of procurement compared to standard expensive IoT sensors and has a small footprint. They considered that different sensors have different communication modes and tried to cope with a heterogenous environment. They also discussed the advantages of their method which include intelligent filtering of sensor data as well as capture and buffering of incoming data while the network connectivity is disrupted. Joshi et al. [15] designed a low-cost basic home automation system to control multiple appliances that can be globally monitored and accessed using low cost Raspberry Pi, Arduino and web server.

Some researchers have carried out works related to personalized and user-centric IoT systems. Jayatilaka et al. [16] proposed an assisted living system where appliances exhibit seamless social interactions with people. They embedded multiple sensors such as thermometer, hydrometer, and scale into appliances (refrigerator, microwave, and trash bin). The appliances used Twitter as a messaging system to send notification messages to authorized people. Wu et al. [17] developed a framework for human-system interaction by analyzing the interactive relationship among services, spaces, and users in a smart home environment. Lee and Lin [18] implemented a situation-aware IoT based system that can detect user activities in a room and control the devices in the room accordingly. Alam et al. [19] worked on predicting user behavior based on human activity pattern. Their approach used episodes of events of home appliances that have on-off states (such as lights, fans, heater, and window blinds) as an input to a sequence prediction algorithm to predict the next activity from previous history. Using multi-sensor data streams, Chen et al. [20] worked on a knowledge-driven real-time continuous activity recognition using multi-sensor data streams in a smart home environment. The approach uses domain knowledge, ontologies, semantic reasoning and classification for activity recognition. Our work is related to developing a platform for smart and user-centric campus environment that provides facilities such as universal access, user-centricity, and support for heterogeneous devices.

III. System Design

A. System Requirement Organization

In this section, we describe the system requirements of our proposed SPACE platform and explain the approaches for implementing a smart campus.

Universal access: End devices and campus facilities should be accessible from anywhere so that users can control devices without physically being present near the devices. SPACE provides universal access by enabling end users to operate all the end devices using a single mobile application.

User-centricity: The system should be simple in terms of deployment, usage, and maintenance for the user. As a consequence of user-centricity, SPACE provides pleasing user experience and user-friendly interface.

Cost effectiveness: The cost of a system includes its deployment, maintenance and the cost of upgrading/adding new components. The cost of deploying SPACE over the existing infrastructure is considerably lower than replacing all the existing components (e.g., lights) in the infrastructure with smart components (e.g., smart bulbs). Physical contact with switches is generally required to control the components. Repeated physical contact results in wear and tear of switches and may lead to accidents. Such accidents can be avoided by replacing physical switches with virtual switches that are controlled through a mobile/desktop application.

Support for heterogeneous IoT devices: Various heterogeneous devices are present in an environment. Such devices have different operations and need different protocols to control them. It is desirable to identify, integrate, and control such devices via a single application so that the user need not use a different application for each end device.

Extensibility: The system needs to be extensible regarding support of both non-smart and already smart devices. It should accommodate various kinds of communication and processing technologies as per the need of the environment in the deployed system. Users should be able to integrate devices with minimum support from the system administrator.

B. System Architecture/Design Overview

The overall architecture of SPACE consists of four main components - local controller, central controller, Device Interfacing Gateway (DIGW), and mobile application. Figure 1 shows the system overview of SPACE.

As shown in the figure, the platform is divided into three layers: User Interface (UI) layer, logical control layer, and physical control layer. A local controller is deployed in each environment such as rooms, offices, and labs. It performs edge computation and it is responsible for managing its local environment. All end devices in an environment communicate with a local controller via DIGW. A DIGW is attached to each of the end devices and is among one of the most important components of the platform. The mobile application can interact with the end devices via central controller or local controller. Each of the components has some specific functions and they interact with one another to fulfill the system requirements. Figure 2 shows the information exchange among the components of SPACE.

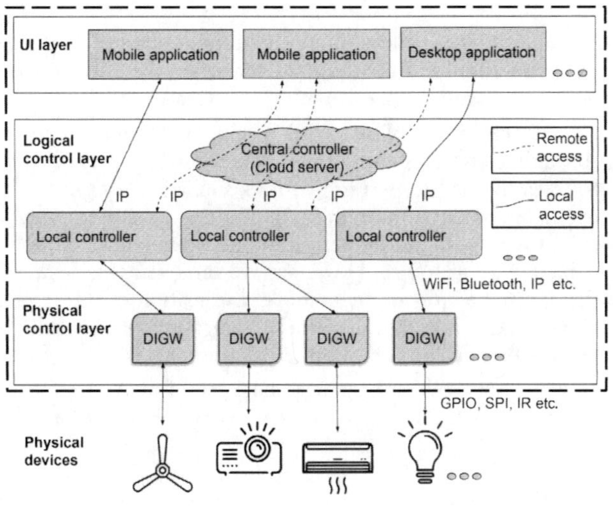

Figure 1. System overview of SPACE

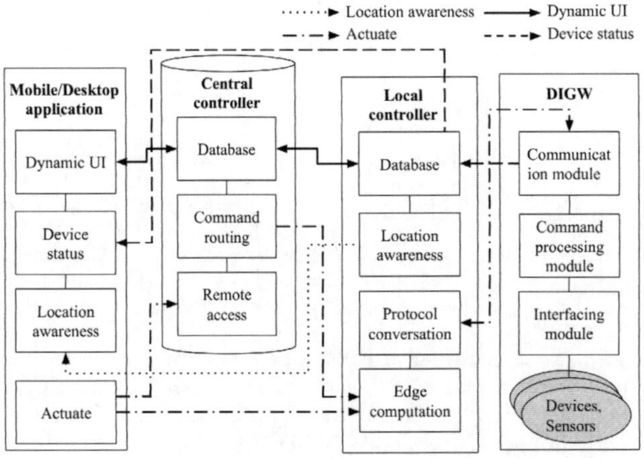

Figure 2. System block information exchange of SPACE

The **Device Interfacing Gateway (DIGW)** is used to proxy and control end devices. Generally, end devices are not capable of communication. To connect these end devices to a network, a DIGW is plugged into each end device. DIGW receives commands from local controller and sends data/feedback from sensors and end devices to local controller, as illustrated in Figure 2. It also enables discovery of end devices. DIGW is comprised of four modules: communication module, command processing module, interfacing module, and power module. The details of each module are explained below.

- The **communication module** takes care of receiving and sending signals over any particular communication protocol like ZigBee, Bluetooth, and Wi-Fi. It does necessary processing of signals to convert them into a standard format understandable by the command processing module.
- The **command processing module** receives commands from communication module, interprets the commands and accordingly calls the right functions that are stored in its memory. The functions then trigger the interfacing module to actuate the command. It also takes care of internal optimization regarding power consumption.
- The **interfacing module** is the physical interface between an end device and DIGW. It consists of actuators such as switches, valves, and infrared (IR) modules that can control the end device. Actuators provide functions such as turning ON/OFF of end devices, modulating control changes, and switching action between different states.
- The **power module** takes care of the power consumed by all the DIGW modules. It is interchangeable with different parts such as adapter, battery, and solar cell.

The **central controller** is responsible for data storage, data processing, command routing, and remote access. The central controller is a cloud server through which all the local controllers and mobile applications can interact. All the information about end devices, room environments, and user information (such as user authentication, and location) are stored in the database of the central controller. The mobile application uses the information present in the database of the central controller for functions such as device status and dynamic UI. The use of cloud service is to provide scalable computing and storage power for developing, maintaining, and running multiple services simultaneously.

The **local controller** is a control unit present in all the environments such as rooms and labs. It is responsible for all the activities happening in its local environment apart from the authentication process, which is taken care of by the central controller. It stores the relevant information of end devices present in its local environment. It supports different communication protocols and acts as a bridge between the DIGW and the central controller. It is responsible for the real-time processing of sensor data in its environment. It is also responsible for protocol conversion. For example, consider a scenario where some end devices speak Zigbee via DIGW, and some other devices speak Wi-Fi and remaining devices speak Bluetooth and Radio-Frequency Identification (RFID). The local controller converts the command request from the mobile application/central controller to the supported protocol and sends the formatted command to the respective DIGW and vice-versa. The local controller broadcasts its location information along with a list of end devices that can be controlled within its environment. This information helps mobile applications to be aware of the location and improves user experience (explained in the next section). If the user is near a local controller, commands from the mobile application reach the local controller earlier before reaching the central controller, and so the command gets executed faster. It performs edge computing which helps in optimizing various latencies such as command execution time.

The **mobile application** gets access to end devices via the central controller or the local controller depending on the location (remote/local) of the user. It has a dynamic UI that changes depending on the location of the user. This feature helps in minimizing the number of manual operations required to perform an action, hence providing a good user experience. The UI of the application reflects consistent information regardless of the technology used at lower layers. For example, two different temperature sensors have the same type of UI even though they are from different manufacturers and use different protocols such as ZigBee or Bluetooth. The mobile application also supports voice commands to control devices.

IV. System Implementation

This section details the implementation of SPACE inside a university (Indian Institute of Technology Hyderabad, India) as a testbed. We assume that, initially, the end devices are not capable of any communication.

A. Technical Components

TABLE I. Software and hardware components of SPACE

Component	Software	Hardware
Mobile application	Operating System (OS): Android K,L,M; Google Speech Application Program Interface (API)	Any smartphone with Internet connectivity
Central Controller	OS: Ubuntu 16.04; Database: PostgreSQL	2.40 GHz quad core Intel Xenon CPU; 8GB RAM
Local Controller	OS: Raspbian	Raspberry Pi (v2,v3), Bluetooth Low Energy (BLE) module
DIGW for air conditioner	Real-Time Operating System (RTOS) and ATtention (AT) commands API; Arduino Interactive Development Environment (IDE)	Espressif Systems (ESP8266EX) [21], IR module
DIGW for room lights	RTOS and AT commands API; Arduino IDE	ATMEGA328P [22]; SPDT relay

Table I presents a concise summary of the various software and hardware elements used by components for implementing the SPACE platform. It may be noted that implementation is done mostly using open-source software.

Figure 3 shows a cropped interface of the mobile application. The sidebar displays information about the user,

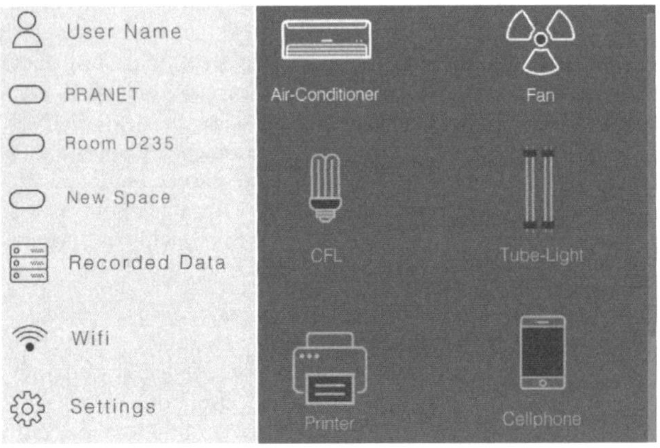

Figure 3. UI of mobile application - side menu and main menu buttons

rooms, recorded data, and available settings. The main menu has clickable icons to control the devices present in a room. The icon changes from grey to blue when the corresponding device changes its state from OFF to ON and vice versa.

The mobile application also supports voice commands through Google Speech API. Certain key phrases are used to train the API to perform actions similar to user clicks. For example, we used the phrase "Lights on" to initiate function calls for turning on lights. The voice command control was deployed in an office. However, we removed this feature in the latest version of the mobile application as the Google Speech API was not accurately detecting the voices and required extensive samples for training data.

Figure 4 shows the block diagram of a local controller along with DIGW and ampere sensors. Here, *Raspberry Pi v3* is used as the local controller for performing edge computation and storing data. Arduino, as well as Single Pole Double Throw (SPDT) relay are used as DIGW to interact with ampere sensors and end devices. Ampere sensors detect the state of devices using the current readings.

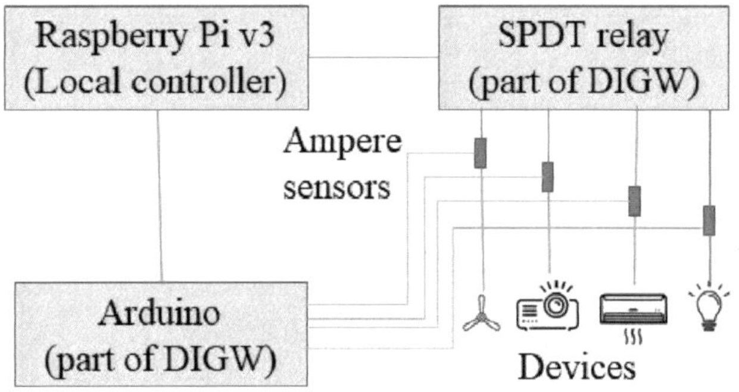

Figure 4. Block diagram of a local controller along with DIGW and ampere sensors

Figure 5 shows the different modules of DIGW used in the real-time deployment of SPACE. All these modules work independently, hence, making DIGW modular. The four modules communicate with each other over General-Purpose

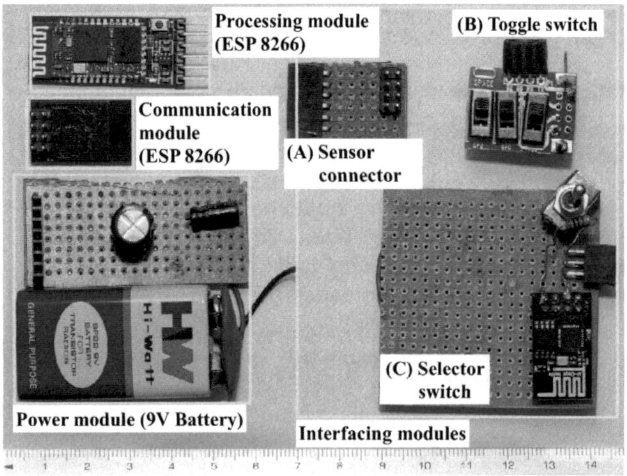

Figure 5. DIGW used in real-time deployment of SPACE

Input/Output (GPIO) interface [23], which is a standardized mode of communication. Consider a case where, after the deployment, the user wishes to change the mode of communication from Bluetooth to Wi-Fi. The user can do so by getting a Wi-Fi module, which is compatible with DIGW and replacing the Bluetooth module by the Wi-Fi module in a plug and play fashion. This feature helps in saving the upgrading cost of the system, as we need not change the whole DIGW to change some particular features of the system.

B. Communication Protocols

Figure 6 shows the information flow with regards to time between various components of the system for executing a command.

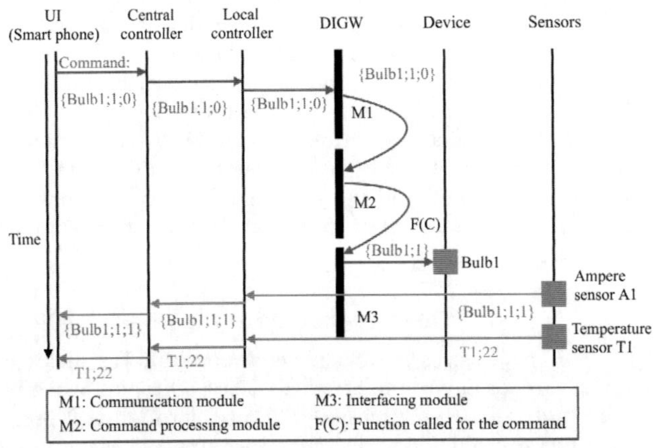

Figure 6. Information flow between components of SPACE

For illustration, we examine two types of information flow: 1) the message flow of user triggered command followed by the sensor data flow that senses the state of the end device after execution of the command, and 2) periodic update of sensor data. Consider a remote user is sending a command to turn on a light bulb using the mobile application. The application generates a command packet consisting of device ID, desired state, and reply status ({Bulb1;1;0}) and passes it to the central controller. The central controller parses the command and routes it to the appropriate local controller. The local controller identifies the light bulb from the device ID and routes the command to the appropriate DIGW, which is connected to the desired light bulb. The communication module (M1) of the DIGW receives the signal from the local controller and converts the signal into a format, which is understandable by the processing module (M2) and then passes the message to M2. M2 then calls the appropriate function F(C) to turn on Bulb1. F(C) gets executed via the interface module (M3), and the light bulb gets switched on. The ampere sensor connected to Bulb1 detects a change in the state after the command execution and sends the sensor data to the mobile phone via the local controller and the central controller, respectively. The application then automatically reflects the new state of the light bulb in the UI. Also, the temperature reading of the room is periodically sent from the temperature sensor (T1) to the mobile application via the local controller and the central controller.

C. Data Structure

Our system implementation used six data types, as shown in Table II.

TABLE II. DATA STRUCTURE OF MESSAGE PACKETS

Data Type	Fields
Authentication	Username, Password, Reply flag
Location	LocationID (IPv6 address), Location SSID
Device	DeviceID, Device name, Device type, LocationID, StateID
Sensor data	SensorID, FloatData
Command	DeviceID, DesireState, Reply
Preset	Room Type, DeviceID, DesireState

Each data type is described as follows.

- **Authentication:** *Username* and *Password* are used for storing the credentials for authorized users. *Reply flag* indicates whether a command is successful or not.
- **Location** is identified by the static IPv6 address assigned to the local controller. In addition, it consists of a human-readable name in the form of an Service Set Identifier (SSID) that in projected in each room.
- **Device** stores the details of a device. The mobile application uses this message packet to know the type and state of devices present in a room.
- **Sensor data** stores the reading of the sensors. This reading is periodically sent to the local controller.
- **Command** is a message triggered by the end user via the mobile application. It contains information regarding the requested action by the end user along with the id of the end device on which the action must be performed.
- **Preset** is used to change the setting of a group of devices for performing a combined task. For example, *lecture preset* is used to turn on AC, projector and turn off lights to prepare for a presentation.

V. EVALUATION

In this section, we discuss the output of implementing the proposed platform. For evaluation, we consider three different room environments: a personal room, a professor's office room, and a computer lab. 10 student volunteers were selected to evaluate various scopes manually.

Universal Access: To test the universal access of the system, the volunteers were asked to control various devices in the rooms via the mobile application. Three different scenarios were considered: 1) when they are inside the room and connected to the university Wi-Fi, 2) when they are at a different location of the institute and connected to the university Wi-Fi, and 3) when they are out of the institute and connected to the Internet using 3G/4G LTE. In all the three scenarios, the volunteers could successfully control all the functions of the system, monitor room temperature, motion inside the rooms, and state of the devices (light, fan, and air conditioner) in real time. This shows that the devices are accessible to the users irrespective of where they are present.

Personalization: The volunteers were asked to install the application and perform the sign-up process on their own.

Using the application, they were asked to add a room and all controllable devices present in the room. The volunteers could arrange the layout of the icons according to their convenience. In average, they took 8 minutes to complete the whole setup under regular Wi-Fi connectivity. This shows that the users could complete the set up and personalize the UI with ease.

Location Awareness: Global Positioning System (GPS) was not used to detect location because of its high power consuming property. A unique SSID, which was projected by all the local controllers, was used to detect the present location of the user. The transmission power of Wi-Fi was controlled to be minimal so that its signal did not penetrate the walls of the room and was available only inside the room. Once a user entered the room, the mobile application picked up the SSID from the local controller and the application dynamically changed its UI, depending on the location (e.g., room, lab, etc.) of the user. This ensured that the user was shown the UI of the room along with devices that could be controlled, rather than seeing the UI of some other room. Consistent observations were made in all the three different room environments. This feature of dynamically changing the UI of the application reduced the number of manual operations a user needs to turn on a device from three to just one.

Cost Effectiveness: Most of the existing IoT solutions use expensive components that are designed for some specific purpose. On the contrary, our implementation uses general readily available inexpensive components such as Raspberry Pi, Arduino, etc. This brings the current cost of the deployed platform to $51 only per room. Each deployed system can accommodate up to 20 end devices. Table III shows the breakdown of the cost of deployment per room.

TABLE III. COST FOR DEPLOYING THE PLATFORM IN A ROOM

Gadget	Price (in USD)	# devices supported
Raspberry Pi v3	35	20
Arduino	6	17
ESP8266	5	1
SPDT	5	8
Misc. devices	5	1
Total	**51**	

Scalability of storage space and processing power: The use of central controller and cloud infrastructure makes the platform scalable in terms of storage space and processing power. Using cloud infrastructure, the storage space and processing power of the central controller can be increased as per the scale of deployment. The storage space and processing power for a local controller depend on the specification of the Raspberry Pi used.

Reaction Time: To test the reaction time and concurrent execution of the commands, we present three instances of command request and the time delays in different stages of execution. The details of the performance of command request through a local controller are shown in Table IV. In the table, the *Number of requests* represent the parallel requests made to the same local controller simultaneously, from different end devices. *Pi execution time* represents the time taken by the local controller to process and forward the command to the DIGW after receiving it from the mobile application. *Communication delay* represents the time taken from the command to go from the mobile application to the local controller. *Net latency* represents the total latency, i.e., the sum of Pi execution time and communication delay. The same user may make multiple requests (e.g., turn on light and AC), but each user is asked to make a different request at the same time. More parallel requests mean more processing load on the local controller and more probability of request drops, hence increasing the reaction time. We observe that the net latency increases with the number of parallel requests. The increase in latency is because of 1) drop of packets by the local controller due to overloading, and 2) Wi-Fi signal delay between the mobile and the local controller. The total delay is consistently low and the system works well even in the situation where 30 different command requests were made concurrently.

TABLE IV. SERVICE PROCESSING TIME COMPARISON OF THREE INSTANCES OF COMMAND EXECUTION

Instance	Number of requests	Pi execution time (ms)	Communication delay delay (ms)	Net latency (ms)
1	5	0.002	0.165	0.167
2	10	0.002	0.213	0.215
3	30	0.003	0.250	0.253

VI. CONCLUSION AND FUTURE WORKS

This paper presented a novel framework for making a smart campus environment called SPACE. Our platform offers user-centric functionality based on user location and preference for controlling devices in the surrounding space through a mobile application. We validated the performance of the SPACE platform through implementation and practical use-cases in a university campus. The modularization property of the DIGW allows SPACE to integrate various modes of communication, power supply, and devices. The proposed platform has high potential to support a wide variety of services and applications on it.

The future work involves polishing the hardware by 3D-printing custom-designed circuit boards and casing with standard design guidelines. This may also help in downsizing and reducing the cost of the local controller and the DIGW. Another direction of future work is optimizing the behavior of the smart campus based on learning of user activity data. Artificial Intelligence and data mining algorithms may be used to predict user activities and actuate the campus facility. Privacy preservation of the user-generated data must be considered for using such data.

REFERENCES

[1] J. Bergman, T. Olsson, I. Johansson, and K. Rassmus-Gröhn, "An exploratory study on how internet of things developing companies handle user experience requirements," in International Working Conference on Requirements Engineering: Foundation for Software Quality. Springer, 2018, pp. 20–36.

[2] M. Swan, "Sensor mania! the internet of things, wearable computing, objective metrics, and the quantified self 2.0," Journal of Sensor and Actuator Networks, vol. 1, no. 3, 2012, pp. 217–253.

[3] T. Sztyler, "Towards real world activity recognition from wearable devices," in Pervasive Computing and Communications Workshops (PerCom Workshops), 2017 IEEE International Conference on. IEEE, 2017, pp. 97–98.

[4] A. Alghamdi and S. Shetty, "Survey toward a smart campus using the internet of things," in Future Internet of Things and Cloud (FiCloud), 2016 IEEE 4th International Conference on. IEEE, 2016, pp. 235–239.

[5] C. Perera, A. Zaslavsky, P. Christen, and D. Georgakopoulos, "Context aware computing for the internet of things: A survey," IEEE Communications Surveys & Tutorials, vol. 16, no. 1, 2014, pp. 414–454.

[6] X. Zhang, R. Adhikari, M. Pipattanasomporn, M. Kuzlu, and S. R. Bradley, "Deploying iot devices to make buildings smart: Performance evaluation and deployment experience," in Internet of Things (WF-IoT), 2016 IEEE 3rd World Forum on. IEEE, 2016, pp. 530–535.

[7] L. Sánchez, V. Gutiérrez, J. A. Galache, P. Sotres, J. R. Santana, J. Casanueva, and L. Muñoz, "Smartsantander: Experimentation and service provision in the smart city," in Wireless Personal Multimedia Communications (WPMC), 2013 16th International Symposium on. IEEE, 2013, pp. 1–6.

[8] D. Georgakopoulos, P. P. Jayaraman, M. Zhang, and R. Ranjan, "Discovery-driven service oriented iot architecture," in Collaboration and Internet Computing (CIC), 2015 IEEE Conference on. IEEE, 2015, pp. 142–149.

[9] I.-I. Pătru, M. Carabaş, M. Bărbulescu, and L. Gheorghe, "Smart home iot system," in RoEduNet Conference: Networking in Education and Research, 2016 15th. IEEE, 2016, pp. 1–6.

[10] M. Nati, A. Gluhak, H. Abangar, and W. Headley, "Smartcampus: A user-centric testbed for internet of things experimentation," in Wireless Personal Multimedia Communications (WPMC), 2013 16th International Symposium on. IEEE, 2013, pp. 1–6.

[11] Hardware Guide, Intel Edison Kit for Arduino. San Val, 2015.

[12] M.-M. Moazzami, G. Xing, D. Mashima, W.-P. Chen, and U. Herberg, "Spot: A smartphone-based platform to tackle heterogeneity in smart-home iot systems," in Internet of Things (WF-IoT), 2016 IEEE 3rd World Forum on. IEEE, 2016, pp. 514–519.

[13] M. E. P. Hernández and S. Reiff-Marganiec, "Towards a software framework for the autonomous internet of things," in Future Internet of Things and Cloud (FiCloud), 2016 IEEE 4th International Conference on. IEEE, 2016, pp. 220–227.

[14] K. Hentschel, D. Jacob, J. Singer, and M. Chalmers, "Supersensors: Raspberry pi devices for smart campus infrastructure," in Future Internet of Things and Cloud (FiCloud), 2016 IEEE 4th International Conference on. IEEE, 2016, pp. 58–62.

[15] J. Joshi, V. Rajapriya, S. Rahul, P. Kumar, S. Polepally, R. Samineni, and D. K. Tej, "Performance enhancement and iot based monitoring for smart home," in Information Networking (ICOIN), 2017 International Conference on. IEEE, 2017, pp. 468–473.

[16] A. Jayatilaka, Y. Su, and D. C. Ranasinghe, "Hotaal: Home of social things meet ambient assisted living," in IEEE International Conference on Pervasive Computing and Communication Workshops (PerCom Workshops). IEEE, 2016, pp. 1–3.

[17] C.-L. Wu and L.-C. Fu, "Design and realization of a framework for human–system interaction in smart homes," IEEE Transactions on Systems, Man, and Cybernetics-Part A: Systems and Humans, vol. 42, no. 1, 2012, pp. 15–31.

[18] S.-Y. Lee and F. J. Lin, "Situation awareness in a smart home environment," in Internet of Things (WF-IoT), 2016 IEEE 3rd World Forum on. IEEE, 2016, pp. 678–683.

[19] M. R. Alam, M. B. I. Reaz, and M. M. Ali, "Speed: An inhabitant activity prediction algorithm for smart homes," IEEE Transactions on Systems, Man, and Cybernetics-Part A: Systems and Humans, vol. 42, no. 4, 2012, pp. 985–990.

[20] L. Chen, C. D. Nugent, and H. Wang, "A knowledge-driven approach to activity recognition in smart homes," IEEE Transactions on Knowledge and Data Engineering, vol. 24, no. 6, 2012, pp. 961–974.

[21] E. S. C. Platform, "Esp8266," Espressif Systems, 2013.

[22] W. Kunikowski, E. Czerwiński, P. Olejnik, and J. Awrejcewicz, "An overview of atmega avr microcontrollers used in scientific research and industrial applications," Pomiary Automatyka Robotyka, vol. 19, 2015.

[23] S. Balachandran, "General purpose input/output (gpio)," Michigan State University College of Engineering. Published, 2009, pp. 08–11.

Towards Modular and Adaptive Assistance Systems for Manual Assembly: A Semantic Description and Interoperability Framework

Amita Singh
Technical University
Kaiserslautern
Email: amitas@kth.se

Fabian Quint
German Research Center
for Artificial Intelligence (DFKI)
Email: mail@fabian-quint.de

Patrick Bertram
Technologie-Initiative
SmartFactoryKL e.V.
Email: bertram@smartfactory.de

Martin Ruskowski
German Research Center
for Artificial Intelligence (DFKI)
Email: martin.ruskowski@dfki.de

***Abstract*—With the advent of Industry 4.0 and human-in-the-loop paradigms, Cyber-Physical Systems (CPS) are becoming increasingly common in production facilities, and, consequently, there has been a surge of interest in the field. In production systems, CPS which assist humans in completing tasks are called assistance systems. Most recent designs proposed for assistance systems in the production domain are monolithic and allow only limited modifications. In contrast, this work considers an assistance system to have a hybrid architecture consisting of a central entity containing the process description (or instructions) and one or more plug-and-play Cyber-Physical Systems to retrieve relevant information from the physical environment. Such a design allows the overall system capabilities to be adapted to the needs of workers and tasks. In this paper, a framework is presented for designing the CPS modules using Semantic Web technologies which will allow (i) interpretation of all data, and (ii) interoperability among the modules, from the very outset. Furthermore, a knowledge description model and ontology development of a CPS module is described. An approach is illustrated with the help of a use case for implementing the framework to design a module, data exchange among modules, and to build a sustainable ecosystem of ontologies which enables rapid development of third-party CPS modules. An implementation using Protégé is provided and future direction of research is discussed.**

***Keywords*—human-centered CPS; assistance systems; adaptive automation; ontology; interoperability.**

I. Introduction

An ever growing catalogue of products, short product life-cycle, competitive product costs, and changing demographics have led to a demand of reactive and proactive production systems that can adapt to the changing needs [1]–[3]. According to the European Factories of the Future Research Association, human-centricity is a prerequisite for the production systems to be flexible and adapt to the changing demographics [4][5]. Thus, major efforts are being made to make adaptive human-centered CPS (H-CPS) where machines and automation adapt to the physical and cognitive needs of humans in a dynamic fashion [6][7].

In this paper, assistance systems are considered as H-CPS in production systems. Assistance systems assess the production process using sensors embedded in the environment and, based on the state of the process, provide instructions to workers through visualisation devices attached to them [8]. Although humans have unparalleled degree of flexibility, i.e., humans can adapt to varying production, major focus is being placed on increasing the flexibility of automation systems that help workers during processes. Emerging developments like modularity, Service-Oriented Architecture (SOA), interoperability by the virtue of common semantic description (e.g., administrative shell [9][10]), and edge-computing [11] are rarely applied to H-CPS.

In this paper, a CPS-based assistance system, which adapts to a worker's need by exploiting the benefits of such techniques is proposed. Such an assistance system has a central system and one or more CPS modules attached to it as shown in Figure 1. CPS modules feed information extracted from the environment to the central system.

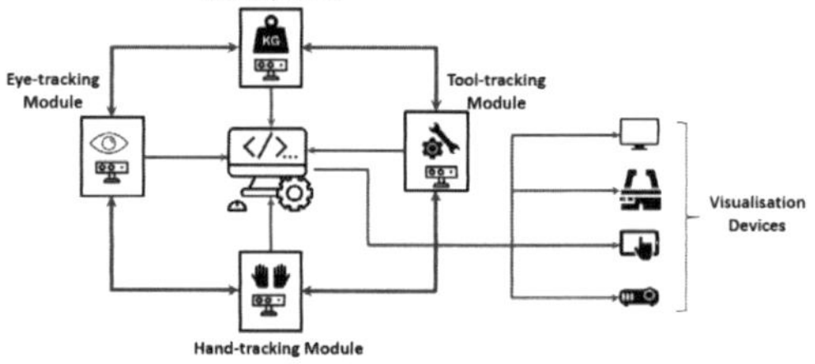

Figure 1. Schematic description of an assistance system.

The central system, in turn, processes this information to assess the state of the process and the worker's needs.

To the best of the authors' knowledge, no design so far allows one module to access and use the data from other modules. In this paper, semantic design of modules and interoperability between different parts of an assistance system are discussed in detail, and consequently, a Semantic Description and Interoperability (SDI) framework is proposed.

In the remainder of the paper, first the related work is presented in Section II and then the concepts of modularity and interoperability are discussed in detail in Section III. In Section IV, the SDI framework for design of modules is presented. Next, the development of such modules is discussed in Section V. Finally, the implementation of an assistance system is simulated using the proposed framework in Section VI, followed by the conclusion and potential future work.

II. Related Work

This work brings together two different areas of research: development of CPS for production, as well as the semantic design of these systems. Related work in both areas are discussed separately and some aspects are discussed in detail.

Assistance Systems. There is significant contemporary research interest in using sensor technology for developing context-aware CPS [8][12]–[14]. Nelles et al. have looked into assistance systems for planning and control in production environment [12]. Gorecky et al. have explored cognitive assistance and training systems for workers during production [13]. Zamfiresu et al. have also integrated virtual reality and a hand-tracking module to help workers during assembly processes [14]. However, they do not consider the modular design of these modules and interoperability between such modules. Very recently, Quint et al. have proposed a hybrid architecture of such a system, which is composed of a central system and modules which can handle heterogeneous data [8]. However, they do not explore standardizing the design of such modules. In this work, a framework for designing CPS modules and an ecosystem for ensuring interoperability across these modules is proposed.

Semantic Design. The Semantic Web is an extension of World Wide Web that promotes common data formats and exchange protocols on the Web through standards. Wahlster et al. [15][16] use Semantic Web technologies to represent and integrate industrial data in a generic way. Grangel et al. [10] discuss Semantic Web technologies in handling heterogeneous data from distributed sources using light-weight vocabulary. Semy et al. [17] describe these technologies as the key enabler for building pervasive context-aware system wherein independently developed devices and softwares can share contextual knowledge among themselves. Semantic Web technology formalisms, such as Resource Description Framework (RDF), RDF Schema and Web Ontology Language (OWL), help solve the major hurdle towards description and interoperability between CPS by annotating the entities of a system. Some of the major advantages of using RDF-based semantic knowledge representation are briefly discussed here:

Global unique identification. Semantic Web describes each entity within a CPS and its relations as a global unique identifier. According to the principles of Semantic Web, HTTP URIs/IRIs should be used as the global unique identifiers [18]. This ensures disambiguation, and retrieval, of entities in the complete system. As a consequence, a decentralised, holistic and global unique retrievable scheme of CPS can be established.

Interoperability. Interoperability is the ability to communicate and interconnect CPS from different vendors. It is vital in order to have cost effective rapid development. According to domain experts [10][16][19], RDF and Linked Data are proven Semantic Web technologies for integrating different types of data. Gezer et al. [20] mention that OWL-S ensures better interoperability by allowing services to exchange data and allowing devices to configure themselves.

Apart from the above mentioned advantages, by using RDF representation different data serialization formats, for example RDF/XML, RDF/OWL can be easily generated and transmitted over the network [10]. Further, data can be made available through a standard interface using SPARQL, a W3C recommendation for RDF query language [21].

Recently, Negri et al. [22] discussed requirements and languages of semantic representation of manufacturing systems and conclude that ontologies are the best way of such representations in the domain. The authors also highlighted importance of ontologies in providing system description in an intuitive and human-readable format, standardization not only in terms of definitions and axioms, but also standardizing Web-services and message-based communication. This not only makes engineering of the system streamlined but also facilitates interoperability between parts of the system. In his seminal work, Nocola Guarino formally defined ontologies both as a tool for knowledge representation and management, as well as a database for information extraction and retrieval [23]. In particular, he describes how ontologies can play a significant role during development, as well as run-time, for information systems.

Further, Niles et al. [24] highlighted the usefulness of upper ontologies in facilitating interoperability between domain-specific ontologies by the virtue of shared globally unique terms and definitions (HTTP URIs/IRIs) in a top-down approach of building a system. Semy et al. [17] also described mid-level ontologies as a bridge between upper ontologies and domain-specific ontologies, which encompass terms and definitions used across many domains but do not qualify as key concepts. Furthermore, Sowa et al. [25] discussed ontology integration and conflicts of data in the process. They conclude that ontology merge is the best way of ontology integration as it preserves complete ontologies while collecting data from different parts of the system into a coherent format. In the remainder of the paper, unless otherwise stated, the definition of ontologies and standards as given by W3C [21] are followed.

Ontologies. Ontologies conceptualise a domain by capturing its structure. In this section, some features of ontologies, which are relevant for the proposed design are discussed. Ontologies are used to explicitly define entities and relations between entities. Figure 2 shows an example of a small ontology, an associated SPARQL query language, and query results obtained during a run-time. Ontologies provide unique global addresses to all entities and relations using HTTP URIs/IRIs . Hence, with the virtue of HTTP URIs/IRIs, entities and relations can be referred to easily from within and outside the system. Ontologies can also be *imported*, which is how definitions of entities and their relationships can be re-used during development time. This feature, as shown in the work later, is crucial in creating an ecosystem of ontologies. During run-time, *individuals* of the entities along with their relationships with each other are created.

Ontology **SPARQL Query** **Result**

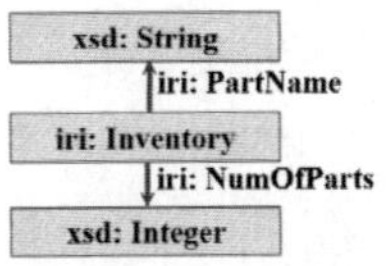


```
PREFIX iri: ...

SELECT ?Name ?Count
WHERE {
  ?Inv iri:PartName ?Name .
  ?Inv iri:NumOfParts ?Count
}
```

Name	Count
M1	10
M2	15

Figure 2. An example of ontology definitions and relations, SPARQL query and results.

To know more about ontologies, the reader is encouraged to visit the W3C standards [21]. The described features are essential while designing and implementing the proposed SDI framework.

III. Modular Design and Interoperability

The assistance system should be designed to be adaptive and flexible, such that it should be possible to combine different CPS with very varying capabilities without requiring extensive configuration from the worker. This flexible design makes it possible to scale the intelligence of the overall system by adding/removing CPS. The paper assumes that the central system contains a process description model, which describes the instructions for a process. The model remains unchanged irrespective of addition or removal of CPS modules. Adding new CPS modules to the central system makes the complete assistance system more aware of its environment and consequently more intelligent.

An assistance system, considered in this work, has hybrid architecture which consists of CPS modules and a central system where each CPS module collects and preprocesses data and feeds information to a central decision-making entity as shown in Figure 1. The central system collects information from all the modules attached to it and decides the next step of the process depending upon the process description model. Next step in the process is conveyed to a worker with the help of visualisation devices as shown in Figure 1. In contrast to a completely centralised or decentralised architecture, in a hybrid architecture, the burden of *making* sense from the raw-data is divided between the CPS modules and the central system: the modules need to preprocess raw data and make minor decisions before reporting it to the central system. The preprocessing step may include operations like analog to digital conversion, computing a parameter which is a function of data from more than one sensor (e.g. numberofParts from totalWeight and weightPerPart), calculating a moving average of a sensor reading, etc. This avoids any computing overhead on both the central system and CPS modules, and consequently makes them more intelligent and context-aware. This division is discussed in detail in Section IV.

A modular design enforces separation of concerns: the central system will only rely on the information *provided* by the modules. As per the traditional modular design, the internal state of the modules, i.e., the implementation details, would ideally be made completely opaque and inaccessible to the central system and other modules. In contrast, in this work, a framework for designing the modules using ontologies is proposed, which will allow the modules to access and use information from each other.

There are several challenges which need to be addressed in order to allow for such interoperability. The paper shows how these can be overcome by semantically annotating the information in each module using ontologies. As discussed in the previous section, an outright advantage of using ontologies is that they can give a unique name, i.e., URIs/IRIs, to *each* piece of information in the complete system thus making it immediately accessible using a simple declarative querying language (SPARQL) as shown in Figure 2 [26]. Moreover, other advantages come naturally with using ontologies, viz. self-documentation, automatic reasoning using description logic for free.

Using ontologies as the tool of choice, the following two questions are considered.

(i) **How to design and semantically annotate a CPS module?** This question is answered in Section IV.

(ii) **How to develop such modules using ontologies?** This issue is discussed in Section V and in Section VI.

Remark. Note that the decision-making algorithm in the central system should be designed in such a way that it does not need to be adapted to accommodate the underlying frequently changing CPS modules, i.e., the assistance system should be able to function without all modules being attached to the system and the modules should be plug-and-play. However, the problem of designing the algorithm is out of the scope of this work.

IV. FRAMEWORK FOR DESIGNING A CPS

In this section, a framework for designing a CPS module and its ontology is proposed as shown in Figure 3. It starts with *what* the module designer wants to achieve by adding a particular CPS to the system, and then determines its boundary, or scope, with respect to the central system. Next, decisions about the *intelligence* of the system are made which, in turn, influence the hardware choices for the module. Finally, a bottom up ontology of a CPS is created and its integration with the central system ontology is described. The framework, and its implementation, are explained with the help of a use case of an inventory module which is shown in Figure 4.

Requirements. At the outset, it is important to understand *why* a CPS module is required. This decision determines the metric used for measuring the effectiveness of a module finally. This objective may range from general, e.g., "increasing the efficiency of a factory", to specific, e.g., "decreasing the number of errors for a particular assembly station".

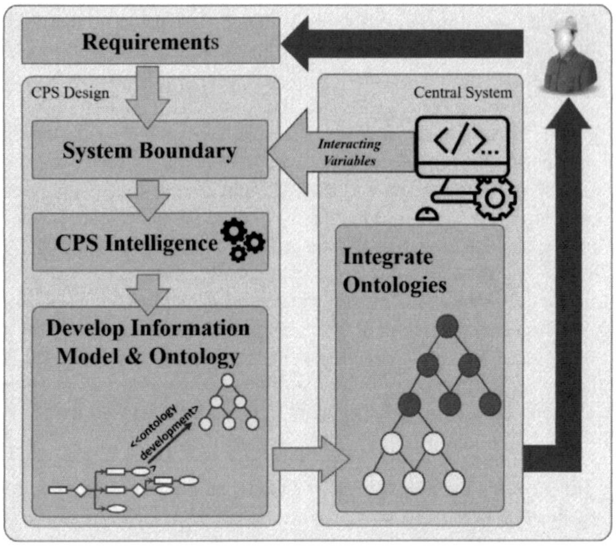

Figure 3. SDI framework for designing a CPS module.

For example, the requirement behind adding an inventory module can be to make the assistance system more aware of the environment in order to better understand the state of the process by the virtue of parts used in the process. This, in turn, improves the ability of an assistance system to help the worker. Keeping the requirements as specific as possible helps with the next step of the design.

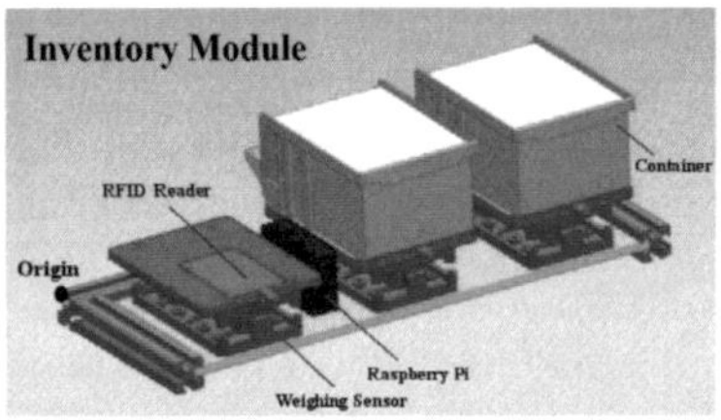

Figure 4. Schematic description of an inventory module

System Boundary. In the next step, the objective needs to be translated into a concrete piece of information that the central system needs from the CPS. An analogy can be drawn between the information which the central system needs and the idea of *minimal sufficient statistic*: the information should be *sufficient* for the central system to arrive at its objective. This information is the *interacting variable* between a CPS module and the central system. In terms of ontologies, the interacting variable needs to have the same URI/IRI in both the central system ontology as well as the ontology of the CPS module. This is ensured by defining the interacting variable in the upper ontology of an assistance system and the CPS module *importing* it.

For example, the central system may need the `total number of parts` for each part on the assembly station from an inventory module. This is the interacting variable for the CPS module.

CPS Intelligence. Once the system boundary is known, i.e., the interacting variable for a CPS module, it is necessary for the CPS to be *intelligent* enough to calculate this information from raw sensor readings. This *intelligence* is manifested in the accuracy/update frequency of sensors and the computational power afforded by the hardware (e.g. Raspberry Pi or Arduino) used to create the CPS module. Calculation of the value of the interacting variable effectively sets a lower bound on this system intelligence, i.e., a CPS should be able to process the data received through sensors to communicate the interacting variable whenever it is needed by the central system, e.g., calculating moving average of raw data every millisecond. The system intelligence can further be improved by using more sophisticated hardware and/or applying better algorithms while processing data, which improves the *quality* of the values calculated by the CPS module for the interacting variable.

Also, note that the CPS module should have the computational power to use ontologies during run-time. However, the restrictions placed by this requirement are mild because ontologies can be made light-weight during run-time [10].

Developing the Information Model & Ontology. After deciding on the hardware to use for a module, an *information model* which is an abstraction of the physical layer is created based on the structural and description models of the physical units present in a CPS module (as shown in Figure 5). The structural model defines physical assets present in a module: it lists all sensors, computational units, communication units and relations between them. The description model describes the properties of these assets. The process model is the process description that exists in the central system and is not changed on addition/removal of CPS modules. Structural and description models of the information model are used to explicitly define the hardware that was decided in the above steps. Figure 5 also shows the structural and description models of an inventory module and the process model contained by the central system.

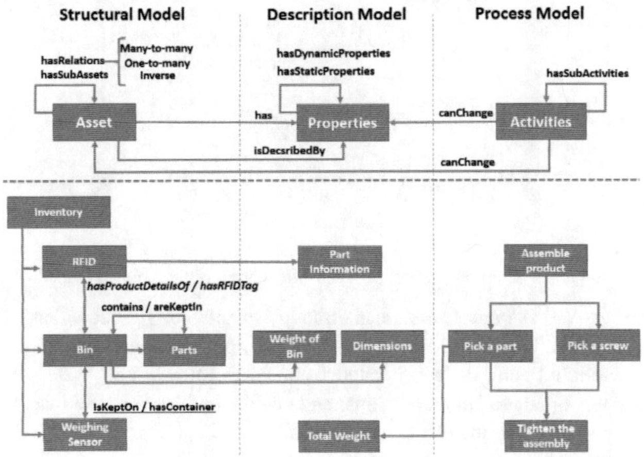

Figure 5. Information model contains structural, description and process models.

The ontology of a CPS module is developed using the information model as a reference. In addition to the entities and relations defined in the information model, the ontology may also contain variables which are the result of *processing* the data gathered by sensors. Finally, the interacting variable(s), which were decided while determining the system boundary, are added to the ontology with appropriate relationships with other entities.

Ontology Integration. In the final step, ontology of the CPS module is merged with the central system ontology. The central system uses the interacting variable for making its own decisions, but also acts as a database for the complete assistance system during run-time. The modules, hence, can query the central system for not only the interacting variables of other modules, but also about the internal entities, which the central system does not explicitly use. The problem of how can the CPS modules be made aware of the various entities which can be accessed is addressed next.

As discussed before, the interacting variables are described in an upper ontology and a mid-level ontology contains descriptions of the entities of *all* modules. To help the ecosystem develop, a committee which consists of all shareholders (central system designers, deployment point managers, module developers, etc.) which oversees the addition to new modules to the ontology would be needed. The upper ontology is kept minimal and is only extended with new interacting variables, i.e. when a new potential CPS module is identified which can aid the intelligence of the central system. The other entities which can be provided by the new module, but which are not needed by the central system, are described in the mid-level ontology. The mid-level ontology acts as a repository of all relevant entities described in all CPS modules. This simplifies the search by engineers for variables provided by other modules. CPS modules `<<import>>` the upper ontology to get the URIs/IRIs of interacting variables and mid-level ontologies to get the URIs/IRIs of the entities of *all* modules.

Instead of having a mid-level ontology, it is possible to have only an upper ontology and ontologies of CPS modules. In such a setting, if one module needs to query for the variables of other CPS module, it then `<<import>>s` the ontology of that particular module. However, this scheme of ontology development may result in reinvention of entities. Thus, a centralised W3C committee like setup [21] which consists of all stakeholders is favoured.

V. Module Development

This section describes at a high level the development of a CPS module and the central system after the design for the module has been included into the upper and mid-level ontologies. During the design of the module, the interacting variable(s) were added in the upper ontology while the mid-level ontology was updated to include all entities which the module could provide, as agreed by all the stakeholders. For the purpose of exposition and to maintain complete generality, it is assumed in this section that the developer creating the module is a third party who intends to develop a newer version of the module from the specification.

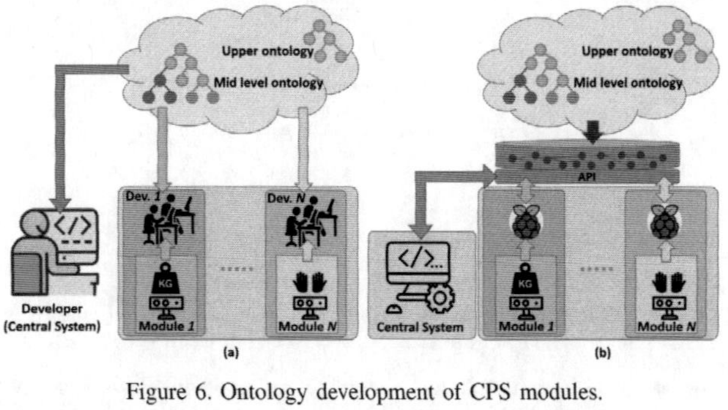

Figure 6. Ontology development of CPS modules.

In the next step towards development of the module, on the one hand, the developer (say, *Dev.* 1) studies the capabilities of the hardware available to her. Here, the developers can leverage the information model and ontology created during the design phase. On the other hand, the developer studies the upper (mid-level) ontology to determine what entities/values they should (could) provide to the central system. This part of the development process is illustrated in Figure 6(a). It should be noted that there is no need for communication or synchronisation between the developers of the different modules or between the developers and the central system developer. The developer `<<import>>s` the upper and mid-level ontologies and creates the module ontology with the remaining (local) ontological entities, and writes code which uses the central system's API and SPARQL queries to update the central system database (as shown in Figure 6(b)).

Lastly, it is advised that Protégé should be used to create the module ontology as (i) it enhances interoperability by using OWL-S, and, (ii) it can automatically generate code using OWL API (Application Programmable Interface), which can ease the burden on the developer. In this work, Protégé is used to create ontologies and the code generated is used to update the ontologies. In the next section, simulation of the central system and an inventory CPS module using Protégé is discussed.

VI. Implementation

In the previous section, the development phase of ontologies was discussed. In this section, the simulation of an assistance system during run-time is discussed. Assistance system ontology is developed in Protégé, a free, open source ontology editor. The code generated using Protégé (as shown in Figure 7) is used to simulate the behaviour of CPS module, via OWL API. This implementation is written in Java. For the ease of exposition, it is assumed in the text that the central system can answer queries sent to it in SPARQL. These queries can be written in a different language or may be provided using an alternate API. However, the use of unique URIs/IRIs to refer to entities in the ontologies is crucial to facilitate interoperability in all implementations.

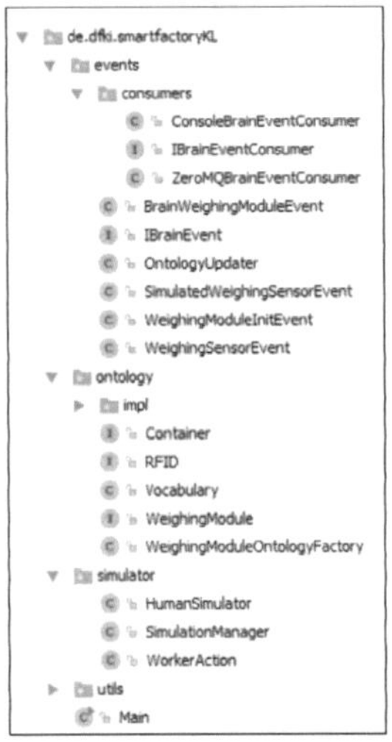

Figure 7. Classes generated by Protégé, based on OWL API. Central system discussed in the paper is referred to as `Brain`.

It is assumed that ontologies of an assistance system, i.e the central system and CPS modules, are developed using the proposed framework. During execution, the ontologies are *populated* by creating *individuals* locally on all modules. During execution, the system goes through three primary stages: (i) intialization, (ii) trigger, and (iii) update, which are shown in Figure 8, and are briefly discussed here:

Initialization. When an assistance system is started, the central system sends an *init()* request to all CPS modules attached to it. This request contains the URI/IRI of the central system. This URI/IRI is address with which all modules identify the central system through the lifetime of the process. In case of hardware malfunction, system restart, or when a new module is attached to the system, the initialization step is executed again.

Trigger. Triggers can be either timer-driven or event-based. Event-based triggers are reported by CPS modules to the central system whereas timer-driven triggers are generated by the central system. Event-based triggers can be events that change the present state of a system to another (valid) state of the system [8]. In case an event occurrence renders no valid state of the system, triggers are not generated. *Trigger()* request is either sent from modules to the central system, as shown in Figure 8, or may be generated internally by the central system clock.

Update. Communication between the central system and CPS modules is pull-based. Upon a trigger, the central system sends a *getUpdate()* reqeust to all modules. Modules send the complete, or a part of, ontologies with the new data values to the central system which, in turn, update its own ontology.

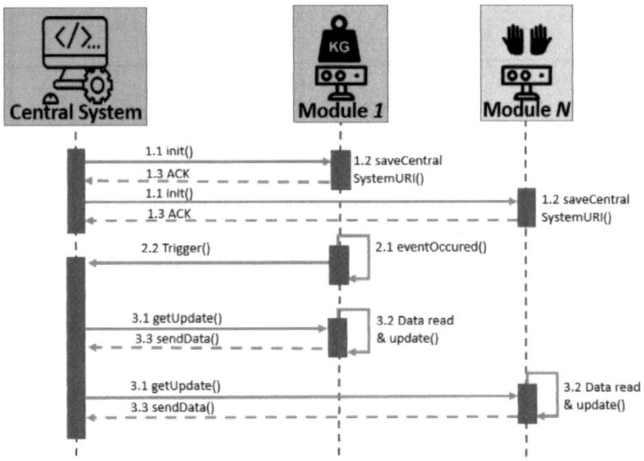

Figure 8. Communication between the central system and CPS modules.

An example implementation is available for download on GitHub [27]. The implementation therein simulates an inventory module (using code generated from Protégé), a central system, and then simulates human actions, updates the ontology on the inventory module using the OWL API, and shows the communication between the module and the central system.

VII. Conclusion

This work is focused on designing a human-centric assistance system used in production which can dynamically adapt to the needs of the workers and tasks using Semantic Web technologies. Assistance systems are considered as consisting of a central system and one or many CPS modules. An SDI framework is proposed to design CPS modules which makes the data of the complete system globally accessible by the virtue of HTTP URIs/IRIs. The SDI framework explained the steps used to decide the boundary between the central system and CPS modules, the performance requirements of hardware, describing modules with the help of information models and finally developing and merging ontologies. It also explains briefly the ecosystem of ontologies consisting of upper, mid-level and module ontologies. The framework is implemented in Protégé using OWL-S. OWL API is used to simulate CPS behaviour and data exchange is demonstrated. However, the proposed framework can be used to design CPS in general: the discussion in the paper was limited to designing a CPS for an assistance system for ease of both exposition and demonstration.

The work assumes that all vendors and third party development use SPARQL as the query language. Calbimonte et al. have discussed how such a problem of multi-vendor multi-querying language can be resolved [28]. It can be incorporated in the SDI framework to make it more robust. Knowledge mapped in ontologies may evolve over time due to modifications in conceptualisation and adaptation to incoming changes. Thus, in future, it is important to establish protocols for versioning of data on Semantic Web as well as understanding the missing data [29]. Another non-trivial task towards adoption of ontologies in real life is setting up committees which oversee the creation and maintenance of upper and mid-level ontologies [30].

The framework results in a repository of data from all modules of the system and interoperability between these modules, thus laying the foundation of plug-and-play production systems. The next important step in the development of assistance systems is to develop a plug-and-play methodology for CPS modules, as alluded to in Section III.

Another important step to make the system deployable is to create global standards: either by defining design and communication standards specific to assistance systems, or by investigating the suitability of existing standards, e.g. RAMI 4.0 [31].

ACKNOWLEDGEMENTS

This work was done as a Master thesis at German Research Center for Artificial Intelligence (DFKI) and TU Kaiserslautern Germany.

REFERENCES

[1] M. M. Tseng and S. J. Hu, "Mass customization," in *CIRP encyclopedia of production engineering*. Springer, 2014, pp. 836–843.

[2] F. Salvador and C. Forza, "Configuring products to address the customization-responsiveness squeeze: A survey of management issues and opportunities," *International journal of production economics*, vol. 91, no. 3, pp. 273–291, 2004.

[3] Y. Koren and M. Shpitalni, "Design of reconfigurable manufacturing systems," *Journal of manufacturing systems*, vol. 29, no. 4, pp. 130–141, 2010.

[4] D. Romero, O. Noran, J. Stahre, P. Bernus, and Å. Fast-Berglund, "Towards a human-centred reference architecture for next generation balanced automation systems: human-automation symbiosis," in *IFIP International Conference on Advances in Production Management Systems*. Springer, 2015, pp. 556–566.

[5] S. Tzafestas, "Concerning human-automation symbiosis in the society and the nature," *Intl. J. of Factory Automation, Robotics and Soft Computing*, vol. 1, no. 3, pp. 6–24, 2006.

[6] P. A. Hancock, R. J. Jagacinski, R. Parasuraman, C. D. Wickens, G. F. Wilson, and D. B. Kaber, "Human-automation interaction research: past, present, and future," *ergonomics in design*, vol. 21, no. 2, pp. 9–14, 2013.

[7] V. Villani, L. Sabattini, J. N. Czerniak, A. Mertens, B. Vogel-Heuser, and C. Fantuzzi, "Towards modern inclusive factories: A methodology for the development of smart adaptive human-machine interfaces," *22nd IEEE International Conference on Emerging Technologies and Factory Automation*, 2017.

[8] F. Quint, F. Loch, M. Orfgen, and D. Zuehlke, "A system architecture for assistance in manual tasks." in *Intelligent Environments (Workshops)*, 2016, pp. 43–52.

[9] E. Tantik and R. Anderl, "Integrated data model and structure for the asset administration shell in industrie 4.0," *Procedia CIRP*, vol. 60, pp. 86–91, 2017.

[10] I. Grangel-González, L. Halilaj, G. Coskun, S. Auer, D. Collarana, and M. Hoffmeister, "Towards a semantic administrative shell for industry 4.0 components," in *Semantic Computing (ICSC), 2016 IEEE Tenth International Conference on*. IEEE, 2016, pp. 230–237.

[11] J. Gezer, Volkan Um and M. Ruskowski, "An extensible edge computing architecture: Definition, requirements and enablers," in *UBICOMM*, 2017.

[12] J. Nelles, S. Kuz, A. Mertens, and C. M. Schlick, "Human-centered design of assistance systems for production planning and control: The role of the human in industry 4.0," in *Industrial Technology (ICIT), 2016 IEEE International Conference on*. IEEE, 2016, pp. 2099–2104.

[13] D. Gorecky, S. F. Worgan, and G. Meixner, "Cognito: a cognitive assistance and training system for manual tasks in industry." in *ECCE*, 2011, pp. 53–56.

[14] C.-B. Zamfirescu, B.-C. Pirvu, D. Gorecky, and H. Chakravarthy, "Human-centred assembly: a case study for an anthropocentric cyber-physical system," *Procedia Technology*, vol. 15, pp. 90–98, 2014.

[15] W. Wahlster, "Semantic technologies for mass customization," in *Towards the Internet of Services: The THESEUS Research Program*. Springer, 2014, pp. 3–13.

[16] M. Graube, J. Pfeffer, J. Ziegler, and L. Urbas, "Linked data as integrating technology for industrial data," *International Journal of Distributed Systems and Technologies (IJDST)*, vol. 3, no. 3, pp. 40–52, 2012.

[17] S. K. Semy, M. K. Pulvermacher, and L. J. Obrst. (2004) Toward the use of an upper ontology for us government and us military domains: An evaluation. Retrieved on 2018-09-20.

[18] C. Bizer, T. Heath, and T. Berners-Lee, "Linked data: The story so far," in *Semantic services, interoperability and web applications: emerging concepts*. IGI Global, 2011, pp. 205–227.

[19] A. Schultz, A. Matteini, R. Isele, P. N. Mendes, C. Bizer, and C. Becker, "Ldif-a framework for large-scale linked data integration," in *21st International World Wide Web Conference (WWW 2012), Developers Track, Lyon, France*, 2012.

[20] V. Gezer and S. Bergweiler, "Cloud-based infrastructure for workflow and service engineering using semantic web technologies," *International Journal on Advances on Internet Technology*, pp. 36–45, 2017.

[21] S. Bechhofer, "Owl: Web ontology language," in *Encyclopedia of database systems*. Springer, 2009, pp. 2008–2009.

[22] E. Negri, L. Fumagalli, M. Garetti, and L. Tanca, "Requirements and languages for the semantic representation of manufacturing systems," *Computers in Industry*, vol. 81, pp. 55–66, 2016.

[23] N. Guarino, *Formal ontology in information systems: Proceedings of the first international conference (FOIS'98), June 6-8, Trento, Italy*. IOS press, 1998, vol. 46.

[24] I. Niles and A. Pease, "Origins of the ieee standard upper ontology," in *Working notes of the IJCAI-2001 workshop on the IEEE standard upper ontology*. Citeseer, 2001, pp. 37–42.

[25] J. F. Sowa *et al.* Building, sharing, and merging ontologies. Retrieved on 2018-09-20. [Online]. Available: http://www.jfsowa.com/ontology/ontoshar.htm

[26] E. Prud *et al.* Sparql query language for rdf. Retrieved on 2018-09-20.

[27] A. Singh. Example implementation of the SDI framework. Retrieved on 2018-09-20. [Online]. Available: https://github.com/AmitaChauhan/SDI-Framework

[28] J.-P. Calbimonte, H. Jeung, O. Corcho, and K. Aberer, "Enabling query technologies for the semantic sensor web," *International Journal On Semantic Web and Information Systems (IJSWIS)*, vol. 8, no. 1, pp. 43–63, 2012.

[29] M. C. Klein and D. Fensel, "Ontology versioning on the semantic web." in *SWWS*, 2001, pp. 75–91.

[30] I. Jacobs. World wide web consortium process document. Retrieved on 2018-09-20. [Online]. Available: https://www.w3.org/2018/Process-20180201/

[31] M. Weyrich and C. Ebert, "Reference architectures for the Internet of things," *IEEE Software*, vol. 33, no. 1, pp. 112–116, 2016.

M-learning as a Motivational Method for Adult Basic and Professional Education

Clayslan Ferreira Xavier, George Mendes Teixeira Santos, Selmon Franco Mascarenhas, Mauro Henrique Lima de Boni, Adelino Rodrigues Soares

Federal Institute of Education, Science and Technology of Tocantins
Palmas, Brazil

Emails: {claysllan, mhldeboni, adelinorsoares}@gmail.com, selmon01@uol.com.br, mtgeorge_@hotmail.com

***Abstract*—It is very important to find ways to improve the teaching methods of adult students enrolled in basic and professional education programs, since these students generally have a deficient education to start with. One way to do so may be using technology to make it easier to access the content to be studied. A mobile application, built according to user-centered design, allows students who own a smartphone to access videos chosen by teachers. In addition, students can answer quizzes as a way to test what they have learned. This mobile application could help these students with the basics of mathematics. After presenting and testing the proposed tool, 55.7% of the students evaluated the tool in a positive way and reported that it improved their understanding of the subject studied.**

Keywords-Mobile Learning; Technology; Education; Adult Education.

I. INTRODUCTION

The National Program of Brazil for the Integration of Basic Education and Vocational Education into the Youth and Adult Education Mode (in Portuguese PROEJA) established by Decree nr. 5.840 [1], of July 13, 2006, has the aim of combining Youth and Adult Education courses with Professional education. PROEJA seeks to teach young people and adults who have not had the opportunity to study in middle and/or high school at the regular age and who also seek to enter a profession. Thus, the youngest age for entering in PROEJA is 18 years old [2].

In general, PROEJA is a modality of teaching involving young people and adults. Thus, teachers must find ways to pass the contents to students in a manner that is dynamic and easy to understand. Especially with this group of students, the creation of a new model of teaching and studying is vital.

Technology enables the use of slides, video-conferencing, collaborative tools, among other technological solutions that can aid the teachers in applying content and improve student's learning experience. Another important point in this learning experience is Mobile learning (M-learning). It is a research field that looks at how mobile applications can collaborate in student learning. M-learning is a very rapidly developing area that has been considered as the future of learning. Mobile devices enhance learning at any moment or place, providing access to learning resources, even outside the school. This flexibility makes it possible for adult learners to minimize their unproductive time, which may enhance their work-education balance [3].

PROEJA students, in general, have had a precarious basic education. This makes the teaching activity even more challenging for the teachers of this program. With math, particularly, this becomes more visible, considering the nature of the competencies acquired. This paper lays out the process for producing a mobile application using available open and free technologies for supporting the teaching and learning process in Mathematics at the Federal Institute of Education, Science and Technology of Tocantins (IFTO). An important objective is to make the contents of the subject attractive and easier for the students.

Therefore, we sought to gather data with the purpose of answering the following research problem: Can the use of technology help teaching math in PROEJA? To do this, we developed an application with a user-centered design so that it was possible to analyze the user experience from the use of this software.

For developing the present study, we used bibliographical and field research, as well as a case study. The bibliographical research was based on scientific publications on user experience and user-centered design. We developed the case study in its entirety through field research at IFTO, campus Palmas, involving the students' profile, their expectations about the tool, general evaluation of the tool and satisfaction survey.

This paper is divided into the following sections: Section 2 presents the work related to the problem; Section 3 describes the proposal presented to solve the problem and Section 4 presents the method used to develop the solution; Section 5 reports the results and presents analysis and discussions, and finally, Section 6 draws conclusions about the project and future work.

II. Related Work

Silva et al. [4] argued the need to search for new methodologies which value learning in order to discover a form of learning that would be significant for PROEJA students. In the study, it was possible to show that mathematical calculations represent the area of study that is the most challenging to the students of this class. Therefore, the authors concluded that they are dealing with a unique audience that needs to be distinguished from the students of other modalities of teaching in several aspects, such as, limited time in the classroom and difficulties in performing work outside the school.

In [5], the authors discussed the effect of M-learning on mathematics learning. The result of this paper showed that utilization of mobile devices increases the motivation of the students. It means that there is a direct and significant relationship between use of mobile devices and student motivation towards mathematics. The authors concluded that M-learning can help to improve students' academic performance.

Saccol et al. [6] perform a real experience in M-learning for training Information Technology (IT) professionals. For this purpose, they developed and implemented a virtual mobile learning environment called COMTEXT, which was designed to support competence development for workers using PocketPCs. In this study, the learners showed interest and excitement for the innovation characteristic of M-learning, especially because they could become connected and use learning resources in different settings.

Mehdipour et al. [7] state that M-learning is emerging as one of the solutions to the challenges faced by education. The main purpose of their study was to describe the current state of mobile learning, benefits, challenges, and barriers to supporting teaching and learning. They concluded that the use of M-learning in classrooms helped the students working interdependently, in groups, or individually to solve problems, to work on projects, to meet individual needs, and to allow for student voice and choice. With access to so much content anytime and anywhere, there are plenty of opportunities for formal and informal learning, both inside and outside the classroom.

In [8], Mahamad et al. proposed M-learning for mathematics by allowing the extension of technology in the traditional classroom in terms of learning and teaching. A survey has been conducted to investigate the use of mobile devices and to determine if primary school students were ready for mobile learning. The result of the survey shows that mobile phones can be useful in learning mathematics as most of primary school students already use them through many communication activities.

III. Proposal

The teaching of mathematics to students through the use of communication technologies is currently widespread in all social strata and is associated with the vast content of information available on the Internet.

Our proposal is to develop an application for mobile devices (App), such as smartphones and tablets, which makes it easy and practical for students to use specific content and mathematics classes, according to the program content, material available on the Internet and free access. In addition, the application will offer quizzes to help students test their knowledge, correct any mistakes in understanding, and allow the teacher to give tests for assessing student performance.

The assumption was that an easy-to-use application containing contents taught in video-lessons for better understanding and quizzes to test knowledge could help students in learning math. Carvalho et al. [9] make it clear that theories and practice associated with information technology in education have repercussions worldwide, precisely because the technological tools offer academic content, objects, spaces, and instruments capable of renewing situations for interaction, expression, creation, communication and information. All this makes learning very different from what has traditionally been grounded in writing and print media.

A. Operating Structure

In general, the system and the App will use the concept of client-service architecture. In this format, the database resides on a remote server and its information is shared through services that are located on the same server as the application's Web service. This Web service will be exposing the services through a RestFul API (Application Programming Interface), which will be used by both the Web system and the App.

According to [10] RestFul API is an architectural pattern that exposes data and functionality through resources accessed via dedicated URLs over HTTP. REST services feature a request-response pattern, where the HTTP methods Post, Get, Put, and Delete on a given resource are mapped to the respective CRUD operations: Create, Read, Update, and Delete. Service responses contain the representation of the requested resource presented in CSV, JSON, XML, or similar formats. This architecture provides greater data integrity because all users are working with the same information.

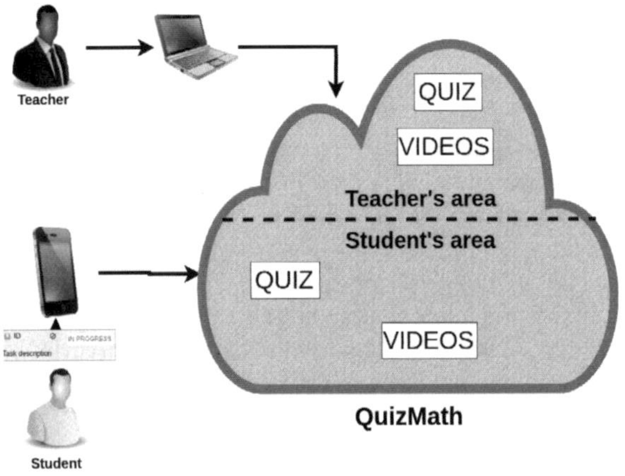

Figure 1. Software Structure.

As can be seen in Figure 1, the system has two aspects: teacher and student. The teacher will be using a Web system, accessed by the browser, and through it will post videos and quizzes for the application. It will also be possible to manage registered students with the application. On the other side will be the students who will use the system through the application that will consume all the information registered by the teachers.

Figure 2. Video Screen.

As can be seen from Figure 2, the video screen lists the video lessons related to the content selected by the student. They will help the student understand the content, thus taking away the doubts that came after the lesson.

We created one server containing all the online services of the application. The database is MongoDB [11] in version 3. We implemented the Web system and Web service using the NodeJS [12] version 8. To develop the application, we used the Ionic Framework [13] of development for mobile applications. The exchange of information from the server to the application is done through JSON files.

IV. Methods

In order to increase the value of this research, we used a case study as a data collection technique. The case study took place a time when it was necessary to survey the current PROEJA scenario, specifically, the mathematics class at IFTO. Based on thisthat could help the students improve in this subject. survey, we develop a tool to solve the problem and check the users' experience with it.

The main aim of this case study was to verify how developing an application helps PROEJA students with learning mathematics as a way to improve their general education, with the purpose of validating the benefit of understanding clearly the basic concepts of mathematics at the IFTO, Campus Palmas, in Palmas, Tocantins, Brazil, in 2018.

First, we used a printed questionnaire about the students' expectations of the proposed tool containing 16 questions; 70 students, 44 women and 26 men, in three PROEJA classes answered the questionnaires. The questions were objective and for most of them we used the Likert scale. This scale ranges from 1 to 5, where 1 represents no interest or total disagreement, level 2 indicates a little interest, level 3 some interest, level 4 interest", and level 5 a lot of interest or totally agree.

After obtaining the results of the expectation questionnaire, we performed an interview with the mathematics teachers of the classes to find out what were the greatest difficulties in teaching of mathematics to this particular group of students and what would be the suggestion of content that could help the students improve in this subject.

Teachers suggested content that was added to the tool's Web system so that it would be consumed by students through the application. Content was written about basic mathematics: operations of addition, subtraction, multiplication, and division; as well as content related to empowerment. After the contents were finalized, we presented the application in the classroom using a digital slide projector.

After presenting the functionalities of the application through the projector, the App was installed on the students' cell phones, to be tested by them. The students watched the videos recorded on the content of basic math operations and soon afterwards they answered quizzes about the proposed subject. The students tested the tool for 2 hours.

Next, a satisfaction questionnaire and conversation with students about software improvements were performed. The questionnaire was given to the same 3 groups of students who answered the previous questionnaire and it was used to analyze user experience and validation of the tool. The questionnaire had 18 objective questions, some subjective questions, and most of them used the Likert scale.

In conclusion, the information was obtained in a sensitive manner through two questionnaires of 16 and 18 questions respectively, related to the proposed tool, applied to mathematics students of the IFTO, Campus Palmas. The research was carried out from April 15, 2018 until June 8, 2018, when the students were available.

The research has a 90% degree of reliability of the data presented and analyzed since, for a total of 90 students with a sampling margin of 5% and with a confidence level of 90%, we would need to reach a sample of 68 answers of the students and we obtained a total sample of 70 answers through the two questionnaires. The sample calculation was automated based on a sample calculation tool published by [14].

V. Results and Discussion

In the questionnaire of expectation, the students were asked which types of mobile device they usually take to school, and it was possible to select more than one option.

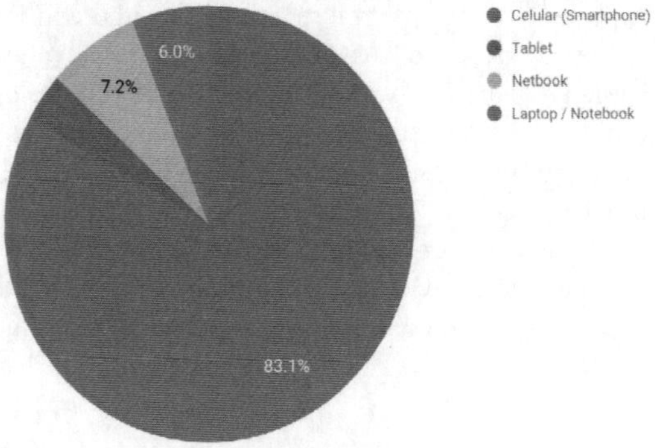

Figure 3. Types of mobile devices usually taken to school.

It can be seen in Figure 3 that all PROEJA students take their mobile devices to school with 83.1% taking their smartphones, followed by 7.2% taking Netbook, 6% taking their laptop and 3.6 % carrying their tablet. It is worth mentioning that developing the mobile application was possible, since the students possessed the devices and took them to the classroom.

Another question from the same questionnaire that students were asked was when they needed to study, but they had to search to find some material if it was more productive to use a smartphone than a computer.

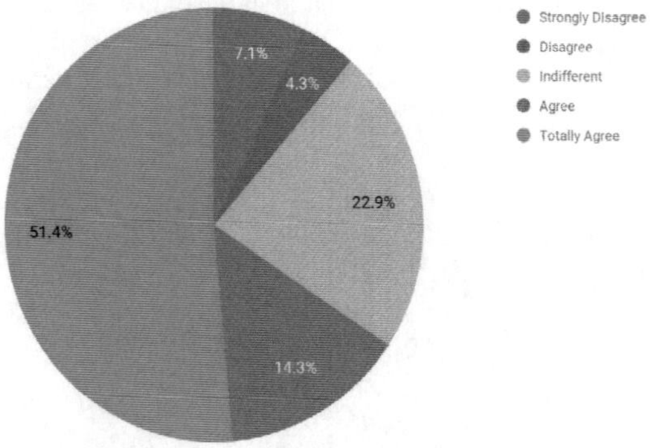

Figure 4. Productivity of the cell phone relative to the computer.

In Figure 4, it can be seen that 51.4% totally agree that a cell phone to study was more productive than using a computer, 14.3% agree with such a statement, 22.9% are indifferent and 4.3% disagree, followed by the 7.1% who disagree completely. It is worth mentioning that adding the agreements gives a percentage of 65.7% of the students. Therefore, it is validated once again that a mathematical study application for the mobile phone would be of great use to students.

Furthermore, some features were presented in which the application would make available in an organized way many videos selected by the teacher as a quiz, through a smart phone, where the student could see the videos and the quiz published by the teacher. In this way, still in the expectation questionnaire, the students were asked if these characteristics made the application a useful tool for the student.

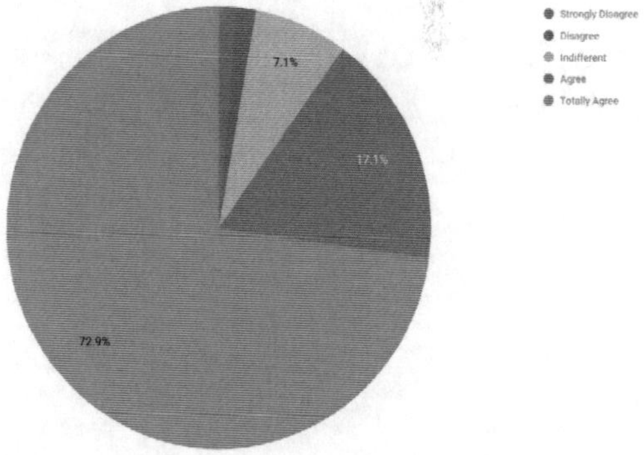

Figure 5. Agreement about application features.

It can be seen from Figure 5 that 72.9% of students agree fully with these characteristics, followed by those who agree, 17.1%, the indifferent add up to 7.1% and those who disagree totaled 1.4%. It is worth noting that adding up only agreement with the first characteristics of the tool accounts for 90% of the students making it possible to create the application again.

Finally, the last question in the expectation questionnaire asked the students if they were interested in using the application as a tool that would help in their classes. Figure 6 depicts the result of this question.

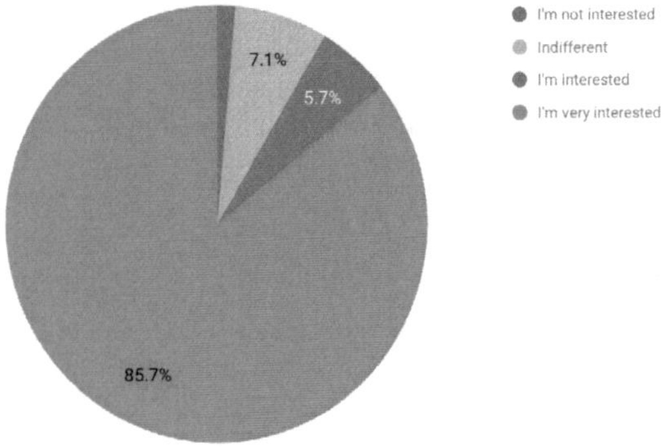

Figure 6. Interest of students regarding the tool.

It can be observed that 85.7% were very interested in the tool as an aid in their classes, 5.7% of them had an interest in the tool, 7.1% are indifferent and only 1.4% of them had no interest in the proposed tool. It is worth mentioning that 93.4% of the students had some interest in using the tool and with this we verified that the students' expectations were high about the proposed application.

After developing the application, presenting to the students and carrying out the tests done by them, we gave a questionnaire of their satisfaction with the proposed application. Students were asked how satisfied they were with the proposed application. Figure 7 depicts the results of this question.

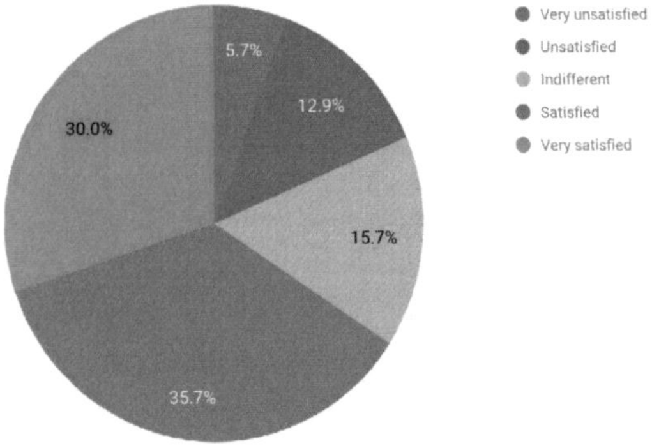

Figure 7. User satisfaction.

It can be observed that 30% of the students were very satisfied with the tool, followed by 35.7% of the students who were satisfied, 15.7% were indifferent, 12.9% were unsatisfied and 5.7% very dissatisfied. The satisfaction was obtained from 65.7% s of the students, and if one subtracts those who were indifferent, only about 18.6% of the students were not satisfied with the tool. We found, therefore, that the overall level of student satisfaction was high.

In order for us to verify whether the application met the expectation created by the students, we asked them in a question in the questionnaire using the Likert scale again. The result can be seen in Figure 8.

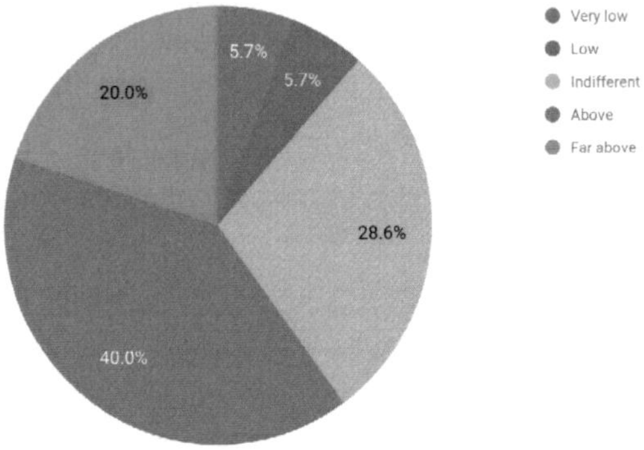

Figure 8. Approval of user expectations.

It can be seen that 20% of the respondents stated that the application was far above their expectations, 40% stated that the application was above their expectations, about 28.6% declared themselves indifferent, 5.7% said the tool was below expectations and another 5.7% said it was far below expectations. It is worth noting that 60% of the respondents stated that the application exceeded their expectations and only 11.4% stated that the application did not meet their expectations. We therefore found that the application has achieved a good user experience by evaluating the application before with the expectation search, during the tests of the users and at the end with the satisfaction survey, the majority of users declared themselves satisfied with the proposed tool.

Finally, to confirm whether the tool would help students in mathematics teaching, students were asked if the use of the tool allowed them to have contact with the same subject, but in a clearer way.

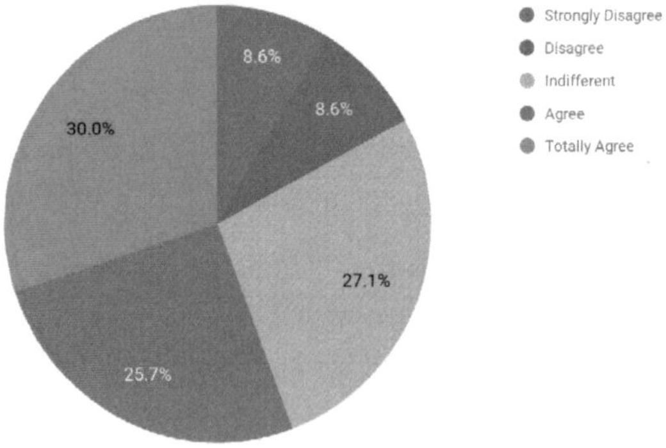

Figure 9. Application learning aid.

According to Figure 9, it can be seen that 30% of the students totally agreed that the application helped them to more clearly understand a math content, 25.7% agreed, 27.1% were indifferent, 8.6% disagreed and another 8.6% disagreed completely. It is worth noting that a total of 55.7% of students agreed that the application made learning the content clearer and easier to understand and only 17.2% were not satisfied. We found that the application brought some benefits for students, such as, learning the content more clearly and easily.

VI. Conclusion and Future Work

Developing the present study allowed an analysis of the needs of PROEJA students and their difficulties in learning mathematics, while allowing us to create an application on demand that could be a tool to aid students in learning. The application is not replacing the teaching models already used, but will be an aid for the class in reinforcing the content studied.

Overall, teachers have shown an interest in working on the topic in the classroom and are looking for ways to be up-to-date, but they still have some difficulties, such as students' lack of knowledge about basic mathematics. Teachers were eager to feed information to the toll by posting a video for the students and questions for practicing math concepts.

Students have also shown considerable interest in the subject and will look through the application to learn about the content. Based on the research data, it can be concluded that 55.7% of the students evaluated the tool positively and reported that it improved their understanding of the subject studied. This way, the application will be a great tool to help students learn, because we concluded that the application had a positive user experience and helped them to learn the content.

Given the importance of the theme, it is necessary to carry out the suggestions and functionalities suggested by the students to make the application a better tool and provide a better user experience, besides conducting research with the teachers about the Web tool that will be used by them, in order to bring new contents to the students.

In this sense, the application of teaching mathematics in PROEJA will allow teachers to mediate the teaching/learning process in a more enriching way, motivating the student to have more desire to learn and helping make learning really meaningful.

References

[1] Brazil, Federal Law nr. 5.840 from July 13th, 2006, Section 1, Page 7 ed., Brasilia, July 2006, official Diary of the Federative Republic of Brazil.

[2] M. R. d. Silva, "The policy of curricular integration within PROEJA: between discourses, subjects and practices," Ensaio: aval. pol. pbl. Educ.,vol. 19, no. 71, June 2011, pp. 307–326

[3] A. Drigas and M. Pappas, "A review of mobile learning applications for mathematics," International Journal of Interactive Mobile Technologies(iJIM), vol. 9, no. 3, 2015, pp. 18–23.

[4] E. O. Silva and E. A. M. Monteiro, "Significant learning in proeja: Experiences of mathematics teaching," Cycle Magazine, vol. 1, no. 2, 2016.

[5] Z. Taleb, A. Ahmadi, and M. Musavi, "The effect of M-learning on mathematics learning," ICPEESY, 2015.

[6] A. Z. Saccol, N. Reinhard, E. Schlemmer, and J. L. V. Barbosa, "M-learning (mobile learning) in practice: A training experience with it professionals," Journal of Information Systems and Technology Management, vol. 7, nr. 2, 2010, pp. 261–280.

[7] Y. Mehdipour and H. Zerehkafi, "Mobile learning for education: Benefits and challenges," International Journal of Computational Engineering Research, vol. 3, June 2013, pp. 93–101.

[8] S. Mahamad, M. N. Ibrahim, and S. M. Taib, "M-learning: A new paradigm of learning mathematics in malaysia," International journal of computer science & information Technology, vol. 2, nr. 4, August 2010.

[9] A. B. G. o. Carvalho, F. M. C. d. S. C. o. Moita, and R. P. d. o. Sousa,Tecnologias digitais na educação. Campina Grande: SciELO, 2011.

[10] L. C. Smith and M. A. Wong, Reference and Information Services: An Introduction: An Introduction. ABC-CLIO, 2016.

[11] Mongo, "Open Source Document Database", MongoDB, 2018. [Online]. Available: https://www.mongodb.com/. [Accessed: 11- Nov- 2018].

[12] N. Foundation, "Node.js", Node.js, 2018. [Online]. Available: https://nodejs.org/en/. [Accessed: 11- Nov- 2018].

[13] Ionic, "Build Amazing Native Apps and Progressive Web Apps with Ionic Framework and Angular", Ionic Framework, 2018. [Online]. Available: https://ionicframework.com/. [Accessed: 11- Nov- 2018].

[14] G. E. d. O. Santos. "Sample calculation: online calculator". , Amostral Calculus, 2018. [Online]. Available: http://www.publicacoesdeturismo.com.br/calculoamostral/ [Accessed: 11- Nov- 2018].

Increasing Throughput and Efficiency of LoRaWAN Class A

Roman Trüb and Lothar Thiele

Computer Engineering and Networks Laboratory
ETH Zurich, Switzerland
Email: {roman.trueb, lothar.thiele}@tik.ee.ethz.ch

***Abstract*—The number of Internet of Things (IoT) devices is expected to increase significantly in the next few years due to the availability of low cost IoT hardware and new application scenarios. As a result, many more wireless IoT devices will share the unlicensed frequency bands. Coordinated channel access is required to increase the efficiency of the frequency spectrum usage. In this paper, we propose two extensions to Long Range Wide Area Network (LoRaWAN) Class A, the *TDMA* and *Burst* scheme, in order to increase the channel utilization and system throughput. Our calculations show that the proposed schemes can provide more than 60% throughput compared to 18% provided by the pure ALOHA scheme used in the current specifications of LoRaWAN. We verify the feasibility of the schemes with an implementation and measurements on eight LoRaWAN end-devices and one gateway.**

Keywords–LoRa; LoRaWAN; TDMA; Burst.

I. Introduction

Wireless Internet of Things (IoT) devices are used for collecting data from environment, industrial monitoring, tracking goods and more. The availability of cheap hardware components for wireless IoT devices and the emerging low-power, long-range communication hardware accelerate the deployment of many more IoT nodes. A significant increase of the number of wireless IoT devices is therefore expected in the next few years.

A large number of battery powered devices makes the frequent maintenance of individual devices infeasible. Therefore, low power requirements of IoT devices are of great importance. Furthermore, it is important to use shared limited resources efficiently, e.g., the frequency spectrum.

In the last few years, different Low Power Wide Area Network (LPWAN) technologies have emerged to connect remote wireless IoT devices to the Internet. Many of these technologies have in common that they trade throughput for increasing the range. In this paper, we focus on Long Range Wide Area Network (LoRaWAN) [1], which is currently one of the most promising LPWAN technologies. What is commonly referred to as *LoRa*, consists of two components: (1) LoRa modulation, a physical (PHY) layer, and (2) LoRaWAN, the corresponding Media Access Control (MAC) layer. The LoRa modulation uses Chirp Spread Spectrum (CSS) with different spreading factors (SFs). We focus on the Class A variant of LoRaWAN since it is best suited for low power end-devices and is widely used. LoRaWAN Class A uses the pure ALOHA protocol to access the channel. This limits the channel utilization to a maximum of 18%. In this paper, we use LoRaWAN Class A as a basis and investigate alternative schemes that allow to use the channel more efficiently while minimizing the additional resource demand in terms of on-air-time.

The development of such a scheme involves the following two main challenges. LoRaWAN Class A does not provide a synchronization on the end-devices. Furthermore, LoRa messages exhibit a long on-air-time, which is problematic given the duty cycle limit of 1%, which is enforced by law in Europe for the corresponding unlicensed EU868 frequency band around 868 MHz.

Based on the analysis of the current channel access scheme and the limitations of the LoRaWAN MAC layer, we propose two schemes to increase the channel utilization for certain use cases. Our analysis shows that the proposed schemes can provide more than 60% throughput compared to 18% throughput of the pure ALOHA scheme used in the current specifications of LoRaWAN.

With this paper, we make the following contributions:

- We identify concepts and strategies to extend LoRaWAN Class A to use the channel more efficiently than the original specification without spending a disproportional amount of resources.
- We propose two schemes, *TDMA* and *Burst*, which provide more throughput and are more efficient in specific use cases and which require only small modification of the LoRaWAN Class A layer.
- We evaluate the proposed schemes with calculations as well as implementations on real LoRaWAN hardware.

We start with discussing related work in Section II and providing relevant background information about the LoRa technology in Section III. In Section IV we analyze suitable transmission protocols. Then, we present our proposed schemes in Section V. We compare the considered schemes with calculations in Section VI. Section VII describes our implementation with real LoRaWAN development hardware and Section VIII provides an evaluation of the implementation. Finally, we conclude the paper in Section IX.

II. Related Work

Adelantado *et al.* give an overview of the limits of LoRaWAN [2]. They investigate the influence of the number of end-devices and also consider the duty cycle limit which is imposed by European regulations [3]. Augustin *et al.* provide an overview of the LoRa modulation and the LoRaWAN MAC layer [4]. The study includes an analysis of the channel capacity of LoRaWAN. Vejlgaard *et al.* investigated the impact of interference on coverage and capacity of the LoRaWAN and the SigFox system [5]. Morin *et al.* investigate the power consumption and the corresponding device lifetime of different

IoT schemes including LoRaWAN [6]. Kim *et al.* propose a dual-channel scheme based on LoRaWAN to allow the data of different categories being delivered with different priorities [7]. Phung *et al.* analyze the packet delivery of LoRaWAN, including acknowledged and not acknowledged Class A transmissions as well as Class C transmissions [8]. Reynders *et al.* propose to use coarse-grained scheduling of transmission power, SF, and time in LoRaWAN networks [9]. Beacons are used for time synchronization. Polonelli *et al.* investigate the use of the slotted ALOHA protocol on top of LoRaWAN [10]. In addition, they propose a simple request-reply based time synchronization, which is similar to the time synchronization used in this work.

To the best of our knowledge, the closest related work is the work of Gu *et al.* [11]. They propose a data network with separated control and data plane. For the control plane, they use LoRaWAN. The data plane is based on a multi-hop ZigBee network. Similar to our work, they add synchronization to LoRaWAN in order to use a Time Division Multiple Access (TDMA) based scheme. In contrast to the work of Gu *et al.*, we do not use a separate control and data plane, we analyze the possibilities for different applications scenarios in general and in addition propose an *Burst* scheme that is advantageous in terms of aggregated throughput and channel use.

III. LoRa Technology

Two components of the LoRaWAN technology can be distinguished: (1) the LoRa modulation and (2) LoRaWAN. In this section, we will discuss the aspects of both layers which are relevant for this work and how to compute the time on air of a LoRa packet.

A. LoRa Modulation (PHY Layer)

The LoRa modulation is the physical layer. It is based on CSS modulation. Similar to the concept of Direct Sequence Spread Spectrum (DSSS), this modulation uses a large spectral bandwidth to improve the robustness. A common bandwidth setting for LoRaWAN is 125 kHz. In addition, the payload information can be distributed over different amounts of time by selecting different *spreading factors (SFs)*. Increasing the SF increases the time needed to send one byte, but also increases the probability of successful transmission with a given Signal-to-noise Ratio (SNR) and therefore increases the feasible range. This allows to trade throughput for range. The physical layer of LoRa has a payload size between 0 and 255 bytes and comprises a Forward Error Correction (FEC) with 4 different coding rates.

LoRa modulation is used on the sub-1 GHz ISM/SDR frequency bands, e.g., the 915 MHz band in North- and South America or 868 MHz and 433 MHz bands in Europe. Those bands do not require a license and are therefore shared with a large range of other devices which use different modulation schemes. Depending on the region, international regulations restrict the use of these bands in different ways. In Europe for example, there are limits on the transmit power and the duty cycle of each transmitting device is limited to 1 % for large parts of the 868 MHz band.

B. LoRaWAN (MAC Layer)

LoRaWAN [1] specifies the MAC layer which is used together with the LoRa modulation. The specification comprises three different types of devices which form a star-of-star topology. At the core, there are one or multiple network servers (NSs), which implement the back-end with the interface to applications in the Internet. Multiple gateways (GWs) are connected to the network server by the Internet Protocol via Ethernet. Each gateway connects multiple end-devices (EDs) via LoRa wireless links to the network server. Three default frequencies are used for end-devices to join a network, data transmissions and fallback. Additional frequencies can be configured manually.

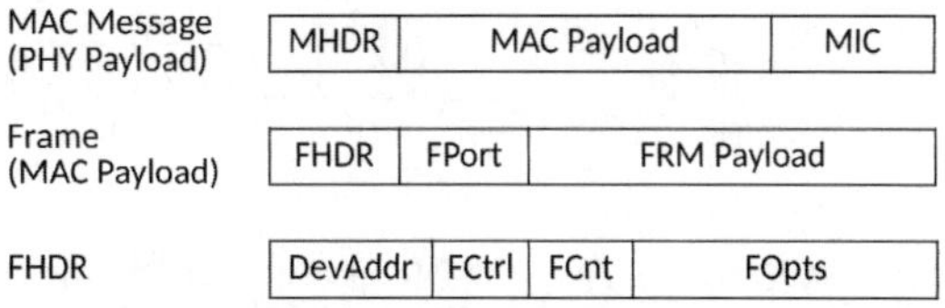

Figure 1. Frame structure of a MAC layer message.

The gateways simply forward messages from the end-devices to the network server and vice versa. A gateway can receive (uplink) messages on different frequencies and with different spreading factors simultaneously. Common gateways feature 8 frequency channels. In contrast to the multi-channel reception, the gateways usually only support to send on a single frequency and a single spreading factor. Most of the available gateways do not support duplex mode, i.e., they cannot receive while transmitting. The network servers manage the connections to the end-devices, keep a state of each end-device and remove duplicate messages originating from different gateways.

LoRaWAN messages are transmitted as payload of a LoRa PHY message. The message structure of data packets is depicted in Figure 1. MHDR is the header of the MAC message. It contains the message type and LoRaWAN version. The MAC payload contains the LoRaWAN frame. The MIC is a message integrity code, which is calculated over MHDR and MAC payload.

The LoRaWAN frame consists of a frame header (FHDR), frame port (FPort) and the frame payload, i.e., the application data. The frame port is a number which specifies which application the data is intended for. The frame header contains the device address (DevAddr), a frame control field (FCtrl) which contains information about the state of the connection, a frame counter value (FCnt), and zero or more MAC layer commands (MAC commands) in the FOpts field.

A LoRaWAN message with 50 bytes of frame payload needs a time-on-air of 176 ms for spreading factor SF7 or 3548 ms for SF12. Accordingly, a device is allowed to send a maximum of 204 messages with SF7 or 10 messages with SF12 in one hour due to the duty cycle limit. This limitation holds for both end-devices and gateways.

The LoRaWAN protocol is divided into three classes. **Class A** provides simple unsynchronized two-way communication between end-devices and network server with focus on the uplink. Downlink messages can be sent only following an uplink message in the so called *receive windows*, which are depicted in Figure 2. Therefore, the downlink throughput and latency are severely limited. **Class B** enabled devices support all features of Class A. In addition, the gateways periodically send beacons to synchronize the end-devices. This allows to

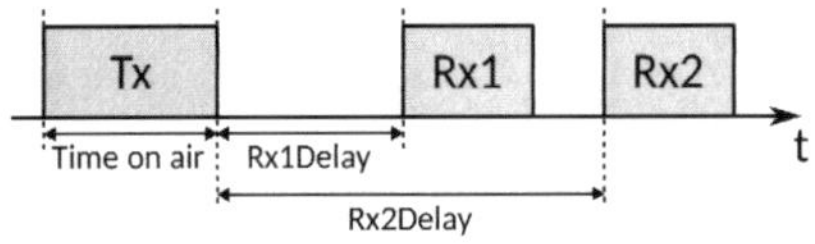

Figure 2. In LoRaWAN Class A end-devices only listen for packets during the defined receive windows.

schedule additional downlink receive windows. With **Class C**, the transceiver of each end-device is constantly turned on, i.e., the end-devices are either receiving or sending at any point in time.

Class B needs additional hardware such as a GPS receiver to keep the gateways globally synchronized since they need to transmit the beacon. Furthermore, Class B is inflexible since all end-devices need to use the same synchronization interval. Currently not many deployed end-devices implement LoRaWAN Class B. Class C is only feasible for devices which have extensive power supply available, which is not the case for scenarios considered in this paper. Because of these reasons, we focus on Class A in this work.

C. Time on air

In order to calculate the on-air-time of a LoRaWAN packet, we use the toa() function (1) given in the SX1276 datasheet [12]. It depends on the number of payload symbols (2) and the symbol duration (3).

$$\text{toa}(PL) = (n_{\text{preamble}} + 4.25 + n_{\text{pl}}) \cdot T_{\text{sym}} \tag{1}$$

$$n_{\text{pl}} = 8 + \max\left(\left\lceil \frac{8\cdot(\text{PL}+13)-4\text{SF}+28+16\text{CRC}-20\text{IH}}{4\cdot(\text{SF}-2\text{DE})} \right\rceil (\text{CR}+4), 0\right) \tag{2}$$

$$T_{\text{sym}} = \frac{2^{\text{SF}}}{\text{BW}} \tag{3}$$

PL is the number of frame (i.e. application) payload bytes. We adapted the formula such that it is valid for application layer payload by adding 13 bytes which correspond to the LoRaWAN overhead under the assumption of not sending any MAC commands in the FOpts field. SF is the spreading factor. We always enable the CRC (CRC $= 1$) and the header (IH $= 0$, *i.e.* implicit header off). We do not make use of the low data rate optimization (DE $= 0$) and use a coding rate of 4/5 (CR $= 1$). For the remaining parameters we use the LoRaWAN default values for the EU868 ISM band according to the LoRaWAN standard [1], [13]: the number of preamble symbols $n_{\text{preamble}} = 8$, and bandwidth of the LoRa modulation BW $= 125\,\text{kHz}$ (default for data rates DR0 - DR5).

IV. Transmission Protocols

In this section, we discuss all channel access and synchronization schemes we consider and mention the restrictions implied by LoRaWAN Class A. Then, we describe the considered schemes to increase the channel utilization, including our two proposed schemes *TDMA* and *Burst*.

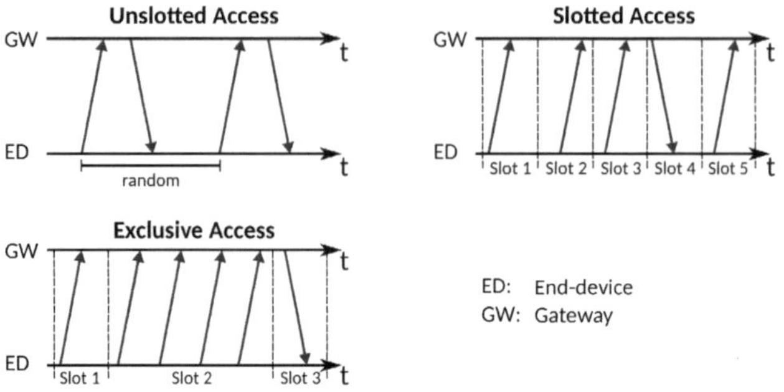

Figure 3. Basic channel access schemes.

A. Channel Access Schemes

Figure 3 provides an overview of the basic channel access schemes considered in this paper. The message exchange between an end-device and the gateway consists of uplink messages that are directed from end-device to gateway and downlink messages from gateway to end-device. Note that in LoRaWAN Class A the time between uplink and downlink messages is fixed, see Figure 2. Depending on the downlink queue in the network server and whether the uplink requests an acknowledgment, the network server transmits a downlink in the receive window or not. In other words, not every uplink message is necessarily followed by a downlink message.

Unslotted Access: End-devices can send messages anytime. Due to this uncoordinated access of the channel, there is a relatively high probability of colliding transmissions.

Slotted Access: The time is partitioned into slots of a fixed length. The end-devices are allowed to access the channel only at the beginning of a slot. This reduces the probability of collisions in comparison to the unslotted protocol. However, the clocks of the end-devices and the network need to be synchronized. In addition, all messages need to fit into the same time slot length.

Exclusive Access: A scheduler determines a time-driven schedule, which defines the assignment of devices to time intervals and frequencies to each device. The resulting schedule, with mutually exclusive channel accesses, precludes message collisions. End-devices need to be synchronized and to receive and store information, which determines the time interval in which they are allowed to access which channel.

B. Time Synchronization

The slotted access and exclusive access scheme require end-devices to be time synchronized. Two options that we consider are shown in Figure 4. The selection is based on the opportunities of the LoRaWAN Class A standard, i.e., sending beacons from the gateways is not possible as downlink messages can only be sent as answer to a previous uplink message.

Request: An end-device and the network server exchange dedicated messages via a gateway to synchronize the clock of the end-device.

Piggy-Back: The request for a time-synchronization is part of a regular data message, which is sent to the network server via a gateway. Synchronization information, like a timestamp, is then part of a downlink message sent from the network

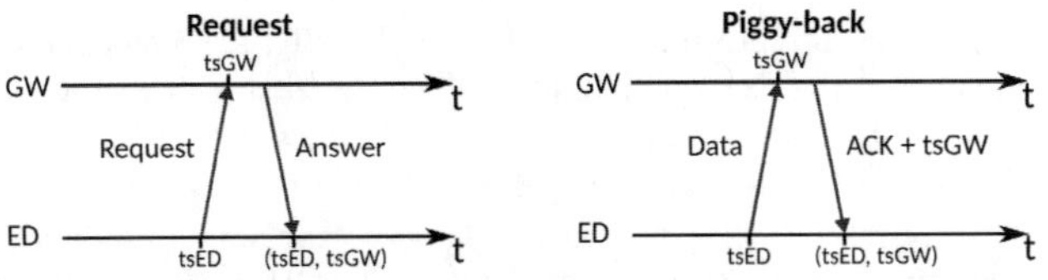

Figure 4. Basic synchronization schemes.

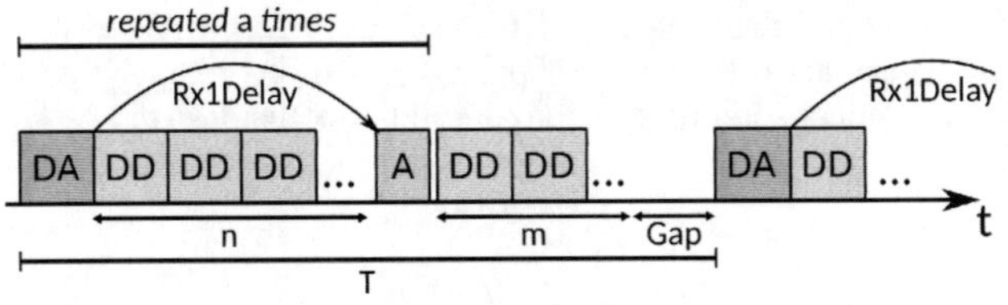

Figure 5. *TDMA* scheme with interleaved acknowledgment/sync packets.

server via a gateway to the end-device. This may be either an acknowledgment or a data downlink message.

C. Considered Transmission Schemes

We will study the following four protocols. They are selected as they represent different extreme solutions of a wide spectrum of possible schemes. Many generalizations and combinations of these four basic schemes are possible.

Pure ALOHA: This protocol has been proposed in [14] and uses the unslotted access scheme and therefore does not require synchronization.

Slotted ALOHA: This scheme has been proposed in [15]. It combines piggy-back synchronization with a partition of the channel in fixed time slots. Depending on the drift of the clock of end-devices, not all uplink messages need be answered by a synchronization message, e.g., a timestamp from the network server. These synchronization messages from the gateway are also subject to message collision.

TDMA: We propose the *TDMA* scheme which takes into account the LoRaWAN Class A specifics. In our scheme, the end-devices repeatedly send data packets D according to a fixed TDMA schedule, see Figure 5. In order to achieve synchronization between the clocks of the end-devices, special data messages (denoted as DA) are answered by acknowledgment messages (denoted by A) from the network server, which include synchronization information. The required rate of the synchronization messages depends on the clock-drift of the end-devices and the required time synchronization accuracy. There are several obvious options on determining such a TDMA schedule and sending it to the end-devices via downlink messages. We propose one possible schedule in Section V-B3.

Burst: For application with non-critical latency demands, we propose a new *Burst* scheme depicted in Figure 6. Multiple messages are aggregated and sent together in a burst. The scheme uses two different LoRa channels (two different frequencies): The *request channel* for coordinating the transmission of burst data messages and to perform time synchronization and the *burst channel* for transmitting bursts of uplink data messages. In order to send a burst, the end-device first needs to request a burst transmission slot from the network server by sending a burst request message on the

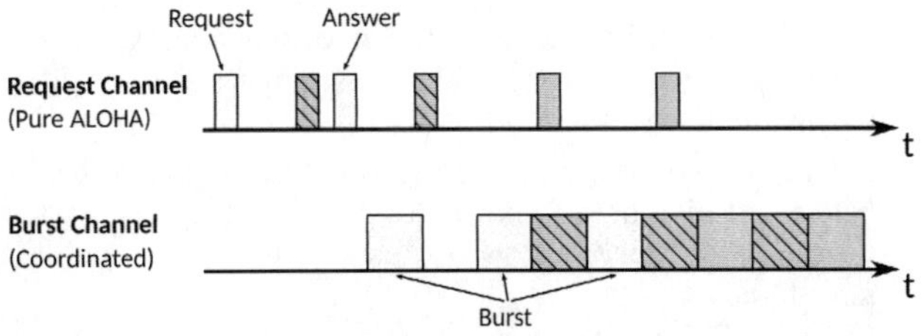

Figure 6. *Burst* scheme with on-demand synchronization with 3 nodes (light, hatched, dark).

request channel. A scheduler on the network server determines which end-device is allowed to send in which time slots.

V. Analysis

In this section, we describe and analyze the considered schemes in order to increase the channel utilization. First, we start defining the model and metrics to compare the different schemes.

A. Model and Metrics

1) Basic Model Assumptions: We suppose that our communication scenario consists of N end-devices and K gateways. We further assume that all end-devices and gateways can reach any other end-device or gateway directly. In general, we assume that every end-device connected to the network generates data of size D with a fixed period T.

Time-On-Air: The on-air-time of a LoRa transmission can be calculated, see Section III-C. We use t_D for the on-air-time of any data uplink packet and t_A for any non-data packet (this includes requests, answer, synchronization, and coordination packets).

Clock Drift: After synchronization, the clocks in the network server and the end-devices will drift apart. We denote the time difference between previous time synchronization and the time when the clock of the end-device is accessed as Δt. The maximal absolute value of the time difference between the end-device and the network server at this point in time is then modeled as

$$\tau(\Delta t) = \tau_0 + \Delta t \cdot \tau_1 \quad (4)$$

where τ_0 is the synchronization error due to the synchronization protocol between the network server and the end-device and τ_1 denotes the clock-drift of the end-device. In order to account for the clock inaccuracy, we expand the actual time-on-air t_D and t_A by a safety margin and define the expanded time for data packets as $s_D = t_D + 2 \cdot \tau(\Delta t_{\max})$ where $\Delta t_{\max}$ is the maximum time between time synchronization updates. We define s_A accordingly.

Duty Cycle Limit: The LoRaWAN standard limits the time, a device is on air, i.e., sending a message. In this paper, we focus on LoRaWAN EU868 and therefore the European regulations (ETSI EN 300 220-1 [3]) apply which enforce a the duty cycle limit of $L = 0.01$ for each device. This also applies to the gateways. According to the regulations, the time interval which is considered to evaluate the adherence to the duty cycle limit is $I = 3600\,\mathrm{s}$. This constraint in terms of duty cycle L and measurement interval I strongly restricts the design space of efficient LoRaWAN based protocols.

2) Metrics for Comparison: In the following, we list the four metrics we are interested in to compare the considered transmission schemes.

The **success probability** P_{succ} is defined as the probability that an attempt of an end-device to transmit a data packet to the network server is successful, i.e., there is no colliding transmission.

We define the **throughput** S as the average accumulated time of successful data message transmissions from all end-devices relative to the total time. If there are in total $M_{\text{succ}}(\Delta t)$ successful message transmissions from any end-device in a time interval of length Δt, then

$$S = \lim_{\Delta t \to \infty} \frac{M_{\text{succ}}(\Delta t) \cdot t_D}{\Delta t} \tag{5}$$

where t_D is the time on air for transmitting a data message.

The **device time utilization** W_d for a specific device d is the average accumulated time the device is (successfully or unsuccessfully) transmitting relative to the total time. For example, if there are $M_d(\Delta t)$ message transmissions from this specific end-device in a time interval of length Δt, then

$$W_d = \lim_{\Delta t \to \infty} \frac{M_d(\Delta t) \cdot t_D}{\Delta t} \tag{6}$$

where t_D is the time on air for transmitting a data message. We denote the device time utilization of an end-device by W_{ED} and the the device time utilization of an gateway by W_{GW}.

The **send efficiency** E is the average accumulated time all end-devices are transmitting data packets which are successfully received relative to the total time all devices are transmitting. For example, if there are $M_{\text{succ}}(\Delta t)$ successful data transmissions, $M_{\text{unsucc}}(\Delta t)$ unsuccessful transmissions, and $M_{\text{sync}}(\Delta t)$ synchronization messages in a time interval of length Δt, then

$$E = \lim_{\Delta t \to \infty} \frac{M_{\text{succ}} \cdot t_D}{(M_{\text{succ}}(\Delta t) + M_{\text{unsucc}}(\Delta t)) \cdot t_D + M_{\text{sync}}(\Delta t) \cdot t_A} \tag{7}$$

B. Considered Transmission Schemes in Detail

In this section, we explain the considered transmission schemes in more detail and provide the corresponding performance analysis.

1) Pure ALOHA Scheme: The LoRaWAN Class A scheme uses the pure, i.e., unslotted, ALOHA scheme for channel access. If the channel access attempts from end-devices are assumed to be Poisson distributed with an average of G accesses per packet time, then the performance metrics are known to be [14]

$$S = G \cdot \mathrm{e}^{-2G} \qquad P_{\text{succ}} = \mathrm{e}^{-2G} \tag{8}$$

In (8), S corresponds to our definition of throughput and G is the number of access attempts per packet time (access rate). The maximum throughput is about $S_{\max} = 18.4\%$, which is achieved for $G = 1/2$. This leads to a corresponding success probability of about $P_{\text{succ,max}} = 0.37$.

In other words, even a low maximal throughput comes with a low success probability. One intuitive measure to increase the success probability is to use positive acknowledgment and retransmission. But this leads to additional channel accesses due to the re-transmitted packets and the acknowledgment for each correctly requested packet. Finally, acknowledgment packets are also subject to collisions. This means we can increase the success probability only by reducing the channel accesses, i.e., by reducing the throughput.

In reality, the duty cycle limit restricts the number of feasible operating points of the pure ALOHA scheme. In our analysis, we want to achieve a throughput S defined by N, t_D and T. We use (8) to calculate $G = \frac{N \cdot t_{\text{Tx}}}{T}$ from S in (9). The actual time-on-air t_{Tx} for each pure ALOHA end-device to generate a total throughput of S is always larger then the theoretical send time required without collisions ($t_{\text{Tx}} > t_D$).

$$S = \frac{N \cdot t_D}{T} \overset{G(S)}{\Rightarrow} G \overset{!}{=} \frac{N \cdot t_{\text{Tx}}}{T} \tag{9}$$

With this, we can determine the end-device time utilization W_{ED} (see (10)). The device time utilization of the gateway is 0 since no transmissions are acknowledged and no synchronization is preformed. The send efficiency is determined by $E = \frac{S}{G}$.

$$W_{\text{ED}} = \frac{m \cdot t_{\text{Tx}}}{T} = \frac{G}{N} \overset{!}{\leq} L \qquad W_{\text{GW}} = 0 \overset{!}{\leq} L \tag{10}$$

Due to retransmissions, a delay has to be accounted for this scheme.

2) Slotted ALOHA Scheme: As in the case of pure ALOHA, the throughput analysis for slotted ALOHA is well known and established [15]:

$$S = G \cdot \mathrm{e}^{-G} \qquad P_{\text{succ}} = \mathrm{e}^{-G} \tag{11}$$

If we assume perfect synchronization with no overhead and no interference on the frequency band (i.e. all transmitted packets are received successfully if they are not overlapping in time), the maximum throughput is about $S_{\max} = 36.8\%$, which is achieved for $G = 1$, where G is the access rate. This would be an improvement by a factor of 2 in comparison to the pure ALOHA protocol in terms of maximally achievable throughput. The success probability remains unchanged with about $P_{\text{succ,max}} = 36.8\%$ for this operating point.

But as we know, the scheme requires the end-devices to be synchronized. Therefore, the actual throughput of a slotted ALOHA system is lower than S and the success probability is lower than P_{succ}. In addition, the rate of acknowledgment packets transmitted by the gateways is limited by the duty cycle limit L. This fact constrains the possible design space for slotted ALOHA further.

3) TDMA Scheme: We propose the *TDMA* scheme which is depicted in Figure 5. The end-devices send a data packet (DD or DA) of fixed size D according to a Time Division Multiple Access (TDMA) schedule. The schedule repeats periodically with period T. In each period, all N end-devices send exactly one data packet. Only a small number $a < N$ of all transmissions are acknowledged (DA packets) in each period in order to keep the overhead low and to comply with the duty cycle limit. The period between synchronization of a particular end-device is $\frac{T \cdot N}{a}$ on average. The acknowledgment A is used to transfer a timestamp from the gateway to the end-device. The acknowledgment slots of multiple periods are evenly distributed to the participating end-devices such that the end-devices are alternately synchronized. In Figure 5, the case for $a = 1$ is depicted. All devices, including the gateways, send on a single frequency.

The LoRaWAN standard specifies the `Rx1Delay` time between the end of the data packet and the corresponding acknowledgment in order to allow the server to react to the received message and to transmit a reply, see Figure 2. During this interval, $n = \left\lfloor \frac{\texttt{Rx1Delay}}{t_D} \right\rfloor$ not acknowledged transmissions are scheduled. This sequence of DA, DD ..., A is repeated a times. The rest of the period is used to schedule m not acknowledged transmissions from the remaining $m = N - a \cdot (n + 1)$ end-devices.

Due to the ETSI duty cycle limit, not all combinations of (N, t_D, T) are possible. The relation for the *TDMA* scheme between payload size D (indirectly given as on-air-time with safety margin s_D) and the period T is given by (12). The application payload and the on-air-time of a packet is linked by the $toa()$ function described in Section III-C.

The relation of the components of one *TDMA* schedule period is given in (12). A non-zero gap (Gap) allows the scheme to be suitable for combinations of parameters which do not exactly fill the *TDMA* schedule. Gap is determined by parameters in (12) (N, t_D, t_A and a).

The constraints due to the duty cycle limit based on the device time utilization are given in (13). The device time utilization due to downlink messages from the network server can be distributed to K gateways.

$$T = (\texttt{Rx1Delay}+s_A)\cdot a + \left(N - \left\lfloor \frac{\texttt{Rx1Delay}}{s_D} \right\rfloor \cdot a\right)\cdot s_D + \text{Gap} \tag{12}$$

$$W_{\text{ED}} = \frac{t_D}{T} \overset{!}{\leq} L \qquad W_{\text{GW}} = \frac{a \cdot t_A}{T} \overset{!}{\leq} L \cdot K \tag{13}$$

L corresponds to the duty cycle limit, see Section V-A1. The send efficiency is $E = \frac{N \cdot t_D}{N \cdot t_D + a \cdot t_A}$.

In the case of no packet loss, the maximum time a clock of an end-device is not synchronized is $\Delta t_{\max} = \lceil \frac{N \cdot T}{a} \rceil$ and the *TDMA* scheme provides a success probability of $P_{\text{succ}} = 1$ since none of the transmissions can be overlapping due to the TDMA schedule.

4) Burst Scheme: As a second scheme, we propose the *Burst* scheme, which is depicted in Figure 6. In contrast to the *TDMA* scheme, in the *Burst* scheme the end-devices are not continuously synchronized. The end-device synchronizes their clock to the network server before sending a burst. Synchronizing for sending a single packet would implicate a large overhead. Therefore, in general the end-devices aggregate data and send multiple packets bundled together in a *burst*.

The proposed scheme uses two different channels: The *request channel* for handling requests and synchronization and the *burst channel* for transmitting the bursts. The request channel is uncoordinated and uses pure ALOHA, whereas the burst channel is coordinated by a scheduler on the network server. There is no explicit acknowledgment but it would be possible to acknowledge the complete transmission of the last burst in the following burst answer.

In order to send a burst, the end-device first needs to request a burst transmission and obtain synchronization by sending a burst request message on the request channel to the network server. The network server maintains a schedule of all scheduled transmissions. With a burst answer transmitted on the request channel, the network server sends a timestamp for synchronization and the information when the end-device is allowed to send the individual packets of the burst. Then the end-devices synchronizes its clock and stands by for sending the burst packets in the designated slots.

The scheduler running on the network server makes sure that no burst can collide on the burst channel. If there are no suitable slots available in the following time interval of length Δt which defines the safety margin $\tau(\Delta t)$, the network server can deny an access to the burst channel. In this case, the end-device tries to request the burst channel again after a backoff time. The backoff time is increased exponentially with every denial. This prevents overloading the request channel if there are simultaneous requests from many nodes.

The LoRaWAN specifications require the end-device to wait with sending a new message until the receive window of the previous message has passed no matter whether the end-device sent a confirmed or unconfirmed message. For this reason, a single burst transmission, which consists of multiple packets, needs to be sent as individual packets with gaps of at least `Rx1Delay` in between.

For the analysis of the performance of this scheme, we assume that the average period between two burst transmissions of a single device is T. The accumulated duration of a burst t_{Burst} and the relation to the burst period T are given in (14). The device time utilization and the corresponding limits are given in (16). Since the messages are sent in bursts, they are not evenly distributed over time, we need an additional constraint, (15), that ensures that the absolute maximal transmitting time within $I = 3600\,\text{s}$ is not exceeded.

$$\begin{aligned} t_{\text{Burst}} &= (n_B + n_G) \cdot s_D \\ T &= N \cdot t_{\text{Burst}} \end{aligned} \tag{14}$$

$$n_B \cdot t_D + t_A \overset{!}{\leq} L \cdot I \tag{15}$$

$$W_{\text{ED}} = \frac{n_B \cdot t_D + t_A}{T} \overset{!}{\leq} L \qquad W_{\text{GW}} = \frac{t_A}{t_{\text{Burst}}} \overset{!}{\leq} L \cdot K \tag{16}$$

n_B indicates the number of LoRaWAN data packets that are sent in a single burst, $n_G \geq 0$ is the number of slots which are unused (gap) following a burst transmission. The unused slots are, in some cases, necessary to keep the aggregated on-air-time (W_{GW}) below the allowed limit L on the side of the gateway. In the *Burst* scheme, the number of nodes is not restricted by the duty cycle limit, as it is the case with the *TDMA* scheme, but depends on the size of the bursts. The success probability of sending the bursts is $P_{\text{succ}} = 1$ since the synchronization and scheduling of the network server makes sure that no transmissions overlap. The probability for a collision on the request channel is supposed to be small since the aggregated on-air-time for acknowledgments by the gateway is limited to $L = 1\%$. The throughput of the

TABLE I. INPUTS AND OUTPUTS OF THE CALCULATIONS.

Input	
D	Application payload size
T	Period with which an end-device sends the application payload
N	Number of participating end-devices
K	Number of gateways
–	LoRaWAN and LoRa modulation parameters

Output	
–	Feasibility
E	Send efficiency
W_{ED}, W_{GW}	Device time utilization
P_{succ}	Probability of a transmission to arrive

entire scheme is determined as $S = \frac{n_B \cdot t_D}{t_{Burst} + 2 \cdot t_A}$ and the send efficiency is given by $E = \frac{n_B \cdot t_D}{n_B \cdot t_D + 2 \cdot t_A}$.

5) Comparison of Slotted ALOHA with TDMA: If we compare slotted ALOHA and the *TDMA* scheme, it is obvious that the minimum synchronization overhead is the same (unless out-of-band synchronization mechanisms are used). In both schemes, all nodes need to be continuously synchronized within the required precision such that packets can be sent inside a time slot. The only difference in overhead is the assignment of each node to slots which exists in the *TDMA* scheme but not in the slotted ALOHA scheme. However, this assignment can be pre-configured (e.g. based on the node's ID), which means that the overhead of the slot assignment of the *TDMA* scheme is negligible. Since the *TDMA* scheme provides a significantly better success probability ($P_{succ} = 1$) it is always beneficial to use *TDMA* instead of slotted ALOHA. Because of this reason, we omit the slotted ALOHA scheme in our calculations which follow next.

VI. CALCULATIONS

In order to compare the three remaining considered schemes, we calculate the previously described metrics.

A. Calculation Model

We numerically evaluate the access schemes described in Section V to obtain the metrics and the feasibility of the considered schemes at different design points. The most important input and output quantities of the calculation are listed in Table I.

The main input of each scheme consists of three parameters, application payload size D in bytes, period between transmissions T of a single end-device in seconds and the number of end-devices N. These three parameters describe the requested throughput. By evaluating the equations of the considered schemes, we determine which areas of the design space are feasible and which scheme provides the best send efficiency.

Further parameters for the calculations are the spreading factor SF, plus further LoRa modulation parameters, which are described in Section III-B and are kept constant for all calculations. In addition, there are parameters which are relevant only for a subset of the schemes: The number of gateways K which is relevant for the *TDMA* and *Burst* scheme, the number of acknowledged transmission a in a *TDMA* period. Another parameter for the calculation are clock offset and drift values which are relevant for the *TDMA* and *Burst* scheme. Based on measurements in Section VIII-A, we assume a clock offset τ_0 of 15 ms and a clock drift of 20 ppm. The application payload D size is a discrete parameter by definition. In order to keep

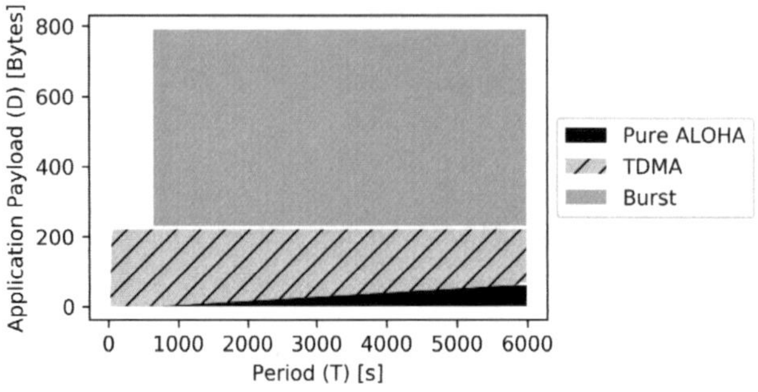

Figure 7. Feasible combinations of period T and application payload D (fixed SF=7 and N=100). The color/hatching indicates the scheme with highest send efficiency E.

the calculations tractable, the application payload D has been sampled with a step size of 10 bytes, the period T with a step size of 20 s. In our model, we consider it infeasible to send multiple packets in a sequence, except for the *Burst* scheme. This limits the application payload D in the *TDMA* scheme to the maximum payload of a LoRaWAN packet (which is 222 bytes for SF7).

B. Calculation Results

In this section, we discuss the results from our calculations in terms of feasibility, send efficiency and throughput.

1) Feasibility and Efficiency of the Schemes: We investigate which scheme is most efficient for a given throughput defined by N, D, and T. In Figure 7 we show an exemplary plot for SF7 and $N = 100$ with 1 gateway. The non-white areas represent the feasible combinations of input parameters. The shading of the area indicates which of the scheme has the best efficiency E. Please note that our assumptions of the model limit the feasibility.

The calculations show that the *TDMA* scheme is feasible and efficient in a large range of periods and payload sizes. For very large periods and small payload size, i.e., low requested throughput, the pure ALOHA scheme has highest send efficiency since the overhead for the continuous synchronization is large compared to the data that should be transmitted. The *Burst* scheme is not feasible for small periods. For lower periods, the device time on the end-device W_{ED} would exceed the duty-cycle limit. For SF7 even for very short periods, the *TDMA* scheme is feasible and provides higher send efficiency. This is expected since the pure ALOHA needs approximately 4 failed transmission to send 1 successful message in the best case of $G = 0.5$. The *TDMA* scheme only needs to send synchronization messages for a fraction of all nodes in each period. The calculations for different spreading factors and different number of end-devices N yield similar insights.

2) Maximum Throughput: In this section, we investigate the maximum achievable throughput of each scheme.

In Figure 8, the throughput S for different number of end-devices N in the case of using only a single gateway is depicted. The *TDMA* scheme can provide significantly higher throughput values compared to the pure ALOHA scheme. However, the maximum throughput for the *Burst* scheme is comparable to the pure ALOHA scheme when using only one gateway.

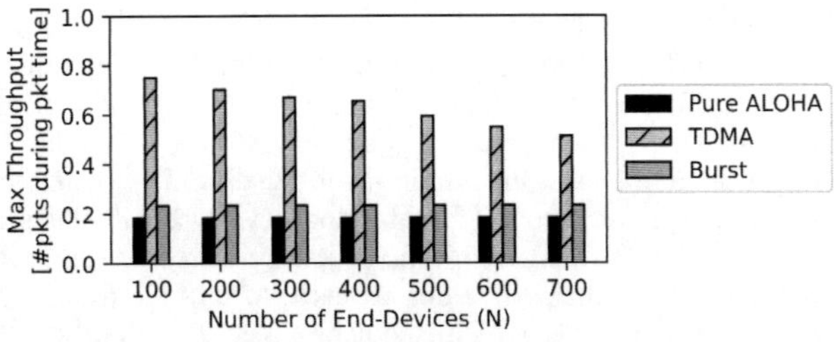

Figure 8. Maximum throughput S for different combinations of period T and application payload D in relation to N (SF=7 and 1 gateway).

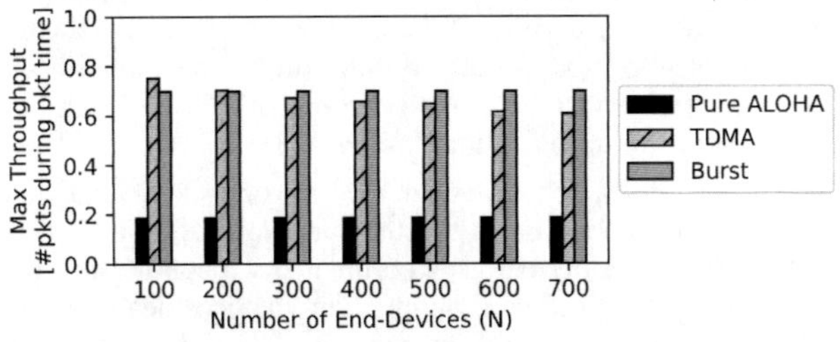

Figure 9. Maximum throughput S for different combinations of period T and application payload D in relation to N (SF=7 and 3 gateways).

If we increase the number of available gateways, we can increase the maximum throughput of the *TDMA* and the *Burst* scheme. In Figure 9, we show the maximum throughput in case of 3 gateways. The calculations show that especially the *Burst* scheme profits from the additional gateways. For the *TDMA* scheme it helps only if the number of end-devices is large. With 3 gateways and SF=7 and less than 300 end-devices, the schemes can provide a throughput up to 70% whereas the pure ALOHA scheme only provides up to 18% throughout.

As shown in Figure 9, the maximum *TDMA* throughput decreases with increasing number of end-devices whereas the maximum *Burst* throughput is constant. For the *TDMA* scheme the overhead to keep nodes synchronized grows with the number of devices. For the *Burst* scheme, the overhead of handling burst requests on the gateway can be kept constant for any N by increasing the period. However, the transferred data per end-device decreases with increasing number of end-devices.

C. Selection of Transmission Scheme

Finally, we will provide guidelines that help to select an appropriate transmission scheme based on the analysis in the previous sections. An overview in the form of a decision tree is given in Figure 10.

In the pure ALOHA scheme, the throughput is constrained by the collisions ($P_{\text{succ}} \leq \frac{1}{2e} = 18.4\%$) which are accepted in order to not require a time synchronization. The *TDMA* and *Burst* scheme have a success probability of $P_{\text{succ}} = 1$ but comprise an overhead due to the necessary time synchronization. The collisions of pure ALOHA and the synchronization overhead of the *TDMA* and *Burst* schemes reduce the send efficiency. In addition, lack of synchronization increases the necessary safety margin $\tau(\Delta t)$. A larger safety margin influences whether a requested throughput can be achieved by a certain scheme but does not influence the send efficiency directly.

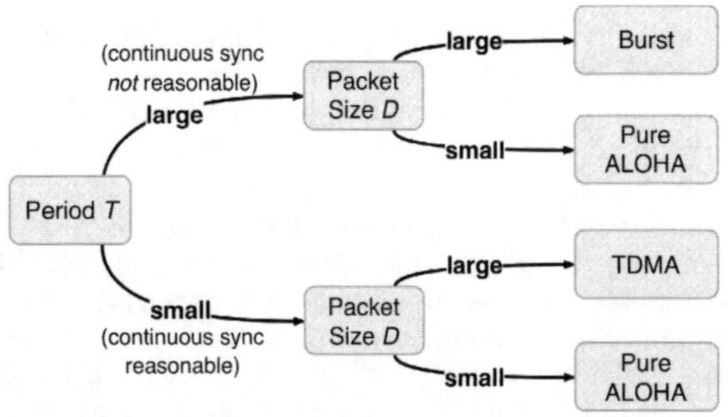

Figure 10. Decision tree for selecting channel access / synchronization scheme.

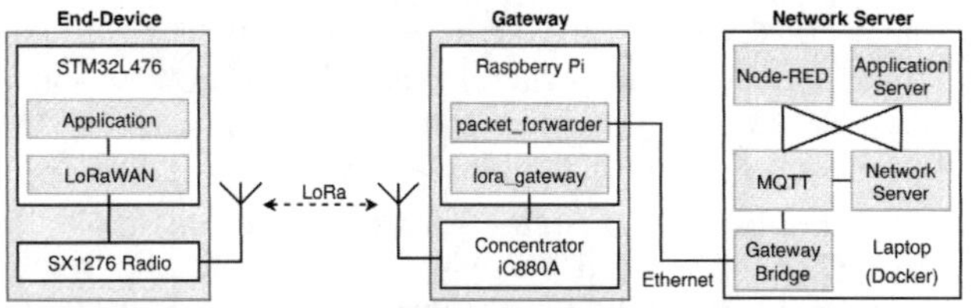

Figure 11. LoRaWAN setup.

If an application requests only a very low throughput (i.e. T large and D small), the pure ALOHA scheme is suitable and provides good send efficiency $E = S/G$, which is large compared to the send efficiency of the synchronized schemes.

For larger requested throughputs there are two cases. If the period T should be small, continuous synchronization of all end-devices is reasonable and therefore the *TDMA* scheme is suitable. If the period T should be large, continuous synchronization is not necessarily reasonable and therefore the *Burst* scheme is more suitable. In certain cases of small period and small packet size, the *TDMA* scheme is not feasible due to the duty cycle limitations. This holds especially for larger spreading factors. In this case, the pure ALOHA is the only option.

VII. Implementation

In this section, we explain the implementation on real LoRaWAN development hardware, which is used to demonstrate the feasibility of the two proposed schemes. The implementation is based on the framework of Polonelli *et al.* [10], which implements the basic mechanism for time synchronization on LoRaWAN development hardware. We extended the framework by a mechanism to enforce frequency channels, using the history of synchronization messages for time synchronization, and the implementation of our proposed *TDMA* and *Burst* scheme.

A. Setup

An overview of the setup which is used in this work is depicted in Figure 11.

1) Network Server: For the network server, we use LoRaServer [16], which is an open source implementation of the corresponding LoRaWAN specifications. We run the different components of the LoRaServer inside different Docker [17] containers on a Lenovo ThinkPad T460s laptop (Intel Core i7-6600U, 2.60 GHz, 19 GiB RAM). The LoRaServer project consists of 3 main parts: the *gateway bridge*, the *network server* block and the *application server*. The gateway bridge is responsible for communicating with the gateway. The network server block implements the LoRaWAN MAC-layer on the server side. The application server manages different user applications and provides a web-interface. The received and transmitted messages are exchanged via the open-source Eclipse Mosquitto MQTT broker [18]. Furthermore, we use a Node-RED [19] container to implement network flows.

2) Gateway: Our LoRaWAN gateway consists of a Raspberry Pi 2 and the iC880A concentrator. This setup supports the simultaneous reception of messages with all spreading factors (SF7 - SF12) on 8 different frequencies. The gateway is connected to the laptop via Ethernet. The software running on the gateway is the *lora_gateway* and *packet_forwarder* from the Lora-net reference project on GitHub [20].

3) End-Device: Each end-device consists of an STM32L476RG microcontroller developer board (Nucleo-L476RG) combined with an *mbed* SX1276 868 MHz LoRa shield. The software running on the end-devices is based on *LoRaMAC-node* from the *Lora-net* reference project on GitHub [20] and the framework of Polonelli *et al.* [10].

B. Time Synchronization

Our proposed schemes require synchronized clocks across end-devices and network server. By default this is not supported with the LoRaWAN MAC layer. Therefore, we add a custom time synchronization to LoRaWAN. The implementation of the time synchronization is based on the implementation described in the work of Polonelli *et al.* [10] and is similar to the scheme used by Gu *et al.* [11].

The implemented synchronization scheme is depicted in Figure 4. This scheme is based on a pair of corresponding timestamps. The end-device takes a local timestamp right before sending a synchronization request. The gateway receives this request and immediately takes the corresponding global timestamp (tsGW). This timestamp is then sent to the end-device in the following synchronization answer message. One such pair of timestamps can be used to calculate the offset between the local and global clocks. This offset is used in the *Burst* scheme. For the *TDMA* scheme, this procedure is repeated, which leads to multiple synchronization pairs. From multiple synchronization pairs, the clock offset and drift are calculated, which can then be used to convert the local timestamp on the end-device to the global time of the network.

C. Enforcing Frequencies

By default, LoRaWAN end-devices choose pseudo-randomly one of the 3 default frequencies to sending LoRa packets. However, our schemes use a fixed assignment of channels to end-devices and in the *Burst* scheme no uncoordinated requests are tolerated in the coordinated burst channel. Therefore, we enforce the end-devices to use the assigned frequency. To implement this, we configure the channel mask on the end-devices such that all but one configured LoRa channels are disabled at any point in time. For this, we make a request to the request/confirm based MAC Information Base (MIB) interface of the LoRaWAN MAC layer.

D. TDMA Implementation

The *TDMA* scheme, proposed in Section V-B3, requires an implementation of a bootstrap mechanism to obtain synchronization and to send messages according to a schedule. The implementation uses the piggy-back synchronization method described in Section VII-B. The end-device re-calculates the offset and drift value each time a new synchronization pair is obtained. The obtained values are used to provide timestamps from a virtual clock, which is synchronized to the clock of the network server due to the synchronization scheme. After boot up and joining the LoRaWAN network, the virtual clock is not yet synchronized and therefore the end-device requests the first synchronization point by sending a dedicated synchronization request message on one of the 3 default LoRaWAN channels. This bootstrap mode is at the same time used for fallback in case the end-device looses synchronization in the case of not receiving a synchronization answer.

In general, a scheduler on the network server can send a schedule to the end-device in the synchronization answer. For the implementation of our experiments, we define the TDMA schedule statically. The individual end-devices determine their send slots based on the current time and the end-device's ID, similar to the implementation of Gu *et al.* [11]. After the bootstrap phase or after sending a data packet, an end-device obtains the current timestamp and together with the ID it determines the time to transmit the next packet and the transmission type (DA, DD or A). In the time between the transmissions, the end-device is put into sleep mode. Timers that are based on the virtual clock are configured to wake the end-device up and send the transmission scheduled by the TDMA schedule.

E. Burst Implementation

The implementation of the *Burst* scheme requires a logic on the end-device to send messages on the assigned channel at the assigned point in time, a scheduler on the network server, and a mechanism to prevent transmitting while receiving a burst data message on the same gateway.

When the end-device wants to send a burst, a synchronization procedure as described in Section VII-B is initiated. In addition to the timestamp, the network server sends the time difference between timestamp and start time of the burst.The end-device then uses the timestamp to synchronize the virtual clock, configures a timer to wake up when the burst should start, and goes into sleep mode. The end-device then alternately sends packets and sleeps in between until all packets of the burst are transmitted. After completing a burst, the end-device sleeps until the start of the next burst. In the implementation for our experiments, we use a configurable interval between sending bursts. The length of this interval is randomized to ensure that the pattern of burst requests changes over time.

The scheduler is implemented as stateful Node-RED flow function. The schedule consists of time slots of size s_D, which are assigned to end-devices which request to send a burst. With this, the scheduler guarantees that the allocated burst patterns do not overlap.

Most of the commercially available LoRaWAN gateways (including the one used for the experiments in this paper) are not capable of full-duplex, i.e., they cannot transmit while receiving. This causes the gateway to miss burst data packets if it sends an answer to a burst request at the same time. We mitigate this problem, by not answering burst requests, if the burst answer would overlap with scheduled burst data packet. Please note, that this problem has no influence on the throughput if two or more gateways are used. For the case of two gateways for example, one gateway can be configured to only receive and the other one to only transmit. The gateways then can periodically switch roles in order to distribute the accumulated transmit time such that the device send time utilization of the gateways is kept below the duty-cycle.

VIII. Evaluation

We perform experiments to verify that our implementation behaves as expected and to demonstrate that our proposed schemes work on real hardware.

A. Synchronization Accuracy

First, we examine whether our assumptions of clock accuracy for the calculations are in accordance with values measured on real hardware. For this, the synchronization accuracy which can be achieved with the implementation is measured. The synchronization implementation is based on the framework of Polonelli *et al.* [10].

We measure the offset between two periodically synchronized end-devices located in the same room. For this, both end-devices synchronize every 10 s with the gateway. In order not to interfere with each other, one of the end-devices runs with a configured offset of 5 s relative to the other end-device. An experiment with 200 transmissions over a time interval of 30 minutes with spreading factor SF7 has been conducted. The the measured offset is is in the range ± 0.0123 s. From these measurements we conclude that $\tau_0 = 15$ ms, which we use in the calculation in Section VI, is a good upper bound for the offset between two synchronized end-devices.

B. Evaluation of the TDMA Scheme

In order to verify that the implementation performs as expected from the calculations, we run the *TDMA* scheme and measure the packet delivery ration (PDR). For the evaluation, we determined a feasible configuration which satisfies all the constraints in Section V-B3 with $N = 64$, an application payload of $D = 50$ bytes, a period $T = 30$ s, and $a = 1$ acknowledged transmission per period. This configuration would ideally lead to a throughput of $S = 25.2\%$ with 1 gateway.

We perform measurements with the mentioned configuration with 8 end-devices and 1 gateway, which are located in the same room. The slots for the remaining 56 end-devices are unused, i.e., no device sends anything during this time. In order to verify the synchronization implementation, we artificially increase in our experiment the synchronization rate such that in every period exactly one of the 8 participating end-devices sends a synchronization request. The measurements includes 253 periods, which corresponds to 127 minutes or 2024 uplink packets.

The resulting packet-delivery-ratio (PDR) for each end-device is plotted in Figure 12. The mean PDR over all 8 end-devices is 99.75%. A probable cause for not receiving all packets successfully is interference from other LoRa transmissions on the same frequency. With this, we demonstrate that an implementation of the described TDMA discipline on top of LoRaWAN is feasible and that the *TDMA* scheme can be implemented on LoRaWAN development hardware.

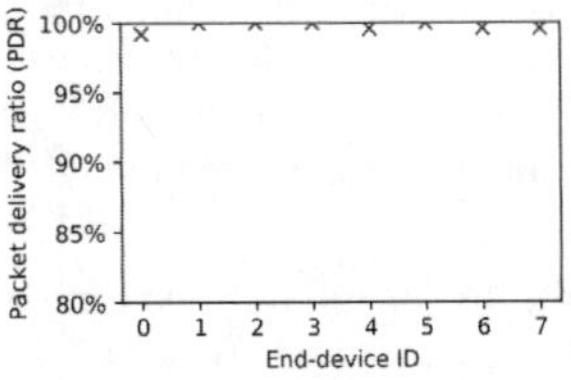

Figure 12. Packet delivery ratios (PDR) of the *TDMA* evaluation.

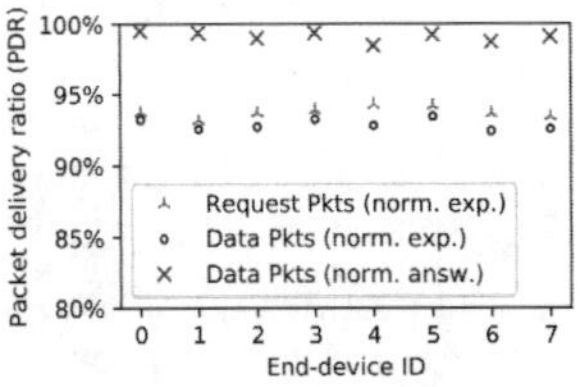

Figure 13. Packet delivery ratios (PDR) of the *Burst* evaluation.

C. Evaluation of the Burst Scheme

In an evaluation experiment, we run the *Burst* scheme implementation to verify that it performs as expected from the calculations. For this, we use the following configuration: $N = 8$, $n_B = 4$, $T = 60.02$ s (95 slots), SF7, $D = 222$ bytes. This leads to a throughput of $S = 31.0\%$. This configuration uses an artificially decreased period T in order to test the system under high load. This means, a single physical device represents multiple virtual devices.

In our experiments, we use the setup of Section VIII-B with 8 end-devices and 1 gateway. The use of 1 gateway means that some burst requests are not answered the first time because the gateway does not send a burst answer while receiving a burst data packet. Therefore, we expect that the amount of positive answers to the the burst requests is smaller than 100%.

The results of the measurements are shown in Figure 13. The star shows the number of burst requests, the circle shows the number of burst data messages of each end-device. Both values are normalized by the expected number of burst requests or data messages, which is calculated using the values of the configuration. The average number of expected bursts from each end-device is 204.96 (absolute number). On average the end-devices received 93.92% of the expected burst requests and 93.04% of the expected burst data packets As expected, both values are lower than the PDR of the *TDMA* evaluation since a significant amount of burst requests is not answered by the network server to allow proper reception of burst data messages. The cross represents the number of received burst data packets normalized by the number of unique burst requests that have been answered by the network server. On average the end-devices received 99.07% of all burst data packets which followed on a answered burst request. This number is comparable with the PDR of the *TDMA* evaluation. In summary, the results show that the implementation of the *Burst* scheme is feasible.

IX. Conclusion

In this paper, we first analyze the existing LoRaWAN Class A scheme. Based on this analysis, we then propose the *TDMA* and the *Burst* scheme, which allow to use the channel more efficiently. The *TDMA* scheme uses a single frequency channel and requires the end-devices to remain synchronized. The *Burst* scheme uses two frequency channels, aggregates data to be sent and requires the devices to be synchronized only when sending a burst. With calculations, we investigate in which scenarios the proposed schemes are advantageous compared to the current version of the LoRaWAN specifications, which uses pure ALOHA. Our analysis shows that the proposed schemes can provide more than 60% throughput compared to 18% provided by the pure ALOHA scheme used in the current specifications of LoRaWAN. With experiments with eight end-devices and one gateway, we demonstrate that the proposed scheme can be implemented on real LoRaWAN development hardware and that only small modifications of the LoRaWAN layer are required.

Interesting future work is the implementation and evaluation with multiple gateways. As discussed in Section VII-E, this would allow to distribute the acknowledgments such that more packets can be acknowledged and the system still complies to the duty cycle limit. Another useful extension is the use of multiple frequency channels with an agreed pseudo random channel hopping sequence for the transmissions to make the schemes more resilient against narrow band interference.

ACKNOWLEDGEMENTS

We would like to thank Emanuele Bedeschi, Tommaso Polonelli, and Davide Brunelli for providing the framework which implements time synchronization on LoRaWAN hardware.

REFERENCES

[1] "LoRaWAN 1.1 Specification," LoRa Alliance, 2017.

[2] F. Adelantado et al., "Understanding the limits of LoRaWAN," IEEE Communications Magazine, vol. 55, no. 9, 2017, pp. 34–40.

[3] "EN 300 220-1 - V3.1.1," European Telecommunications Standards Institute (ETSI), 2017.

[4] A. Augustin, J. Yi, T. Clausen, and W. M. Townsley, "A study of LoRa: Long range & low power networks for the internet of things," Sensors, vol. 16, no. 9, 2016, p. 1466.

[5] B. Vejlgaard et al., "Interference impact on coverage and capacity for low power wide area IoT networks," in Wireless Communications and Networking Conference (WCNC), 2017 IEEE. IEEE, 2017, pp. 1–6.

[6] É. Morin, M. Maman, R. Guizzetti, and A. Duda, "Comparison of the device lifetime in wireless networks for the internet of things," IEEE Access, vol. 5, 2017, pp. 7097–7114.

[7] D.-Y. Kim and S. Kim, "Dual-channel medium access control of low power wide area networks considering traffic characteristics in IoE," Cluster Computing, vol. 20, no. 3, 2017, pp. 2375–2384.

[8] K.-H. Phung, H. Tran, Q. Nguyen, T. T. Huong, and T.-L. Nguyen, "Analysis and assessment of LoRaWAN," in Recent Advances in Signal Processing, Telecommunications & Computing (SigTelCom), 2018 2nd International Conference on. IEEE, 2018, pp. 241–246.

[9] B. Reynders, Q. Wang, P. Tuset-Peiro, X. Vilajosana, and S. Pollin, "Improving Reliability and Scalability of LoRaWANs Through Lightweight Scheduling," IEEE Internet of Things Journal, 2018.

[10] T. Polonelli, D. Brunelli, and L. Benini, "Slotted ALOHA Overlay on LoRaWAN – a Distributed Synchronization Approach," in IEEE International Conference on Embedded and Ubiquitous Computing (EUC 2018).

[11] C. Gu, R. Tan, X. Lou, and D. Niyato, "One-Hop Out-of-Band Control Planes for Low-Power Multi-Hop Wireless Networks," arXiv preprint arXiv:1712.06056, 2017.

[12] "SX1276/77/78/79 Datasheet," Semtech Corporation, 2017.

[13] "LoRaWAN 1.1 Regional Parameters," LoRa Alliance, 2017.

[14] N. Abramson, "THE ALOHA SYSTEM: another alternative for computer communications," in Proceedings of the November 17-19, 1970, fall joint computer conference. ACM, 1970, pp. 281–285.

[15] L. G. Roberts, "ALOHA packet system with and without slots and capture," ACM SIGCOMM Computer Communication Review, vol. 5, no. 2, 1975, pp. 28–42.

[16] "LoRa Server, open-source LoRaWAN network-server," https://www.loraserver.io/, [retrieved: September, 2018].

[17] "Docker," https://www.docker.com/, [retrieved: September, 2018].

[18] "Eclipse Mosquitto," https://mosquitto.org/, [retrieved: September, 2018].

[19] "Node-RED," https://nodered.org/, [retrieved: September, 2018].

[20] "LoRa network ," https://github.com/Lora-net, [retrieved: September, 2018].

Countermeasure to Human Recognition Error for Agent-based Human Tracking System

Masaru Shiozuka[†‡], Tappei Yotsumoto[†],
Kenichi Takahashi[‡], Masashi Nishiyama[‡], Takao Kawamura[‡], Kazunori Sugahara[‡]

[†]System Engineering Department,
Melco Power Systems Co. Ltd.
Kobe, Japan
email: {Shiozuka.Masaru@zd, Yotsumoto.Tappei@zb}.MitsubishiElectric.co.jp

[‡]Graduate School of Engineering,
Tottori University
Tottori, Japan
email: {takahashi, nishiyama, kawamura, sugahara }@tottori-u.ac.jp

Abstract—**Human monitoring systems are widely deployed in companies, schools and elsewhere for the prevention of crimes. Such systems require operators to monitor information sent from monitoring devices, such as cameras and/or beacon sensors. To reduce the burden of operators' work, we have proposed an automatic human tracking system based on mobile agent technologies. The system succeeded in tracking persons when Radio Frequency IDentifier (RFID) sensors were used as monitoring devices. However, it sometimes causes human recognition error when using a camera. In this paper, we propose a method to address human recognition error. In this method, an agent changes his/her behavior according to a distance computed from pictures taken by a camera. Experiments using the proposed method showed that the rate of successful human tracking improved even in an environment where human tracking error often occurred.**

Keywords-Human Tracking; Mobile Agent; Camera; Sensor.

I. INTRODUCTION

As security measures of companies and our daily lives, various kinds of systems, such as an entrance control system for monitoring suspicious persons, have been introduced. However, if the number of sensors and tracking targets increases, tracking all targets becomes difficult. Therefore, we propose a mobile agent-based tracking system using neighbor relations of sensors in the environment where each sensor is located discretely [1]-[3]. This system consists of sensors, tracking nodes, mobile agents and a monitoring terminal. The system uses cameras and/or beacons as sensors. In this system, a node with a sensor analyzes data received from its sensor, therefore, the processing load of data analysis is distributed in each node.

One agent has the features of one target person. The agent moves among nodes by detecting the features of the target person. An operator can know the location of the target by checking the location of its corresponding agent. Since sensors are installed in discrete locations, such as an entrance and passage crossings, a person is often not caught in any sensors. Therefore, we proposed a method to predict which sensor may catch the target person next [1]. The method calculates neighbor nodes of each sensor based on the value of each sensor's detection range, the map of the floor and the locations of the installed sensors. Since the method enables us to calculate neighbor nodes, the system can predict which sensor may catch the target person next.

The system, however, sometimes fails to track a target person due to the uncertainty of sensors. Even if the system uses RFID sensors, the system sometimes fails to receive a signal from a RFID tag. Therefore, we have proposed a method to find hidden neighbor relations [2]. In this method, when an agent loses a target, a new bypass is constructed between the node where the target is lost and the node where the target is found. This method can achieve continuous tracking of a person.

When beacons or RFID are used as sensors, a unique ID is included in the signal from the sensor. Thus, a person is uniquely identified; we do not need to consider human recognition error. A system using cameras, however, causes human recognition error. When the system uses cameras, the system extracts the features of a person from a picture taken by a camera. Here, the features cannot always be extracted accurately. For example, when tracking a person with brown hair color, his/her hair color may be recognized as black under the intensity of the light. As a result, it may cause human recognition error.

Several research studies on human tracking using cameras have been proposed. Wenxi et al. [4] propose a method to predict the migration route of a person in a crowd by using high-order particle filter and online-learning. Jin et al. [5] propose a group structure to improve tracking accuracy in a situation when the detection ranges of cameras overlap. These are not applicable to a situation where sensors are installed discretely. Babenko et al. [6] and Zhang et al. [7] propose an online classifier to improve tracking accuracy of a single object. Cho et al. [8] propose a method to create neighbor relationships among cameras automatically. However, they require a central server to collect and manage data from cameras. If the number of cameras increases, the system requires expensive machines because of the increased computational cost.

In this paper, we propose a method to address human tracking errors. When we use a camera as a sensor, human recognition error occurs because a person is identified by the difference (hereafter, called "distance") between the features of a target and features extracted from a picture taken by a camera. Therefore, a person who is not a target may be recognized as the target; a person who is a target may not be recognized as being the target. To address such cases, we introduce the concept of *reliability*. Since the reliability is calculated from several pictures, agents can keep tracking even if the distance computed from a picture is accidentally low or high. In experiments, we confirmed that it is possible to track persons with high accuracy even in a situation where human recognition error occurs.

The remainder of this paper is structured as follows. Section II introduces the overview of our human tracking system. Section III proposes a method to correct human recognition error. In Section IV, the proposed method is evaluated, and Section V concludes the paper.

II. Human Tracking System Based on Mobile Agent Technologies

We have developed an automatic human tracking system based on mobile agent technologies [1]. In this system, a mobile agent tracks one person called "target." All the targets are tracked by each agent automatically. An operator can know the location of each target by its corresponding agent.

A. System Overview

Figure 1 shows the overview of the system. The system consists of targets, sensors, nodes, agents and a monitoring terminal. A target is a human tracked by agents. A node has a data analysis function and an execution environment for agents. An agent moves across nodes along the migration of a target. The location of a target is displayed on the monitoring terminal through the location of the agent.

B. Tracking Flow

When a person comes into the detection range of the sensor, the corresponding node catches its signal. If the person is not tracked by any agent, the node generates an agent with his/her features e.g. facial features and beacon IDs. Hereafter, we call it as "a target agent." The target agent distributes its copies called "copy agents" to its neighbor nodes. Neighbor nodes are calculated by a method described in Section II-C. The set of a target agent and copy agents is called as "a group." When the target is detected in the group, a copy agent which detects the target becomes a new target agent. Thus, the target is tracked by the new target agent. The original target and copy agents are subsequently erased. The new target agent distributes its copy agents to its neighbor nodes. In these steps, a person can be tracked by agents.

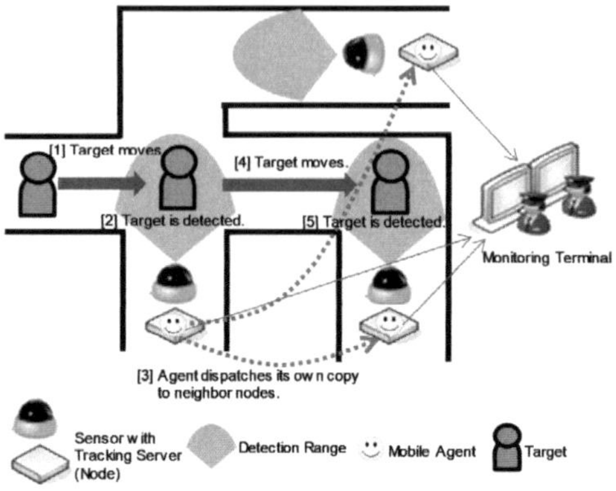

Figure 1. Overview of the Proposed System

C. Method to Calculate Neighbor Nodes

To predict which sensors may detect a target next, we have proposed a method which calculates neighbor nodes based on each sensor's detection range and the locations where sensors are installed. In this method, the following points are defined:

- Branch points (passage crossings): B_i
- Sensor points (sensor locations): S_i
- Detection points (between two branch points, between two sensor points and between a branch point and a sensor point): D_i

Matrix X of $|S| \times |P|$ is defined from the detection range of all sensors. S is a set of sensor points and P is a set of all points (branch points, sensor points and detection points). Element X_{ij} of matrix X is defined as (1).

$$X_{ij} = \begin{cases} 0, & \begin{array}{c} where\ detection\ range\ of\ sensor \\ S_i\ does\ not\ include\ point\ P_j. \end{array} \\ 1, & \begin{array}{c} where\ detection\ range\ of\ sensor \\ S_i\ includes\ point\ P_j. \end{array} \end{cases} \quad (1)$$

Next, we define an adjacency matrix Y of $|P| \times |P|$. Element Y_{ij} of matrix Y is defined as (2).

$$Y_{ij} = \begin{cases} 0, & \begin{array}{c} where\ point\ P_i\ and\ point\ P_j \\ are\ not\ neighboring\ each\ other. \end{array} \\ 1, & \begin{array}{c} where\ point\ \ P_i\ and\ point\ P_j \\ are\ neighboring\ each\ other. \end{array} \end{cases} \quad (2)$$

When $E_{ij} \geq 1$ in (3), the neighboring sensor exists $(n-1)$ points away from the detection range of sensor S_i.

$$E = X \cdot Y^n \cdot X^T \quad (3)$$

TABLE I. SENSORS' DETECTION RESULT AND REAL EVENT

Real Events / *Sensor*	*No Person Exists*	*Person P1 Exists*	*Person P2 Exists*	*Person P1 and P2 Exist*
Undetected	True Detection	Non-Detection	Non-Detection	Non-Detection
Person P1 is Detected	False Detection	True Detection	False Detection	True Detection and Non-Detection (※1)
Person P2 is Detected	False Detection	False Detection	True Detection	True Detection and Non-Detection (※1)
Person P1 and P2 are Detected	False Detection	True Detection and False Detection (※2)	True Detection and False Detection (※2)	True Detection

※1 One person is detected but another person is not detected.
※2 Other person except existing persons are detected
Note) False detection never occurs if we use a Beacon/RFID sensor

Even if the neighboring sensors can be calculated in (3), the number of points between the detection ranges of two sensors is unknown. In other words, n is unknown. Therefore, the points which are not included in the detection range of all sensors are eliminated from matrix X and Y. Matrix X' is generated from matrix X by eliminating all the points in column j that satisfy (4).

$$\sum_{k=i}^{m} X_{kj} = 0 \quad (4)$$

Further, X_{ik} is set to 1 if $X_{ij} = 1$ and $X_{jk} = 1$. This prevents a route from being cut off by the elimination of a point. Similarly, matrix Y' is generated from matrix Y by eliminating all the points in column j and row j. Then, the neighbor sensors can be calculated in (5).

$$E' = X' \cdot Y' \cdot X'^{T} \quad (5)$$

In (5), we can find all neighbor nodes calculated from all tracking route.

D. Issues To Be Tackled

The system can track a person continuously if sensors detect a target person correctly. However, a sensor has uncertainty, thus, it sometimes fails to detect a target.

Therefore, we have to tackle the uncertainty of the sensors. We, first, discuss the uncertainty of sensors by the comparison between a sensor's detection result and a real event, shown in Table I. Real events are put on the column, and sensors' detection results are on the row. In this table, "True Detection" means that a target is correctly detected. "False Detection" means that other person except existing person is detected. "Non-Detection" means that a target is not detected where the target exists. Tracking misses when "False Detection" or "Non-Detection" occurs.

When we use a beacon as a sensor, "False Detection" does not occur. Therefore, we have proposed a hidden neighbor relation in [2]. In experiments using the hidden neighbor relation, we have confirmed that the tracking accuracy improved. However, the problem of "False Detection" is remained. In the next section, we propose a method to improve tracking accuracy even if "False Detection" occurs.

TABLE II. EXAMPLE OF HUMAN RECOGNITION RESULTS

Input Picture	*Pictures Ordered by Distance*			
P1_Front	P2_Right	P1_Right	P3_Back	...
	2.760	3.208	3.476	...
P1_Left	P1_Right	P3_Back	P2_Right	...
	2.119	2.679	3.117	...

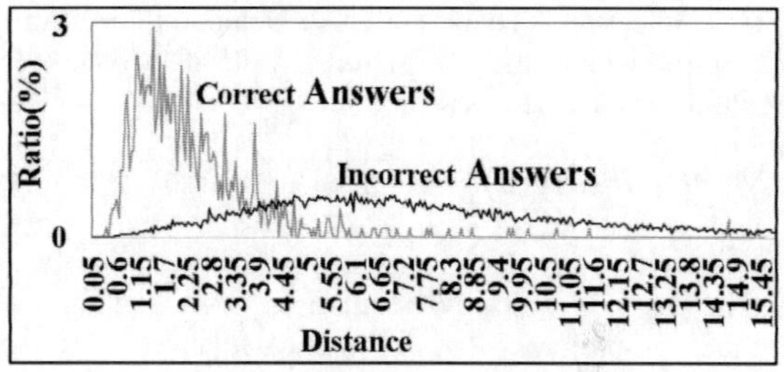

Figure 2. Distribution of Correct/Incorrect Answers

III. DEALING WITH TARGET RECOGNITION ERROR

When we use a camera as a sensor, target recognition error occurs because a person is not uniquely identified. Therefore, a person who is not a target may be recognized as the target; a person who is a target may not be recognized as the target. The former causes "False Detection", and the latter causes missing the target by "Non-Detection." Also, two or more persons may be recognized as the same target. In this section, we, first, explain an example of target recognition error.

A. Example of Target Recognition Error

As an example, we show a person recognition method proposed by Nishiyama [9]. It uses a picture database named SARC3D [10] included in PETA dataset [11]. The SARC3D consists of pictures of 50 different persons. Each person has four pictures taken from four directions, front, back, left and right. Therefore, the SARC3D has 200 pictures in total. 100 pictures are used as training data for parameters' setting. Table II shows a part of distance computed from an input picture and other pictures in remained 100 pictures. The smaller value means an input picture and other picture is similar. For example, P1_front picture (taken from the front of person P1) is most similar to P2_Right (taken from the right side of person P2), and second similar is P1_Right (take from the right side of person P1).

The distribution of distances are shown in Figure 2. Correct answer means the distance between two pictures of the same person. Incorrect answer means the distance between the pictures of other person. From Figure 2, we can see the distance of the same person tends to be low, and the distance of other person tends to be high. However, the distance of correct answers and incorrect answers overlap. Even if a distance is low, it is not always a correct answer. Even if a distance is high, it is not always an incorrect answer. In other words, when the distance between the pictures of other person becomes accidentally low, human recognition error occurs. This causes "False Detection."

B. Reliability

Each picture taken by a camera is certainly different even if they are the pictures of the same person. This sometimes causes that a distance computed from a person who is not a target is lower than a distance computed from a target person. As shown in Figure 2, the graphs of correct and incorrect answers have an overlapping part. That is, even if the distance is low, it may be an incorrect answer. This causes "False Detection." To avoid "False Detection," we introduce *reliability* which uses n pictures instead of one picture. Reliability is defined as (9).

$$reliabilitiy(n) = 1 - \prod_{i=1}^{n}(1 - P(x_i)) \quad (9)$$

In (9), x_i is a distance computed from a picture, n is a number of pictures used for the calculation of reliability. When n is 3, we use continuous three pictures taken by one camera to recognize a target or not. $P(n)$ is a function that returns a precision for a distance x_i. Since the function $P(n)$ depends on a person recognition method, we have to make function $P(n)$ based on a person recognition method. An agent recognizes a person as his/her target if equation (10) is satisfied.

$$reliability(n) > p_n \quad (10)$$

In (10), p_n is the threshold value. The threshold value enables us to control "False Detection" rate. If the threshold value p_n is high, "False Detection" decreases, but missing a target increases. The threshold value p_n is low, "False Detection" increases.

In addition, even if the "False Detection" rate is low, two or more agents which are tracking different targets may recognize the same person as their each targets. In this case, "False Detection" should occur except on one agent. Therefore, we adapt group expansion described in the next section without the decision of their target. In the same reason, we adapt group expansion when two or more different persons are recognized as the same target.

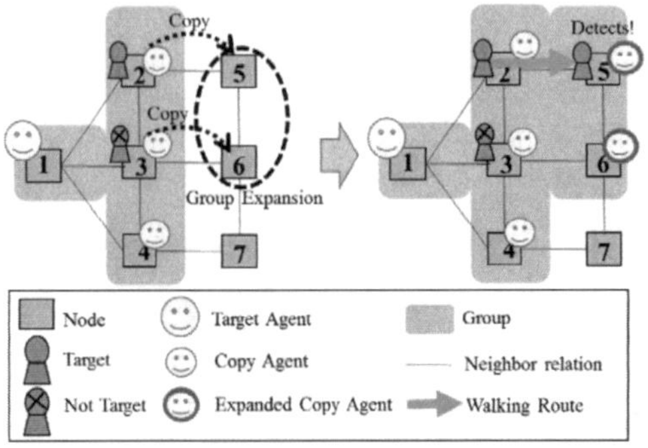

Figure 3. Example of Group Expansion

C. Group Expansion

If p_n is high, "False Detection" decreases, but missing a target increases. To decrease the problem of missing a target, we expand a group. A group consists of a target agent in a node which found a target last, and copy agents in its neighbor nodes. The agents try to find a target within their nodes. When an agent misses a target, the target may go out of the monitoring area covered by their nodes. Therefore, we expand a group to cover the outside of the monitoring area. An agent misses a target in the following cases.

- Case1: Non-Detection occurs.
- Case2: Reliability is less than a threshold value.
- Case3: Two or more different persons are recognized as the same target.
- Case4: Two or more agents which are tracking different persons recognized the same person as their target.

We do not mention Case 1 in this paper, since this case is already addressed in [2]. We, first, mention Case 3. Here, we suppose that a target agent stays in node 1, copy agents stay in node 2, 3 and 4 in Figure 3. Then, both agents in node 2 and 3 find target candidates. Since a target is one person, we cannot determine which person in node 2 or 3 is the target. Therefore, when the target moves to node 5 or 6, the agents lose the target. Then, a group is expanded to cover neighbor nodes of node 2 and 3 (node 5 and 6 in Figure 3). Since node 5 and 6 are monitored by group expansion, the target can be tracked continuously. In a similar way, a group is expanded in Case 4.

Case 2 is different from Case 3 and 4. We cannot find expanded nodes because there is no person who is likely to be a target. Therefore, we make a group expansion condition. The group expansion condition is defined as (11).

$$reliability(i) > p_i \ (0 < i < n) \quad (11)$$

An agent uses n pictures to calculate reliability. When reliability calculated from n pictures of the target is accidentally low, the agent recognizes the target as a non-target. In equation (11), pictures less than n are used as group expansion condition. Therefore, the group expansion condition is satisfied, if the distance of one picture is high. When the group expansion condition is satisfied at some, a group is expanded to cover its neighbor nodes. By group expansion, missing rate of a target can be reduced.

IV. Experiments

We implemented a simulator to evaluate our proposed method. In this simulator, we evaluated whether persons can be tracked correctly in situations where person recognition error occurs. As a picture recognition method, we use the person recognition method proposed in [9], but we can apply any other person recognition method.

A. Simulation Settings

Figure 4 shows the map used in this simulation. There are nine cameras installed in each node. Since our system is implemented in distributed manner, the number of cameras does not affect our system performance. Maximum eight persons are walking at the same time. Table III shows the walking route of each person. Each person moves between nodes in 5 seconds. For example, person P1 starts at node 1, reaches at node 2 in 5 seconds and finally reaches at node 9 in 40 seconds.

In this simulation, we fix n on 3, therefore, three pictures are used to calculate reliability. The threshold p_n is set up to be "False Detection" rate under 5%.

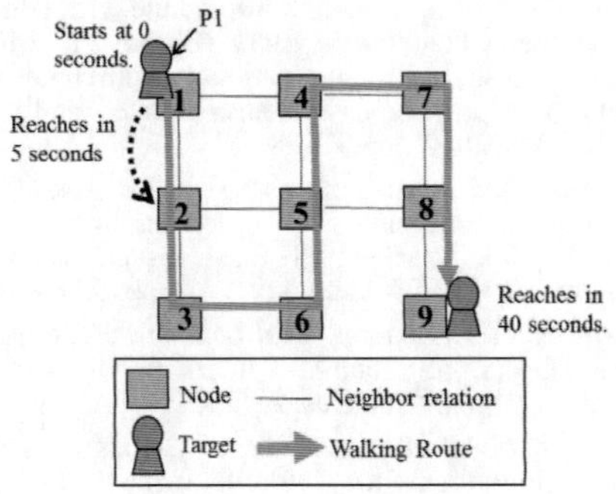

Figure 4. Simulation Map

TABLE III. WALKING ROUTE

Target ID	Walking Route
P1	1→2→3→6→5→4→7→8→9
P2	9→8→7→4→5→6→3→2→1
P3	3→2→1→4→5→6→9→8→7
P4	7→8→9→6→5→4→1→2→3
P5	1→4→7→8→5→2→3→6→9
P6	9→6→3→2→5→8→7→4→1
P7	3→6→9→8→5→2→1→4→7
P8	7→4→1→2→5→8→9→6→3

In this simulator, a distance computed from a picture is given as follows:

Rule1: If the target of an agent is in the detection range of a sensor, an agent randomly get a distance from the set of correct answers in Figure 2.

Rule2: If the target of an agent is not in the detection range of a sensor, an agent randomly get a distance from the set of incorrect answers in Figure 2.

In these rules, a target recognition error can be produced. For example, when a target is not appeared in, an agent gets distance from the set of incorrect answers according to rule 2. If the distance is low, the agent recognizes that the target is there even if the target does not exist. Then, a target recognition error occurs.

Regarding group expansion, we implemented Case 2 and 3 in Section III-C except Case 1 and 4.

B. Tracking Results of Two Persons

In this simulation, two persons, P1 and P2 are walking in the map at the same time. Figure 5 shows the tracking result of P1. We can see an agent can track P1 exactly behind 3 seconds. The reason of being 3 seconds behind is that 3 seconds are necessary to take three pictures. Figure 6 shows the tracking result of P2. When P2 moves to node 4, the reliability did not exceed the threshold p_n. Therefore, the agent cannot follow with P2. However, copy agents are distributed to node 1 and 5 (Figure 7) which are neighboring nodes of node 4, since the group expansion condition is satisfied at node 4. After that, when P2 moves to node 5, P2 is detected at node 5. As a result, the agent can continue the tracking.

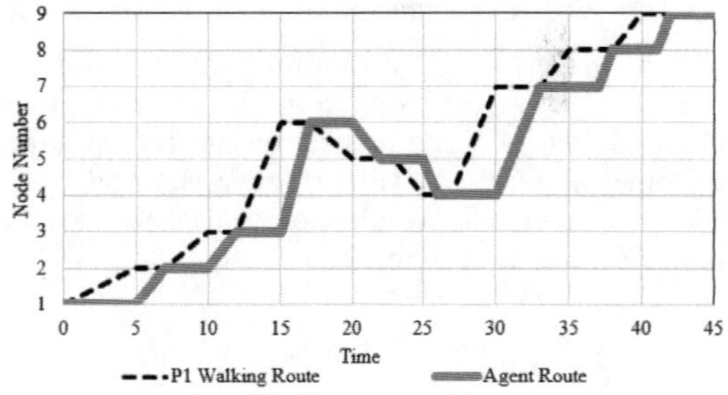

Figure 5. Tracking Result of P1

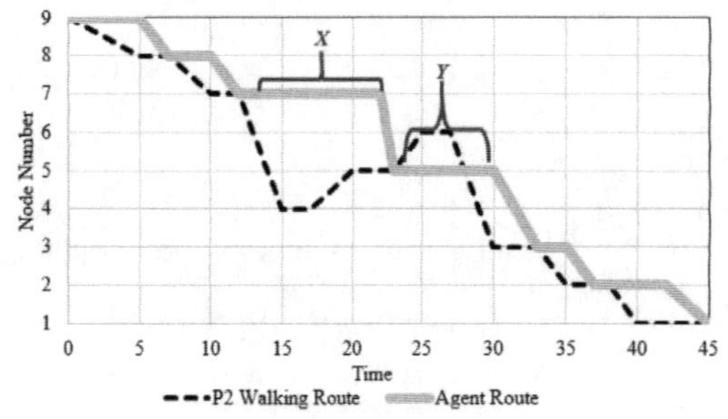

Figure 6. Tracking Result of P2

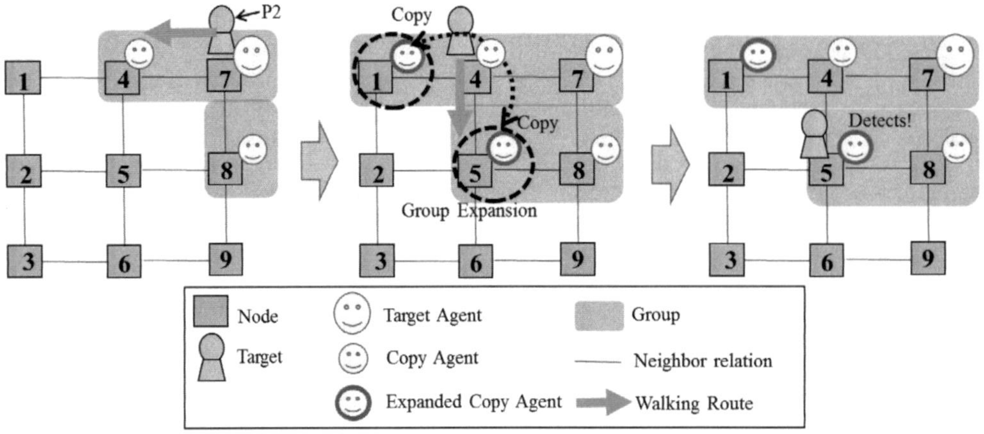

Figure 7. Tracking Results of P2 Group Expansion at Node 4

C. Tracking Results of One to Eight Persons

Figure 8 shows the tracking results of one to eight persons. The results are the average of 20 simulations. Figure 8 shows the rate of that a target and its corresponding agent are on same node. As shown in Figure 8, even if the number of targets increases, the tracking success rate does not fall. In the case of 8 persons, the tracking success rate is 92.5%. For comparison, we make a system that regards a person with smallest distance as a target. The comparative system regards a person with smallest distance as a target. In this comparative system, when the number of persons increases, the tracking success rate falls greatly. In the case of 8 persons, the tracking success rate is 67%.

V. CONCULSION AND FUTURE WORK

In this paper, we extend the method proposed in [2] to address target recognition error. In this extension, we introduced two concepts, reliability and group expansion. The simulation results show the success rate of target tracking is improved. We plan to evaluate the soundness of our method in a real environment.

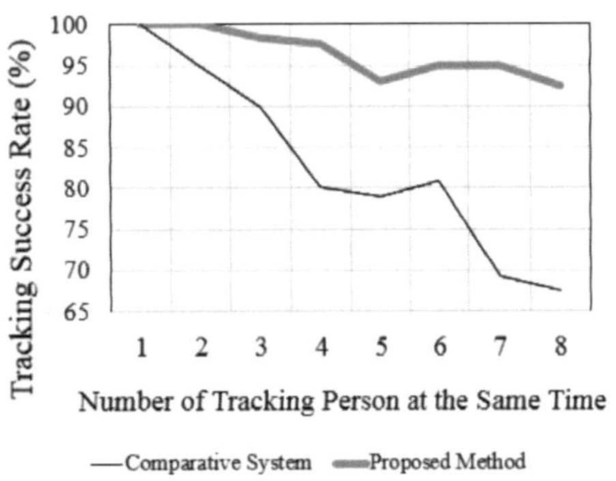

Figure 8. Tracking Result of One to Eight Persons

REFERENCES

[1] T. Yotsumoto et al., "Automatic Human Tracking System using Localized Neighbor Node Cluculation," Sensors & Transducers, Vol. 194, No. 11, pp. 54-61, 2015.

[2] T. Yotsumoto, M. Shiozuka, K. Takahashi, T. Kawamura, and K. Sugahara, "Hidden neighbor relations to tackle the uncertainness of sensors for anautomatic human tracking," 2017 Second IEEE International Conference on Electrical, Computer and Communication Technologies (ICECCT 2017), Coimbatore, India, pp. 690-696, 2017.

[3] M. Shiozuka, T. Yotsumoto, K. Takahashi, T. Kawamura, and K. Sugahara, "Implementation Example with Ultra-Small PCs for Human Tracking System Based on Mobile Agent Technologies," 11th International Conference on Mobile Ubiquitos Computing, Systems, Sercies and Technologies (UBICOMM2017), pp. 73-78.

[4] L. Wenxi, C. Antoni, L. Rynson, and M. Dinesh, "Leveraging long-term predictions and onlinelearning in agent-based multiple person tracking," IEEE Transactions on Circuits and Systems for Video Technology, 25.3, pp. 399-410, 2015.

[5] Z. Jin and B. Bhanu, "Multi-camera Pedestrian Tracking using Group Structure," International Conference on Distributed Smart Cameras, Article No. 2, 2014.

[6] B. Babenko, M.-H. Yang, and S. Belongie, "Robust Object Traccking with Online Multiple Instance Learning," IEEE Transactions on Pattern Analysis and Machine Intelligence, Vol. 33, Issue 8, pp. 1619-1632, 2011.

[7] L. Zhang and L. van der Maaten, "Preserving Structure in Model-Free Trackin," IEEE Transactions on Pattern Analysis and Machine Intelligence, Vol. 36, No. 4, pp. 756-769, 2014.

[8] Y.J. Cho, S.A. Kim, J.H. Park, K. Lee, and K.J. Yoon, "Joint Person Re-identification and Camera Network Topology Inference in Multiple Camera," arXiv:1710.00983, 2017.

[9] M. Nishiyama et al., "Person Re-identification using Co-occurrence Attributes of Physical and Adhered Human Characteristics," 23rd International Coference of Pattern Recognition (ICPR), pp. 2086-2091, 2016.

[10] SARC3D, http://www.openvisor.org/sarc3d.asp, September, 2018.

[11] Y. Deng, P. Luo, C. Loy, and X. Tang, "Pedestrian attribute recognition at far distance," ACM Multimedia, pp. 3-7, 2014.

Application of Machine Learning Techniques to Situational Risk Assessment Based on Accident Database

Ryuta Watanabe, Keisuke Yamazaki, Tsuyoshi Nakajima
Department of Information Science and Engineering
Shibaura Institute of Technology, SIT
Tokyo, Japan

e-mails: {ma18109, ma17123, tsnaka}@shibaura-it.ac.jp

Abstract— **It is challenging to prevent various kinds of offenses, such as bicycle theft or street snatching. Machine learning techniques, like Support Vector Machine (SVM) and Bayesian Network (BN), are considered to be promising technologies to assess the risk of such offenses. However, applying these technologies is not easy and some problems include preparation of missing data, providing reasons, and multi –level classification of risks. In this paper, we propose a method to solve these problems. We applied our proposed method on an example of risk information provision system on bicycle parking lots; the results showed the effectiveness of the proposed method.**

Keywords; Machine learning; Support Vector Machine; Bayesian Network; Risk Assessment.

I. INTRODUCTION

It is challenging to prevent various kinds of offenses, such as bicycle theft or street snatching. PredPol, which predicts crimes by using data of past offenses, has been used in the city of Santa Cruz, California, USA, and, as a result, contributed to decreasing the crime rate of that city [1].

The risk of accidents for a specified situation should be assessed using many factors, and so it is difficult to model crime occurrence mechanism mathematically. Machine learning techniques like Support Vector Machine (SVM) and Bayesian Network (BN) are considered to be promising technology for this purpose.

However, we have the following three problems for applying the techniques. The first problem is preparation of missing data. Machine learning techniques require as learning data both accident data that occurred in the past and non-accident data that did not occur. The problem is that, in general, non-accident data do not exist in the database, and, in addition, accident data in the database often have missing items in it. We should prepare such missing data and data items. The second problem is provision of reasons. Most machine learning techniques do not present reasons for the assessment results, which makes the user is doubtful of the results because he does not recognize why the situation is unsafe. The third problem is multi-level classification of risks. Machine learning techniques can classify the situation into safe or unsafe. Such a classification alone could not satisfy the user needs for determining what behavior to take. Although some techniques can provide the probability for the result, it is unlikely to be the real probability for the occurrence of the accidents due to the first problem.

We propose a method to solve the above three problems when using machine learning techniques to assess the risk of a specified situation based on accident database. As target machine learning techniques, we use SVM [2] and BN [3].

The rest of the paper is structured as follows. Section II describes an Internet of Things (IoT) system, as an example to which the proposed method is applied. Section III addresses the three problems, and the Section IV provides the method for solving them. We conclude the work in Section V.

II. A RISK INFORMATION PROVISION SYSTEM ON BICYCLE PARKING LOTS

This section describes an IoT system, as an example to which the proposed method is applied: Risk information provision system on bicycle parking lots [4], called RaBiPL.

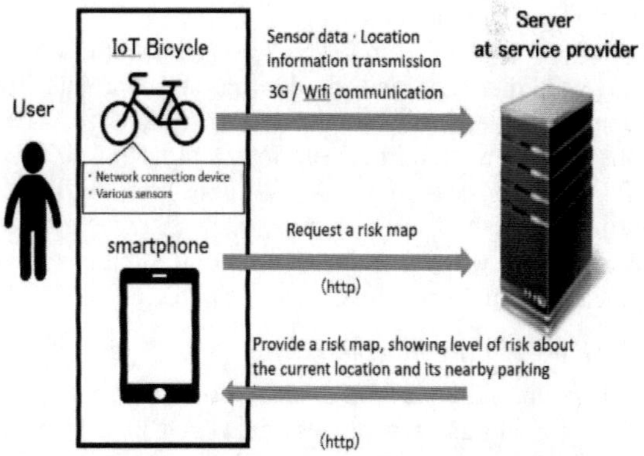

Figure 1. Risk information provision system on bicycle parking lots (RabiPL)

Figure 1 shows what devices the system uses and how it works. The system provides risk information for a specified situation to prevent from bicycle theft. This system works with IoT bicycles [5], which have various sensors and 3G/WiFi connection. The server of the system at the service provider site gets environmental information, based on which it assesses the risk of theft for the situation. The results are provided to the user's smart device upon request. The server performs the risk assessment by analyzing the environmental information stored on the server.

TABLE I. ENVIRONMENT INFORMATION

Information to be obtained		Method
1) Properties of bicycle		Obtaining from the information the user registered
2) Regional characteristics		Using publicly available database to extract information on specific region (using GPS sensor)
3) Time (hour, day, season)		Obtaining from the time the user request issues
4) Information on surrounding environment	Pedestrian traffic	Using human detection rate (using human sensor)
	Weather	Querying the weather service about weather information on specific region (using GPS sensor)
	Lightness	Obtaining directly from sensor data (using illuminance sensor)
	Temperature and humidity	Obtaining directly from sensor data (using temperature / humidity sensor)

Environmental information includes:
(1) Properties of bicycle, such as model and price,
(2) Regional characteristics, such as the number of crimes,
(3) Time, such as time zone and day of week, and
(4) Surrounding environment, such as pedestrian traffic.

TI shows the four types of environmental information and the method to obtain it.

III. RESEARCH PROBLEMS

A. *Problem1: Preparetion of missing data*

Machine learning techniques require as learning data both accident data that occurred in the past and non-accident data that did not occur.

The problem is that in general, non-accident data do not exist in the database, and in addition, accident data in the database often have missing items in the data.

In the case of RabiPL, their victims report many bicycle thefts, and their data are available on the Web [6], but each data may have missing elements, such as bicycle's color, and weather in which it occurred. Of course, there is no data for the situation where bicycle thefts did not occur.

B. *Problem2: Provision of reasons*

Most machine learning techniques do not present reasons for the assessment results, which makes the user doubtful of the results because he does not recognize why the situation is unsafe.

In the case of RabiPL, if the system informs its user that the risk that bicycle theft will occur in his situation is high, only the result may not convince him to stop parking there.

Problem3: Multi-Level Classification of risks

Machine learning techniques can classify the situation into safe or unsafe. Such a classification alone could not satisfy the user needs for determining his behavior to take.

Although some techniques provide probability of the result, it is not a true value for the accidents. Therefore, it is necessary to show how high the risk is at multiple levels so that the user can easily decide what to do.

In the case of RabiPL, users want to know that his situation is not risky, a little risky, risky, or very risky so that he can make a decision on whether he will park or not, considering his need to do it.

IV. PROPOSED METHOD AND ITS APPLICATION

A. *Preparation of missing data*

We propose a method to solve the three problems mentioned in Section 3 and describe its application.

1) *Proposed method for preparation of missing data*

To solve Problem 1, we propose the following method to prepare accident data with missing data items and non-accident data.

- Missing data items in accident data:
  - What can be obtained with sensors: field work
  - Others: randomly created value
- Non-accident data (the same number as that of the accident data) :
  - Place (Randomly selected from where the accidents did not occurred)
  - Time (Randomly selected)
  - Others:
    - What can be obtained with sensors: field work
    - Others: randomly created value

"Field work" is to go where the specified situation can be realized to collect data by using sensors.

2) *Application to RabiPL*

- Missing data items for theft occurrence data:
  - Using the theft data on the Web [6]
  - Obtaining regional characteristics from a Web service by searching by the current location
  - Missing data:
    - Information on surrounding environment (traffic lights, illuminance, etc.): obtaining the data items by "field work" at the place where theft occurred
- Non-theft occurrence environment data:
  - Randomly selecting the same number of non-theft data where no theft occurred in the publicly available list of the bicycle parking lots
  - Getting location of the lots
  - Randomly selecting time and properties of the bicycle
    - Obtaining regional characteristics from location with the Web service
    - Collecting non-theft environmental data with field work

In the "field work", we collected data for five minutes to use the average value of the measured sensor data.

Using the above method, we made 25 theft occurrence environmental data in the perfect form and created 25 non-theft data, and we were able to prepare 50 cases in total.

B. Provision of reasons

To solve Problem 2, we propose the following method to provide reasons and describe its application.

1) Proposed method for providing reasons

We adopt Bayesian Network [3] as the applied machine learning technique, which is a probabilistic graphical model (a type of statistical model) that represents a set of variables and their conditional dependencies via a Directed Acyclic Graph (DAG). [6].

When using BN, intermediate nodes are chosen to explain the reasons for the assessment results, which have been an established common sense through statistical analysis conducted so far.

Then, after the assessment, choose the factors from those with higher risks than thresholds as the reason of the assessment.

2) Application to RabiPL

From the analysis on the theft of bicycles [7], we select the following four major factors as the intermediate nodes of the BN.

- Existence of those who want to steal
- Low possibility of detection
- Attractiveness of the bicycle
- Easiness to steal

Then, we link all the factors to the intermediate nodes. With regard to RabiPL, we linked all the environmental information items to the four intermediate nodes, as shown in Figure 2.

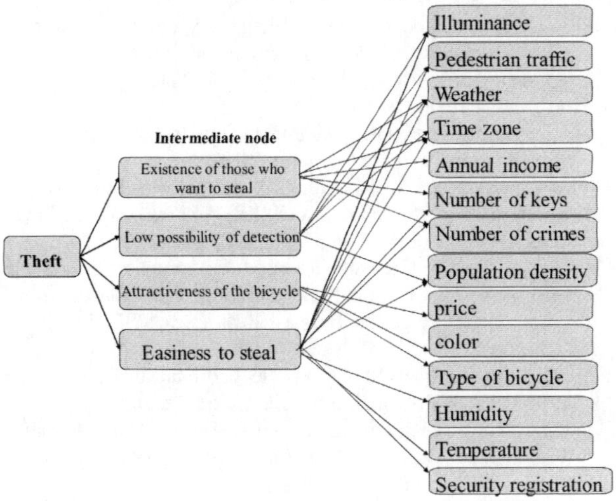

Figure 2.Relationship between intermediate nodes and environment information

Figure 3 shows an example to show the reason of the assessment result.

- The user wants to know why theft risk is high.
- The system selects the intermediate nodes that are the major contributors of the result. In this case, two nodes: "Low possibility of detection" and "Easiness to steal" are chosen.
- The system selects the environmental information items that contribute to the probability of the intermediate nodes and exceed the threshold. In Figure 4, two items: "Pedestrian traffic" and "Time zone" are chosen.

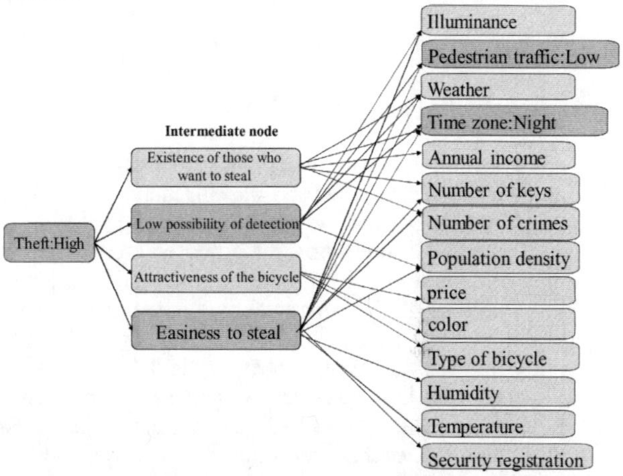

Figure 3.Relationship between intermediate nodes and environment information 2

- The system provides abstract and detailed reasons for the user, by using the intermediate nodes and environmental information items, as shown in Figure 4.

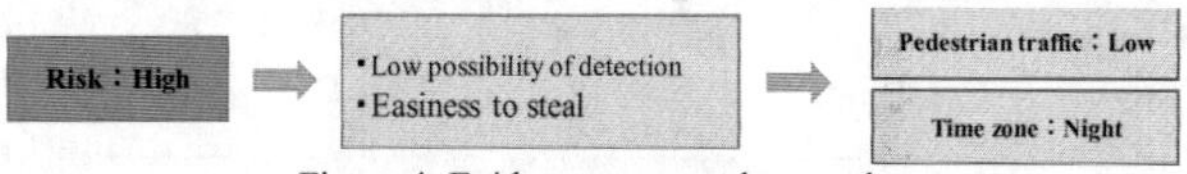

Figure 4. Evidence presented example

C. Multi-Level classification of risks

To solve Problem 3, we propose the following method to provide multi-level classification of risks and describe its application.

1) Proposed method for multi level risk classification

We also adopt Bayesian Network as the applied machine learning technique, which provides a probability value with the result. As mentioned before, the value is not the real probability of the occurrence of the accidents because of the Problem 1.

Therefore, we propose the following method to classify the result into *N* levels based on its probability value.

n: the number of data items.

d_k : k th data item (k =1, . . . , n)

a) Create a sequence S_d by sorting in descending order of probability values

$$S_d = (d_1, d_2, \cdots, d_n)$$

Where $P(d_i) < P(d_{i+1})$

b) Divide the sequence into N as follows.

$$S_i = (d_{l^i}, \cdots, d_{m^i})$$

Where $i = 1, \ldots, N$

$$l^i < \frac{n}{N}(i-1)$$

$$m^i \geq \frac{n}{N} i$$

c) Let a data d be at level K when satisfying the following equation.

$$P(d_{m^{k-1}}) < P(d) \leq P(d_{m^k})$$

Where $P(d_{m^0}) = 0$

$$P(d_{m^N}) = 100$$

2) Application to RabiPL

In the case of RabiPL, we set the number of classification level to three: high, medium and low. The number of training data used was 30, including 15 theft data and 15 non-theft data.

Figure 5 illustrates how the proposed method determines threshold values to classify a probability value into a certain level. In Figure 5, the horizontal axis is the probability value of the learning data: d_i, and the vertical axis is the sequence number i. The sequence numbers: 10 and 20 divide the set of learning data into three levels, and so the corresponding probability values P1 and P2 can be used as the thresholds that classify a probability value into a certain level: low, medium, or high.

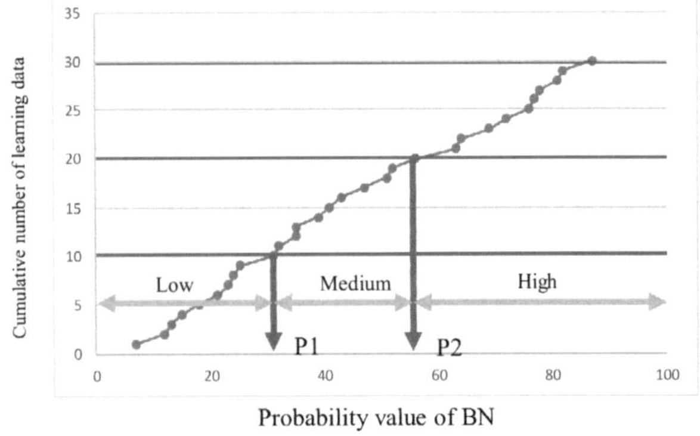

Figure 5. How to determine the risk

We use six theft data and four non-theft data as test data to evaluate the assessment results using the thresholds that the proposed method determined. Based on this data, the evaluation was made on multiple levels of risk determination.

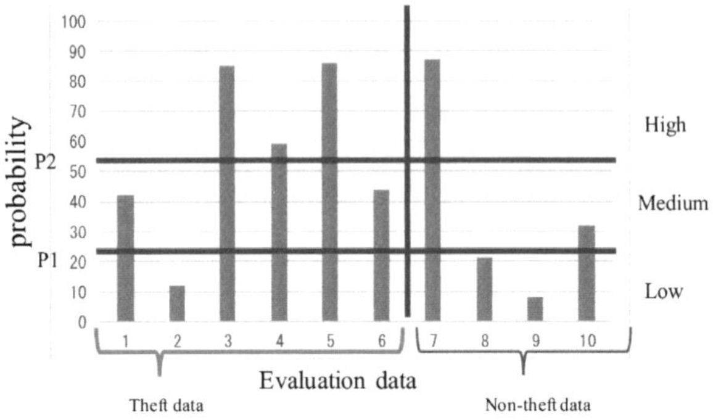

Figure 6. Evaluation on risk assessment

Figure 6 shows the probability values for test data, in which data 1-6 are theft data and data 7-10 are non-theft data. From this result, five out of six theft data are classified into high or medium level, and three out of four non-theft data are classified into low or medium level. This result shows this method gives us a good classifier of the inferred results.

V. CONCLUSION

We proposed a set of methods to solve three problems that machine learning techniques have when they are applied to the risk assessment based on accident database. We applied the proposed methods to risk assessment for bicycle theft, which shows a good performance of the methods, although a relatively small number of data are used for the experiment.

The proposed methods should be applied to risk assessment for other types of accidents so that it can prove useful more widely.

REFERENCES

[1] E. Huet, "Server And Protect: Predictive Policing Firm PredPol Promises To Map Crime Before It Happens," Forbes, No. 2, 2015.

[2] C. C. Chung, and C. Lin, "LIBSVM: a library for support vector machines," ACM transactions on intelligent systems and technology, Vol. 2, No. 3, Article 27, 2011

[3] Bayesian Network http://nlp.dse.ibaraki.ac.jp/~shinnou/zemi2006/zemi06-bayesnet.html [accessed October 2018]

[4] K. Yamazaki and T. Nakajima, "A risk information provision system on bicycle parking lots," IEEE International Congress on Internet of Things (ICIOT), pp. 162-165, 2017.

[5] C. Kiefer and F. Behrendt, "Smart e-bike monitoring system: real-time open source and open hardware GPS assistance and sensor data for electrically-assisted bicycles," IET Intelligent Transport Systems, Vol. 10, No. 2, pp. 79-88, 2016.

[6] CSI bicycle police 24 hour: bicycle theft map (in Japanese): http://www.cycle-search.info/csi/tabid/56/Default.aspx.

[7] S. D. Johnson, A. Sidebottom, and A. Thorpe, "Bicycle theft," Washington, DC: US Department of Justice, Office of Community Oriented Policing Services, 2008.

Wearable Spirometry: Using Integrated Environment Sensor for Breath Measurement

Alejandro Baucells Costa, Bo Zhou, Orkhan Amiraslanov and Paul Lukowicz
German Research Center for Artificial Intelligence (DFKI), Kaiserslautern, Germany
Technical University of Kaiserslautern, Kaiserslautern, Germany
{Alejandro.Baucells_Costa, Bo.Zhou, Orkhan.Amiraslanov, Paul.Lukowicz}@dfki.de

***Abstract*—In this work, we present and evaluate a concept for using an integrated environment sensor as a wearable spirometer. Unlike a standard spirometer that by design is fairly bulky, our device can be unobtrusively integrated into various configurations suitable for long-term use in everyday settings (open headset, regular face mask, and professional sports mask). The sensor measures the transient change in air pressure, humidity and temperature in front of wearers' mouth and nostrils. We present our hardware design and signal analysis methods needed to extract breathing rate information. We compare the results with a standard spirometer. Moreover, a calibration between the BME280 sensor and the spirometer is performed, having both working in parallel. We show that our approach is able to distinguish between normal breaths and deep breaths, as well as to capture the period and magnitude of the breath cycles, with a wearable device that can be used in everyday scenarios, as well as sport activities. The classification accuracy is 96% in face mask settings and 82% in an open headset setting. We also show that the sensor is able to approximate air volume by comparing the sensor's pressure channel to the spirometer's flow rate results.**

Keywords*–*Wearable technology; Head-mounted sensing; Spirometry; Respiration detection.

I. INTRODUCTION

Nowadays, wearable devices have a wide range of capabilities to monitor users' vitals and physical activities, such as heart rate and the number of steps taken; however, there has been a lack of emphasis on breathing detection during everyday scenarios.

Spirometry is an important established medical procedure to determine lung capacity and oxygen intake [1]. Studies have shown oxygen intake has a direct correlation with body composition and physical conditioning, such as cardio-respiratory performance [2][3]. Spirometry is important not only in physical fitness related activities but also in one's daily professional life.

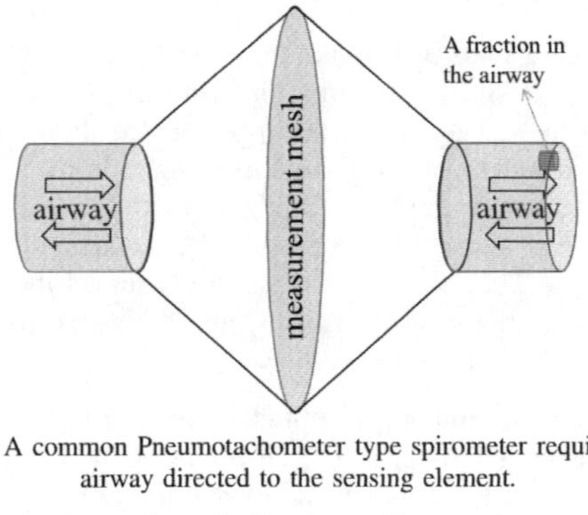

Figure 1. A common Pneumotachometer type spirometer requires all the airway directed to the sensing element.

Sigh rate is a clear indication of mental stress [4], and sufficient deep breathing can also effectively reduce stress and anxiety [5][6]. Lung capacity is also an indicator of development or stage of recovery of various illness [7][8].

However, all of the spirometry is carried out under a testing environment such as in a lab or clinic. As mentioned in various studies, such an environment cannot fully reflect every aspect of the participants' daily life [9]. The traditional digital pneumotachometer spirometer requires a fine mesh of typically 7 cm in diameter as the sensing element, as well as a mouthpiece that directs all the airflow into the sensing element, as illustrated in Figure 1. This is because the standardization of spirometry requires a laminar airflow passage that has a total resistance to the airflow at $14L \cdot s^{-1}$ smaller than $1.5cmH_2O \cdot L^{-1} \cdot s^{-1}$, considering any mechanical structure between the person and the sensing element including tubing, valves, filters, etc., as well as water vapor condensation [1]. Therefore, it is not practical to transform the traditional spirometer into a wearable device.

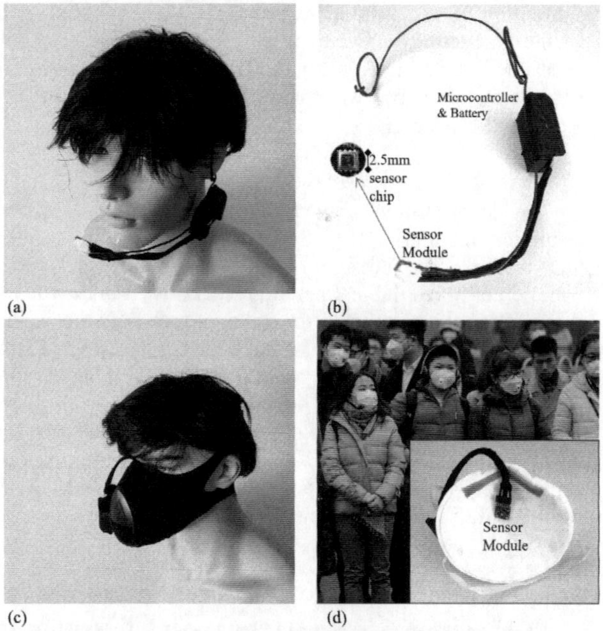

Figure 2. (a) (b) prototype as an open-air headset. (c) prototype fitted into a professional training mask (TRAINING MASK 3.0). (d) prototype fitted into a regular dust respirator (3M 8710E) [10].

The contribution of this work is three-fold:

- We have developed a wearable system to continuously monitor respiration using a small atmosphere monitoring Integrated-Circuit (IC) sensor.
- We compare our system with an off-the-shelf hand-held spirometer. The result proves there is a consistent relationship between the two different sensors during breathing.

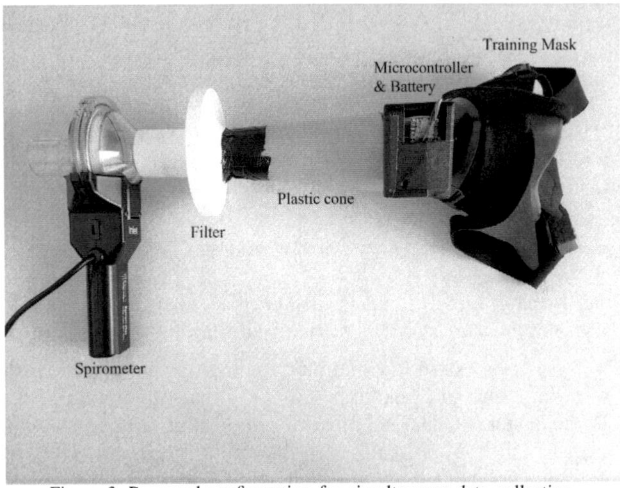

Figure 3. Proposed configuration for simultaneous data collection.

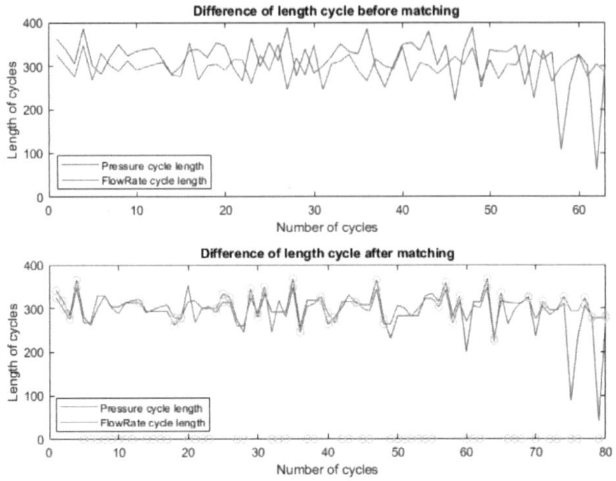

Figure 4. A difference of length cycle before vs. after thresholding

- We demonstrate that our system alone is capable of detecting breathing instances, and recognizing between normal and deep breaths.

The rest of the paper is structured as follows: In Section II, the state-of-the-art is reviewed. In Section III, the form factors of this work are described. In Section IV, the hardware and the configuration of the system are described. In Section V, we explain the first of the performed studies regarding the calibration of the system: experiments, data processing, and results. In Section VI, we expose and explain a use case study: experiments, data processing, and results. Finally, in Section VII, we conclude our work and mention new ideas to further evaluate the system.

II. Related Work

A wide range of wearable technologies is being developed in respiratory monitoring [11]. Some examples are belt transducers that measure the change of chest perimeter such as the commercially available Pneumotrace II by AD Instruments; sternum or belly positioned smartphones recording the accelerometric signals [12]; sound based wheeze detection [13] and breathing rate detection [14]; and deriving breathing rate from pulse oximetry [15]. However, as the sensors are not directly positioned in the air flow passage, most of the modalities focus on breathing rate and not on air volume during the respiration act, and are prone to noise and motion caused influences, thus most of the studies conducted require the wearers to remain still.

III. Form Factors

In this work, we measure the parameters of a fraction from the airflow including pressure, temperature, and humidity. These physical parameters can be measured by miniature integrated sensors, such as the Bosch BME280 with the dimension of 2.5 mm-by-2.5 mm (Figure 2(d)).

There are already several form factors where the sensors can be integrated. In many professional workplaces, there are slim headsets that position a small microphone in front of the mouth. Particularly in Asia, respiratory masks are commonly used to fend off pollen, epidemic, and pollution. While the acceptance of such surgical masks may be a matter of debate in other cultures, fashionable designs are already emerging to improve the acceptance, such as Vogmask and Airinum. In sports, there are also training masks that restricts the air intake to increase the training intensity, such as Training Mask [16] in Figure 2(c).

IV. Prototype

We integrate the small BME280 sensor (Bosch) in each of these form factors to examine the output as the wearers do normal and deep breathing. The different settings (headset, training mask and cotton mask) are shown in Figure 2. In the headset case, the airflow out of the mouth and nostril are not directed to be focused on the sensor; for both of the masks, the sensor is in a closed chamber. The cotton mask has a filtering effect on both the inflow and outflow of air. The training mask does not have a filter, but an adjustable valve.

The system consists of a BME280 sensor measuring pressure (units in Pascal); temperature (units in Celsius) and relative humidity (units in percent) (Figure 2(d)). In our pilot study prototype, we use an Adafruit BME280 module. But the actual sensor measures only 2.5 mm, which can be easily integrated into any headpiece/mouthpiece form factors. The sensor readout is controlled by an ATMEL microcontroller through an I2C bus. The microcontroller then communicates with an RN42 module via UART, forwarding the data to an Android application for visualization and recording sensor data.

V. System Calibration

A. Experiment

Our goal is to investigate how the sensor data relates to an off-the-shelf spirometer in estimating the volume of air. For that reason, we are interested in capturing the actual breathed volume from both sensing systems running in parallel. In Figure 3, the proposed configuration is depicted, which consists of the spirometer and the training mask connected to each other using a plastic cone sealed on both extremes by a black tape. To evaluate this setup, 5 participants are asked to perform the following 4 experiments:

1) 3 seconds inhale, 3 seconds exhale,
2) 3 seconds inhale, 3 seconds retaining the breath, 3 seconds exhale and 3 more seconds sustaining. The whole sequence is considered a cycle,
3) monitoring breathing while watching a video,

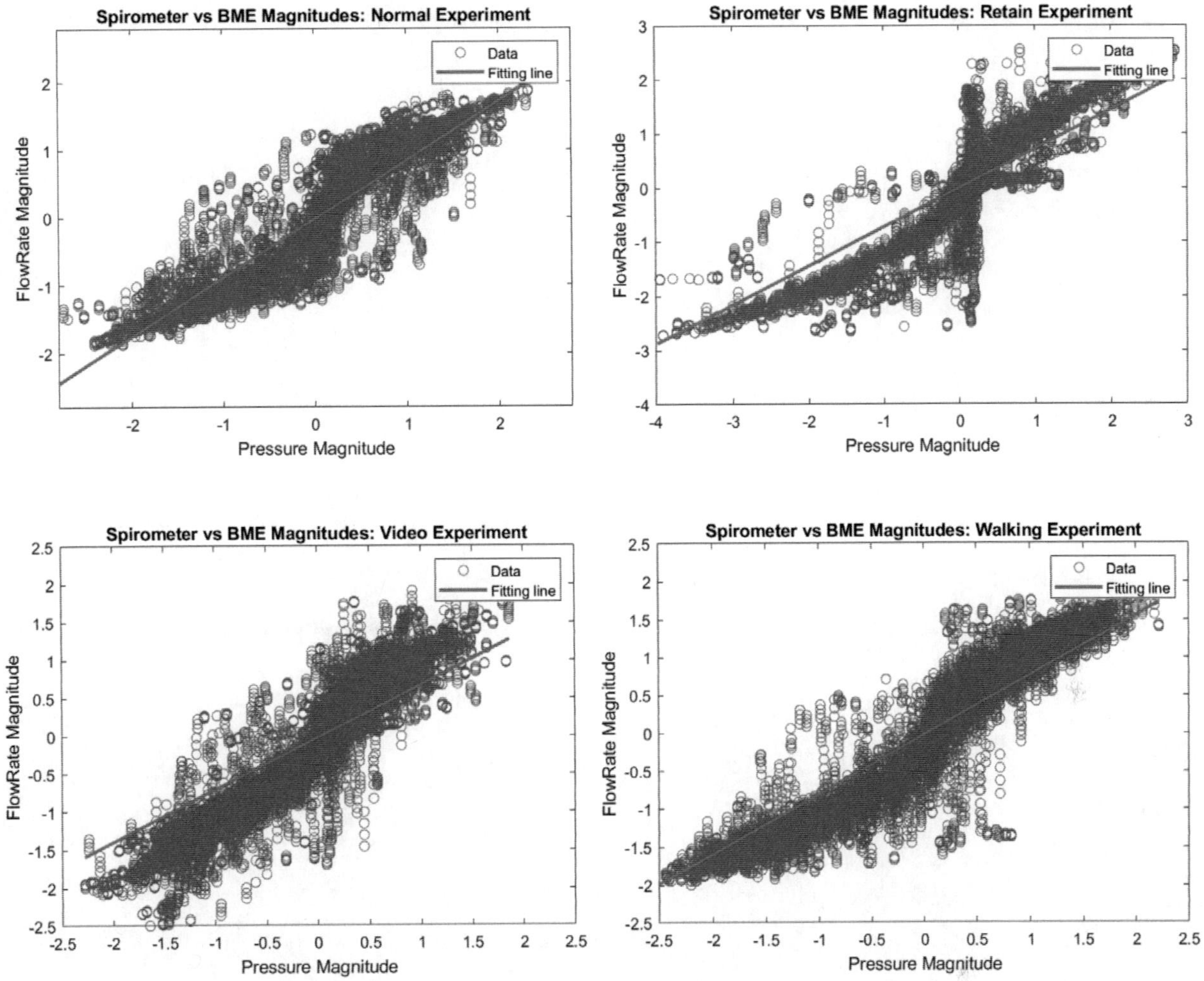

Figure 5. Magnitude relation between spirometry and BME sensor for participant 1

4) monitoring breathing while walking outdoors.

The height range of the participants is between 160 cm and 190 cm, and the weight ranges from 52.3 kg and 100 kg.

TABLE I. MAGNITUDE RELATION PARAMETERS FOR ALL PARTICIPANTS AND EXPERIMENTS

Participant	Experiment 1	Experiment 2	Experiment 3	Experiment 4
1	std=0.328 slope=0.931 mar=0.234	std=0.442 slope=0.897 mar=0.307	std=0.310 slope=0.806 mar=0.222	std=0.278 slope=0.951 mar=0.1970
2	std=0.380 slope=0.896 mar=0.260	std=0.553 slope=0.933 mar=0.438	std=0.235 slope=0.954 mar=0.1503	std=0.292 slope=0.923 mar=0.192
3	std=0.166 slope=0.976 mar=0.128	std=0.260 slope=0.937 mar=0.176	std=0.174 slope=0.958 mar=0.118	std=0.254 slope=0.943 mar=0.166
4	std=0.6478 slope=0.751 mar=0.437	std=0.524 slope=0.793 mar=0.432	std=0.470 slope=0.772 mar=0.345	std=0.390 slope=0.900 mar=0.2711
5	std=0.531 slope=0.822 mar=0.328	std=0.344 slope=1.10 mar=0.244	- - -	std=0.245 slope=0.941 mar=0.181

For a more precise measure of the breathed volume, we let the users perform these 4 experiments using the mask with the sensor on it and the spirometer in parallel so that the two sensors can simultaneously capture the sequences of breathing cycles. All the experiments are recorded for 7 minutes. The Experiment 1 and 2 are performed with help of an Android application, which is intended to guide the users throughout a series of breathing routines for calming, relaxing or helping against stress. It is necessary to mention that the application has been only used to provide a visual guide to the participants, but the sequences described in there have not been followed accordingly. The third experiment is recorded while watching a video and the latest, walking outdoors. The latter two do not follow any determined cycle, only normal breath events are captured. The participants are asked to perform three fast initial exhalations as a synchronization point to facilitate the posterior analysis of the signals.

B. Calibration Data Processing

Since the study involves multiple units, every experiment recording is normalized so that the average value is 0 and the standard deviation is 1.

The fact that the BME280 sensor and spirometer are placed at different locations in the airway passage may cause the signals from the two instruments to differ from each other. Especially the BME280 may be facing the nostrils and the mouth of the user in a different location and angle, because the facial structure of everyone is different. This may also contribute to deviations of the signal quality across participants.

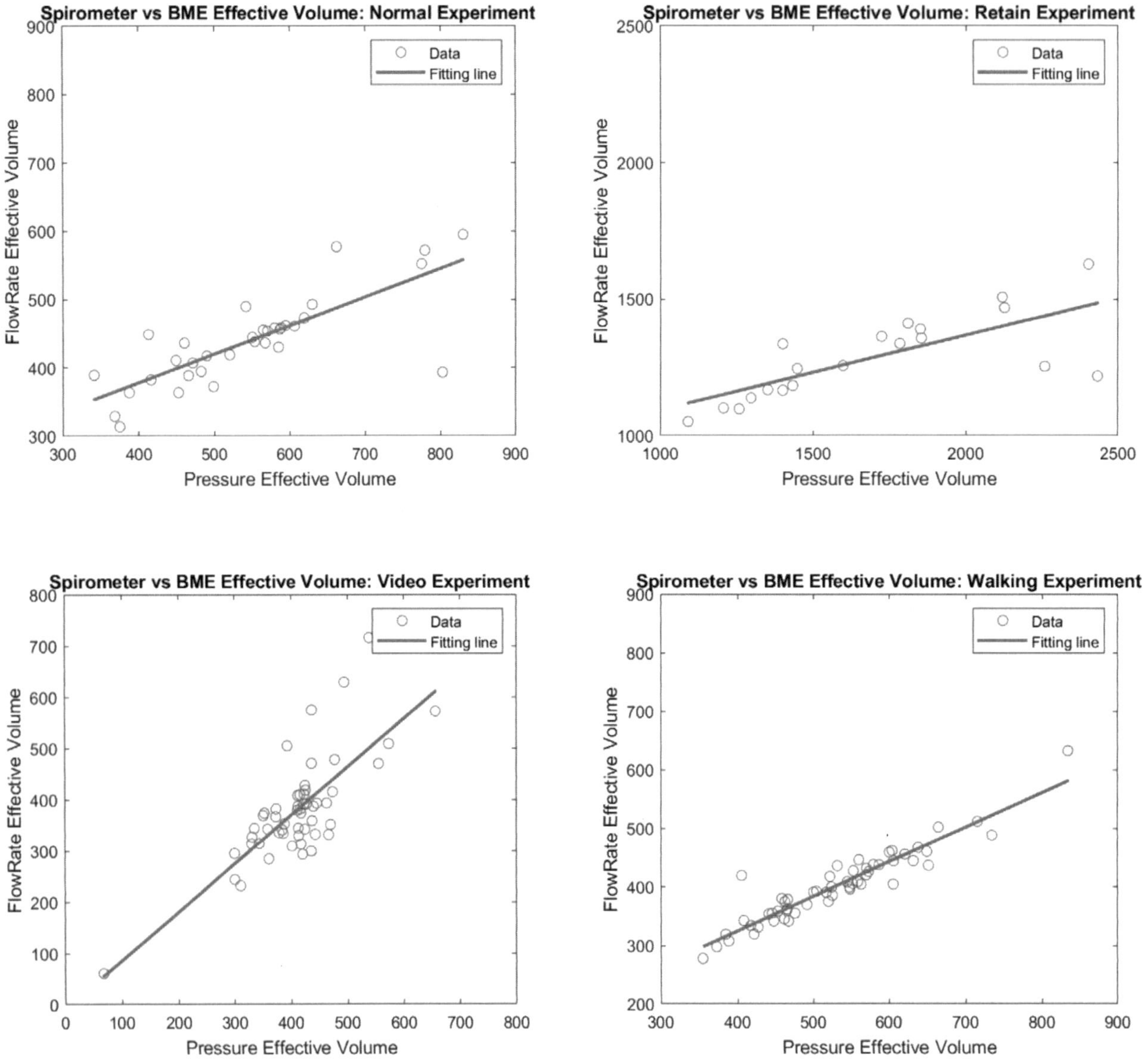

Figure 6. Effective volume relation between spirometry and BME sensor for participant 1

We chose the pressure sensor channel because it measures a similar physical parameter to the spirometer. Due to de-synchronization between the two sensors, a previous processing of the signals is necessary in order to compare the two sensors regarding matching breathing cycles. The spirometer and BME280 sensor signals are normalized and interpolated, matching their different time steps. We apply simple average filtering to remove small fluctuations in the signal samples. Then, the signals are segmented by peak detection: positive and negative peaks are located based on a prominence threshold of 20% of the signal's standard deviation. From the detected peaks, we calculate the length between each negative peak location corresponding to a breath cycle. An example is shown in Figure 4 (top). Due to interpolation, the cycles might not be perfectly aligned so a subtraction of this delay is needed, making the length of cycles from both sensors match better.

Then, we want to match the cycles that have similar length in both sensors. But there may be missing or false positive cycles in either sensor, therefore the solution is to find similar patterns in the change of cycles in both sensors. Thus *Dynamic Time Warping (DTW)* is used to match the patterns in the change of cycle lengths by finding the best matches. The result is also shown in Figure 4 (bottom). From the DTW result, it is obvious that while some cycles match exactly, some have greater differences. Except for the cases where the two cycles are actual different events, this may also be caused by the fact that from one sensor, one cycle is repeated by the DTW to 'stretch' this point so that later patterns can match the other sensor. An empirical threshold is set to eliminate those cycles whose distance is not reasonable. In Figure 4, the green marks on the plot indicate the cycles accepted by the threshold, and those at zero are rejected.

After this data processing, most of the accepted cycles are matching each other. Figure 7 illustrates 10 cycles of both sensors cycles after processing.

C. Results

Once subtraction for alignment and threshold for outlier elimination have been set, we extract each of those acceptable cycles to perform a deeper analysis. Those selected ones are once again interpolated and plotted. For a clearer picture of their correlation, we plot the magnitude of the pressure channel (BME280) against the magnitude of the flow rate (spirometer), resulting in Figure 5. Every point corresponds to a sensor sample. A clear positive relation is noticeable for all 4 cases. Around 0 there is a vertical belt area, where a large dispersion caused by airflow delay from the BME280 sensor's location to the spirometer, and misalignment between the two sensors, making the variance around that area larger than in the regions located on the extremes. It is especially visible in the retain experiment. Thus this vertical belt is removed in the following evaluations.

We use linear fitting within each experiment's BME280 sensor' pressure channel and spirometer's flow rate scatter plot. The vertical distance from a sensor sample point to the fitting line is the residual, which tells us how far the flow rate value of this point is away from the fitting line with the same pressure value. We use the mean value of the absolute residuals (*mar*) as a measure of how dispersed the data is away from the fitting line.

In Table I, the values for all 5 participants and the 4 experiments are depicted. Due to faulty hardware, experiment 3 for participant 5 failed.

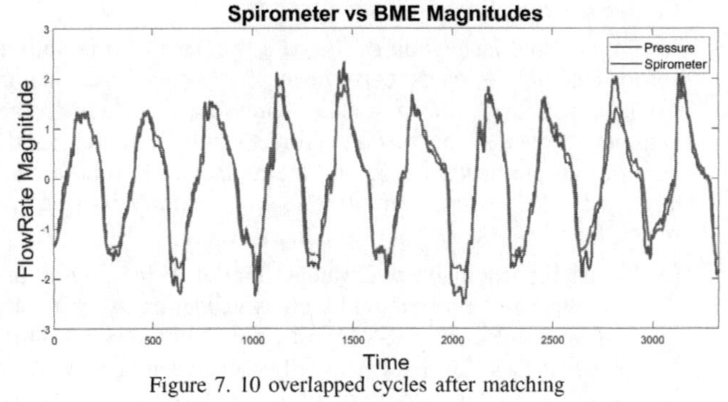

Figure 7. 10 overlapped cycles after matching

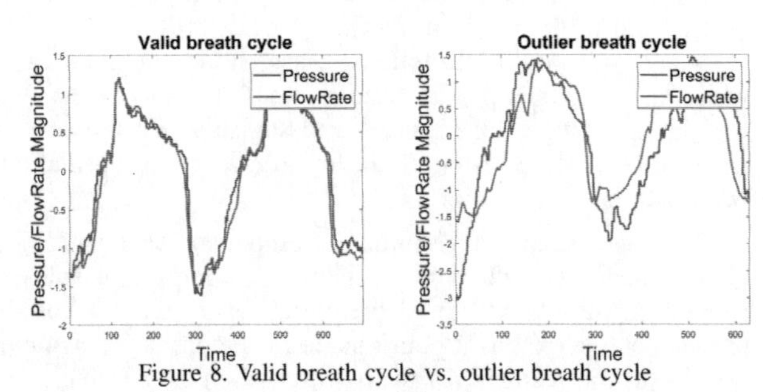

Figure 8. Valid breath cycle vs. outlier breath cycle

Even though it depends on the subject and experiment, it is possible to observe that often the *mar* values of Experiment 2 are the largest. This can be contributed to the retaining and sustaining parts of the breathing cycles described as part of Experiment 2. These assumptions could explain such values in Table I.

Later on, we calculate the 6th feature, the *Effective Volume* (explained in Section VI-B), on both training mask and spirometer data because this feature has a positive correlation with the amount of air breathed. In Figure 6, every point corresponds to a detected breathing cycle showing a linear dependency between the *Effective Volume* of pressure channel and the *Effective Volume* of the spirometer's flow rate. This means that the estimation of air volume of BME sensor and the spirometer are positively correlated. In the subplot up left of Figure 6, there are a few breathing cycles which are not close to the fitting line.

To illustrate these outlier cycles, we plot in Figure 8 one valid detected cycle against one of these such outliers so the difference between them can be observed. These outliers may not exactly be the same breathing event because the peak-to-peak distances of the two instruments do not match each other.

VI. USE CASE STUDY

A. Experiment

For the headset, training mask and cotton mask cases, we invited 4, 7 and 4 people to perform experiments according to the following sequences:

1) 5 deep breaths, apnea for 5-8 seconds, and 5 more deep breaths,
2) a continuous series of 5 normal breaths, 5 deep breaths, 5 normal breaths, and 5 deep breaths,
3) a continuous series of 5 deep breaths, 5 normal breaths, and 5 deep breaths
   For the training mask, the participants performed all of the 3 sequences once while seated in a room, and once walking in a hallway.

For the cotton mask and headset, only seated data is recorded. When people wear a headset, the piece pointing at the mouth may have varying distances to the mouth. Therefore, in the headset case, we let the participants adjust the piece with 2 cm, 4 cm, and 6 cm distance to the lips, and recorded the 3 sequences once in each distance.

The height range of the participants is between 160 cm and 190 cm, and the weight ranges from 52.3 kg and 100 kg. An example of the resultant signals from the second sequence in each of the cases can be observed in Figure 9. We use a spirometer SPR-BTA Inlet Vernier for reference, letting the 7 participants from the training mask perform the same sequences with the spirometer while seated. The spirometer airflow signal of the same participant from Figure 9 is shown in Figure 10.

From Figure 9, it is obvious that pressure, temperature, and humidity behave differently in the three settings. In the open-air headset setting, the air pressure is greatly influenced by the environment and only gives visible peak under a deep breath. Temperature and humidity offer a distinguishable signal, but have a drifting effect: both values increase with continuous deep breath and decrease with a normal breathing. The average values of all three channels are also lower than the other two settings which are in a closed chamber.

In the cotton mask setting, the humidity is always saturated to 100% due to the filtering material blocks humidity from dissipating. Pressure and temperature show clear distinguishable signals for normal and deep breathing. The temperature still

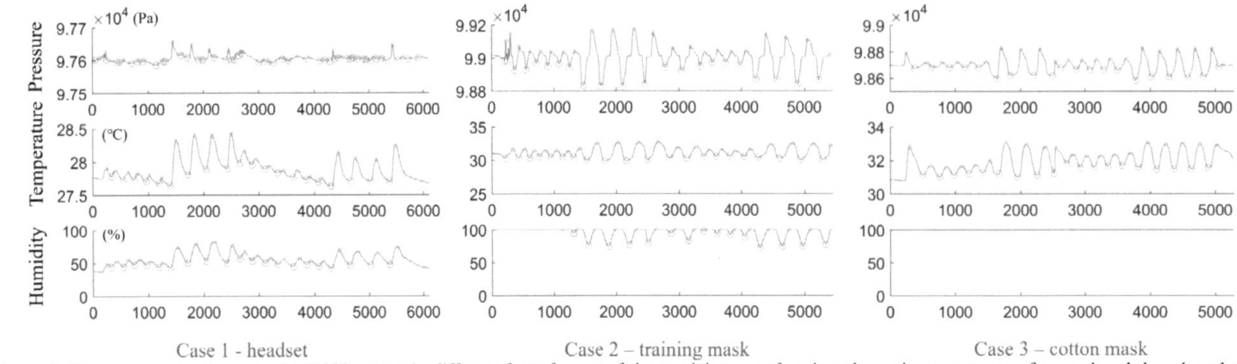

Figure 9. Signal examples from the BME280 sensor in different form factors of the participant performing alternating sequences of normal and deep breaths, the sampling rate is 50Hz

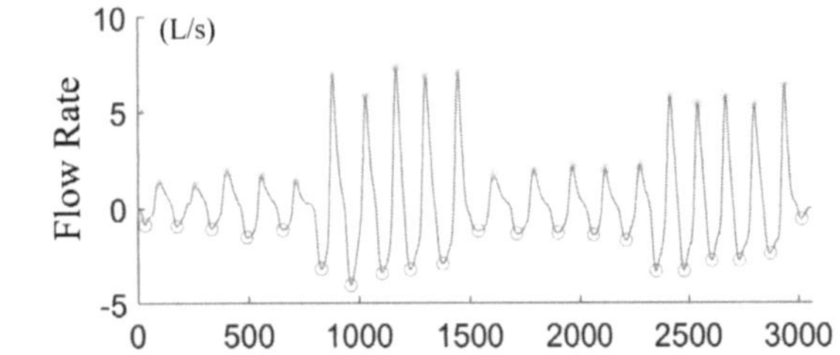

Figure 10. Signal example from the spirometer of the participant performing alternating sequences of normal and deep breaths, the sampling rate is 50Hz

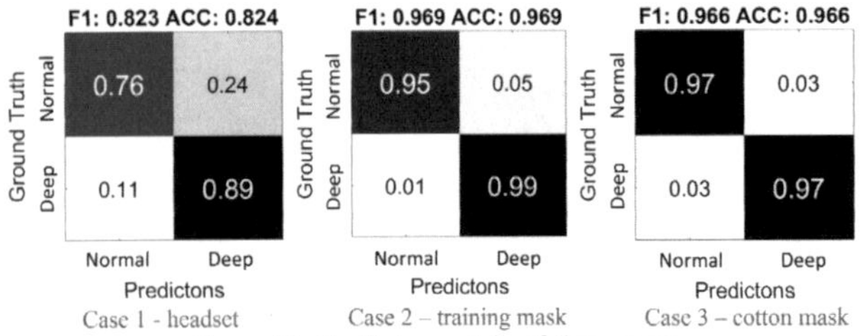

Figure 11. Confusion matrix of three cases

shows slight drifting, which is possibly contributed by the heat isolation property of the material.

In the training mask setting, the pressure and temperature showed a similar response with the cotton mask. The difference of the training mask is that the air flow in and out of the mask is an open, unfiltered airway. This contributes to less shifting in the temperature value, and the humidity is also no longer always saturated.

B. Machine Learning Data Processing

First, the same normalization method is applied to the signal for every experiment recording in its entirety. We apply simple average filtering with a kernel size of 1-by-15 to remove small fluctuations in the signal sample. The signal is then segmented by peak detection: positive and negative peaks are located based on a prominence threshold of 20% of the signal's standard deviation, as shown in Figure 9. Since the experiment only included normal breathing paces, if there are multiple negative peaks within 2 seconds, only the deepest peak is kept. A negative peak between two positive peaks is marked as a segment point, the signal between two of these points is taken as one breathing instance or one window. Every instance is manually annotated as ground truth by assigning normal and deep breath labels. The precision and recall of detecting a breath through said peak detection are 95.6% and 99.1%.

For every breathing instance $D(t)$, we calculate the following features to represent the signal:

1) average value of $D(t)$,
2) absolute range: $max(D(t)) - min(D(t))$,
3) standard deviation of $D(t)$,
4) kurtosis of $D(t)$,
5) length of the window (negative peak-to-peak distance),
6) effective volume: first $Base(D(t))$ is calculated as the linear function that connects $D(first)$ and $D(last)$, then the sum value of $D(t) - Base(D(t))$ is taken as the effective volume.

C. Recognizing Breath Types

From visual inspection of the data, we selected the optimal sensor channel for every case: headset - temperature, training mask - pressure, cotton mask - pressure. Although other channels may also be possible for a candidate, such as the humidity in the headset case and the temperature in both mask cases, how to combine different sensor channels will be part of the future work.

For each participant, we evaluate how well the normal and deep breaths can be separated by cross-validation using a cubic Support Vector Machine (SVM) classifier with the six features. Figure 11 shows the result as confusion matrices. The value in every cell is the summary of the individual results and normalized to the total amount of ground truth samples. The accuracy is above 96% in training mask and cotton mask cases, while 82.4% in the open-air headset case. This also agrees with the signal examples in Figure 9 and suggests that the sensors perform better in a restricted airflow for detecting normal and deep breaths.

Next, we use the Neighborhood Component Analysis (NCA) [17] to decide which features play more important roles in separating the two different breathing types. NCA takes the prediction accuracy as a goal function of additionally assigned weights to the features for every observation as variables. The goal function is continuously differentiable, thus the local maxima point can be found with optimization algorithms, where a combination of the feature weights results in a maximum prediction accuracy.

We use the `fscnca` method implemented in the Matlab Machine Learning Toolbox with default settings to perform

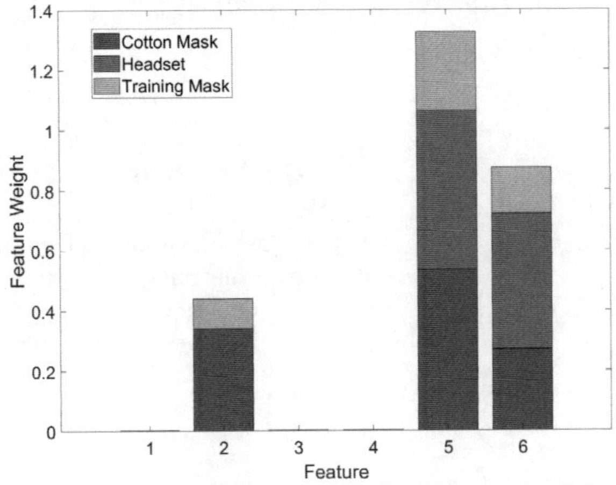

Figure 12. Feature weight after neighborhood component analysis.

NCA on a per-person basis, and then calculate the average weight for each feature within every form factor. The resulting featherweights are shown in Figure. 12. A higher value means the corresponding feature is more relevant for recognition. From the result, the 5th feature (window length) and the 6th feature (effective volume) are more relevant in all three form factors. For the cotton mask and training mask form factors, the 2nd feature (absolute range) is also relevant. The remaining features have close to zero weight. This result can be used to further optimize the feature calculation process.

VII. Conclusion and Future Work

From our pilot study, it is clear that the integrated atmosphere sensor, which measures air pressure, temperature and humidity, can be used to detect breathing events and distinguish normal and deep breaths in different form factors including face masks and an open-air headset, thanks to the small footprint of the sensor. The algorithm consists of simple filtering, peak detection, and 6 features are calculated. The sensor is also shown to be able to estimate the air volume by comparing with a spirometer.

In our future work, we will work on improving the accuracy of detecting deep and normal breaths for the reasons that this form factor is more acceptable and can be integrated with other head-mounted wearable devices, such as headphones or smart glasses. In particular, we will investigate utilizing more than one channel instead of selecting a single optimal channel, or using two opposite-facing sensors as a differential setting to reduce the influence of the environment.

We will also conduct experiments in outdoor or more active scenarios, and use case studies especially in sport and fitness, including user feedback and assisted training.

References

[1] M. Miller and J. Hankinson, "Standardisation of spirometry," European respiratory journal, vol. 26, no. 2, 2005, pp. 319–338.

[2] E. Buskirk and H. Taylor, "Maximal oxygen intake and its relation to body composition, with special reference to chronic physical activity and obesity," Journal of applied physiology, vol. 11, no. 1, 1957, pp. 72–78.

[3] H. Taylor, E. Buskirk, and A. Henschel, "Maximal oxygen intake as an objective measure of cardio-respiratory performance," Journal of applied physiology, vol. 8, no. 1, 1955, pp. 73–80.

[4] E. Vlemincx, J. Taelman, S. De Peuter, I. Van Diest, and O. Van Den Bergh, "Sigh rate and respiratory variability during mental load and sustained attention," Psychophysiology, vol. 48, no. 1, 2011, pp. 117–120.

[5] E. Vlemincx, J. Taelman, I. Van Diest, and O. Van den Bergh, "Take a deep breath: the relief effect of spontaneous and instructed sighs," Physiology & Behavior, vol. 101, no. 1, 2010, pp. 67–73.

[6] R. Brown and P. Gerbarg, "Sudarshan kriya yogic breathing in the treatment of stress, anxiety, and depression," Journal of Alternative & Complementary Medicine, vol. 11, no. 4, 2005, pp. 711–717.

[7] T. Kavanagh et al., "Peak oxygen intake and cardiac mortality in women referred for cardiac rehabilitation," Journal of the American College of Cardiology, vol. 42, no. 12, 2003, pp. 2139–2143.

[8] J. Stocks and P. H. Quanjer, "Reference values for residual volume, functional residual capacity and total lung capacity," European Respiratory Journal, vol. 8, no. 3, 1995, pp. 492–506.

[9] F. Swart, M. M. Schuurmans, J. C. Heydenreich, C. H. Pieper, and C. T. Bolliger, "Comparison of a new desktop spirometer (spirospec) with a laboratory spirometer in a respiratory out-patient clinic," Respiratory care, vol. 48, no. 6, 2003, pp. 591–595.

[10] "Chinadaily." [Online]. Available: https://www.ChinaDaily.com.cn [retrieved October 2018]

[11] A. Aliverti, "Wearable technology: role in respiratory health and disease," Breathe, vol. 13, no. 2, 2017, p. e27.

[12] F. Landreani and A. Martin-Yebra, "Respiratory frequency estimation from accelerometric signals acquired by mobile phone in a controlled breathing protocol," in Computing in Cardiology, 2018, pp. 1–4.

[13] S. Li, B. Lin, C. Tsai, C. Yang, and B. Lin, "Design of wearable breathing sound monitoring system for real-time wheeze detection," Sensors, vol. 17, no. 1, 2017, p. 171.

[14] A. Martin and J. Voix, "In-ear audio wearable: Measurement of heart and breathing rates for health and safety monitoring," IEEE Transactions on Biomedical Engineering, vol. 65, no. 6, 2018, pp. 1256–1263.

[15] A. Fusco, D. Locatelli, F. Onorati, G. Durelli, and M. Santambrogio, "On how to extract breathing rate from ppg signal using wearable devices," in Biomedical Circuits and Systems Conference (BioCAS), 2015 IEEE. IEEE, 2015, pp. 1–4.

[16] "Training mask l.l.c." [Online]. Available: https://www.trainingmask.com [retrieved October 2018]

[17] W. Yang, K. Wang, and W. Zuo, "Neighborhood component feature selection for high-dimensional data." JCP, vol. 7, no. 1, 2012, pp. 161–168.

Searching for Temporal Dependencies in the Privacy Concerns of Location-Based Service Users

Antonios Karatzoglou

Karlsruhe Institute of Technology
and Robert Bosch,
Corporate Sector Research
and Advance Engineering
Germany
Email: antonios.karatzoglou@kit.edu
antonios.karatzoglou@de.bosch.com

Julia Anken,
Florian Banscher,
Lukas Diewald

Karlsruhe Institute of Technology
Germany
Email: {julia.anken,
florian.banscher,
lukas.diewald}
@student.kit.edu

Michael Beigl

Karlsruhe Institute of Technology
Pervasive Computing Systems
Germany
Email: michael.beigl@kit.edu

***Abstract*—As the number of Location-Based Service (LBS) users grows steadily worldwide, the need for data protection and privacy-respecting methods and standards grows with it. There exists a big variety of privacy enhancing approaches by now. However, very few seem to have explored the impact of time on people's sense of privacy. In this work, we attempt to answer the question whether and to what degree privacy concerns with respect to location sharing are time-dependent or not. For this purpose, we designed and carried out 2 different user studies, a Web survey and a 4-week long experimental study. Our analysis shows evidence towards an existing dependency between time and the users' willingness to share their location. Moreover, the effect appears to be highly user-specific and correlates with certain personal features, such as conviviality and the general personal view on privacy and data protection.**

Keywords*—*Data protection and Privacy; Location Based Services; Semantic Trajectories and Locations.

I. INTRODUCTION

In recent years, mobile service providers rely increasingly on context and in particular on location awareness in order to raise the quality of their service. As a result, the number of Location-Based Service (LBS) users has experienced enormous growth worldwide. Only in the US, it has been doubled in the last 5 years and expected to reach 242 million in 2018 [1]. Location-Based Services go nowadays beyond the sole knowledge of the coordinates of some single point on a map, e.g., for navigation purposes. Moreover, they make use of additional knowledge about the location, such as its type, corresponding activities and its opening hours, in order to be able to provide targeted recommendations to the users. In this case, this kind of semantically enriched locations may be referred to as *semantic locations* and the corresponding trajectories as *semantic trajectories* [2]. Semantic trajectories support an application-oriented and thus a more sophisticated way for modeling, analyzing and predicting human movement patterns like in [3]–[6]. Since most modeling approaches are data-driven, a large amount of tracking data is necessary in order to achieve a good performance. However, large high-quality datasets are hard to find. Rising privacy concerns and strict privacy guidelines further aggravate this problem. Two recent reports underpin this fact and show that almost half of teen and over a third of adult smartphone app users have turned off the location tracking feature at some time on their phones or tablets because they worried about who might access their data, [7] and [8].

Due to this fact and due to privacy becoming a generally very important issue of our data-overflowing society, many developers and researchers lay their focus on finding new methods to protect the privacy of LBS, and not only, users. This led to the emergence of so called *Privacy Enhancing Technologies (PET)* [9] and *Privacy by design* approaches [10]. These aim at taking human values and privacy explicitly into account and incorporating them into the development process of services, while at the same time acting in accordance with the data protection laws. There exists a great variety of different approaches and ideas behind these methods. In the location and tracking scene, current works base primarily on spatial obfuscation techniques, such as GPS grid masking [11] and spatial cloaking [12] to name but a few. According to these techniques, certain location types or spatial areas that are considered to be sensitive, such as hospitals, are being *obfuscated* either by reducing the spatial resolution or by anonymizing single individuals behind a bigger group of people.

However, the aforementioned methods are static and despite the dynamic nature of human behaviour none seems to have investigated the impact of time on the users' privacy concerns so far. In the presented work, we attempt to explore whether and to what degree time affects the users' sensitivity when it comes to providing information about their location. In other words, we want to find out if there exist situations, in which a user experiences a certain location sometimes more and sometimes less critical in terms of revealing the particular location. For instance, a visit to a bar in the evening might for some users be alright to share, whereas a visit to the same bar in the morning not, especially when social standards and values are taken into account. Adapting to this kind of potential temporal privacy concerns would make location-based applications more trustworthy and user-friendly. In order to explore such temporal effects, we conducted and evaluated 2 user studies, an online survey and a 4-week long experimental study. During both studies, the participants were asked to provide information about their willingness to reveal their location together with a brief explanation.

The rest of this work is structured as follows. In Section II, we provide a brief overview on some of the most related work in the field of privacy and privacy protection. Sections III and IV describe in their first parts the details of our two user studies. Their second parts include our evaluation results and interpretations. Finally, in Section V, we summarize our work and provide some concluding thoughts.

II. Related Work

The first part of this section provides insight into some basic work in the theory of privacy and privacy protection. The second part gives a short overview of location protection related work used in Location-Based Services.

A. Privacy Theories

A big variety of privacy theories has been developed so far. Here, we discuss two of these theories, which have been most frequently applied over time and verified by diverse studies: the privacy theory by Westin and the privacy regulation theory by Altman [13].

The privacy theory by Westin was developed in 1967 [14]. In his work, Westin regards privacy as

> *the claim of individuals or groups, to determine for themselves when, how and to what extend information about them is passed on to others.*

When privacy is viewed in the context of social interaction, Westin describes it as

> *the wilful and temporary withdrawal of a person from the general society.*

His theory supports the existence of different levels of privacy that can be determined based on the following four states (or dimensions) of privacy: *Solitude, Intimacy, Anonymity* and *Reserve* and their corresponding degree of achievement. In addition, Westin found in [15] that the driving factors behind privacy attitudes depend on the one hand on the individual's level of distrust in companies or institutions and on the other hand on her fears of technology abuse, a fact that applies very well to our LBS use case. Westin's fundamental work led to the development of scales for measuring privacy such as the Marshall dimensions of privacy preferences described in [16].

Altman's privacy regulation theory [17] extends and refines in part Westin's work. In Altman's view, privacy is a dynamic rather than a static interaction withdrawal process, in which individual people (or groups of people) selectively control the access to themselves. In particular, his theory takes into account that people may open themselves to others at a certain time and close themselves off at another time. Thus, people's desired privacy level changes over time, a fact that can be attributed to different external or internal factors. Altman further describes an optimization process with two ends and an optimal interaction level somewhere in the middle. On the one hand, there is the end with too much interaction and on the other hand, the end with too little interaction. Both ends are considered to be unsatisfactory. The ideal privacy level, i.e., the optimal level of interaction lies in-between, can change over time and is different for each person. Finally, Altman's theory considers a set of behavioural mechanisms that can serve to achieve the desired level of social interaction and thus, of privacy. Verbal, para-verbal and non-verbal behaviour, as well as, similar to Westin's work, physical (territorial) distance and isolation from the rest represent some of them.

Westin's and Altman's work has been often applied and adapted respectively to match the requirements of our technocratic society, in which the physical world merges increasingly with the virtual one. Work, such as in [18] and [19], extend privacy by adding the notion of roles and boundaries in the virtual space and defining in this way virtual territories.

B. Privacy Protection Methods for Location-Based Services and Applications

Due to location being a strong personal identifier, privacy protection methods are an essential part of LBS. The location history of LBS users reveals loads of private and sensitive information about the user, which in turn may be used to provide deep insights into their personal lives, their identity, as well as into their personality and character. This makes location data particularly critical. Therefore, their protection is of great importance. There exist various location protective approaches. *k-anonymity* and *l-diversity*, represent two of them and are briefly introduced below.

k-Anonymity is a so called spatial *cloaking* technique. It builds up a coarse, *cloaked* area over the location of a single LBS user and enlarges it until $k-1$ other persons (users) are included in it [12] [20]. By doing so, the LBS provider or an attacker cannot distinguish an individual entry of a single user from at least $k-1$ other entries in the cloaked area and thus the single user remains unidentifiable. It is self-evident that the value of k plays a significant role in the performance of k-Anonymity.

The so called Feeling-based Privacy model of Xu et al. relies on the k-Anonymity method and considers privacy and its protection as a feeling of the user [21]. For this reason, it is difficult to find a practicable value for k and thus to reduce the feeling of the individual user to a numerical value. In the Feeling-based Privacy model, a user is able to set indirectly his desired anonymity level by defining spatial areas in which he generally feels secure and comfortable, the so-called *public* regions. The entropy of the selected areas is used to describe their popularity, which in turn is used as the anonymity level for subsequent requests to the LBS, and must be guaranteed to the user. The result is a more personalized version of k-Anonymity. However, both approaches wouldn't work if the $k-1$ other users were in a group, that is, if the corresponding $k-1$ (user-ID, location)-tuples contain same sensitive values as, for example, the same exact location. In this case, the cloaked area would be small and might fall inside a large critical location such as a hospital area. This would allow an attacker to still know the whereabouts of a user.

l-Diversity was introduced to solve this problem [20] [22]. This method extends the k-Anonymity approach by ensuring that the (user-ID, location)-tuples of a certain cloaked area contain at least $l-1$ different location types. This leads to a further enlargement of the cloaked area until it covers $l-1$ different locations.

In the aforementioned methods, the exact position is abstracted by including other users or different locations into the region of interest. This makes it difficult for LBS providers or an attacker to gather private and sensitive information and draw conclusions upon it. However, semantic information about the $k-1$ included locations can still become problematic for both models. For example, it is imaginable that a cloaked area contains only semantically similar places. In this case, it would be possible for an attacker to assign a semantic meaning to the whole area. This could be for instance the case if the cloaked area consisted solely of health service places, such as hospitals or medical specialists. An attacker could conclude that users from this cloaked area have either health problems or know people that have health problems or work in the health service domain. Similarly, if the cloaked area referred to a university campus, an attacker could conclude that the users are either students or belong to the academic staff. Although personal information is being revealed in both cases, the first (hospital) case is regarded as a more critical piece of information. Thus, locations show a different degree of sensitivity depending on their type. For this reason, recent approaches aim at protecting the semantics, that is, the meaning of locations as well, such as in Damiani et al.'s framework [23]. Lee et al. present in their work also such a *semantic cloaking* method, where cloaked areas are built up based solely on *different* semantic location types [20].

Finally, in [24], Marconi et al. extend the core idea of Xu et al. by interpreting feelings as dynamic, time-varying features. In their work, they define and evaluate new attacker models that have additional access to temporal information, such as the distribution of anonymized entries over the day. It could be shown that as soon as the factor time is included in the attacker models, the privacy protection assumed in the Feeling-based Privacy model could not be maintained. Moreover, their work is in line with our assumption that when it comes to privacy, time plays a major role. In contrast to the presented work, both Marconi et al. and Xu et al. evaluate their work on synthetic data and their focus lies primarily on the optimization of depersonalization servers.

III. User Study I

A. Overview - Description

Our first study included two parts. The first part aimed at establishing possible connections between demographic as well as personality characteristics and the sense of privacy among the participants. In the second part, we focused on learning more about the use of LBS running on smartphones with respect to privacy and willingness to share their location. For this purpose, we confronted the participants with the question whether they believe that the sense of privacy is time-dependent in various contexts. The goal was to identify the circumstances, with respect to time, under which, people would most likely reveal their data. In addition, the obtained data of this first study served also an additional purpose, namely as basis for the design and the content of our app in the main, experimental study described in the following Section IV. That is, we used the gained data in order to modify the app accordingly and be able to provide our participants with a high usability. This is particularly important when conducting a long user study, because users tend to close or remove apps with low usability more often.

For the purpose of our first study, we used the Google Forms online survey platform [25]. We asked a total of 52 people, which we recruited via email. Approximately three fourths of the participants were 18-25 years, with most being in education (e.g., college or university students or trainees). The rest of the participants were uniformly distributed within the range of 25-65 years old. In addition, three fourths were male and about 80% show a strong to very strong affinity for technology.

B. Evaluation

Due to the limited space, in this section we will focus on the most interesting findings. Figure 1 shows an interesting but also expected trend with regard to location data protection and the personality trait of conviviality. It can be seen that the more sociable and extrovert people are, the less they care about the protection of their location data. That is, people that enjoy being more often with other people are more relaxed with the idea of sharing their location, even with other parties. In Figure 2, we can see the relation between location data protection and whether the participants consider privacy to be time-dependent or not. It is apparent that particularly people who do not pay big attention to the protection of their location data, do not consider privacy to be time-dependent. The other way round, a large part of the people that care for their privacy and to whom location data protection is important, consider the sense of privacy to be changing over time. Our correlation analysis resulted in a two-tailed significance of 0.03 and a Pearson correlation coefficient of -0.302, which underpins the indication of an inverse correlation between the two items. Figure 3 presents the results of the belief that privacy is a time-dependent feature in relation to the participants' affinity for technology. What stands out in this figure is that solely

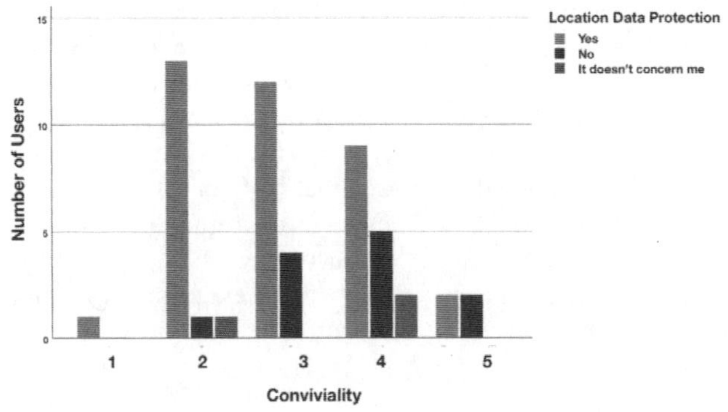

Fig. 1. Conviviality vs. Location data protection.
1: self-effacing and introvert, **5**: sociable and extrovert.
"**Yes**" represents: "Yes, Location data protection is important to me".

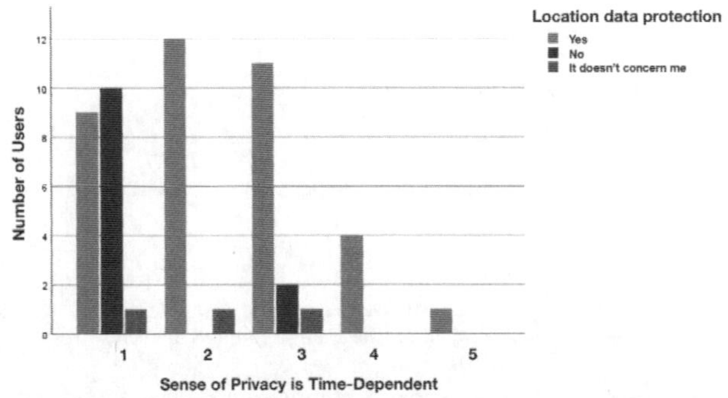

Fig. 2. Time-dependent sense of privacy vs. Location data protection.
1: "No, it isn't time-dependent", **5**: "Yes, it is time-dependent".
"**Yes**" represents: "Yes, Location data protection is important to me".

people with a strong affinity to technology take the view that privacy is indeed a time-dependent feature. This can be partly attributed to the fact that people interested in technology, know more about its potential, both positive and negative one. Thus, they might be more aware of situations where sharing location data can be critical and where flexible, time-dependent privacy rules could be of great importance. In general, it has been

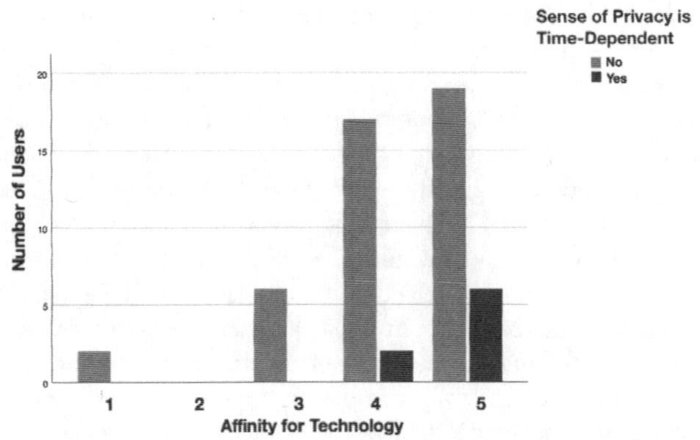

Fig. 3. Affinity for technology vs. Sense of privacy is time-dependent.
1: "I'm not interested in technology", **5**: "I'm very interested in technology".

noticed that the interviewees have very divergent views on data protection and privacy. Some participants were not interested in data protection at all and have no problem being tracked everywhere and at any time. Other, however, consider data protection to be extremely important and want to be tracked as little as possible or even not at all. A significant group of the participant lie in-between by stating that they agree with sharing their location data only when it is necessary or brings practical benefits with it, e.g., for navigation purposes.

IV. User Study II

A. *Overview - Description*

This section discusses our experimental study. Scope of this study was to identify existing time-dependencies with respect to privacy concerns in a real-world dataset scenario and confirm this way the results of our survey described in the previous Section III. During our experiment, we tracked a total of 10 mobile phone users over a period of 4 weeks. In addition to the GPS tracking running in the background, the users were asked to provide additional information or answer a small set of questions whenever they changed their location as described below:

- **Location type:** E.g., "restaurant", "chinese restaurant", etc.
- **Purpose of visit:** E.g., "Eating with friends/family", "celebrating Christmas party", etc.
- **Would you share this location at any time?** "Yes", "No". In case of "No", the user is additionally asked to add the reason.
- **Rating bar:** The user is asked to rate the experienced intrusion of his privacy with respect to sharing her current location, whereby
  1 star = "Uncritical, I have no problems with being tracked right now".
  5 stars = "Critical, I don't want people to know where I am right now".
- **Description:** E.g., "Critical, because no one should know that I am at a party," or "Not critical, because everyone knows that I am working here anyway".

For this purpose, we designed and implemented an Android tracking and annotation app illustrated in Figure 4. During the user study, both GPS and annotation data were encrypted and stored locally in the users' own devices in order to comply with the data protection guidelines. Each app user was assigned with a random User-ID. The per User-ID anonymized data were then transmitted to us after the study was over. Finally, we offered 3 Amazon coupons to the 3 participants that used our app at most, that is, with the most annotated entries, as an additional incentive for the participants of our study.

B. *Evaluation*

First, we preprocessed the data by filtering out inconsistencies and missing values. The filtered data were then organized in tables according to the type of information, e.g., "user-ID",

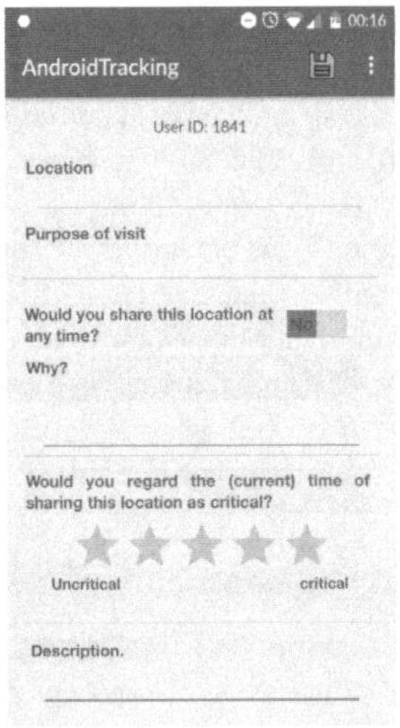

Fig. 4. Screenshot of our Android tracking and annotation app.

"timestamp", "location label", "purpose", etc. We evaluated potential temporal dependencies in our data with regard to following aspects:

- Absolute time of day., e.g., 12:35pm, etc.
- Aggregated time of day in blocks:
  - 6am-10am: "morning"
  - 10am-12am: "mid-morning"
  - 12am-14pm: "midday"
  - 14pm-17pm: "afternoon"
  - 17pm-21pm: "evening"
  - 21pm-6am: "Night"
- Aggregated time in special blocks (events):
  - During the week
  - Weekend
  - Non-lecture period & Holidays
  - Christmas (24-26/12)
- Location category (based on the Foursquare venue taxonomy [26])
  - Residence
  - Work
  - Food
  - Business & Services
  - University
  - Culture & Entertainment
  - Nightlife
  - Natur & Leisure time
  - Travel & Traffic
  - Event
  - Others

The evaluation with respect to the location category is important in order to identify and exclude eventual impacts of the location type on the criticality rating of sharing the current location (from now on referred to as *privacy rating*).

We analyzed the data of each user both separately and combined. All in all, we had a total of 157 entries, which corresponds to an average of 5.61 entries per day. We calculated an average privacy rating of 1.847 and a standard deviation of 1.287, with 1 and 5 representing the least and the most critical score with regard to sharing the location at the corresponding moment, respectively. This is a relative low score. However, the data showed that 4 of our 10 users had no privacy concerns at all when it comes to sharing their location. They showed a permanent privacy rating of 1, regardless of time and place. This fact puled our average privacy rating down. Figure 5 presents the corresponding privacy rating

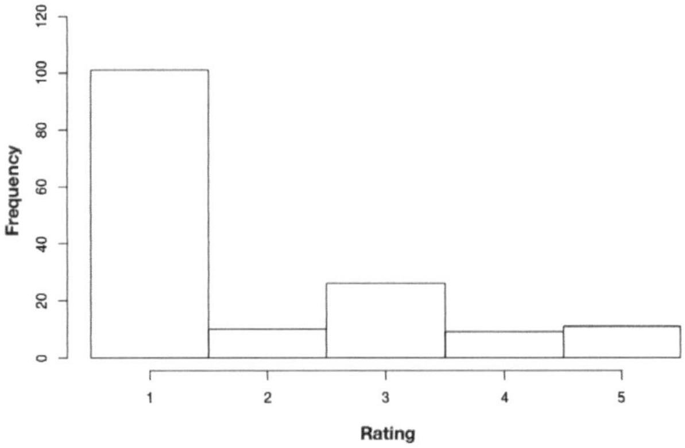

Fig. 5. Privacy ratings distribution over all users. 1 and 5 represent the least and the most critical private rating score respectively.

distribution. The rating score 3 stands out as the second most frequently chosen rating. As being the middle rating value, it could be interpreted as users having occasionally substantial but not extreme concerns over their location privacy. The rest of the ratings are almost evenly spread out. Figure 6 contains the privacy ratings of all users distributed over the time of day. It can be seen that the privacy ratings are spread out over the range 1 to 5 without forming any identifiable patterns with respect to time. We can see the dense concentration of 1 values that reflects the ratings of the aforementioned "biased" users. We can also see the second dense concentration of 3 values. At first glance, despite the results of our first study, time appears to have no effect on the users' privacy concerns. However, after analyzing the data of single users separately, we could indeed find evidence of temporal dependencies. Figure 7 shows the privacy rating distribution over time for user ID4775. What is striking in this figure is that the particular user stated to be more sensitive when it comes to sharing her location in the afternoon hours between 14pm-20pm. A similar effect could be partly observed in other users as well. However, it should be noted here that high ratings came often in combination with certain location categories as well, such as outdoor and nightlife locations or friend's homes. Thus, it might be the location types that affect at most the users' sense of privacy. On the other hand, since certain locations are visited only during specific times, this could be again indirectly interpreted as a time-dependent effect as well, an effect that appears to be rather user-specific.

In Figure 8, we aggregate the time of day into 6 blocks.

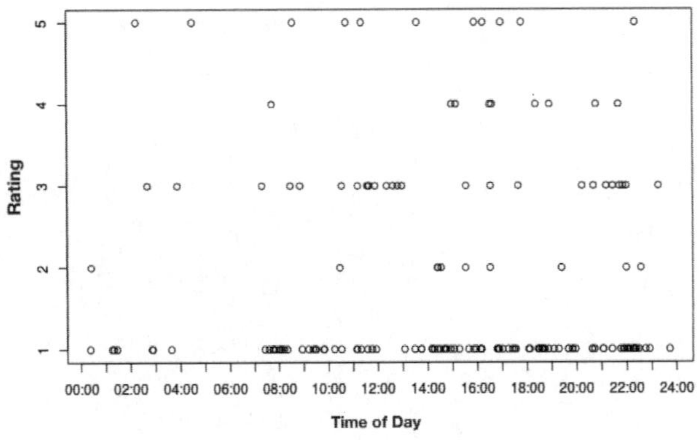

Fig. 6. Privacy ratings of all users over time of day. 1 and 5 represent the least and the most critical private rating score respectively.

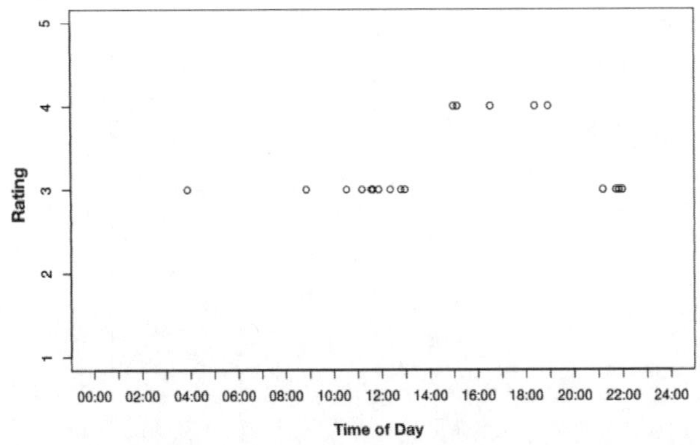

Fig. 7. Privacy ratings of user ID4775 over time of day. 1 and 5 represent the least and the most critical private rating score respectively.

Interestingly, both the mid-morning and the midday show an elevated average privacy rating of 2.24 and 2.33. However, at the same time, both show the least recorded entries, which may have affected to a certain degree the averages. Furthermore, no

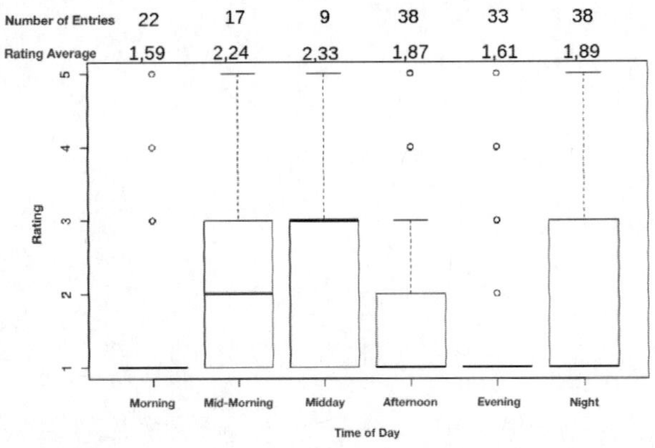

Fig. 8. Privacy ratings of all users over aggregated time blocks. 1 and 5 represent the least and the most critical private rating score respectively.

significant differences could be observed when we compared the ratings of during the week with the ones of the weekend. The Christmas period seemed to be having a slight effect on some users as we could observe a slight raise of high criticality rating values in the particular period (24-26 December). This could be attributed to the fact that people tend to concern more about their location privacy in their free time, when they are going out and when they are visiting relatives and close friends. Finally, an interesting result could be observed with regard to the location "home". Although "home" is a generally highly private location, the privacy ratings do change significantly over time, a fact that once again underpins our hypothesis that privacy concerns are time-dependent.

V. Conclusion

Recent research has been increasingly working on developing ways to protect the users' location data, with most focusing on spatial or semantic obfuscation techniques. However, very few seem to have investigated the impact of time on the users' privacy concerns. In the presented work, we attempt to explore time as a factor influencing the willingness of users to provide information about their location. In order to achieve this, we conducted 2 separate user studies, an online user survey as well as a 4-week long experimental study. Our analysis revealed slight, yet still present, evidence of an existing dependency between time and people's sense of privacy. The effect seems to be user-specific and is more common in people that are strong advocates of data protection. Certain personality traits, such as conviviality, also appear to play a significant role on the existence of time-dependencies. Overall, the presented results strengthen the need for dynamic, time-dependent location data protection techniques.

Acknowledgment

The authors would like to thank all of our user study participants, as well as Corbinian Grimm, Dennis Brüstle and Kevin Kellner for their contribution to the Android app design.

References

[1] eMarketer. (2015) Key trends in mobile advertising. [Online]. Available: https://www.statista.com/statistics/436071/location-based-service-users-usa/

[2] C. Parent *et al.*, "Semantic trajectories modeling and analysis," *ACM Computing Surveys (CSUR)*, vol. 45, no. 4, p. 42, 2013.

[3] A. Karatzoglou, H. Sentürk, A. Jablonski, and M. Beigl, "Applying artificial neural networks on two-layer semantic trajectories for predicting the next semantic location," in *International Conference on Artificial Neural Networks*. Springer, 2017, pp. 233–241.

[4] A. Karatzoglou, S. C. Lamp, and M. Beigl, "Matrix factorization on semantic trajectories for predicting future semantic locations," in *Wireless and Mobile Computing, Networking and Communications (WiMob),*. IEEE, 2017, pp. 1–7.

[5] J. J.-C. Ying, W.-C. Lee, T.-C. Weng, and V. S. Tseng, "Semantic trajectory mining for location prediction," in *Proceedings of the 19th ACM SIGSPATIAL International Conference on Advances in Geographic Information Systems*. ACM, 2011, pp. 34–43.

[6] A. Karatzoglou, D. Köhler, and M. Beigl, "Purpose-of-visit-driven semantic similarity analysis on semantic trajectories for enhancing the future location prediction," in *2018 IEEE International Conference on Pervasive Computing and Communications (PerCom) Workshop Proceedings*. IEEE, 2018.

[7] J. L. Boyles, A. Smith, and M. Madden, "Privacy and data management on mobile devices," *Pew Research Center's Internet & American Life Project*, 2012.

[8] Zickuhr, "Location-based services," *Pew Research Center's Internet & American Life Project*, 2013.
[9] Y. Wang, "Privacy-enhancing technologies," in *Handbook of research on social and organizational liabilities in information security*. IGI Global, 2009, pp. 203–227.
[10] M. Langheinrich, "Privacy by design?principles of privacy-aware ubiquitous systems," in *International conference on Ubiquitous Computing*. Springer, 2001, pp. 273–291.
[11] D. E. Seidl, P. Jankowski, and M.-H. Tsou, "Privacy and spatial pattern preservation in masked gps trajectory data," *International Journal of Geographical Information Science*, vol. 30, no. 4, pp. 785–800, 2016.
[12] L. Sweeney, "K-anonymity: A model for protecting privacy," *Int. J. Uncertain. Fuzziness Knowl.-Based Syst.*, pp. 557–570, 2002.
[13] S. T. Margulis, "On the status and contribution of westin's and altman's theories of privacy," *Journal of Social Issues*, vol. 59, no. 2, pp. 411–429, 2003.
[14] A. F. Westin and O. M. Ruebhausen, *Privacy and freedom*. Atheneum New York, 1967, vol. 1.
[15] A. Westin, "Opinion surveys: What consumers have to say about information privacy," *Prepared Witness Testimony, The House Committee on Energy and Commerce*, 2001.
[16] N. J. Marshall, "Dimensions of privacy preferences," *Multivariate Behaviour Research*, vol. 9, no. 3, pp. 255–272, 1974.
[17] I. Altman, "Privacy regulation: Culturally universal or culturally specific?" *Journal of Social Issues*, vol. 33, no. 3, pp. 66–84, 1977.
[18] N. Zhang, C. Wang, and Y. Xu, "Privacy in online social networks," 2011, CiteSeer.
[19] M. Moloney and F. Bannister, "A privacy control theory for online environments," in *System Sciences, 2009. HICSS'09. 42nd Hawaii International Conference on*. IEEE, 2009, pp. 1–10.
[20] B. Lee, J. Oh, H. Yu, and J. Kim, "Protecting location privacy using location semantics," in *Proceedings of the 17th ACM SIGKDD International Conference on Knowledge Discovery and Data Mining*, ser. KDD '11. ACM, 2011, pp. 1289–1297.
[21] T. Xu and Y. Cai, "Feeling-based location privacy protection for location-based services," in *Proceedings of the 16th ACM Conference on Computer and Communications Security*, ser. CCS '09. ACM, 2009, pp. 348–357.
[22] A. Machanavajjhala, D. Kifer, J. Gehrke, and M. Venkitasubramaniam, "L-diversity: Privacy beyond k-anonymity," *ACM Trans. Knowl. Discov. Data*, 2007.
[23] M. L. Damiani, C. Silvestri, and E. Bertino, "Fine-grained cloaking of sensitive positions in location-sharing applications," *IEEE Pervasive Computing*, no. 4, pp. 64–72, 2011.
[24] L. Marconi, R. Di Pietro, B. Crispo, and M. Conti, "Time warp: How time affects privacy in lbss," in *Information and Communications Security*, M. Soriano, S. Qing, and J. López, Eds. Berlin, Heidelberg: Springer Berlin Heidelberg, 2010, pp. 325–339.
[25] Google. (2018) Google forms. [Online]. Available: https://www.google.com/forms/
[26] Foursquare. (2018) Venue categories. [Online]. Available: https://developer.foursquare.com/docs/resources/categories

An Efficient Self-Organizing Node Deployment Algorithm for Mobile Sensor Networks

Mahsa Sadeghi Ghahroudi, Alireza Shahrabi, and Tuleen Boutaleb

School of Computing, Engineering and Built Environment
Glasgow Caledonian University, Glasgow, UK
Emails:{ Mahsa.Sadeghi, A.Shahrabi, T.Boutaleb}@gcu.ac.uk

***Abstract*—Wireless Sensor Networks (WSNs) constitute the platform for a broad range of applications, such as those related to national security, surveillance, military, health care, and environmental monitoring. Maximising coverage using resource-constrained nodes is usually a goal to provide the expected quality of service for these applications. This problem has been studied extensively in recent years, especially when the connectivity and energy efficiency are of high significance. In this paper, we propose a new distributed move-assisted algorithm, called SODA, to efficiently provide the maximum coverage for WSNs with self-organising mobile nodes. SODA is based on a deployment algorithm recently reported in the literature which is inspired by the equilibrium of molecules. However, while SODA's transition from chaos to order is faster, the final coverage provided by SODA is also insensitive to the initial deployment of the nodes and no specific level of coverage during the initial deployment is required. This is achieved by detecting the local network density and adjusting the partial force applied at each step in each neighbourhood accordingly. Our extensive simulation study shows the advantages of SODA including lower power consumption, as well as faster and more effective coverage.**

Keywords–coverage; distributed wireless sensor network; energy efficiency; node deployment.

I. INTRODUCTION

Wireless Sensor Networks (WSNs) are being used in many different applications in the world, particularly with the proliferation of Micro-Electro-Mechanical Systems (MEMS) technology which has promoted the development of smart sensors [1]. These applications vary from entertainment, travel, retail, and industry to medicine, and emergency management [2] [3].

In WSNs, providing adequate coverage is a fundamental problem that has gained much attention recently [4] with the aim to provide the maximum sensing coverage over the Region of Interest (ROI). The required coverage can be achieved by proper deployment of sensors after the initial deployment. Therefore, random deployment of mobile sensors does not guarantee the expected coverage in the ROI.

The mobile sensor deployment algorithms in WSNs are classified as centralised or distributed [5]. The distributed method is fault tolerant, scalable, and cost-efficient and, hence a more popular method in wireless sensor networks [6] [7]. Distributed deployment of sensors does not rely on a centralised node, i.e., sink, to decide on all the sensors movements. In the distributed strategy, every sensor can communicate with its neighbouring nodes to decide about its movement at each step. The communication method, the data sent and received, and also the communication and sensing range are some of the essential parameters to be specified in every distributed deployment algorithm.

In different algorithms, different methods are used for communication between neighbouring nodes to increase the coverage in the area [7]–[12]. Some algorithms are inspired by observing some natural phenomenon behaviours to cope with the distributed sensor network requirements. For example, neighbourhood movement theory that is seen in the animal aggregation movements, like birds migration, is applied in a deployment algorithm proposed in [13]. In this deployment algorithm [13], sensors move based on the average of the neighbour's positions and, as a result, create a uniform sensor placement to achieve the required coverage. In another study [14], an algorithm is proposed for a distributed sensor network in which the equilibrium of molecules inspires sensor movement. This algorithm can provide full coverage after a rather high number of steps and provides a somewhat high initial coverage percentage over the initial deployment. Another deployment algorithm using a clustering approach to achieve better power usage and coverage has also been proposed in [14] with the same concept for sensor movements. However, none of them considers assumptions like the initial deployment of sensors in the antagonistic environment in which manual deployment of sensors is not possible. For instance, a sensor network could be deployed near the crater of a volcano to measure temperature, pressure, and seismic activities [15] or it could be deployed as part of security surveillance in military operations [6]. Therefore, the initial deployment of sensor nodes with a certain percentage of initial coverage is not always possible.

In this paper, we aim to develop a distributed deployment algorithm, called Self-Organizing Deployment Algorithm (SODA) for mobile sensor networks. Our primary goal is to achieve maximum coverage within an acceptable range of energy consumption and time cost. The SODA is based on the Distributed Self-Spreading Algorithm (DSSA) [14], which is inspired by the equilibrium of molecules. SODA addresses the DSSA limitations, such as sensitivity to the minimum percentage of initial deployment coverage, the long transition time from chaos situation to order, and limitations in providing the appropriate coverage for single-point-deployment scenarios, where all nodes are initially located over a single sub-area, such as one corner or at the centre of the area. The superiority of SODA is due to the adjustment of partial force where the network is dense locally.

The rest of the paper is organised as follows. Section II presents an introduction to DSSA followed by the SODA

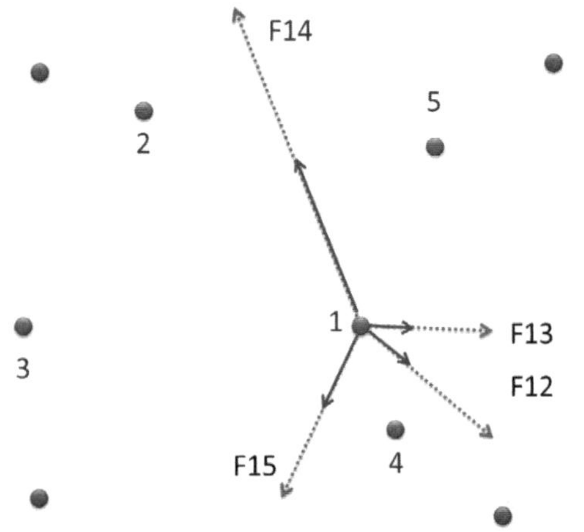

Figure 1. Partial forces in between sensor 1 and its neighbours.

solution in Section III. The performance evaluation section to describe the simulation specification and results is under Section IV while our conclusions are drawn in Section V.

II. A BRIEF REVIEWING OF DSSA

The DSSA is inspired by the equilibrium of molecules, which balances the energy of the particles to remain in their locations. This balance is caused by particles, which stay in their lowest energy point with the same distance from each other in a distributed manner. Similarly, the optimal spacing in between sensors creates the required coverage.

In DSSA, it is assumed that sensors are randomly distributed in an area. Sensors can communicate with each other if they are located within their communication range, called C_R, and can sense their environment with the sensing range, S_R. The communication between sensors is performed in order to find their neighbouring nodes and to exchange the requisite information. The collected information is then used to decide about the appropriate location of each node to provide the required coverage for the area. Every sensor node executes the DSSA after an initial step.

In the initial step of the DSSA, the communication range, C_R and sensing range, S_R values are given, which are dependent on sensors' specifications that are the same for all the sensors. The initial location of sensors is specified in a 2D vector (p_0). The higher dimension for sensor locations, is possible by adding another component to the location vector. The $threshold1$ and $threshold2$ are two parameters that can check the exit points of the algorithm and should be defined in the initial step, which are explained in the following sections. Another important variable is $\mathcal{M}$ which is the expected density in the sensor network. Expected density is the average number of sensors in a one-hop neighbourhood. The expected density is calculated by $\mathcal{M} = (\frac{N.\pi.C_R^2}{A})$, where C_R is communication range, S_R is sensing range, N is the number of sensors, and A is the size of the ROI. In addition to expected density, D represents the local one-hop neighbourhood density of every sensor. The expected density and local density control the movement of the sensors.

The central core of DSSA is the partial force that moves the sensors. This force is dependent on the current location of sensors, the distance in between every two neighbouring sensors, and the local density. Local density and partial force have a direct relationship, that is the same as the movement of particles in physics, which follow Coulomb's Law.

The partial force at step n for a sensor and its neighbouring sensor is a repulsive force calculated as:

$$f_{(i,j)} = \frac{D^i}{\mathcal{M}^2}(C_R - |p_n^i - p_n^j|)\frac{p_n^j - p_n^i}{|p_n^j - p_n^i|} \tag{1}$$

p_n^i stands for the position of sensor i at step of n, and D^i stands for the local density of sensor i at step of n. As appears in (1), the magnitude of partial force depends on the position of the nodes. If any neighbour of the sensor, like sensor j, has a higher value in one dimension then the magnitude of that force is positive and negative otherwise.

For every sensor node, the total force that moves that sensor is the cumulative force of all neighbouring nodes in its one-hop neighbourhood. The movement is independent of the movement of any other sensor node inside or outside of the neighbourhood. This process is executed as long as the conditions for stopping the algorithm are not satisfied. These conditions are:

- *Oscillation Check*: The execution of the algorithm at each node is stopped when it reaches its oscillation limit. Oscillation happens when a sensor moves back and forth between almost the same locations consecutively. The number of oscillations is counted by oscillation count, O_{count}. The distance that a sensor moves back and forth is called $threshold1$, and oscillation limit, O_{lim}, is the maximum number of oscillations until the sensor stops its movement. A sensor stops its movement if its O_{count} equals the O_{lim}.
- *Stability Check*: If a sensor moves less than a $threshold2$ over a number of steps, it can be concluded that it has reached its stable position and it can stop its movement. To count the number of these steps, a variable, $StabilityLimit(S_{lim})$, is defined. The stability check is useful if a sensor breaks down or has reached stable status.

III. SELF-ORGANIZING DEPLOYMENT ALGORITHM (SODA)

A. DSSA limitations

The concept of partial force and the background idea of equilibrium of molecules, make DSSA a prominent solution in WSN to achieve full coverage. However, many assumptions in DSSA are not feasible. Sensitivity to the minimum percentage of initial coverage, initial uniformity, non-single-point-deployment are some assumptions in DSSA, which cannot be applicable in the realistic scenarios. In addition to these assumptions, the high order of time for DSSA from chaos to order state has been observed as one of the challenges. These assumptions and challenges in DSSA are:

1) Single-point-deployment: In many applications in sensor networks like chemical sensitive environment or borders, single-point-deployment is the only way to initially locate the sensors since it is not feasible to uniformly locate the sensors. In DSSA, the initial deployment of sensors is considered to be uniformly distributed in the ROI where in some

```
procedure INITIALIZE
    P ← an array includes all the sensors locations
    $C_R$ ← communication range of sensors
    $S_R$ ← sensing range of sensors
    D ← calculated local density
    $\mathcal{M}$ ← calculated expected density
end procedure

procedure SODA(Until all the sensor nodes are stable)
    Calculate local density for the sensor
    if Sensor i is not stable then
        if Local density > Expected Density ($\mathcal{M}$) then
            Partial Force is ← $Fnew_n(i, j)$
        else
            Partial Force is ← $f_n(i, j)$
        end if

        Update next step position for the sensor

        Check for oscillation
        if Oscillation happens then
            Increase $O_{count}$
            if $O_{count} > O_{limit}$ then
                Move the sensor to centriod of
                oscillation points and make it stable
            end if
        end if

        Check for stability
        if Sensor node is stable then
            Increase $S_{count}$
            if $S_{count} > S_{limit}$ then
                make the sensor stable
            end if
        end if
    end if
end procedure
```

Figure 2. SODA Algorithm.

environments random deployment of sensors is not possible. Therefore, single-point-deployment is a necessity in most of the applications, which initially causes a high local density in a part of ROI.

The partial force in DSSA depends on the local density and distance in between sensors. An illustration of a sensor node and its neighbours in the DSSA is shown in Figure 1. The blue forces are for a scenario where $sensor1$ and 4 blue sensors in the $sensor1$'s neighbourhood are in the area, and the red forces are for another scenario that 4 more red sensors are added in the current area. The size of the partial forces has a direct relationship with their distance to the $sensor1$ and the local density. Therefore, the partial force for a closer sensor like sensor 4, $F14$, is greater than, the partial force for sensor 2, $F12$. In another scenario, if the local density of a sensor increases by adding some sensors (i.e. red sensors in Figure 1), the values of the partial forces even for previous sensors increase, that are shown as red forces.

For scenarios where the density is quite high in a sub-region, the high force moves all the sensors with an unreasonable intensity to the corners. The $\frac{D}{\mathcal{M}^2}$ shows the density factor in the partial force. The $\frac{D}{\mathcal{M}^2}$ parameter is large when sensor i is surrounded with many sensor neighbours. In the dense areas $(C_R - |p_n^i - p_n^j|)$ affects the partial force inversely. The adjacent sensor node creates a larger force in comparison to the sensor, which is far apart and not in the dense area. Therefore, the intense move that is caused by $\frac{D}{\mathcal{M}^2}$ is known as the density factor, which is large in this case. Also the small distance between sensors, which causes $(C_R - |p_n^i - p_n^j|)$ parameter to be closer to C_R. Addressing these issues can improve the performance of the deployment algorithm for all scenarios including the single-point-deployment cases.

2) Sensitivity to the minimum percentage of initial coverage: In order to achieve the best coverage, a minimum coverage during the initial deployment is required in DSSA. The random deployment of the sensors using enough number of sensors in most cases provides more than 90% initial coverage of the ROI [14]. Obtaining a high percentage of coverage during the initial deployment is unreasonable as this level of uniformity for the initial deployment is impossible for most of the practical applications. Therefore, we aim to address this issue.

3) A long process from chaos to order state: In DSSA, the partial force is the key concept. The partial force in a single-point-deployment is large at the few first steps of the algorithm, which causes chaos in the system. The chaos situation proceeds to a stable state as the effect of it decreases by lower partial force. In the DSSA, the order state happens in the last steps of the algorithm before the full coverage is achieved. Therefore, the DSSA needs a long time to reach a stable state.

B. Self-Organising Deployment Algorithm (SODA)

Self-Organising Deployment Algorithm (SODA) is proposed to overcome the limitations mentioned earlier in DSSA. All those limitations are originated from the DSSA uniformly treating of any local area regardless of the density of each neighbourhood. Whereas, the partial force should depend on the density of each neighbourhood to adjust the intensity of applied partial forces in different circumstances. The number of sensors and expected density are two parameters that should determine the intensity of the applied partial force. Adjusting the applied force during the first few movements of each sensor is especially significance to avoid moving nodes chaotically. The partial force is stateless (has no information about the previous and next layout). Therefore, the number of sensors in the neighbourhood and the expected density at the end of the algorithm are used as a guide to control partial force to behave as it is expected.

The detail of this algorithm is presented in Figure 2. In SODA, two steps are considered: initialisation step and force calculation step. The SODA initiates its process by initialising the P, C_R, S_R, D, and calculating $\mathcal{M}$, which is the expected density. After initialisation, SODA is executed at each node as long as the node is unstable. An unstable node is defined as a

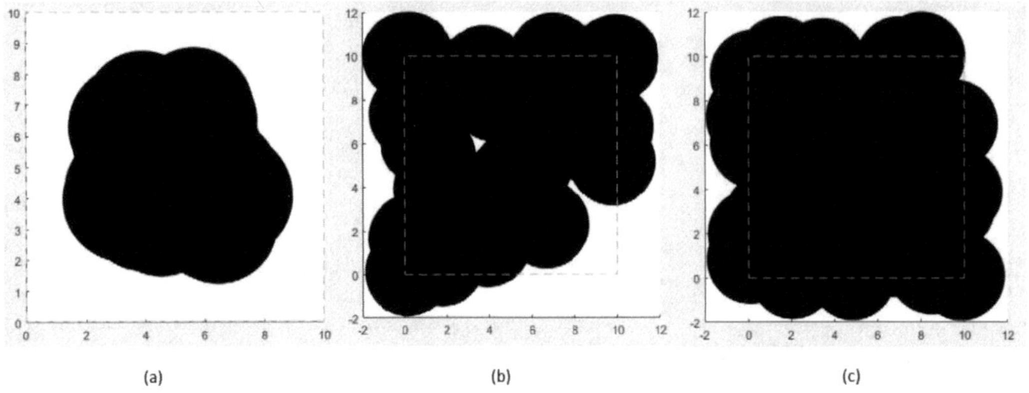

Figure 3. Covered area in a 10x10 region, 30 sensor nodes, $C_R = 4$ and $S_R = 2$: (a) Initial deployment. (b) Final coverage by DSSA. (c) Final coverage by SODA.

node in which has not been reached its oscillation or stability point.

The partial force at each node is calculated based on the local density at each neighbourhood. Equation 1 is used when the local density is lower than the expected density. The following equation is used otherwise:

$$Fnew_n(i,j) = \frac{D}{\mathcal{M} \times N}(C_R - |p_n^i - p_n^j|)\frac{p_n^j - p_n^i}{|p_n^j - p_n^i|} \quad (2)$$

where the applied force is reduced in the dense neighbourhood. In this equation, D, M, and N are local density, expected density and the number of neighbours, respectively. C_R stands for communication range, and p shows the positions of the sensors.

IV. Performance Evaluation

A. Simulation Specifications

The DSSA and SODA algorithms are simulated in a 10 x 10 region using Matlab. The C_R and S_R are assumed 4 and 2, respectively. The $threshold$ for oscillation and stability is considered to be 0.1522, the same as what is used in DSSA performance study [14]. The sensor nodes are considered to be randomly distributed around a point, which is chosen randomly in the ROI. The initial coverage for each scenario is different as the deployment point is chosen randomly. The final coverage by running DSSA in one scenario is presented in Figure 3(b), where this algorithm covers 97.2% of the area. These results are based on 30 sensor nodes, $C_R = 4$ and $S_R = 2$ in a 10 x 10 area. In this deployment, the whole coverage of the requested area is not achieved. The final coverage by SODA for the same initial deployment is presented in Figure 3(c). The initial coverage of 40.76% , presented in Figure 3(a), has resulted in a full coverage by SODA.

The final coverage and the mean travelled distance by every sensor are measured for the different number of deployed sensors in two areas: a 10 x 10 small area and another 20 x 20 area. To obtain reliable results, every experiment is repeatedly executed a number of times for every chosen deployment point, and the average results are taken. The value of $threshold$ for oscillation and stability in 20 x 20 area is considered to be half of the value of $threshold$ in a 10 x 10 area, which is 0.0761. This is because the $threshold$ should be smaller in larger areas since the same number of sensors needs more accurate movements in a larger area to be able to cover the area more efficiently.

B. Results

1) Area Coverage: The initial covered area and the final coverage of DSSA and SODA algorithms are shown in Figures 4 and 5, respectively. The initial coverage for both algorithms is the same because the initial deployment in both experiments is identical. As expected, the final coverage area provided by each algorithm is increased by increasing the network size (i.e., number of sensors). However, the results from the figures show an improvement in the covered area obtained by SODA compared to the DSSA's results in both scenarios. This difference decreases as the number of sensors increases. Therefore, the improvement in coverage descends as the number of sensors increases. It applies to both scenarios. In SODA a dense initial deployment can be locally recognised and very close sensors can be separated gradually regardless of the initial percentage of the coverage. Therefore, the coverage provided by SODA is 10% increased in sparse scenarios where the network is not crowded with sensors. The effectiveness of coverage in SODA in larger networks is more noticeable than in smaller networks. As can be seen from Figure 4, SODA continuously performs well and can achieve up to 20% higher coverage than that of DSSA in an area of 20 x 20.

2) Mean distance: Figures 6 and 7 show the mean distance travelled by every node in both DSSA and SODA. The total distance travelled by every node before reaching a stable state is not appropriate for comparison. Therefore, the mean distance is calculated to compare DSSA and SODA from this perspective. The mean distance is important in case of power usage, and movement mobility of every sensor, which at last causes network stability. Figures 6 and 7 show that the SODA has a smaller mean distance and in result uses less power generally in both areas. The correct movement of the sensors in SODA decreases the transition time from chaos to order state in comparison to DSSA algorithm. The applied partial force in SODA considers the local density and sensor numbers that

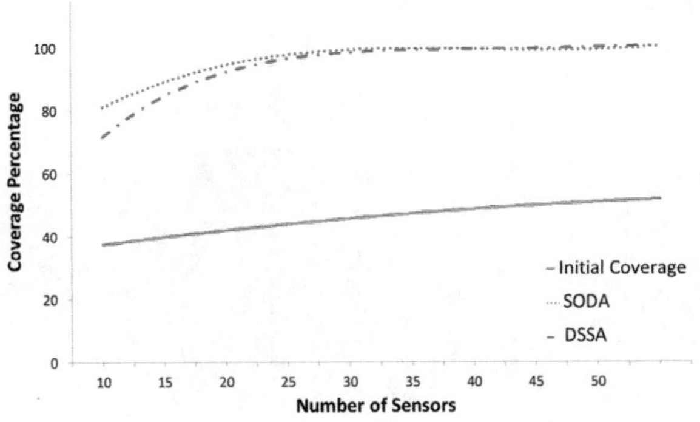

Figure 4. The area coverage in 10 x 10 region

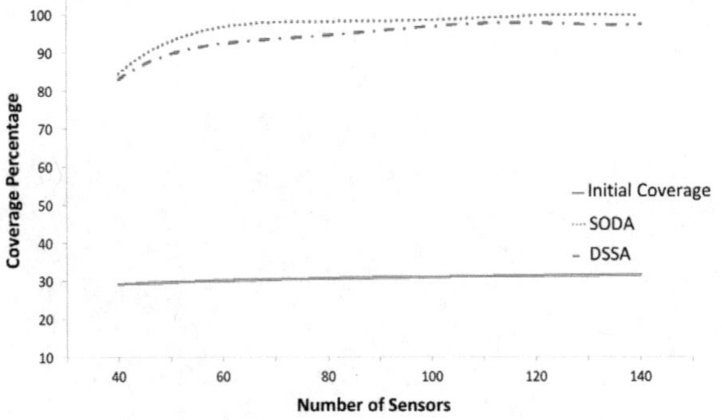

Figure 5. The area coverage in 20 x 20 region

causes more appropriate movements. The proper movement causes the sensors to reach their steady state sooner.

The behaviour in Figures 6 and 7 show that by increasing the number of sensors, the mean distance that every sensor travels rises and very slowly decreases after a while. In Figure 8, three different number of sensors are simulated in the SODA algorithm, and this image is captured after three runs. Based on Figures 6 and 7, the mean distance that every sensor travels increases as the number of sensors increases and then decreases after a while. The turning point in Figure 6, for instance, is 110 sensors. The result of the simulation in Figure 8 shows 6.52, 7.36, and 6.53 as mean distance of 150, 115, and 80 sensors respectively. This data confirms the result from Figures 6 and 7.

The theoretical reason behind this behaviour is the distribution of the sensors. In any size of the area, the mean distance of every sensor node increases as the number of sensor increases. The increase of sensor numbers leads to the higher partial force for every sensor node that causes more movements. However, this increment behaviour stops after a certain point, which is called the Optimal Number of Sensor (ONS). The ONS is where the full coverage of an area is achieved. Although, before ONS point the mean distance of sensors increases, the reduction in mean distance is seen after this point. This behaviour is also based on the density of sensors after this point. The number of neighbours for every sensor increases as the total number of sensors increases. The distribution of these neighbours is asymmetric before ONS point. It makes partial force to be large; however, when the number of sensors is greater than the ONS, the node arrangement in every neighbourhood tends to be more symmetrical and hence, their forces counterbalance every other. Consequently, less force implied shorter movement, which results in a lower mean distance.

V. Conclusion and Future Works

Coverage can be considered as the practical measurement of wireless sensor networks due to its direct impact on the network performance. Many factors, such as sensors technical specifications, network topology and most importantly, deployment algorithms influence the designated coverage. Maximising coverage using the resource constrained nodes is usually the goal of any deployment algorithm.

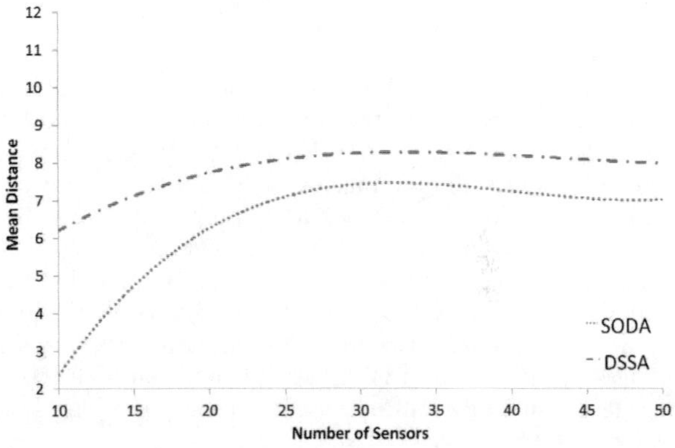

Figure 6. Mean distance in 10 x 10 region

In this paper, we have proposed SODA for mobile sensor networks. SODA is based on the DSSA that is reported in the literature, which is inspired by the equilibrium of molecules to provide the required coverage. However, the effectiveness of DSSA is highly dependent on the initial deployment of the nodes and also subject to providing a minimum initial coverage. These issues have been addressed in SODA. Furthermore, SODA's transition from chaos (i.e., initial deployment) to order (stabilised nodes) state is faster.

In our performance study, the performance of SODA has

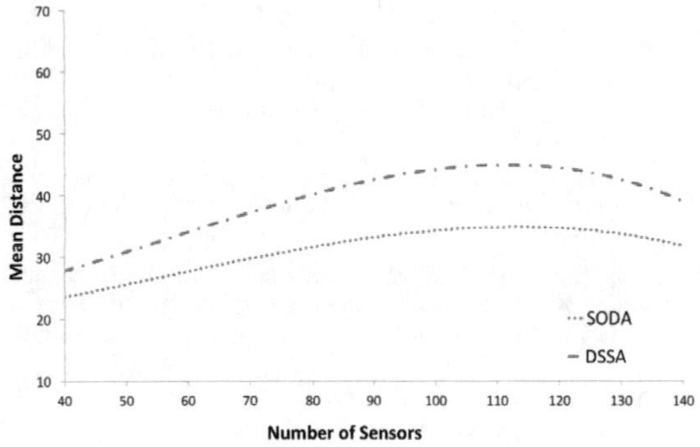

Figure 7. Mean distance in 20 x 20 region

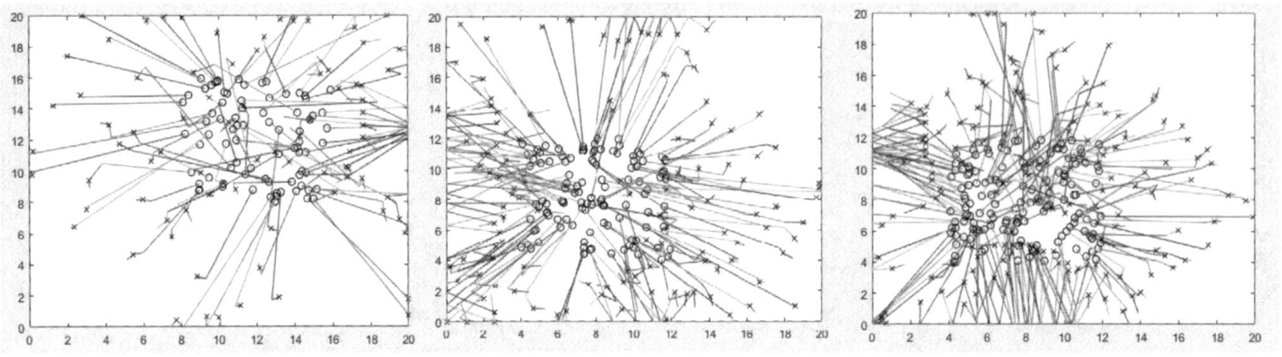

(a) (b) (c)

Figure 8. Sensors movements in 20x20 region: (a) Movements of 80 sensors. (b) Movements of 115 sensors. (c) Movements of 150 sensors.

been compared to DSSA, by simulating both algorithms in Matlab and measuring the final percentage of the coverage, and the mean distance travelled by every node. Simulation results confirm the advantages of SODA to achieve a more uniform distribution of nodes after applying the algorithm and hence a better coverage. The SODA solution has improved the final percentage of coverage by 10% and the mean distance has been reduced by 10% to even 60% in comparison to those of DSSA. The faster transition from chaos to order causes the faster symmetric form of each neighbourhood with less mean distance for every sensor and consequently resulting in lower power consumption.

In more realistic scenarios, WSNs can be used in a large area, where the ROI can be divided into multiple sub-regions for easy deployment. Finding an optimal solution to provide a trade-off between the number of sub-region and the designated coverage can be a direction for future work. Additionally, extending SODA to be able to utilise two-hops neighbouring information, or even more, when calculating the partial force at each neighbourhood may yield benefits beyond those of one-hop SODA. As another line, we are going to study this in the future.

REFERENCES

[1] J. Yick, B. Mukherjee, and D. Ghosal, "Wireless sensor network survey," Computer networks, vol. 52, no. 12, 2008, pp. 2292–2330.

[2] H. Alemdar and C. Ersoy, "Wireless sensor networks for healthcare: A survey," Computer networks, vol. 54, no. 15, 2010, pp. 2688–2710.

[3] G. Tuna, V. C. Gungor, and K. Gulez, "An autonomous wireless sensor network deployment system using mobile robots for human existence detection in case of disasters," Ad Hoc Networks, vol. 13, 2014, pp. 54–68.

[4] D. Tao and T.-Y. Wu, "A survey on barrier coverage problem in directional sensor networks," IEEE sensors journal, vol. 15, no. 2, 2015, pp. 876–885.

[5] T. J. Chowdhury, C. Elkin, V. Devabhaktuni, D. B. Rawat, and J. Oluoch, "Advances on localization techniques for wireless sensor networks: A survey," Computer Networks, vol. 110, 2016, pp. 284–305.

[6] A. Ghosh and S. K. Das, "Coverage and connectivity issues in wireless sensor networks: A survey," Pervasive and Mobile Computing, vol. 4, no. 3, 2008, pp. 303–334.

[7] A. Simonetto and G. Leus, "Distributed maximum likelihood sensor network localization," IEEE Trans. Signal Processing, vol. 62, no. 6, 2014, pp. 1424–1437.

[8] B. Horling, R. Vincent, R. Mailler, J. Shen, R. Becker, K. Rawlins, and V. Lesser, "Distributed sensor network for real time tracking," in Proceedings of the fifth international conference on Autonomous agents. ACM, 2001, pp. 417–424.

[9] A. Baranzadeh and V. Nazarzehi, "A decentralized formation building algorithm with obstacle avoidance for multi-robot systems," in Robotics and Biomimetics (ROBIO), 2015 IEEE International Conference on. IEEE, 2015, pp. 2513–2518.

[10] J. Liang and Q. Liang, "Design and analysis of distributed radar sensor networks," IEEE Transactions on Parallel and Distributed Systems, vol. 22, no. 11, 2011, pp. 1926–1933.

[11] V. Nazarzehi, A. V. Savkin, and A. Baranzadeh, "Distributed 3d dynamic search coverage for mobile wireless sensor networks," IEEE Communications Letters, vol. 19, no. 4, 2015, pp. 633–636.

[12] H. Mahboubi, K. Moezzi, A. G. Aghdam, K. Sayrafian-Pour, and V. Marbukh, "Distributed deployment algorithms for improved coverage in a network of wireless mobile sensors," IEEE Transactions on Industrial Informatics, vol. 10, no. 1, 2014, pp. 163–174.

[13] C.-F. Cheng, T.-Y. Wu, and H.-C. Liao, "A density-barrier construction algorithm with minimum total movement in mobile wsns," Computer Networks, vol. 62, 2014, pp. 208–220.

[14] N. Heo and P. K. Varshney, "Energy-efficient deployment of intelligent mobile sensor networks," IEEE Transactions on Systems, Man, and Cybernetics-Part A: Systems and Humans, vol. 35, no. 1, 2005, pp. 78–92.

[15] G. Werner-Allen, K. Lorincz, J. Johnson, J. Lees, and M. Welsh, "Fidelity and yield in a volcano monitoring sensor network," in Proceedings of the 7th symposium on Operating systems design and implementation. USENIX Association, 2006, pp. 381–396.

Vessel Profile Indicators using Fuzzy Logic Reasoning and AIS

Konstantinos Chatzikokolakis[*], Dimitrios Zissis[*†] and Giannis Spiliopoulos[*]
[*]MarineTraffic, London, United Kingdom
[†]Department of Product & Systems Design Engineering, University of the Aegean, Greece
email: konstantinos.chatzikokolakis@marinetraffic.com, dzissis@aegean.gr, giannis.spiliopoulos@marinetraffic.com

Abstract— **Early vessel profiling and risk assessment is a critical component of advanced maritime tracking systems, required by a number of maritime stakeholders including custom controls, port authorities, coastguards and others. This paper reports on the development of a fuzzy logic reasoning tool for generating maritime vessel profile indicators through the Automatic Identification System (AIS). The report describes the need and the underlying statistical methods applied, which are based on Fuzzy Logic Reasoning, for finding potential profile indicators and classifying vessels to a degree of "risk", thus requiring further examination and monitoring. Under conservative assumptions, some preliminary results about the probabilities and boundaries of potential indicators are presented and discussed.**

Keywords-AIS; Maritime Domain Awareness; Anomaly Detection; Fuzzy Logic System.

I. INTRODUCTION

Maritime Domain Awareness (MDA) is the effective understanding of activities, events and threats in the maritime environment that could impact global safety, security, economic activity or the environment [1]. Recent advancements in Information and Communications Technologies (ICT) have created opportunities for increasing MDA, through better monitoring and understanding of vessel movements. The International Maritime Organisation (IMO) identified this issue as affecting the safety and efficiency of navigation and initiated a work program named e-Navigation to reduce the "confusion of profusion". The IMO defines e-Navigation as: "the harmonised collection, integration, exchange, presentation and analysis of maritime information onboard and ashore by electronic means to enhance berth to berth navigation and related services, for safety and security at sea and protection of the marine environment" [2]. e-Navigation is expected to contribute to safer waterways, reducing accidents and environmental incidents through improved situational and traffic awareness both afloat and ashore [3].

Sea transport surveillance has been ineffective in the past decades due to lack of data, but nowadays tracking technology (i.e., Automatic Identification System, AIS) has transformed the problem into one of data overload [4]. For the last decade AIS has been inseparable part of the modern maritime industry. The original purpose of the system was to reduce collision risks, by providing vessels' crews the necessary traffic information. The AIS transponders are capable of communicating in range of a few kilometres (i.e., less than 50km) and although the AIS system was not designed to be monitored in a centralised method, the maritime industry has been extremely interested in such systems (e.g., MarineTraffic, etc.).

Positional data together with the departure and destination ports transmitted in AIS messages can be used for route prediction and in conjunction with vessel's speed, time of arrival prediction is possible. Performing complex operations over such large datasets can give extra insights besides route prediction. For instance, combining route forecasts for multiple vessels can provide early warnings of possible collisions (by determining whether vessels' routes will meet in space and time) and actual route data can be used to perform various kinds of complex analytics (e.g., root-cause analysis in case of forensic investigation). In addition, improving the route analysis process can offer to various maritime stakeholders (e.g., shipping companies, charterers, insurance companies and port authorities) the opportunity to perform risk analysis and understand better any possible threats of vessels' manoeuvres, or even perform environment impact assessment, providing CO_2 emissions and fuel consumption predictions. Ultimately, AIS historical data can be used to determine actual sea lanes, their capacity and port connections, produce realistic vessel operational profiles that determine the normal behaviour of specific vessel types, detect any anomalies (i.e., irregular behaviour) and much more.

Anomaly is a "strange" deviation from a vessel's normal behaviour, meaning that it is inconsistent with, or straying from what is usual, normal or expected, or because it is not conforming to rules, laws or regulations [5]. Detecting an anomaly can be defined as a method that supports situation assessment by indicating objects and situations that deviate from the expected behaviour and thus may be of interest for further investigation. The understanding of the complex maritime environment and a vessel normal behaviour though, can never be limited to simply adding up and connecting various vessel positions as they travel across the seas. A combination of static information such as reporting information, vessel's flag (i.e., country), ship's owner, vessel's name, IMO and Maritime Mobile Service Identity (MMSI) and destination port with dynamic information such as speed/course changes, proximity with other vessels or structures, etc., is needed to classify possible abnormal ship's behaviour. An anomaly can be classified as either static or dynamic depending on the vessel's characteristics that distinguish the behaviour as anomaly. Static anomalies are related to vessel's identification information mismatches or irregular changes. This information includes vessel's flag, IMO, MMSI, vessel's name and owner company. In addition, irregular changes in destination reported from AIS messages (particularly when the vessel is under-way) is a potential indicator of risk. Combining such information with port inspections or incident reports that prove vessels are not conforming to regulations can also assist in anomaly detection; thus, classifying a vessel as potentially riskier than others and worthy of further investigation and monitoring. Dynamic anomalies are mostly related to vessels' voyages and deviations from these. Speed or course changes, proximity with other vessels, and mismatches between the ship type and the sea lane (or zone) travelling are aspects that could constitute a dynamic anomaly.

In this paper, we propose a decision support system that evaluates modifications of vessel identities and mismatches between reported destinations and actual port calls to determine possible risks (i.e., static anomalies). As this is a complex problem that requires the evaluation of multiple criteria while relying on inexact or partial knowledge obtained from the analysis of the AIS messages, we introduce a fuzzy-logic based mechanism that maritime stakeholders can use to detect risk indicators and classify vessels.

The rest of this paper is structured as follows; Section II provides the state-of-the-art analysis for anomaly detection. Then, Section III presents the proposed Fuzzy Logic (FL) Reasoner and Section IV provides the analysis of the correlation of the FL inputs with the produced output. Finally, Section V concludes our work and discusses possible future extensions.

II. Related Work

Static anomaly detection is mostly treated as a decision-making process driven by risk identification/assessment in the related literature. Two classes of solutions are dominant in this perspective; the ones relying on probabilistic risk assessment and the ones using fuzzy logic as a relaxation approach to the definite boundaries of probabilistic approaches. Probabilistic risk assessment has been introduced as a solution for the assessment of risk in the maritime domain in [6]. In [7], the authors applied a Bayesian simulation for the occurrence of situations with accident potential and a Bayesian multivariate regression analysis of the relationship between factors describing these situations and expert judgments of accident risk, to perform a full-scale assessment of risk and uncertainty. A fuzzy approach that evaluates the maritime risk assessment when applied to safety at sea and more particularly, the pollution prevention on the open sea is introduced in [8]. The proposed decision-making system exploits a set of open datasets combined with human expert experience to perform information analysis and define the risk factor. Besides this solution, other approaches [9][10] also rely on Fuzzy-Bayesian networks to model maritime security risks.

Dynamic anomaly detection is highly related to efficiently handling vast amount of mostly positional data. Previous works have been focused on extracting knowledge regarding motion patterns from AIS data in support of MDA including numerous methods of supervised and unsupervised clustering data mining techniques. In their work [11], Pallotta et al. propose the TREAD methodology as a method of automatically learning a statistical model for maritime traffic from AIS data in an unsupervised way as a framework for anomaly detection and route prediction. A statistical analysis upon AIS data to extract motion patterns, predict vessel movements and detect possible anomalies in their itineraries is introduced in [12]. In relation to AIS and sea ports research, AIS data are used in [13] to model maritime terminals operations, specifically focusing on the Port of Messina. In [14], the authors introduce a two-step methodology for anomaly detection that attempts to deal with the scalability issues caused by the vast amount of raw AIS data by distributing the learning process. Firstly, a density-based clustering algorithm that uses spatial and voyage information is used to distinguish "normal" vessel positions from the "abnormal". Then, the labelled dataset is fed as training data into a distributed supervised learning algorithm running on Hadoop.

Spatial join queries, which combine trajectory datasets and a spatial objects dataset based on spatio-temporal predicates, have high computational requirements, which often lead to long query latencies. In [15], Ray et al. propose a parallel in-memory trajectory-based Spatiotemporal Topological join (PISTON), a parallel main memory query execution infrastructure designed specifically to address the difficulties of spatio-temporal joins. Generally, the methods which are used in the context of anomaly detection are based on statistical/probabilistic models [16]–[19], such as the Gaussian Mixture Model (GMM) and the adaptive Kernel Density Estimator (KDE) [12][20], Bayesian networks [21]–[24], but also neural networks [25]–[27] and hybrid approaches [28].

A number of prototype systems have been developed for experimental and operational reasons. For example, SeeCoast [29] is installed at Kount Harbor Operations Center in Portsmouth, Virginia. The system uses the Hawkeye system to fuse video data with radar signals and AIS messages to produce fused vessel tracks in or close by the port and reliably detect anomalies on such tracks. SCANMARIS [30] is a feedback-based system tested at "Centre Régional Opérationnel de Surveillance et Sauvetage Corsen" on Ouessant traffic management. It uses a rule-based learning engine to process data fused from maritime traffic imagery, alert operators based on the rules defining anomalies and adapt its operation through the operators' feedback. LEPER [31], which was tested successfully at the Joint Interagency Task Force South (JIATF South), is a system that performs primitive geohashing using a military grid reference system upon which it decomposes ship's trajectories into sequences of discrete squares and uses Hidden Markov Model to calculate transition probabilities between grid locations. The predicted location is compared with the vessel's position (determined by the speed and heading of the vessel) and if the distance between these two positions is above a predefined threshold, an anomaly is raised. Other notable prototypes that currently exist are SECMAR [32], FastC2AP [33] and MALEF [34].

In our work, we introduce a Fuzzy Logic Reasoner in which the thresholds of the Fuzzy Logic Rules are based on statistical analysis and not on experts' view.

III. FUZZY LOGIC REASONER FOR ANOMALY DETECTION

Fuzzy logic was first introduced in [35] by Lotfi Zadeh and relies on the theory of fuzzy sets. Contrary to the classical set theory, such sets contain element with degree of membership. This approach exploits the notion of degree in the verification of a condition, enabling conditions to be in intermediate states between the states of conventional evaluations, thus allowing variables to be "partially" true, or "not definitely yes" etc. Such notions can be formulated mathematically and processed by machines, giving thus a more human-like interaction between the programmer and the computers [36]. Fuzzy logic has been selected for static anomaly detection as it is considered to be an ideal tool when dealing with imprecise or contradictive data, which can be modelled adequately with fuzzy sets, and combined with human logic [37].

A Fuzzy Inference System (FIS) is the fundamental implementation of fuzzy logic schemes comprising three key elements, namely the fuzzifier, the inference engine and the defuzzifier. The first element is responsible for transforming crisp values (e.g., real, integer, natural number, etc.) to fuzzy degrees of membership to states (i.e., values between the [0,1] interval). Then, the inference engine exploits a set of if-then rules compiled by experts to link the inputs with the outputs and afterwards it collects and aggregates all the outputs of every rule into one fuzzy set. Multiple aggregation schemes have been proposed and applied relying on the maximum value, summing up the outputs or performing a probabilistic analysis on the produced fuzzy set. The sum aggregation is the most common one and also the one applied in our Fuzzy Reasoner. Finally, the defuzzifier aggregates the outcomes of all the fuzzy rules defuzzifies them to a single crisp value which is the output of the Fuzzy Reasoner.

Thus, in order to define the FIS, the set of inputs and the output of the rule set should be defined. In the context of static anomaly detection, the inputs are the vessels' static characteristics and the output is the fuzzy anomaly detection indicator. Table I sums up the rule set that drives the Fuzzy Inference System. Each rule is a union of conditions that when met the corresponding output is triggered (based also on the fuzzy degree). Thus, each set of input values may match to multiple rules with a certain degree. The defuzzifier will take this fact into account when transforming the fuzzy values into a crisp output.

The proposed Fuzzy Reasoner (FR) produces a vessel anomaly indicator which captures the behavior of the vessel according to its static characteristics. The FR takes into consideration three inputs, namely "flag changes frequency", "name changes frequency" and "destination changed/port arrival deviation". "Flag changes frequency" captures how many times a vessel has changed its flag over a specific time period. Although this is not a de facto metric of abnormal behavior, frequent changes may be linked with fraudulent registrations or other illegal activities [38]. Furthermore, in order to minimize the probability of false negative cases (i.e., falsely assuming a vessel to be performing abnormaly), we take into account only flags that according to Paris MoU organization perform poorly [39]. "Name changes frequency", similarly to the previous input is the input that captures how many times a vessel has transmitted a different vessel name through its AIS transponder in a specific time period and it is another indicator that a vessel may be trying to spoof its messages and hide its identity (e.g. O Ka San vessel that falsely transmitted its name to be Sarisa) [38]. Destination changed/Port Arrivals deviation: This input captures the mismatches between the number of destination ports a vessel reports through its AIS transponder compared to actual port arrivals. The latter have been produced through spatial analysis of the vessels' reported positions and the ports locations. The metric for this input is calculated based on. (1). Finally, the output of the Fuzzy Inference engine is an indicator for vessel anomaly that the related stakeholders should further investigate its compliance to international safety, security and environmental standards.

$$\text{Deviation} = 1 - \#\text{Dest\_changed} / \#\text{Port\_Arrivals} \quad (1)$$

As depicted in Table I, we have selected two Membership Functions for the first two inputs labeled as Low and High and three Membership functions (i.e., Low, Normal and High) for the third input. This decision was due to the nature of the inputs. More specifically, "flag change frequency" and "name change frequency" are bounded in the [0, +∞) range with zero being the less risky situation (i.e., normal) while the "destination changed/port arrival deviation" is bounded in the [-∞, 1) range with zero being the normal situation, in which case the reported number of destinations is equal to the actual port arrivals.

TABLE I. FUZZY LOGIC RULES

Rule No.	Inputs			Output
	Flag changes frequency	*Name change frequency*	*Destination changed/Port Arrivals deviation*	*Vessel anomaly indicator*
1	Low	Low	Low	Medium
2	Low	Low	Normal	Low
3	Low	Low	High	Medium
4	Low	High	Low	Medium
5	Low	High	Normal	Low
6	Low	High	High	Medium
7	High	Low	Low	High
8	High	Low	Normal	Medium
9	High	Low	High	High
10	High	High	Low	High
11	High	High	Normal	High
12	High	High	High	High

Although the Fuzzy Logic ruleset is compiled by experts, determining the shapes and the boundaries of the membership functions for each input is a difficult process that should be carefully designed. In our approach, shapes and boundaries are determined based on statistical analysis of observed flag changes, name changes and destination changed/port arrivals mismatches. The data used in this study is an AIS dataset provided by MarineTraffic, covering the entire globe and collected during 2017.

Multiple shapes for the membership functions can be used relying on the nature of each input (i.e., the data distribution) with the triangular, trapezoidal and Gaussian being the most commonly used. In our system, triangular membership functions have been used for the flag change frequency and the name change frequency, because at certain values we are certain about the state that they are capturing. On the other hand, for the destination changed/port arrivals input gaussian membership function has been used for exploiting the continuous and non-negative nature of this membership function at the definition domain. Finally, Gaussian membership function has also been applied on the output for its smoothness in the decision-making process.

In order to determine the boundaries of the Membership Functions of each input, we have calculated the probability distribution of each input. Figure 1, Figure 2 and Figure 3 show the Cumulative Distribution Function (CDF) for the vessel flag changes, name changes and destination reported/arrival deviation respectively. As shown in Figure 1, most of the vessels (i.e., 91%) have made one or two flag changes in 2017, thus the boundary between the low and the high membership function of this input is set to two.

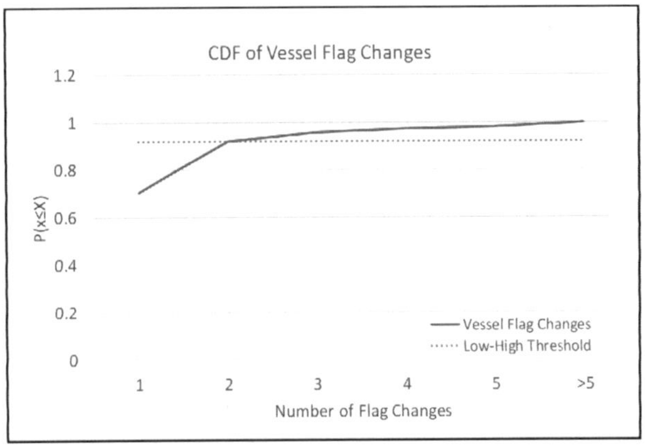

Figure 1. Cumulative Distribution Function of number of vessel flag changes

Figure 2 highlights the CDF for the Vessel name changes. The curve in this case is smoother compared to the Flag Changes and most of the vessels (i.e., 89%) have four or less name changes in a full year. Thus, the boundary between Low and High is set to four for this input.

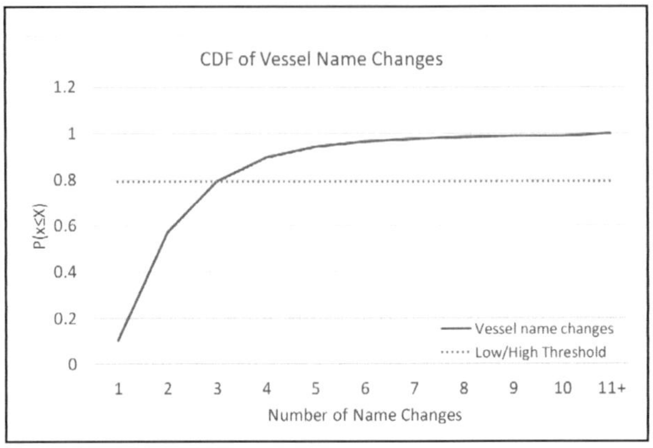

Figure 2. Cumulative Distribution Function of number of vessel name changes

Finally, Figure 3 highlights the CDF for the destination reported/port arrival deviation. This input is calculated based on (1) and normal behavior for a vessel would result in deviation equal, or near to zero. There are two cases of anomalies included in (1). If the deviation is near 1 then the destinations reported are much less than the actual arrivals which implies that the vessel's crew is not reporting vessel's itineraries. On the other hand, if the deviation is negative for a vessel, then this means that it changes its destination more frequently than its actual voyages, which is an abnormal and possibly risky situation. Thus, in this case we have three membership functions, Low, Normal and High capturing these three possible situations. The boundaries are such that Low and High deviation correspond to 7.5% of the vessels each and Normal corresponds to 85%.

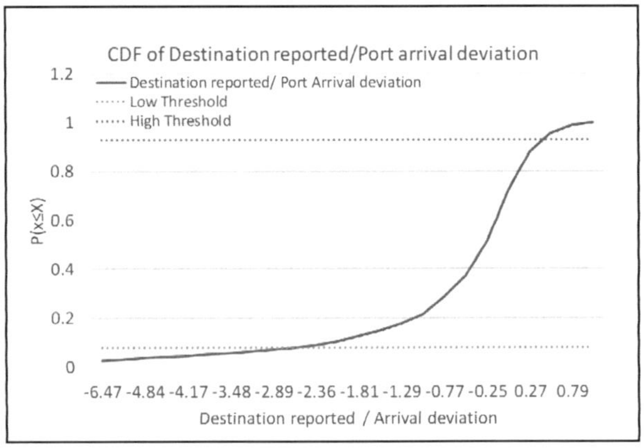

Figure 3. Cumulative Distribution Function of destination reported/port arrival deviation

IV. Discussion and Conclusions

Detection and classification of vessels to profiles of vessels requiring further monitoring is a requirement of many maritime authorities. In this work, we suggest a tool which makes use of Fuzzy Logic Reasoning and exploits open maritime tracking data, such as that collected through the AIS to build such indicators.

We notice that frequent flag and vessel name changes are strong indicators of vessels operating outside normal behavioral patterns. Specifically based on the distribution and while taking into account the uncertainty of the data, we detect that most of the vessels (i.e., 89%) have four or less name changes in a full year, while the majority of vessels (i.e., 91%) have made one or two flag changes. Our broader goal is that of building an expert system of automatic anomaly detection for both positional and static data transmitted by vessels, which would increase the effectiveness of the system and high-level situational understanding. In our future work, we will perform thorough experimental evaluations of our fuzzy inference algorithms in combination with positional anomaly detection.

ACKNOWLEDGMENT

This project has received funding from the European Union's Horizon 2020 research and innovation programme under grant agreement No 732310.

REFERENCES

[1] B. Santos and K. Lunday, "Maritime Domain Awareness-International involvement to promote maritime security and safety," Proc. Mar. Saf. Secur. Counc. Coast Guard J. Saf. Secur. Sea, pp. 24-28, 2009.

[2] IMO MSC 85/26/Add.1 Annex 20 – Strategy for the development and implementation of e - Navigation (section 1.1). London: International Maritime Organization

[3] e-Navigation Strategic Action Plan, US Committee on the Marine Transportation System, 1200 New Jersey Avenue, SE, 2012.

[4] L. Millefiori, D. Zissis, L. Cazzanti, and G. Arcieri, "Computational Maritime Situational Awareness Techniques for Unsupervised Port Area," NATO Unclassified Reports, Science and Technology Organisation Centre for Maritime Research and Experimentation, La Spezia, Italy, 2016.

[5] J. Roy and M. Davenport, "Categorisation of Maritime Anomalies for Notification and Alerting Purpose," in: NATO Work. Data Fusion Anom. Detect. Marit. Situational Aware., 2009.

[6] T. Bedford and R.M. Cooke, "Probabilistic risk analysis : foundations and methods," Cambridge University Press, 2001.

[7] J.R.W. Merrick and J.R. Van Dorp, "Speaking the Truth in Maritime Risk Assessment," Risk Analysis, 26(1), pp. 223-237.

[8] J.-F. Balmat, F. Lafont, R. Maifret, and N. Pessel, "A decision-making system to maritime risk assessment," Ocean Eng. 38, pp. 171–176, 2011. doi:10.1016/j.oceaneng.2010.10.012.

[9] A. G. Eleye-Datubo, A. Wall, and J. Wang, "Marine and offshore safety assessment by incorporative risk modelling in a fuzzy-Bayesian network of an induced mass assignment paradigm," Risk Analysis, vol. 28, no. 1, pp. 95-112, 2008.

[10] Z. Yang, S. Bonsall, and J. Wang, "Fuzzy Rule-Based Bayesian Reasoning Approach for Prioritization of Failures in FMEA," IEEE Trans. Reliab. vol. 57, pp. 517–528, 2008. doi:10.1109/TR.2008.928208.

[11] G. Pallotta, M. Vespe, and K. Bryan, "Vessel Pattern Knowledge Discovery from AIS Data: A Framework for Anomaly Detection and Route Prediction," Entropy, vol. 15, no.6, pp. 2218–2245, 2013. doi:10.3390/e15062218.

[12] B. Ristic, B. La Scala, M. Morelande and N. Gordon, "Statistical analysis of motion patterns in AIS Data: Anomaly detection and motion prediction," 2008 11th International Conference on Information Fusion, Cologne, 2008, pp. 1-7.

[13] S. Ricci, C. Marinacci, and L. Rizzetto, "The Modelling Support to Maritime Terminals Sea operation: The Case Study of Post Messina," Journal of Maritime Research vol. 9 (Issue 3), pp 39–43 (ISSN: 1697–4840), 2014.

[14] B. Huijbrechts, M. Velikova, R. Scheepens, and S. Michels, "Metis: An integrated reference architecture for addressing uncertainty in decisionsupport systems," Procedia Computer Science, vol. 44, pp. 476–485, 2015.

[15] S. Ray, A. Demke Brown, N. Koudas, R. Blanco and A. K. Goel, "Parallel in-memory trajectory-based spatiotemporal topological join," 2015 IEEE International Conference on Big Data (Big Data), Santa Clara, CA, 2015, pp. 361-370. doi: 10.1109/BigData.2015.7363777.

[16] A. Dahlbom and L. Niklasson, "Trajectory clustering for coastal surveillance," 2007 10th International Conference on Information Fusion, Quebec, Que., 2007, pp. 1-8. doi: 10.1109/ICIF.2007.4408114

[17] D. Lindsay and S. Cox, "Effective probability forecasting for time series data using standard machine learning techniques," in Pattern Recognition and Data Mining, 2005, pp. 35–44. doi:10.1007/11551188.

[18] G.K.D. de Vries and M. Van Someren, "Machine learning for vessel trajectories using compression, alignments and domain knowledge," Expert Systems with Applications, vol. 39, 2012, pp. 13426–13439.

[19] K. Kowalska and L. Peel, "Maritime anomaly detection using Gaussian Process active learning," 2012 15th International Conference on Information Fusion, Singapore, 2012, pp. 1164-1171.

[20] R. Laxhammar, G. Falkman and E. Sviestins, "Anomaly detection in sea traffic - A comparison of the Gaussian Mixture Model and the Kernel Density Estimator," 2009 12th International Conference on Information Fusion, Seattle, WA, 2009, pp. 756-763.

[21] F. Johansson and G. Falkman, "Detection of vessel anomalies - a Bayesian network approach, in: 2007 3rd Int. Conf. Intell. Sensors, Sens. Networks Inf., IEEE, 2007: pp. 395–400. doi:10.1109/ISSNIP.2007.4496876.

[22] A. Nicholson, F. Cozman, S. Mascaro, A.E. Nicholso, and K.B. Korb, "Anomaly detection in vessel tracks using Bayesian networks," Int. J. Approx. Reason. 55, 2014, pp. 84–98.

[23] R.O. Lane, D.A. Nevell, S.D. Hayward, and T.W. Beaney, "Maritime anomaly detection and threat assessment," 2010, pp. 1–8.

[24] F. Fooladvandi, C. Brax, P. Gustavsson, and M. Fredin, "Signature-based activity detection based on Bayesian networks acquired from expert knowledge," 2009, pp. 436–443.

[25] N. Bomberger, B. Rhodes, M. Seibert, and A. Waxman, "Associative Learning of Vessel Motion Patterns for Maritime Situation Awareness," in: 2006 9th Int. Conf. Inf. Fusion, IEEE, 2006: pp. 1–8. doi:10.1109/ICIF.2006.301661.

[26] B.J. Rhodes, N.A. Bomberger, and M. Zandipour, "Probabilistic associative learning of vessel motion patterns at multiple spatial scales for maritime situation awareness," in: 2007 10th Int. Conf. Inf. Fusion, IEEE, 2007: pp. 1–8. doi:10.1109/ICIF.2007.4408127.

[27] S.-B.C. Sang-Jun Han and Kyung-Joong Kim, "Evolutionary Learning Program's Behavior in Neural Networks for Anomaly Detection," in: N.R. Pal, N. Kasabov, R.K. Mudi, S. Pal, S.K. Parui (Eds.), Neural Inf. Process., Springer Berlin Heidelberg, Berlin, Heidelberg, 2004. doi:10.1007/b103766.

[28] J.B. Kraiman, S.L. Arouh, and M.L. Webb, "Automated anomaly detection processor," in: A.F. Sisti, D.A. Trevisani

(Eds.), Proc. SPIE 4716, Enabling Technol. Simul. Sci. VI, 128, International Society for Optics and Photonics, 2002: pp. 128–137. doi:10.1117/12.474940.

[29] M. Seibert et al., "SeeCoast port surveillance," in: M.J. DeWeert, T.T. Saito, H.L. Guthmuller (Eds.), 2006: p. 62040B. doi:10.1117/12.666980.

[30] M. Morel et al., SCANMARIS Project – Detection of Abnormal Vessel Behaviours, in: NATO Work. Data Fusion Anom. Detect. Marit. Situational Aware. (NATO MSA 2009), La Spezia, Italy, 2009.

[31] C. Griffin, "Learning and Prediction for Enhanced Readiness: An ONR Office 31 Program," in: Present. to TTCP MAR AG-8, 2009.

[32] M. Géhant, V. Roy, J.-P. Marmorat, and M. Bordier, "A Behaviour Analysis Prototype for Application to Maritime Security," in: NATO Work. Data Fusion Anom. Detect. Marit. Situational Aware. (NATO MSA 2009), La Spezia, Italy, 2009.

[33] DARPA, Fast Connectivity for Coalitions and Agents Project, Fact Sheet, 2005.

[34] J. Tozicka, M. Rovatsos, M. Pechoucek, and S. Urban, "MALEF: Framework for distributed machine learning and data mining," Int. J. Intell. Inf. Database Syst. 2 (2008) 6. doi:10.1504/IJIIDS.2008.017242.

[35] L.A. Zadeh, "Fuzzy sets," Inf. Control. 8, 1965, pp. 338–353. doi:10.1016/S0019-9958(65)90241-X.

[36] L.A. Zadeh, "Making computers think like people," IEEE Spectr. 21, 1984, pp. 26–32. doi:10.1109/MSPEC.1984.6370431.

[37] K. Chatzikokolakis, P. Spapis, A. Kaloxylos, G. Beinas, and N. Alonistioti, "Spectrum sharing: A coordination framework enabled by fuzzy logic," in: 2015 Int. Conf. Comput. Inf. Telecommun. Syst., IEEE, 2015: pp. 1–5. doi:10.1109/CITS.2015.7297761.

[38] https://thediplomat.com/2018/09/fake-flags-at-sea-sanctions-enforcement-and-ship-identity-falsification/ (Accessed on 08/10/2018)

[39] https://www.parismou.org/2017-performance-lists-paris-mou (Accessed on 08/10/2018)

Graph Theory and NoSQL Database Applied to School Scheduling Problem

Jocivan Suassone Alves, Luídne da Silva Mota, Carlos Henrique Correa Tolentino
IFTO - Federal Institute of Education,
Science and Technology of Tocantins
Palmas, Tocantins, Brazil
Email: {suassone, luidne}@gmail.com, chtolentino@ifto.edu.br

***Abstract*—This paper presents a graph-based model for the school scheduling problem. A Web system was developed using the Neo4J graph-oriented non-relational database management system. The results show that investing in the modeling and use of a fully compatible database management system is worth the cost and effort, since the execution time for the algorithms was highly satisfactory. The modeling is extensible and supports representation of other aspects of the problem, while the architecture of the solution allows each of its components to be optimized without impacting the others, favoring the development of future work.**

***Keywords*–Graph; Scheduling Problem; Neo4j.**

I. Introduction

School scheduling is a problem that affects educational institutions around the world. That is the case with the IFTO - Federal Institute of Education, Science and Technology of Tocantins, a public institution for secondary, technical and college education. The campus in the state capital Palmas alone, has 29 courses at different educational levels and more than 250 teachers.

This problem has already been used as a case study to validate several modeling and optimization techniques and there are many software products that help solve it. On the other hand, the cost of this software makes it difficult for public institutions with scarce resources to acquire it. In this way, the task is usually dealt with by a single person or team, who are usually overwhelmed. This fact increases the chances of obtaining inconsistent class scheduling as a result.

According to Sousa et al. [1], the problem of generation of schedules is NP-Complete, which means that it can-not be solved with polynomial runtime algorithms and the exact methods, meaning that, algorithms that always return the optimal solution normally run for prohibitive computational times. However, according to Saviniec et al. [2], for that reason, the approach to the problem must be made by heuristic methods which, although not guaranteeing an optimal solution, are able to generate satisfactory solutions in an acceptable runtime.

Due to nature of the problem, which requires robust tools for solving it, the human cost involved, the constant changes in the courses offered by the institutions, as well as the inconstancy of relationship between teachers-courses-students and other peculiarities of the public sector, it is appropriate to propose a solution that fits the IFTO profile using free tools and to explore its positive aspects.

Because school resources are better used in didactic and pedagogical than in administrative activities, this work presents the development stages of software for performing the automatic generation of class schedules for the IFTO - Campus Palmas. The main objectives are to provide:

- Graph-based modeling, which allows the use of low complexity algorithms;
- Storage in a graph-oriented NoSQL database, which makes object-relational mapping unnecessary, since it is common in this type of software, allows more efficient queries and runs part of the algorithm on the server itself;
- Use of an architecture of independent modules that allows the improvement of each one without impact on the others;
- Use of the Iterated Local Search (ILS) meta-heuristic to explore the solution search space.

Once the objectives are reached, a reduction of the effort, especially human, is expected in the assembling of the course timetable.

This work is organized as follows: After the Introduction, Session II presents related works, Session III presents the proposed modeling and formulation of the problem, Session IV presents the methodology and Session V presents the results. Finally, Section VI presents some considerations and future work.

II. Related Work

The main difference between the works that approach this topic using meta-heuristics is the modeling and the heuristic basis for solving each particular instance of the problem. In Freitas et al. [3], the class scheduling problem is solved using Genetic Algorithms and binary arrays for storing each solution. They developed a software called Kayrós, using Java programming language and the data is stored in an object-oriented database supported by DB4 6.0. The solution proposed in Viera et al. [4], also uses Genetic Algorithms but the modelling is based on an array where each element is a four-field structure (course, teacher, schedule[], vacancy[]). The last two are also arrays.

In Cassemiro et al. [5], a hybrid solution based on genetic algorithms and Tabu search was proposed. The model supported in a three-dimensional array was developed to allow the optimization of some aspects of the problem using a target function that considers, among other values, the number of collisions in each individual of the population, treating them as penalties.

A similar approach to this work was performed by Saviniec et al. [2]. Such an approach involves three algorithms based on ILS that are implemented separately and in combination and do not present any mechanism for storing the results. Despite the good results, modeling the problem involves complex mathematical elements that are not easy to reproduce.

In Catarino et al. [6], the performance of a relational database (MySQL) is compared to the performance of a NoSQL (Neo4J) [7]. The results show an advantage for the MySQL database for a small amount of data. However, as the amount of data increases the performance of Neo4J becomes higher. Finally, in Côrrea et al. [8], the performance of two databases was compared, considering insertion, update and query operations. The NoSQL database ran the inserts at 38% of the time in the relational database. In the update and consultation operations, the percentages were 6.46% and 2.69%, respectively.

III. Graph-Based Modelling

Generating schedules is a problem associated with school activity. Each teaching institution has particularities that need to be represented in the model. Such a model should also be able to store a solution to the exposed problem. In addition, the aspects to be optimized must be present.

The amount of constraints involved influences the complexity of the algorithm that solves the problem. In this way, generically, [2][9] one may classify the constraints into two main groups:

- Strong constraints (essential for solution consistency):
  - a teacher cannot teach two courses at the same time;
  - one class can not be in two courses at the same time;
  - classes of the same course must be held on the same day;
  - courses must be scheduled in the course in which the course is offered.
- Weak restrictions (non-essential):
  - avoid windows in the teachers' timetable;
  - minimize the number of days each teacher will be in the classroom;
  - If classes of the same course are not all on the same day, they should not be on consecutive days.

In this work, only the strong constraints were observed.

This work represents the elements of the scheduling problem using a graph in the form $G = (V, E)$ form, in which V is formed by the following subsets, which represent the different types of elements described as vertices:

- $P = \{p_1, ..., p_k\}$ represents the teachers;
- $D = \{d_1, ..., d_l\}$ represents the courses;
- $T = \{t_1, ..., t_m\}$ represents the classes;
- $H = \{h_1, ..., h_n\}$ represents possible schedules (week day and time interval).

The set of edges is also composed by typified edges, representing constraints and associations between the different types of vertices:

- $RH = \{rh_1, ..., rh_l\}$ represents the constraints between H elements connected to other P subset elements. For example, where a $rh \in RH$ connects a $p \in P$ to a $h \in H$ it means that p is unavailable for scheduling in h interval;
- $PA = \{pa_1, ..., pa_m\}$ associates teachers and courses, it defines that a $p \in P$ teacher will be the chair of a $d \in D$ course;
- $TD = \{td_1, ..., td_n\}$, which represents the courses and their respective classes.

Figure 1 shows a graphical representation of $G = \{V = \{P, D, T, H\}, E = \{RH, PA, TD\}\}$.

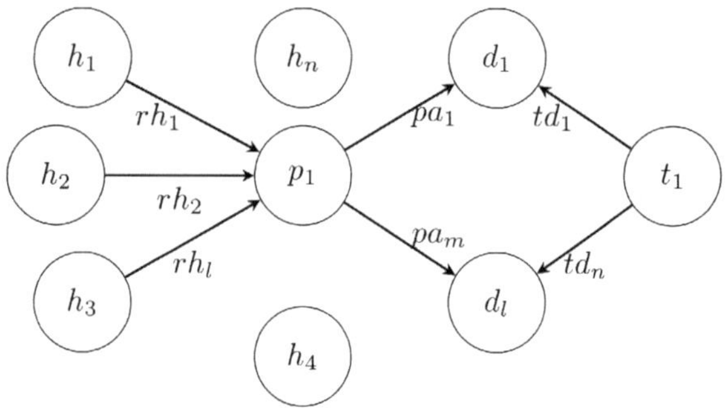

Figure 1. Graph-based model.

To represent the solution of the problem by indicating at which time each class will be performed, the following types of edges are added to the set $E = \{RH, PA, TD\}$:

- $HAT = \{ht_1, ..., ht_n\}$ associates a class with a schedule;
- $HAP = \{hp_1, ..., hp_n\}$ indicates that a teacher is in class at a given time;
- $HAD = \{hd_1, ...hd_n\}$ defines that the classes of a given course are performed at a certain time.

Considering the extension of the model with the inclusion of HAT, HAP and HAD edges, it becomes complete. Figure 2 illustrates a simplified scheduling where the highlighted edges hp_1, hd_1 and ht_1 says that the teacher p_1 teaches the d_1 course for t_1 class. In the same way, the highlighted edges hp_2, hd_2 and ht_2 says that teacher p_1 teaches the d_2 course for t_1 class.

IV. Materials and Methods

In order to achieve the objective of offering a low-cost tool for the IFTO, only free distribution software was used in the development of this work. To store the problem data to be captured and inserted into the model, the NoSQL Neo4J DBMS was used. This graph-oriented database allows the model to be stored in its original format, requiring no object-relational mapping that would increase the computational cost of the system. In addition, the Cypher language [10], used for data manipulation, allows the algorithm to determine the class scheduling to run on the server itself.

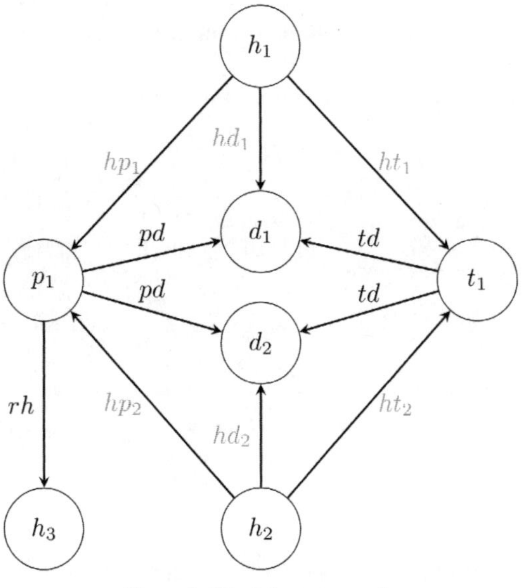

Figure 2. Schedule represented.

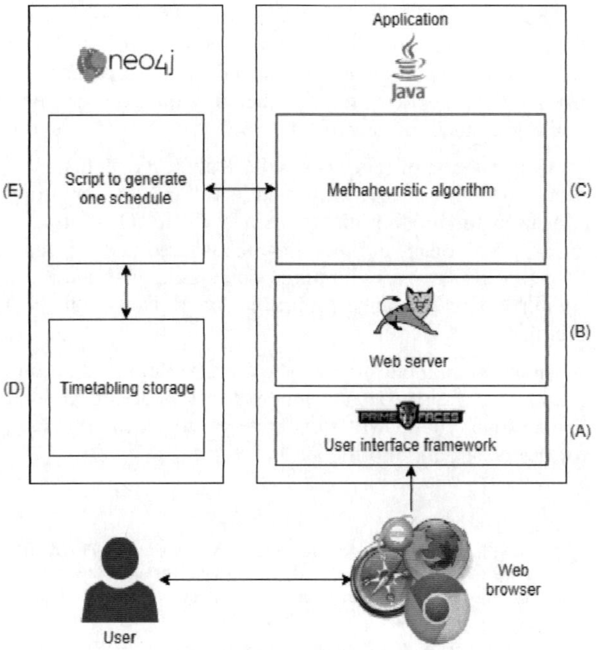

Figure 3. System architecture.

To explore the solutions space the meta-heuristic ILS was used. This stage of scheduling is performed by an application written in Java. The user interface is based on the PrimeFaces framework [11], running on a Tomcat 9.0 Web server. Finally, the Web system was developed using NetBeans IDE 8.2 [12]. Figure 3 illustrates the system architecture.

Looking at Figure 3, the bottom block represents the user view. On the right, the three internal blocks represent: (A) a framework to assist the user interface (which is optional), (B) the Web server and (C) the metaheuristic coded in a programming language. Note that these elements are independent and can be optimized and replaced without affecting the others, preserving compatibility.

The left block represents the DBMS, which includes storage in (D) and scheduling in (E). The main interaction occurs between blocks (C) and (E) where (C) receives and evaluates the schedules generated in (E).

V. Results

The algorithm developed to generate the schedules of a single course $d \in D$ related to a class $t \in T$ and a teacher $p \in P$, written in the Cypher language, is shown in Listing 1.

Listing 1. Internal Algorithm on Cypher Language.

```
1  match(t:Class)-[td:ClassCourse]->(d:Course
       {code: id })<-[pd:TeacherCourse]-(p:
     Teacher)
2  match(h:Schedule)
3  where not (h)-[:ClassSchedule]->(p) and
     not (h)-[:ClassSchedule]->(t) and not
     (p)-[:RTeacherSchedule]->(h)
4  with d, t, h, p limit 1
5  optional match(d)<-[ha:ClassSchedule]-(:
     Schedule)
6  with d, t, h, p, d.ClassPerWeek as nClass
     , count(ha) as nHad
7  where nHad < nClass
8   create(h)-[:ClassSchedule]->(p)
9   create(h)-[:ClassSchedule]->(t)
10  create(h)-[:ClassSchedule]->(d)
```

Having d (course) as input, line 1 finds the class t and the teacher p. The available schedules (line 2) are filtered so that only those free of any constraints remain (line 3). Next, line 5 checks if the course has already been scheduled, if the selected time interval is sufficient for the classes of the course (line 7), and in this case, if the connection between p, t, and d is made with the chosen time interval h (lines 8, 9 and 10), inserting the appropriate edges. Adapting structured logical reasoning to the Cypher language paradigm was a challenge encountered at this stage of the work.

Figure 4 shows the execution flow of the ILS. The algorithm presented in Listing 1 composes block 1, indicated. Note that the scheduling is not complete until all the subgraph $G = \{D\}$ is visited and each $d \in D$ has been associated with a interval $h \in H$ by an edge.

Steps 1, 2, and 3 of Block 1 in the Figure 4 are executed by DBMS, whereas the external steps to that block are executed by the application. Thus, different scheduling solutions can be generated from several courses sorting in array D [].

The tests were carried out considering that the association between teachers and courses, classes and courses and the constraints were previously defined, for example, by the school managers. Therefore, the problem is summarized in staggering the classes, since the possible conflicts were previously solved. To perform the tests, two scenarios were created: scenario 1, simpler, with 15 courses, 5 teachers, 3 classes and 20 schedules and scenario 2, more complex, containing 50 courses, 19 teachers, 10 classes and 20 schedules. The chart in Figure 5 illustrates the comparison of runtime in seconds with the PowerCubus software [13].

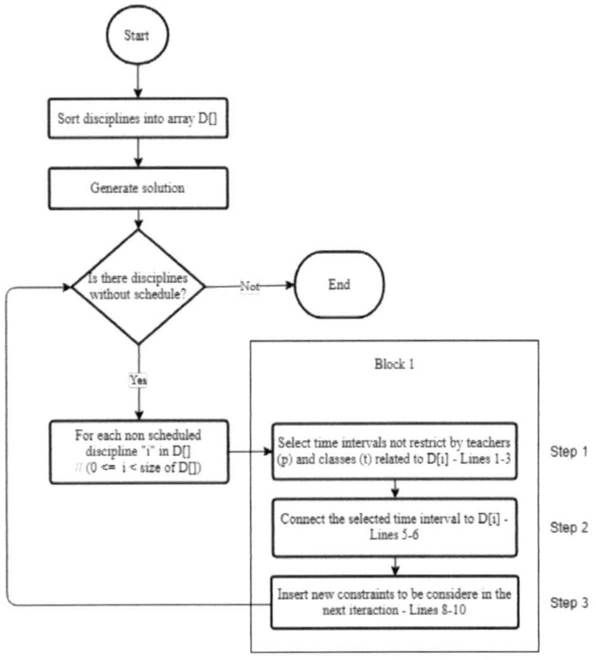

Figure 4. Algorithm flowchart.

As one can see, the runtime of the solution proposed in this article is only 12.5% of the time spent by the PowerCubus software in the scenario 1. Scenario 2 could not be tested in the PowerCubus software because it is limited to a free version. However, the solution proposed in this article in the second scenario was executed using only 30% of the time spent by the PowerCubus software compared to the first scenario. Thus, even for a more complex case, our solution obtained a significantly more satisfactory result.

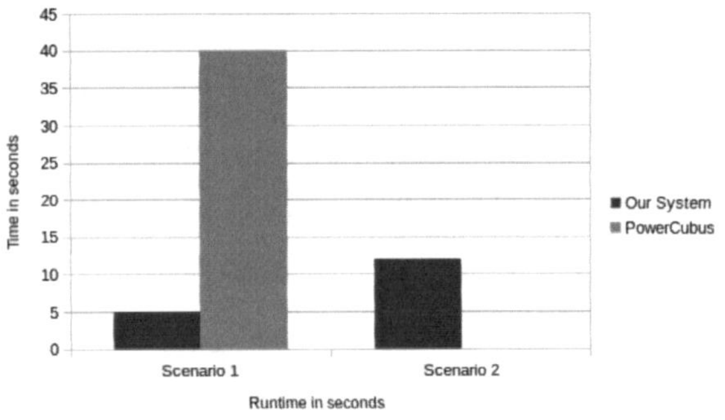

Figure 5. Our System x PowerCubus.

Finally, Figure 6 illustrates the interface developed and presents the result of scheduling for a single class.

VI. Conclusion and Future Work

The proposed modeling was efficient in representing the aspects of the scheduling problem. The model is general enough to allow inserting of new data, such as other types of constraints. The ILS presented satisfactory solutions and the algorithm executed directly in the graph-oriented DBMS was consistent and quick to execute. Note that the graph-oriented database allows queries to be performed without the need to cross-out data in cross and joins the are common in relational databases, being more direct and much faster. Furthermore, since Neo4J does not limit the storage of nodes, the solution proposed in this article allows us to deal with instances of any size for the proposed problem, meaning that it, it can be used in the long term by the IFTO.

Continuation of this work will involves the inclusion of the weak restrictions previously mentioned and also environment allocation for holding classes. Since the IFTO offers courses in different areas and requires the shared use of facilities such as classrooms, swimming pool, sports gym, auditoriums, computer labs, among others, this functionality will be very useful.

In addition, the user interface must be upgraded to improve usability, because, despite automated scheduling generation, human intervention will still be necessary in the process, e.g. for inserting data into the system.

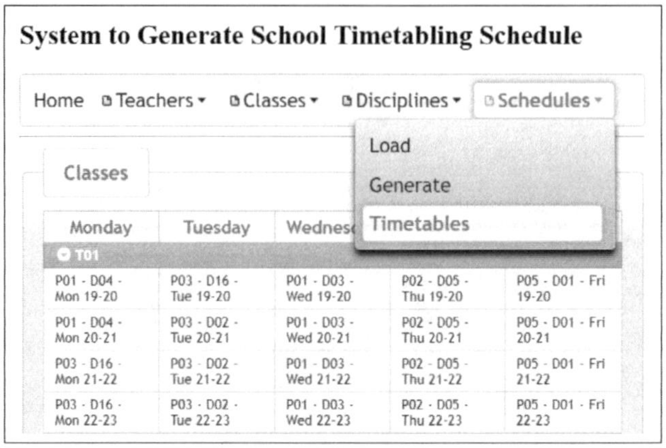

Figure 6. Web page: Screenshot schedule for single class.

References

[1] V. N. d. Sousa, A. C. Moretti, and V. A. d. Podestá, "Programação da grade de horário em escolas de ensino fundamental e médio [Schedule the timetable in elementary and middle schools] ," Pesquisa Operacional [Operational Research], vol. 28, 2008, pp. 399–421.

[2] L. Saviniec, A. A. Constantino, W. Romão, and H. G. Santos, " Solving the High Timetabling Problem to Optimality by Using ILS Algorithms," Simpósio Brasileiro de Pesquisa Operacional, September 2013.

[3] C. C. Freitas, P. R. B. Guimarães, M. C. M. Neto, and F. J. R. Barboza, "Uma Ferramenta Baseada em Algoritmos Genéticos para a Geração de Tabela de Horário Escola [A Tool Based on Genetic Algorithms for School Timetable Generation]," Faculdade Ruy Barbosa (FRB) – Salvador – BA - Brasil, September 2014.

[4] F. Vieira and H. Macedo, "Sistema de Alocação de Horários de Cursos Universitários [System of Time Allocation of University Courses]," Um Estudo de Caso no Departamento de Computação da Universidade Federal de Sergipe, São Cristovão, Brasil [A Case Study in the Computer Department of the Federal University of Sergipe, São Cristovão, Brasil], vol. 7, no. 3, March 2011.

[5] M. V. d. S. Cassemiro, "Desenvolvimento de um Modelo Híbrido Baseado em Algoritmo Genético e Busca Tabu para Resolução do Problema de Quadro de Horários Escolar [Development of a Hybrid Model Based on Genetic Algorithm and Tabu Search for Problem Resolution of School Schedules]," Simpósio Brasileiro de Pesquisa Operacional,

Salvador – BA - Brasil [Brazilian Symposium on Operational Research, Salvador – BA - Brazil], September 2014.

[6] M. H. Catarino, "Integrando banco de dados relacional e orientado a grafos para otimizar consultas com alto grau de indireção [Integrating relational and graphical database to optimize queries with high degree of indirection]," Instituto de Matemática e Estátistica da Universidade Federal de São Paulo, São Paulo - Brasil [Institute of Mathematics and Statistics of the Federal University of São Paulo, São Paulo - Brasil], November 2017.

[7] "The Native Path to Graph Performance," URL: https://neo4j.com/business-edge/native-path-to-graph-performance/ [accessed: 2018-10-14].

[8] T. d. S. Côrrea, D. E. C. d. Almeida, and A. F. G. Neto, "Comparação entre banco de dados relacional e não relacional em arquitetura distribuída [Comparison between relational and non-relational database in distributed architecture]," III Seminário de desenvolvimento em soa com cloud computing e conectividade, Instituto Nacional de Telecomunicações – INATEL [III Seminar of development in sounds with cloud computing and connectivity, National Institute of Telecommunications - INATEL], September 2017, ISSN: 2447-2352.

[9] E. A. Abdelhalim and G. A. El Khayat, "A Utilization-based Genetic Algorithm for Solving the University Timetabling Problem (UGA)," Alexandria Engineering Journal, vol. 55, March 2016, pp. 1395–1409.

[10] "Intro to Cypher," URL: https://neo4j.com/news/explorando-o-cypher-a-linguagem-de-pesquisas-em-grafo-do-neo4j/ [accessed: 2018-10-14].

[11] "Why PrimeFaces," URL: https://www.primefaces.org/whyprimefaces/ [accessed: 2018-11-11].

[12] "NetBeans IDE - The Smarter and Faster Way to Code," URL: https://netbeans.org/features/ [accessed: 2018-11-11].

[13] "PowerCubus," 2016, URL: http://www.powercubus.com.br/ [accessed: 2018-10-04].

A Solution for Mobility Protocols Evaluation

Thierry Silva Pereira

Federal Institute of Education, Science and Technology of Tocantins (IFTO)
Palmas, Brazil
Email: thierrysilvaee@gmail.com

Abstract—**The motivation of the research project proposed in this article is to show means and results for overcoming the challenges of maintaining an uninterrupted connection on wireless mobile networks, which is becoming more and more necessary for users who increasingly require ubiquity when accessing voice and video services. These services become a critical case when used together, since high transmission rates are needed. A possible option in this scenario is the use of smartphone oriented networks, considering their recent support for packet-switched services evolution. This article presents the implementation of an app for mobile devices, that can be used with the Android or IOS operating systems, which provides a thorough mobility protocol evaluation.**

Keywords–Technology; Mobility; Handover; Latency; Wireless Networks.

I. INTRODUCTION

Due to the increasing demand for services that require strict compliance with network requirements, such as, voice and video applications, along with the ubiquity of these services, the issue of always keeping mobile devices users well connected when moving among networks with different administrative domains, has proved to be a challenge. During the handover period, the user may suffer longer delays than desired or even data loss. This effect ends up decreasing the quality of information, and this situation becomes especially critical when one is dealing with multimedia data in communication.

Effectiveness in the delivery of a service or provision quality assurance in transmission and reception of a flow is related to some variables that can be crucial in a computer network application. They are almost always related to the technology that was used, how the transmission flow was made and, very often, to the functional requirements of the application that will benefit from the network architecture. Analyzing the context of mobility and convergence, the requirements in the control of the limits of each parameter of these variables are even more important, since they can be a determining factor as to whether or not to deliver a particular package. Thus, network technologies need to work in such a way that can promote transparency to the users, from the point of view of utilization of the service, providing full support to mobility and data continuity.

Beside the need that involves the support of connection and continuity of data traffic, there is the additional challenge of integration among wireless services. Interfaces without coupling present additional challenges, because they are very frequently found in networks with many different administrative domains. In such situations, it is noted that one network does not provide a coupling to another, and, as a result, there is management of different IPs addresses, leading to the need for rigorous studies to evaluate the impact of a migration process among heterogeneous networks, as presented in Al-Surmi [1] and Fernandes [2].

The Internet was not originally designed to support device mobility. Considering the existing infrastructure and all the main protocols used in the Transmission Control Protocol/Internet Protocol (TCP/IP), layer model, these have limitations which make it difficult to use them for mobility scenarios. The Mobile Internet Protocol (MIP), described in Perkins [3], has been widely disseminated, studied and used as a solution to the mobility problem in IP networks, leading to some implementation of this protocol. However, in some studies, such as Kodaly [4] and Mohamed [5], its application has become practically unfeasible, since it was based on providing architectures in extremely controlled and poorly functional environments.

This study proposes to implement a mobile app that is able to provide results of certain mobility protocols evaluations. For the next step in future work, it is proposed to measure and evaluate the handover latency values using the Specialized MIP (SMIP) protocol, as presented in Monteiro [6], analyzing the feasibility of mobility in networks. The efficiency of these protocols will be experimentally and numerically evaluated in a given scenario, from the viewpoint of network latency and its involvement in certain types of traffic or applications. The results obtained from the evaluation of the mobility protocols will be available in the created app and disseminated to the scientific community.

This paper is organized into the following sections: after the Introduction, in Section II the work listed presents the research carried out, showing the theoretical references that were used and a brief description of each one. Section III provides the proposal of this article, as well as the materials used for app planning and implementation and the methodology applied to carry out the research. Section IV presents the results obtained with the use of the app. In Section V, we conclude this paper and suggest directions for future work.

II. RELATED WORK

Technology is everywhere today. Studies are pursuing solutions in order to provide ubiquitous information for the most diverse problems. Mobile devices have a crucial role in this information dissemination process.

The largest number of studies found about mobility protocol evaluations show experiences with mobile IP in complex and specific environments. An example can be seen in [7], where authors demonstrate the use and performance of IP protocol in a smart bridge environment. This particular research proposal is to introduce and characterize a protocol architecture based on IP to achieve applications in, for example, smart meters and inverters.

In another case, the authors in [8], address and evaluate the mobile IP in a Pay-TV environment, showing its efficiency in that specific scenario. Some weaknesses related to maintenance of user privacy, can be highlighted, such as insider attack and user traceability attack.

In [9], results are presented for the use of IP protocol in a Virtual Private Network (VPN) environment, allowing terminal mobility for the user of that VPN. This was based on aggregation of two or more internet mobile accesses and is able to provide a higher end-to-end available bandwidth due to an adaptive load balancing algorithm. This research also proposes a neural network approach for predicting the main Key Performance Indicators (KPIs) values at a given geographical point.

Thus, with a view to continue pointing in the direction of using mobile apps for troubleshooting in the context of mobility, this research presents the implementation of an app that provides information about the research that will be carried out during the postgraduate course in Telematics.

III. PROPOSAL

When thinking about mobility in networks with different administrative domains, the biggest challenge is the increase in handover latency. Taking this scenario into account, it is possible to adopt certain procedures that enable implementation of mobility under specific circumstances, provided that certain requirements are established. These requirements range from defining which layer mobility will be introduced into, to the most efficient application of the algorithm or protocol that will perform the actual implementation.

The proposal of this research is to create an app that will provide information about the research. The research has the purpose of evaluating and measuring handover latency using specific protocols, seeking solutions that are workable for use on current mobile devices.

In order to find the best way to seek information and present it in a practical, easy-to-read and understandable way for the users, a plan of action was devised for the project. Figure 1 shows the architecture of the solution, as well as the steps and sequence of actions that were executed for implementing the proposal of this research.

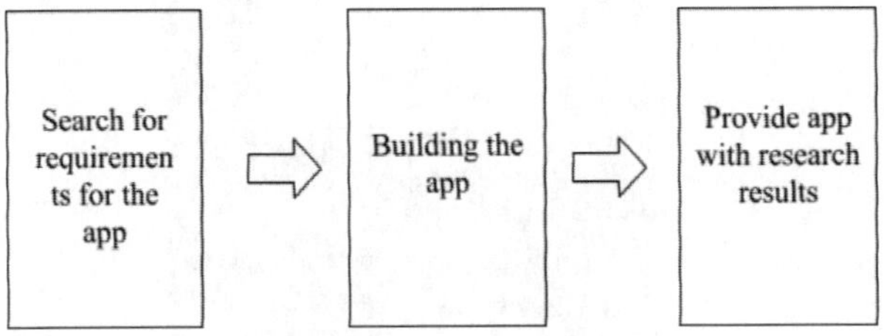

Figure 1. Solution architecture

A. Materials

This research was developed during the postgraduate degree course in Telematics. The research group work was consolidated in meetings held in the laboratory reserved for the postgraduate course of the Federal Institute of Education, Science and Technology of Tocantins (IFTO), and some meetings were also attended by video conference.

The efforts during the first meetings were concentrated on solving problems that have been proposed to groups by professors in the postgraduate course. It involved several debates with the intention of finding ways of how the various parts of the project would be executed. After the presentation of all problems that had been proposed, the other meetings were focused on the search for practical and highly applicable solutions for teaching and learning. Current and easily usable tools such as YouTube [10], Gmail [11], Classroom [12], WhatsApp [13], Google Drive [14] and Google Docs [15]were used for the video conference.

In order to develop the app proposed in this research, the following items that will be described as follows were used: Computers (Desktop and a Dell notebook) using Linux and Windows operating systems, respectively, both with Internet access, a Web platform that enables the creation of mobile apps, the AppSheet, Google Drive for storing required content for the application of the implementation, Google Docs for editing of the files that will be made available in the app and YouTube for sharing videos. The mobile device for testing was a Motorola Moto tt^5 plus smartphone.

B. Methodology

This subsection will present the steps and methodological technologies adopted for implementation of the proposed project in this work. The app was developed for smartphones, tablets or any device with an Android or IOS operatingsystem, with a view to providing information about the research that will be performed.

The first stage of the project was collection of information that deals with mobility among heterogeneous networks. Initially, requirements and functionalities were developed for the system in question: project description, protocol used, testing environment, objectives, problems, advantages, challenges and team work.

Once the requirements were established, part of the implementation of the app started. For this purpose, we used a specific tool, AppSheet, a platform Web site that enables creation of apps for mobile devices without the need for having extensive experience in mobile application development. The AppSheet was created in 2014 and the tool is employed by users in more than 220 countries, making it possible to create apps that meet specific needs from a spreadsheet, simply and quickly.

A spreadsheet was created to show implementation of the app containing information that will be available, as well as images related to the texts, files to help in data interpretation and videos. In order to enter the platform, it was necessary to sign in with a Gmail account and allow the tool to have access to the file saved on the drive. Editing to the app is done in a very simple and practical way.

The AppSheet platform interface is shown in Figure 2, where the functionalities provided by the tool have been displayed. This figure points out the options for app editing, the tables that were used for app construction, the conditions established for proper functioning and a presentation of an app

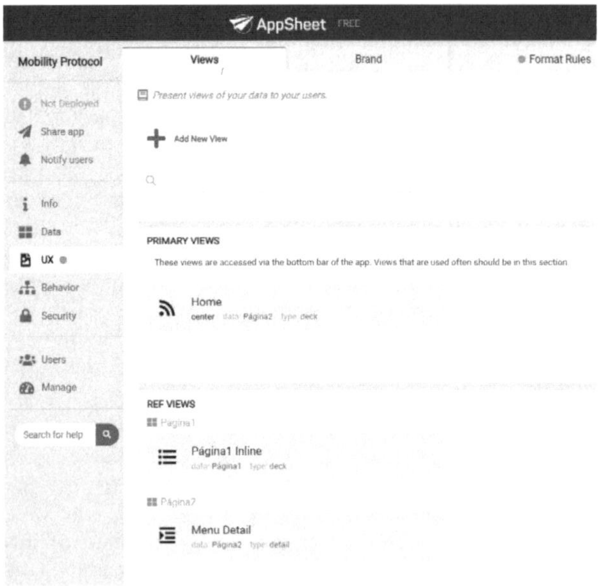

Figure 2. AppSheet

already in operation, in other words, an app simulation on a mobile screen.

After the app began to take shape, final adjustments were made in terms of information presentation and the colors used to make project more visually attractive.

Research on mobility protocol evaluation will be done later on during the postgraduate course. For this first stage the efforts were concentrated on creating the app. The results obtained, the methodology and how the test environment was assembled will be also presented for the app developed in this research.

IV. Results

In this section, the results obtained will be presented for implementation of the app using the AppSheet, which was described in the previous section.

In order to optimize the dissemination of information relevant to solutions that address the heterogeneity of wireless networks, an application was created to provide the results of the research that will be carried out during the postgraduate course. The manner in which the information will be provided will provide a very concise and dynamic understanding.

The initial prototype of the app was built from the requirements and features surveyed during the course of the research. A spreadsheet was created in Google Documents and from this, an application was implemented on the AppSheet Web platform. Figure 3 illustrates some of the app screens after it was ready. Figure 3 (a) shows the screen when we press the button named Project, connecting the path to the Project Description part and to the Project Motivation that encourages further research. Figure 3 (b) illustrates the application screen when the Goals button is clicked; it shows the user the General Purpose and Specific Objectives buttons.

The overall goal of protocol evaluation shown in Figure 3 (b) is to try to always keep mobile device users well connected when moving among different administrative domain networks and provide higher quality and reliability among connections. The specific objectives are to facilitate the reestablishment of connections, decrease registry data traffic in a mobility environment and create mechanisms that reduce the latency and quantity of packet losses during the handover process.

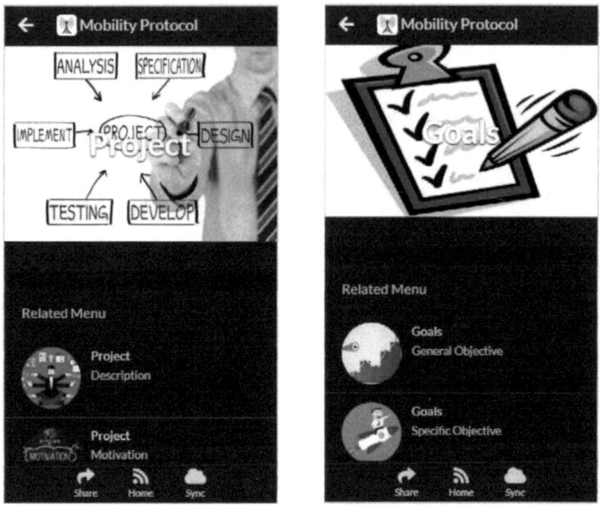

(a) (b)

Figure 3. App implementation

The process for installing the app on mobile devices is easy. The AppSheet must be installed first. The app developed is called Mobility Protocol and after installation on the smartphone, the first screen presentation provides a brief summary of what the app is all about, the motive and reason for its creation. Figure 4 shows the screen application shortly after installation on a device mobile with Android or IOS system.

Figure 4. Home screen

The main mission of the app in question is to inform and educate users about a very specific topic, which is the evaluation of mobility protocol. As a result, the model of structure plan used will be the index architecture model. For applications with a specific purpose, this type of structure is the best option. Figure 5 presents an organized menu for the app after adoption of the index architecture template. Figure 5 (a) has a print screen showing the top of the app main menu. In the app, there are several buttons in the main menu, and Figure 5 (b) illustrates the bottom section after scrolling vertically.

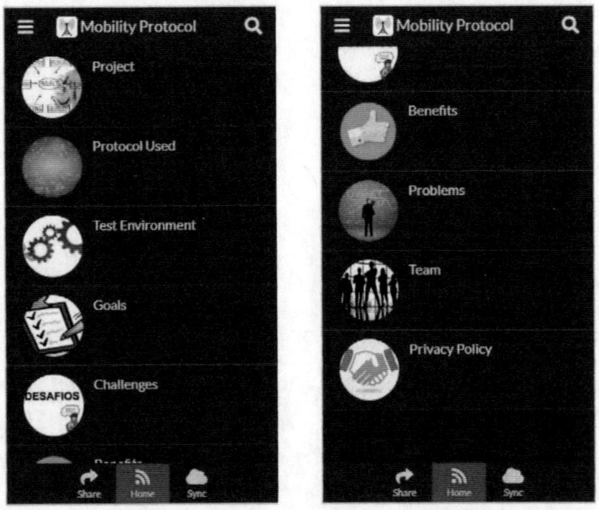

(a) (b)

Figure 5. Home

In a constant effort to optimize the application developed so that users always have a good experience and proper usability, the app has a feature for users to leave suggestions, ideas for possible improvements and/or compliments. The button that allows this connection between the user and the developer is called Feedback and is available in the upper left menu of the app, allowing the user to send the text to the email that the developer registered during creation of the project. The app created has not yet been shared with the academic community and other users who will use it, and we will thus not be able to provide any feedback from possible users at this stage. Figure 6 illustrates the menu where this resource can be found.

Through the development and usability tests performed, we have implemented the app that was proposed for this project. Simple texts were used for better understanding of the information that is being transmitted, the images illustrated in each topic are related, whenever possible, to the texts of each information and the colors have been chosen in order to achieve harmonization in the app set.

V. Conclusion and Future Work

Technology has made a major contribution to education, as demonstrated by the use of television, multimedia equipment and computers over the last few decades. However, because of continuing modernization, the latest mobile technologies deserve attention and can be applied in education, given that and a large part of the population already has access to a high-tech mobile device.

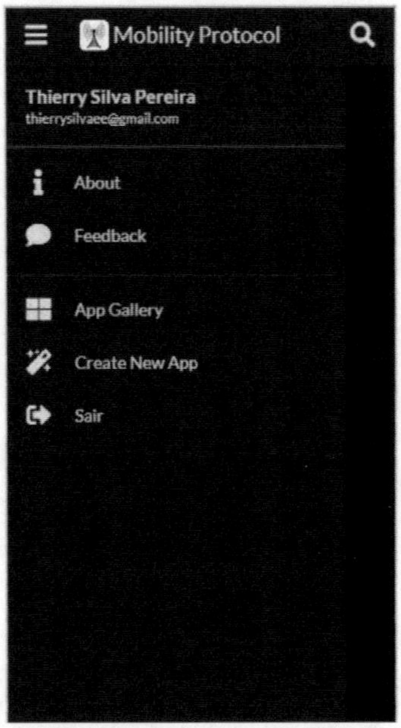

Figure 6. Menu

Although it is not a new topic and has already been dealt with by several academic researchers, the IP mobility management problem still deserves attention, especially in environments where the networks used by the mobile device do not have coupling and are located in many different administrative domains. Such scenarios are becoming more and more common and the quest for solutions is being treated with a focus on mobile devices.

This research is focused on the development of an app for mobile devices that will provide pertinent information for research. It will be carried out during the postgraduate course in the Telematics laboratory, where tests were performed for evaluation of mobility protocols, as a requirement for obtaining a specialist certificate.

The Mobility Protocol Assessment app has proved promising in its ability to provide a contribution to education, because it can aid in learning within the classroom, by providing more dynamics and better presentation of the information in an enlightening manner.

Therefore, in this context, the app developed meets the central objective of the research, which is to present useful information to the user and to show in a simple way how to apply them. However, the Mobility Protocol Assessment tool will not solve the mobility problem between heterogeneous networks by itself, and will always require research on the mobility issue and sharing of the results on the app.

As a suggestion for future work, this app can be disseminated throughout the academic community of the Federal Institute of Education, Science and Technology of Tocantins, in an effort to seek optimized versions. In parallel, there will be a search for solutions for mobile device mobility when moving along networks of different administrative domains, an issue that will always provide room for new academic research.

REFERENCES

[1] I. Al-Surmi, M. Othman, and B. Mohd Al, "Mobility management for IP-based next generation mobile networks: Review, challenge and perspective," Journal of Network and Computer Applications. Volume 35, Issue: 1, 2012, pp. 295–315, Elsevier.

[2] S. Fernandes and A. Karmouch, "Vertical Mobility Management Architectures in Wireless Networks: A Comprehensive Survey and Future Directions. Communications Surveys Tutorial," IEEE. Volume: 14, Issue: 1, 2012, pp. 45–63, IEEE.

[3] C. E. Perkins, "IP Mobility Support," IETF RFC 3344, August 2002.

[4] R. Kodaly and C. E. Perkins, "Mobile IPv4 Fast Handover," Internet Draft, Mobile IPv4 Working Group, 2006.

[5] A. Mohamed, A. Irfani, and D. Holton, "Handoff Mechanism in Mobile IP," IEEE, 2009.

[6] C. C. Monteiro, "An Environment to Support the Integration of Heterogeneous Wireless Networks," Doctoral thesis. Presented to the Department of Electrical Engineering, University of Brasilia, 2012.

[7] S. Rinaldi, F. Bonafini, P. Ferrari, A. Flammini, E. Sisinni, D. Di Cara, N. Panzavecchia, G. Tinè, A. Cataliotti, V. Cosentino et al., "Characterization of ip-based communication for smart grid using software-defined networking," IEEE Transactions on Instrumentation and Measurement, 2018.

[8] S. B. Far and M. Alagheband, "Analysis and improvement of a lightweight anonymous authentication protocol for mobile pay-tv systems (full text)," arXiv preprint arXiv:1808.09493, 2018.

[9] F. Beritelli, G. Capizzi, G. L. Sciuto, M. Woźniak, D. Połap, K. Ksiażek et al., "A smart vpn bonding technique based on rtt analysis and neural network prediction." International Journal of Computer Science & Applications, vol. 15, no. 1, 2018.

[10] "YouTube," 2018, URL: http://www.youtube.com/ [accessed: 2018-08-06].

[11] "Gmail," 2018, URL: http://www.gmail.com/ [accessed: 2018-08-06].

[12] "Classroom," 2018, URL: http://www.classroom.google.com/ [accessed: 2018-08-06].

[13] "WhatsApp," 2018, URL: https://www.web.whatsapp.com/ [accessed: 2018-08-06].

[14] "Google Drive," 2018, URL: https://www.drive.google.com/ [accessed: 2018-08-06].

[15] "Google Docs," 2018, URL: https://www.docs.google.com/ [accessed: 2018-08-06].

ConstruNET - A Collaborative Tool to Provide Offers of Construction Supplies

André Praça de Almeida Pinheiro, Jeverson de Sousa Barbosa Lima, Mardenn Robledo Rodrigues Coelho and Rafael Pereira Trancoso Borges
Federal Institute of Education, Science and Technology (IFTO), Palmas, Brazil
E-mails: {apracapinheiro, contatojeverson, mardennsk8, rafaelptb}@gmail.com

Abstract—**This article deals with the theoretical and practical aspects of developing an app called ConstruNET. It was created by a research group in the Graduate Program in Telematics of the Federal Institute of Education, Science and Technology of Tocantins, Brazil (IFTO). This solution was developed with available Web applications and has the goal of providing users with information about offers from a list of construction supplies sold by stores in the city of Palmas - Tocantins - Brazil. The purpose is to show the importance of an app such as ConstruNET to aid the search for building material products, as well as to avoid the waste of time and money in construction activities. This article demonstrates the planning, conception and utilization of ConstruNET as a mobile technology app directed towards civil engineering construction supplies.**

Keywords-Collaborative tools; App; Construction; Mobile Devices; Internet.

I. Introduction

The advent of globalization has brought access to various technologies that greatly facilitate communication and interaction between people. Today, people have several services at their fingertips in ways that were impossible ten years ago. This is because of the opportunity for acquiring mobile devices and Internet access services.

The use of smartphones and tablets has increased the production of applications, making it possible to solve day-to-day problems. Today, it is possible to verify the prices of several products online, as well as to compare them, evaluating them and pointing out what needs to be improved.

This paper is structured into six parts. After the Introduction, in Section 2, the publications related to this research are presented. In Section 3, we present the problem and its justification, besides the general and specific objectives established for the project. In that section, we describe how we used the physical relationship diagram and virtual tools in meetings of the research group. In Section 4, we present the online survey and statistical graphics. In Section 5, we present our overview of ConstruNET.

II. Related Works

Mobile devices play a fundamental role in the information dissemination process.

Research works are aimed at finding a solution that would allow people to search prices of civil engineering construction supplies in a given region. Appsheet® [1] was the main tool for development of mobile applications because it is easy to use and low-cost.

The authors in [2] show how the Appsheet® tool was used for calculating water consumption of the reference plants, presenting an easy way for data storage and for developing an application. The tool is an alternative for data storage and management.

The researchers in [3] use the Appsheet® tool for developing a solution for providing a low-cost electronic data collection tool for a health facility survey study. They created an online application using the Appsheet® tool functionalities.

In [4], the authors use the Appsheet® tool to develop a Web solution to support decision-making. The Appsheet® tool was used as the main tool for development and the authors realized the advantages of the Appsheet® tool, considering its operation and ease of programming, as well as its database robustness.

The researchers in [5] present a database model totally based on the Appsheet® tool, showing its performance and ease of operation. They address the use of the Appsheet® tool in building a database for facilitating location and development of a warehouse management system.

The use of a mobile application that aims to save time and money for users when they need to search prices for products and / or building materials in their city is the focus of this paper.

III. Proposal

According to Meireles [6] citing the 29ª Annual Survey of Information Technology (IT) Usage conducted by GVCia (Center for Applied Information Technology of the Getúlio Vargas Foundation), in the year 2018, Brazil already has about two hundred and twenty million active smartphones, proportionally well over one smartphone per inhabitant. Even with this information and the increasing use of mobile applications, there is a lack of tools that facilitate daily tasks. For example, when there is a need to make a small renovation, there is almost always inconvenience in obtaining offers of construction materials, tools and accessories from the stores, along with the best prices.

ConstruNET was born with the proposal of presenting to the user a solution that uses a mobile application to facilitate access to a list of offers of construction material products from several stores in Palmas, the state capital of Tocantins.

The general purpose of this article is to provide an app for the population that allows a comparison of prices of construction materials in the main stores of a given locality, allowing the consumer to quickly find a better price, thus reducing the time spent on construction or remodeling.

Additionally, there are three specific objectives of our work:

- Allow the consumer to register the building material products whose information will be shared.
- Provide a list of products containing their respective prices and the stores that are offering them.
- Provide maintenance tips that will assist the consumers in resolving minor repairs or renovations to their homes.

A. Materials

ConstruNET was planned and documented using tools from the Google family (Docs [7], Sheets [8], Slide [9], Classroom [10] and Forms [11]). We considered User-Experience and Usability for developing the APP using a spreadsheet with Nielsen Heuristics [12] and a document in Card-sorting format.

The ConstruNET app prototype was created using the AppSheet® tool. The physical resources used during development included mobile devices for tests such as a Samsung® GT-7102 smartphone, a Motorola® MOTO G5 Plus smartphone, a Samsung® A9 Pro smartphone and a Samsung® Galaxy S7 smartphone, all of them connected in WI-FI 802.11n internal networks and 3G and 4G mobile networks.

All physical equipment was from the Telematics and Application Laboratory at IFTO (Federal Institute of Education, Science and Technology of Tocantins).

B. Methods

The idea of ConstruNET was conceived during face-to-face meetings and through distance learning (Google Classroom tool) in the graduate program in Telematics, carried out at the Telematics and Applications in Education Laboratory at the Federal Institute of Education and Technology, Palmas, Brazil from March to August of 2018 and was based on the Problem Based Learning (PBL) methodology.

The data collection instrument consisted of an online questionnaire from the Google® Forms tool, shared and answered by one hundred and seventeen users in Palmas and who evaluated the feasibility of creating an application that could offer prices from construction materials. During the Telematics Graduate classes, the Google Docs tools were used to prepare documents that supported the application test, Google Sheets spreadsheets for the AppSheet® tool Database and the results were shown using Google Slide. The Google Classroom tool served as the basis for communication between the teacher and the students.

In the second stage of planning, the skeleton, design and usability plans, and the Nielsen Heuristics worksheet based on the needs of the online survey constructed using the Google Sheets and Google Forms tools, were also thought out and idealized through card-sorting for ten users with the objective of testing their views regarding issues of application navigability. The presentation of the results was done by the Google Slide tool.

In the creation phase, the ConstruNET prototype was designed, using the AppSheet® tool. The application was initially created with four screens, where the offer list sessions, stores, products and categories were made available. Given its hybrid nature, the AppSheet® tool made it possible to make use of the application on the Android® and IOS® platforms through its access database.

As a result of the planning and design processes, ConstruNET was designed and operates according to the diagram in Figure 1 below:

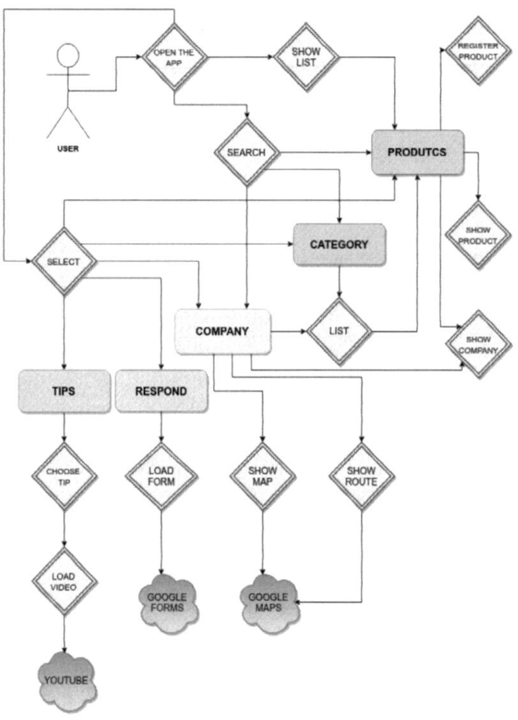

Figure 1. Relationship Diagram.

When the users run the ConstruNET application, they view the list of available products sorted in alphabetical order and from the lowest to the highest price. In the initial screen, the user can search for a product (product module), category (category module) or company (company module). On the initial screen, the user can also select the module tips, answer survey, company, category and products for visualization.

If the user has selected the item related to the company search, the search result will be the company entered by the user. As a result, detailed company data such as name, address, telephone number, storefront photo, map with company location and available company products will be shown. Also in relation to the company, the application uses a map to invoke the Google Maps® [13] tool and a route is drawn from the user's GPS location to the company location.

When the user chooses a category search, the application shows the categories of products available, e.g., hydraulic or electric and when a category is selected, a list is shown with all products registered in the selected category.

If the user chooses the tips module, the APP will present a list with simple maintenance procedures that can be performed by the user without the need of a professional. When the user selects a tip, the system loads the YouTube® [14] video for viewing within the ConstruNET application.

The module responds, when accessed by the application user, by loading a form created in the Google Forms® tool, which contains a survey on the use of the ConstruNET application, which may or may not be filled out by the user.

The products module is the most important of the application, because it is what contains the information for which the system is intended to be created. The user, when accessing this module, can register a product, view product details and view the company that sells the product. In the product details is presented an image of the product, the selling price, the company that offers the product, technical specification and description and the category of the product. Also in the product description, the user can access data for the company that sells the product and the category of the product, presenting all products registered in the category.

In the main list with the products registered, the user has the option of registering a new product. In the product register, it is necessary to fill in the product, price, company and category fields. Optional fields are image (product photo), description and specification.

For tests using the ConstruNET functionality, a copy of the application in developer mode and six copies of it in a limited mode for six invited users in the city of Palmas-Tocantins were installed in four smartphones of the graduate students.

IV. Results

ConstruNET was conceived during face-to-face meetings through distance learning (Google Classroom tool) of the Graduate Program in Telematics, held at the Telematics and Applications in Education Laboratory of the Federal Institute of Education, Science and Technology, Palmas, Brazil, during the period from March to August of 2018 and was based on Problem Based Learning-PBL methodology.

The data collect instrument consisted of an online survey from the Google® Forms tool, shared and answered by one hundred and seventeen users in Palmas, which evaluated the development viability of creating an application that could provide prices / offers of construction materials.

TABLE I. SURVEY QUESTIONS

Number	Questions
1	Gender
2	Age
3	Have you bought any kind of construction and / or maintenance material?
4	At home, who usually performs minor repairs / maintenance?
5	How do you usually buy your materials, tools and / or accessories to use in your building or home?
6	How much do you use building and / or maintenance materials?
7	Would a search application that provides information on building and/or maintenance materials be useful when shopping?
8	Would you like an app that shows the lowest price of a building material, tool or accessory for maintenance in the stores in your area?
9	Would you like to receive a quote for all the materials you need, at the lowest prices, from the application?
10	Would you like the application to show tips about minor repairs that you can do yourself?
11	Would you like the app to showcase supplies, tools, and / or accessories for stores in your area?
12	How much do you think the app will help in saving time and money at the time of purchase?

The initial study pointed to a need for the application and in light of the results, the prototype of the ConstruNET has the following functionalities:

- Product registration.
- List of products and information of companies that sell them.
- List of companies that sell building materials.
- List of categories.
- Viewing details of a product.
- Viewing details of a company.
- View of the route of a customer to a selected company.
- Maintenance tips.

Some screenshots of functionalities in the ConstruNET prototype are shown in Figures 2 and 3.

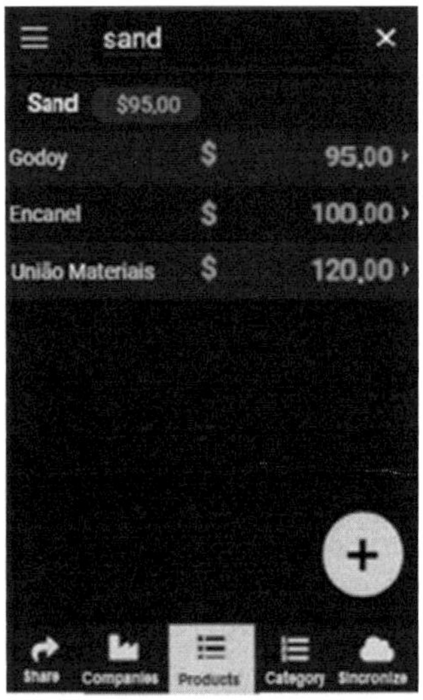

Figure 2. List of products

Figure 3. List of companies

A. *Data Analysis*

In Figure 4, we can see that 67% of the public, who answered the survey are male with an average age of about 18-40, as shown in Figure 5.

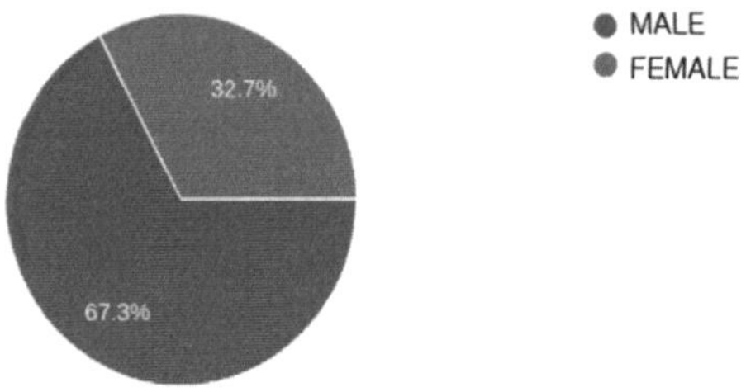

Figure 4. User gender

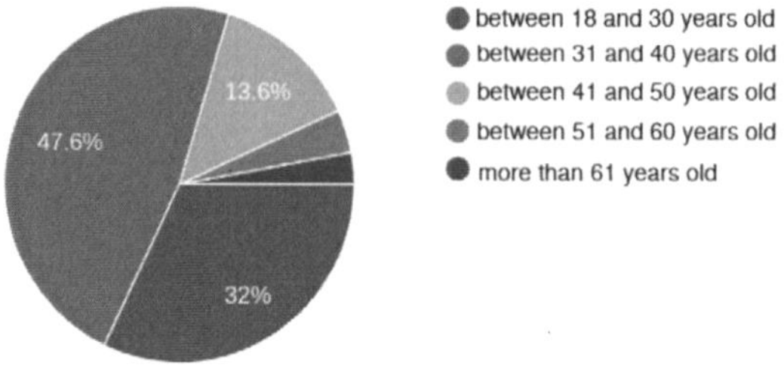

Figure 5. User ages

According to Figure 6, 91% have already bought some type of construction material, about 46% have already made minor repairs to their home and only 26% call a specialized professional.

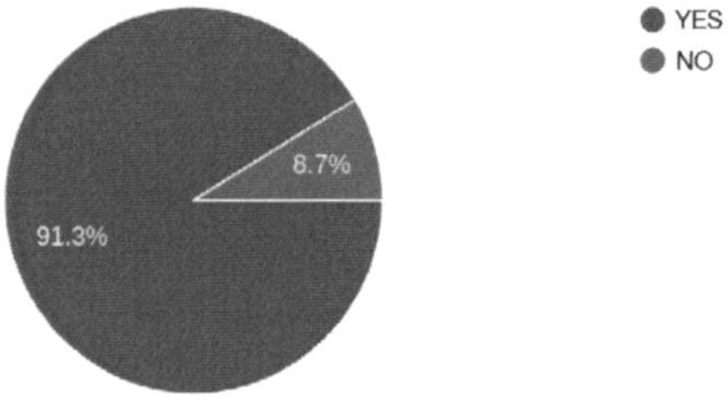

Figure 6. Users who purchased materials

An interesting figure is that 78% buy building materials from physical stores and about 95% would find it much more interesting to have an app that could resolve budgets, make comparisons, and show offers for construction materials from a variety of stores for a possible future purchase.

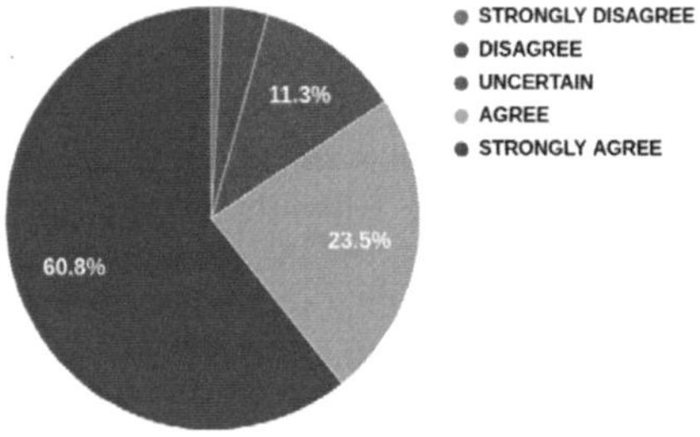

Figure 7. Users would like an application that helps them save time and money

It is also worth mentioning in Figure 7 that 60.8% of those interviewed would like an application that helps them save time and money when shopping.

In addition to the results presented, ConstruNET will provide the features of:

- Informing the location of the closest companies that contain the product searched by the user.
- Generating a budget
- Comparing prices.
- Ranking the users in relation to the veracity of the information inserted.

- Authentication of the user through Social Networks.

Additionally, application features will be verified through field testing to assess usability and user acceptance.

V. CONCLUSIONS AND FUTURE WORK

Usability issues in ConstruNET were handled with due attention by the application development team. In evaluating it, several techniques were used that inform indicators to be improved, both in navigability, as well as design and interaction with the end user.

Jakob Nielsen's Heuristics were used in the application, with the evaluation of some specialists and light of the result, it was verified that ConstruNET has a good set of colors that assist its users, besides providing a better visualization of the app at any time of the day, in addition to saving the battery of the mobile device on which it is installed. Another positive point is that the application has a unique font, making it easier to identify, changing only the font size, and the words are well associated with their respective functions. The structure of the screens is consistent, which facilitates learning how to use ConstruNET.

Points for improvement are the inclusion of titles and sections informing where the user is and translation of help and error messages. Images should be standard size and aligned on all screens. One point also to be improved is understanding of the product screen in relation to the information that should be highlighted.

As assessed in the evaluation, the application should also go through future implementations, such as social networking login and migration from the Appsheet® tool (where it currently is) to the Ionic platform.

Although the prototype was developed with limited Web applications, ConstruNET presents itself as a good solution to the proposal for which it was conceived. In future updates, the suggestions captured by the users will be covered through research and testing using the application during the prototyping phase.

ConstruNET is at the service of users of mobile technology, and through its announced offers it facilitates the planning of small reforms, as well as expediting decision-making in the acquisition of materials for construction.

REFERENCES

[1] Appsheet, Available from: <https://www.appsheet.com/>.Accessed: Nov, 2018.

[2] Phairoj Samutrak and Chalit Kangvaravoot, “Application to Calculate Potential Evapotranspiration”. International Journal of Applied Computer Technology and Information Systems, Vol 7. No.1, 2017, pp.35-40.

[3] Sylim PG, Santos-Acuin CC. "Development of A Low-Cost Electronic Data Collection Tool for A Health Facility Survey Study: Lessons Learned in the Field". J Int Soc Telemed eHealth 2016; 4:e27.

[4] Quinn Alexander J.,Bederson Benjamin B. "Appsheet: Efficient use of web workers to support decision making". Available from:<http://www.cs.umd.edu/hcil/trs/2011-26/2011-26.pdf>. Accessed: Nov, 2018.

[5] Ojha, Vinit. "Facility location and development of warehouse management system for cross channel Business Model". Available from: <http://14.139.205.163:8080/jspui/bitstream/123456789/92/1/2015PGMFMS03.pdf>. Accessed: Nov, 2018.

[6] F. S. Meireles, “29th Annual Survey of IT Usage 2018”, Available from: <https://eaesp.fgv.br/sites/eaesp.fgv.br/files/pesti2018gvciapp t.pdf>. Accessed: Nov, 2018.

[7] Google Docs, Available from: <https://www.google.com/docs/about/>. Accessed: Nov, 2018.

[8] Google Sheets, Available from: <https://www.google.com/sheets/about/>. Accessed: Nov, 2018.

[9] Google Slides, Available from: <https://www.google.com/slides/about/>. Accessed: Jun, 2018.

[10] Google Classroom, Available from: <https://classroom.google.com>. Accessed: Nov, 2018.

[11] Google Forms, Available from: <https://www.google.com/forms/about/>. Accessed: Oct, 2018.

[12] J. Nielsen, Usability Engineering. Academic Press, Boston, ISBN 0-12-518405-0 (hardcover), 0-12-518406-9 (softcover). Japanese translation ISBN 4-8101-9009-9.

[13] Google Maps, Available from: <https://www.google.com/maps/about/>. Accessed: Jun, 2018.

[14] Youtube, Available from: <https://www.youtube.com/>. Accessed: Oct, 2018.

The Use of E-portfolio as Collaborative Tool for a Creative Economy

Arich Andrade Rocha, Irlley José A. C. Branco,
Jonh Leno Fernandes and Mauro Henrique L. de Boni

Federal Institute of Sciente, Technology and Education
Palmas, Tocantins, Brazil
E-mails: arichandrade@gmail.com, irlleyjacb@gmail.com,
jonhleno.fer@gmail.com, mauro@ifto.edu.br

Abstract—**This article presents a tool for helping someone who needs to hire a freelance worker. Through a research performed by the authors, the results show that the Tocantins, the newest Brazilian state, has a big number of migrants from other states who have difficulty getting into the job market because they have no references. It also contributes to adaptation difficulties. Thus, the app can help both the local economy and the migrants by giving them an opportunity to take care of their families with dignity. To accomplish that, we used a tool called AppSheet, a framework based on components, to develop a prototype and verify the acceptance of the proposal.**

Keywords-E-portfolios; Collaborative; Professionals; Freelance; Sharing Economy; Opportunity.

I. INTRODUCTION

Currently, the inevitable and constant interactions between human being and technology haves increased in proportions never verified before. The use of smartphones has become as common as the tradition of sending letters in the last century. Smartphones are not only useful for sending messages, they perform many functions that transform them into an important tool for data storage, content creation, media access and collaboration with other persons.

According to IBGE (Brazilian Institute of Geography and Statistics) [1] by 2015, approximately 88% of the Brazilians who have a smartphone do not leave their home place without it, which proves how dependent society is on this device and indicates to the internet has allowed almost 97% of the Brazilian population to obtain access to information in real time, share their information as well, and interact with people and make transactions in various perspectives.

Given this, the rise of the Collaborative Consumption (CC) or sharing economy, the peer-to-peer-based activity of obtaining, giving, or sharing the access to goods and services, coordinated through community-based online services has been noticed. It has been motivated mostly by economic gains. In Brazil, this environment is promising to freelance workers.

In this sense, questions arise: "what to do when we have leaking in the kitchen, air conditioning that does not work, malfunctioning power sockets, a poorly finished floor, torn clothes, etc.?" These may be very common problems, but are not simple tasks to find a professional who can solve them and, even more difficult, to know whether the work offered is reliable. It is even harder to identify how reliable a given worker is when the usual method for finding professionals is based on WhatsApp groups, family opinion and store catalogues.

Based on this common problem of thousands of people, and thinking of providing a practical and safe solution for hiring freelance workers, it was decided to develop an application that unites several types of information in a single place, either for those who need to find a freelance worker and also for those who intend to offer their services. The application main goal is to make easier the professionals' meeting with potential clients.

This application is a showcase for the freelance workers, a place where all the information, such as the description of the work offered and the professional agenda will be detailed for anyone who accesses it. It will also make it more practical since it will optimize the search for a given professional, for example to fix the problems described before. The advantage of e-portfolio is that it provides a powerful way to collect and share information from professionals, gathers in one place, jobs, knowledge, skills, and attributes acquired during the person's lifetime, generating enormous potential in attracting many more clients. In the context of the search for optimizing the time and quality of the work effort, technology has proven to be an excellent ally in the life of the freelance workers and their clients. Currently, it is possible to have applications that facilitate and organize the entire work routine, and so, the idea of the 'TÔ aqui' (meaning: I'm here – in Portuguese) App came up.

In order to address this subject and report on the experience, the rest of the paper is organized as follows: in Section II, relevant related work on the topics is presented; in Section III, we discuss the research paper proposal, with specifications for materials and methods; in Section IV, the results of the research are presented, through analysis of the data collected and the development tool; in Section V, we present our final conclusions.

II. RELATED WORKS

To check if the goals of the users are reached, Maguire [2] shows that the development team must visualize the translation of functional requirements into technical requirements and prototypes. To do this, mock-ups, storyboards, or prototypes are created and tested sequentially and iteratively with intended users. Wong [3] introduced a method that address an applied user-centered and user-experience product development. The Designers need to identify their target users during the design process either in design, system or interface. These user profiles are based on the characteristics, interest, cultural beliefs, gender, social groups and lifestyle of the target group.

A good user experience is very important for the success of interactive products. Schrepp [4] demonstrates that user experience questionnaire can be used to help the design team measure the user experience of a product quantitatively.

Peer-to-peer markets, as showed by Zervas [5], have emerged as alternative suppliers of goods and services traditionally provided by long-established industries. The authors explore the economic impact of the sharing economy by studying the case of Airbnb, a platform form short-term accommodations.

III. PROPOSAL

Tocantins is one of the 27 states of Brazil. As the newest state in the country, it is a developing frontier area, and its inhabitants historically have been mostly of Indigenous and mixed European-Indigenous ancestry and, in 2015, its population was approximately 1.497 million people. To better understanding the situation, the migration of different people from different regions causes a conflict because of few references in people lives. One example is, the lack of reliability when choosing a professional to perform a particular service.

Imagine the following situation: A housewife needs a plumber as it is leaking in the kitchen. How does she find a professional of her confidence, since she has no technical knowledge about the problem, and especially since she is new in town, and does not know any professionals in the area?

Taking advantage of this problem, we are working on the development of a application for mobile devices, such as tablets and smartphones, that can gather information on a single platform, bringing reliability when choosing a freelance worker to proceed with the execution of a given service. In Section A we will work with more details about the application.

A. Materials

In order to create this app, we used the AppSheet, a web application development platform that does not necessarily require advanced programming knowledge to quickly and easily transform an idea into an app. This tool was chosen, since it is a tool that promotes the manipulation of information in a ubiquitous way: visualization, insertion, editing, and deletion of data at any time, since the given platform connects to highly available tools, such as the Google Drive. The Google form is a free tool that has enabled us to extract the information outside the academic field, helping us to define and model the application's visual display with more specific content.

The application is made available in a collaborative perspective. That means that the information presented in the application will not be responsibility of the creator of the application. Collaborative Consumption (CC) is increasingly transforming human interaction; one example is the exchange of experiences, services, and products; what is called Sharing Economy when it is related to financial gains.

Thus, the application can reach a huge number of users: those looking for a professional and / or those professionals who wish to expand their business. Furthermore, for the best application navigation and to encourage the user to contribute with relevant information, all views of the application will be developed with the purpose of making it intuitive for users, to make sure they will have no problem in finding any particular data, and to ensure a good user experience (UX). The screens and the icons are easy to identify, allowing the customer to register, view, and update the information.

Figure 1. Views Flowchart example

As showed in Figure 1, the navigation from login screen and a given registered professional screen is made in only three clicks. The usability of the application was simplified as much as possible. So, even the users without experience in using apps will successfully find a professional according to their needs.

B. Method

After choosing the platform, the app interface has been defined in a collaborative way through presentations and discussions during the Telematics Post-Graduation Program classes in order to provide a user-friendly visual experience that meets the previously identified need which is, in this context, to provide to the potential clients the information they need to establish contact with a professional who can execute a given work.

To identify the need of such an app, it was made a query application. It was developed as a survey with 10 questions, which can be seen in Table 1. Those questions were inserted in Google Form platform. In order to serve a larger audience, the online link of the form was made available through the social networks, such as Facebook, WhatsApp, and Instagram. With the data collection at the end of the questionnaire, answered by a total of 83 people, we were able to provide a solution to the problem presented.

IV. RESULTS

The use of technology in solving problems has become a common thing in people's lives. Mobile devices are a technology that can, ubiquitously, enable fast access to information, exchange of messages, payments, among others. To make sure there is a need of an app to help people to find a freelance worker with the needed capabilities we applied a survey showed at the Table 1. This survey has ten questions about how often people need freelance workers, how they find them, and their opinion on an app that could help them in these situations.

The results of this research were obtained by interpreting the data collected by a survey evaluation developed in Google Forms. This was done to verify the viability of the application on the market, since until then we were basing ourselves solely on our own need. The questions involved topics about the customer's need to search for a professional, how often they would use the app, which are the most wanted professionals, among others.

TABLE I. QUIZ

Query
1. How old are you?
2. How often do you need a freelance worker?
3. When you need a freelance worker, which resource or method do you use to find one?
4. Would you use, or do you already use, an app on your smartphone to find freelance workers?
5. Which categories of professionals do you need most often?
6. What information about this professional would be essential for you to hire a service?
7. How often do you use your smartphone?
8. For what purpose to you use your smartphone the most?
9. As for the number of apps on your smartphone, how many would you say you have installed?
10. How would an application about freelance workers be considered by you?

A. Data Analysis

According to Figure 2, we conclude that the app would be feasible, since approximately 80% need a freelance worker from time to time.

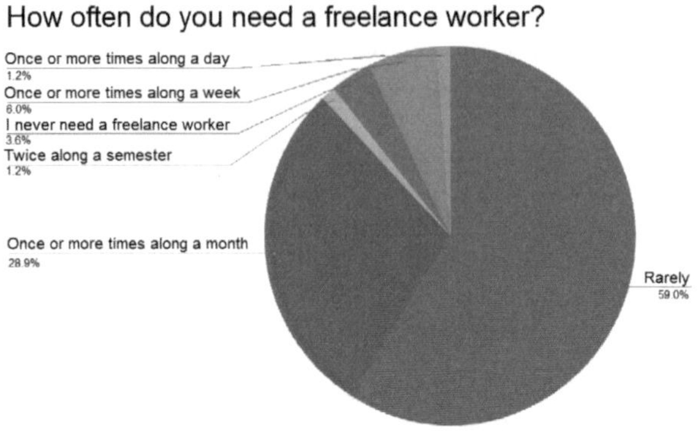

Figure 2. Result of the survey applied.

Other needs verified:

- Identification of the most wanted freelance services:

The results showed that the four most sought after professions are: Masons, Electricians, Mechanics, and Computer Science Technicians;

- The app user possible age range:

By weighted average, it was verified that the average age of our possible users is 32 years;

- Essential information the app most provide for supplying a service:

As can be seen in Figure 3, potential users consider important information to qualify the professional, such as vocational courses, technical courses, or even a higher level course; professional experience such as, places where they have already performed some service; and lastly the one that stood out most as requirements by the users, evaluation of the professional by other people, that is, the importance of the evaluation influences when choosing a professional.

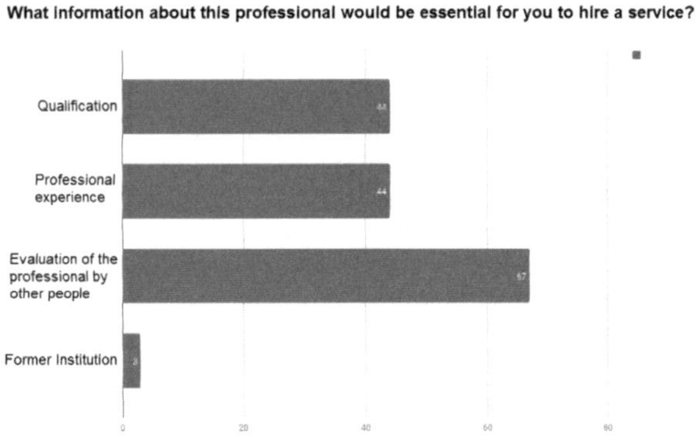

Figure 3. Result of the survey applied.

- And finally, how necessary would this app be:

According to Figure 4, the evaluation of possible users regarding the need for such an app, the result shows that approximately 85% of people questioned consider the app to be essential or necessary.

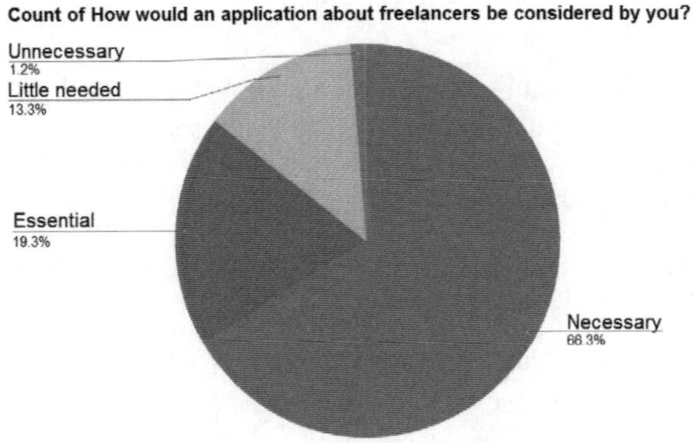

Figure 4. Result of the survey applied.

B. Development Tool

Since it is a development tool based on visual components and the organization of the data arranged in the spreadsheet, here are some screens of the application and the development process.

Figure 5 show the app screens: first, the list of freelance workers category, the second shows the registration screen of a given freelance worker category, such as "mason", for example. And lastly, the list of professionals registered in a certain profession category.

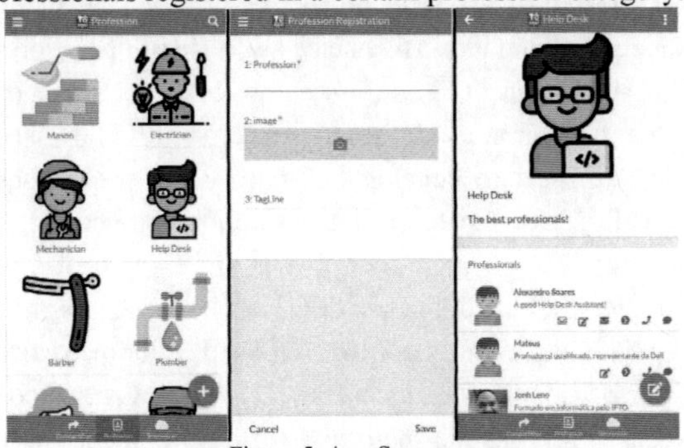

Figure 5. App Screens

Figure 6 shows the professional registration screen, and the description of a particular professional.

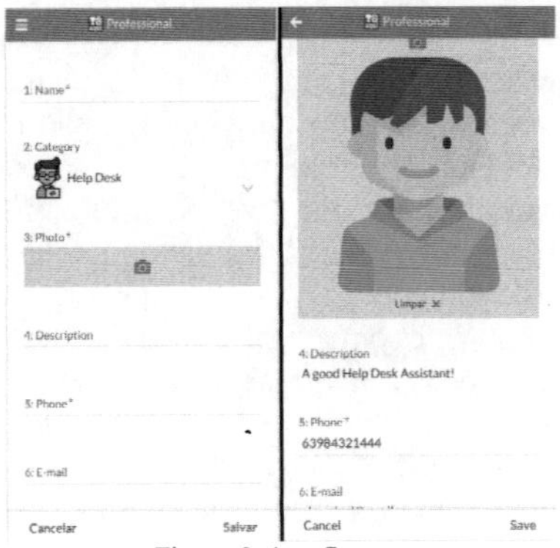

Figure 6. App Screens

V. Conclusion and Future Works

Apps are used for a variety of services around the world. In this scenario, the "TÔ aqui" project presents itself as a reliable and viable option for a person looking for a professional to do domestic chores, as for the professionals who need to advertise their activities and work to earn a living. In an unstable job market, offering options for people to work and thus survive, motivate us to contribute even more to the development of this app.

Therefore, in order to continue pointing towards the use of mobile applications to solve problems, from the perspective of mobility, this work presents the possibility of gathering information on trust and credibility in a collaborative environment that will bring more security to the user at the moment of choosing a professional by showing suggestions, evaluations, and opinions left by other users.

References

[1] Brazilian Institute of Geography and Statistics. IBGE: *National Household Sample Survey*. [Online]. Available from:https://ww2.ibge.gov.br/english/estatistica/indicadores/trabalhoerendimento/pnad_continua/default.shtm

[2] M. Maquire, "Methods to support human-centered design" International Journal of Human-Computer, vol. 55, pp.587-634. 2001. doi:10.1006/ijhc.2001.0503 .

[3] M. C. Wong, C. W. Khong and H. Thwaites "Applied UX and UCD Design Process in Interface Design," Procedia – Social and Behavioral Sciences, vol. 21, pp.703-708. 2010. doi:10.1016/j.sbspro.2012.08.228.

[4] M. Schrepp, A. Hinderks and J. Thomaschewski "Applying the User Experience Questionnaire (UEQ) in Different Evaluation Scenarios" International Conference of Design, User Experience, and Usability. pp.383-392. 2014. doi: 10.1007/978-3-319-07668-3_37

[5] G. Zervas, D. Proserpio and J. W. Byears, "The Rise of the Sharing Economy: Estimating the Impact of Airbnb on the Hotel Industry" Journal of Marketing Research, vol. 54, pp.687-705. 2017. doi: 10.1509/jmr.15.0204

Gas-TO - a Case Study in Project-based Learning

José Itamar M. de Souza Júnior, Diego Ferreira de Miranda, Yuri Antonio S. de Souza
Federal Institute of Science and Technology of Tocantins
Palmas, Brazil
E-mails: {jhoseju, diegofinformatica, yantonio1992}@gmail.com

Abstract—**This paper presents a case study of Project-based Learning applying translational research. The novelty proposed consists in how the Project-based Learning approach can be used to obtain a solution for a problem in society. The supporting project is a real-life problem, about filling up on gas. Its development was planned in phases: bibliographical research, survey for obtaining the level of interest for the solution proposed, prototype and deployment of Gas-TO. We employed strategies to ensure that the proposed development methodology can be carried out by any academician, regardless of their area of training, thus ensuring an interdisciplinary methodology for developing solutions for the community.**

Keywords-Project-based Learning; methodology; mobile technologies; application.

I. INTRODUCTION

Nowadays, quick and easy access to information has become a necessity [1] and has motivated the development of applications used by users in general [2].

In this scenario, when we consider applications that have information about filling stations in state of Tocantins in Brazil, we identify that there are no instruments to provide online and cooperative information about filling station locations and fuel distributor names and about how much fuel there is in each one. This was confirmed by searching for this kind of application on Play Store and App Store.

Therefore, our goal is to apply the concept of translational research [3] in order to obtain a solution to the problem described. To that end, all authors use the knowledge they have acquired beforehand in writing contributions. We use Project-based Learning - PBL to integrate the several life and technical backgrounds of our team members [4][5], in order to find a way to achieve a positive and collaborative solution for informing people where it is less expensive to buy gasoline.

Therefore, we have developed an application named Gas-TO. Our goal was to develop a collaborative application [6], in which data updates can be made by the users [7]. Thus, through PBL we have developed a solution that offers users the price, location, and distributor name of each filling station. In developing of this app, we used tools that made it possible to develop an app without high-level programming [8].

The rest of the paper is organized as follows. In Section II, we present some relevant related work. In Section III, we present the proposal of the article and the methodology used. Next, in Section IV, we show the results obtained. Finally, in Section V, we discuss the results and conclude with possible future directions.

II. RELATED WORK

In this section we will present some works that use the Google Appsheet as an easy way for developing solutions involving database and cellular applications, in order to show the real importance of the Google AppSheet tools for facilitating database development and operation.

Thus, the authors in [9], show how the AppSheet was used for calculating water consumption by the reference plants, presenting an easy way for storage and development an application.

In the same way, the authors in [10], address use of the AppSheet for building a database for facilitating location and development of a warehouse management system. The authors present a database model totally based on Google Appsheet, showing its performance and ease of operation.

The authors in [11] address a low-cost electronic data collection tool for a health facility survey study. They used a Google Appsheet to develop this tool, using the appsheet functionalities for create an online application, showing its efficiency.

On the other hand, the use of Google Appsheet is shown in [8], where the authors use the tool for development a web solution to support decision making. In this work, Google Appsheet is used as the main tool for development and the authors note the advantages of the Appsheet, considering its operation and programming facility, as well as the its database robustness.

III. PROPOSAL

Our proposal can be described as an application for showing information about price, location and distribution of filling stations at Tocantins State - Brazil. This application was created using a cooperative approach. That means the users can update the data according to their experiences as customers.

The app enables easy navigation for the user and has a structure and mechanisms that aim to encourage user collaboration. The app was developed in order to ensure that the user is able to view of the registered filling stations, and is thus able to choose to register a new filling station, verify the prices by type of fuel and/or update information, as represented in Figure 1.

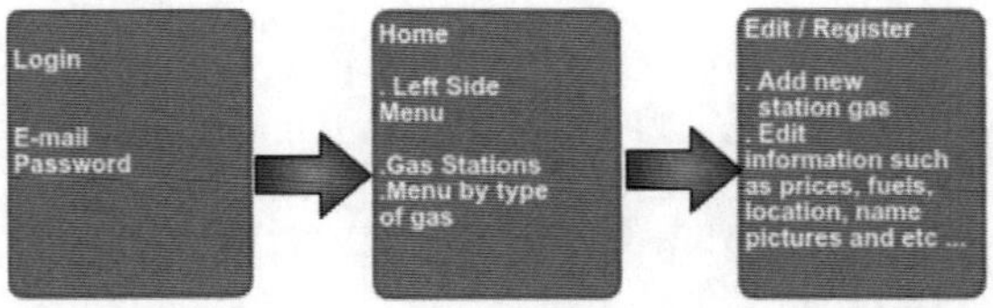

Figure 1. Flowchart.

A. *Materials*

The choice of tools was strongly influenced by the limiting factor of technical feasibility, considering the heterogeneity of the group, as well as the weekly workload that each member of the group had available for developing the application. The selected tool (AppSheet) supports the methodology proposed in this work and was presented to the Telematics class. It was used as the main tool for development of the Gas-TO application.

The AppSheet is defined as a smart platform that does not need to use a programming language to obtain apps, enabling people who are not experts in Information Technology to use it without difficulty [12]. The AppSheet has a simple structure, as shown in Figure 2.

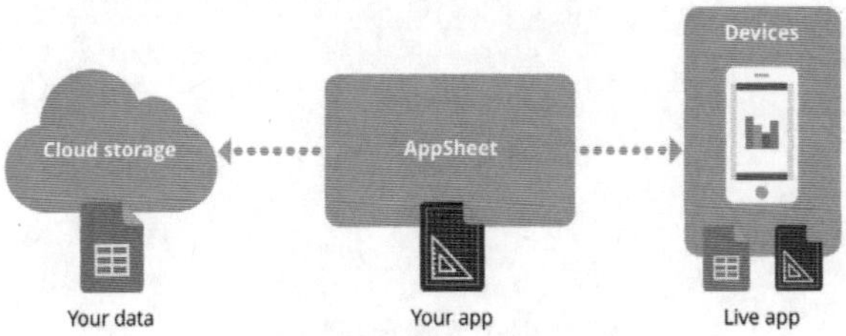

Figure 2. AppSheet Architecture.

The development of this work, would not be possible if we used a complex development tool or if we needed to use programming languages, considering the time we had. Because of that, we choose to develop Gas-To with AppSheet, which allowed us to develop the app within the scheduled time.

After choosing the development tools, we conducted a survey with possible future users of the application to measure the degree of interest in the proposed solution. 71.6% of them indicated that they would use an application like the one presented in this solution. For applying all the surveys, we used Google Forms, a free service for creating forms online. With Google Forms, the user can produce multiple-choice searches, make discursive questions, request numerical-scale evaluations, and use other options [13]. Consequently, we obtained feedback on a number of issues that guided the development of our work and validated our methodology.

IV. RESULTS

We applied an online form for drivers in Tocantins State to verify their interest in using the application and to indicate what information about filling stations is most important for them. With the survey we obtained 74 answers. These answers influenced the development of the application, since they demonstrated the real degree of interest in it.

Figure 3 presents the answers to the question: When you are you going to fill your tank, what is most relevant to you? For 59.5% it is the price, for 27% it is the distributor and 13.5% answered that distance is the most important factor.

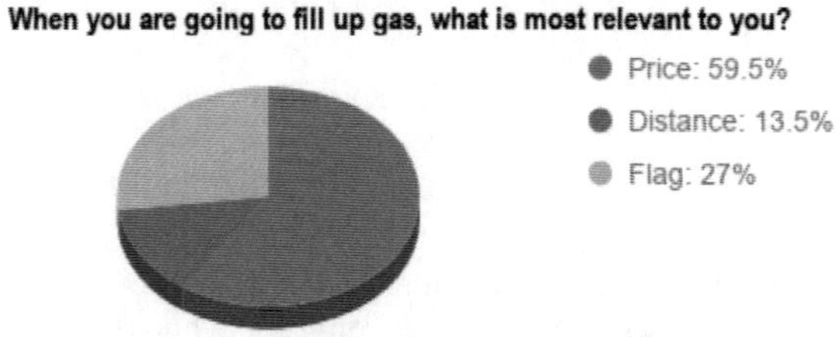

Figure 3. What is most import when filling up?

Figure 4 presents the answers to the question: Would you use an application that tells you about fuel prices, and the location of the filling stations? Zero means little interest in the use and 10 much use interest. The maximum level of interest was shown by 71.6% of the drivers; 13.5% answered 9; 6.8% answered 8; 5.4% answered 7; 1.4% answered 6 and 1.4% answered 1.

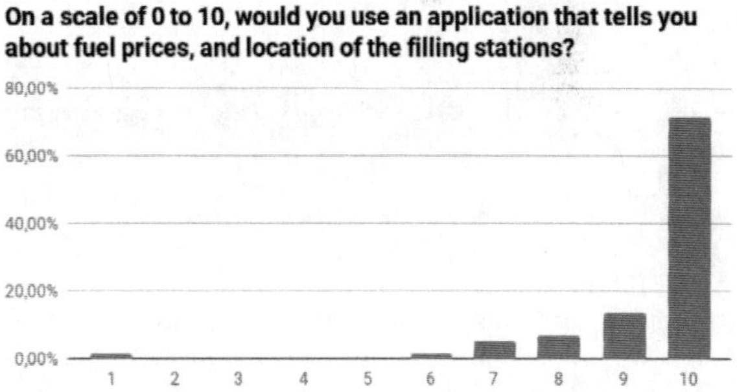

Figure 4. Would you use an application that tells you about fuel prices, and the location of the filling stations?

We considered the answers shown in Figures 3 and 4, in implementing the function to present the ranked list of the filling stations, as shown in Figure 5.

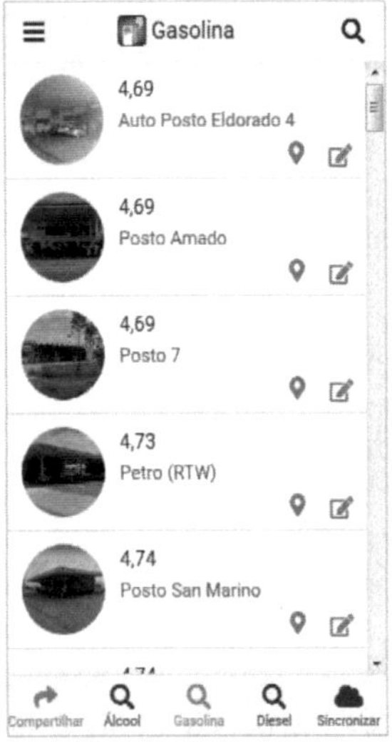

Figure 5. App screen.

Figure 6 presents a summary of the answers to the question: What type of fuel do you use in your vehicle? We can see that 90.3% answered that they use regular gasoline, 22.2% said they use premium gasoline, 20.8% answered that they employed ethanol and 5.6% answered that they used diesel.

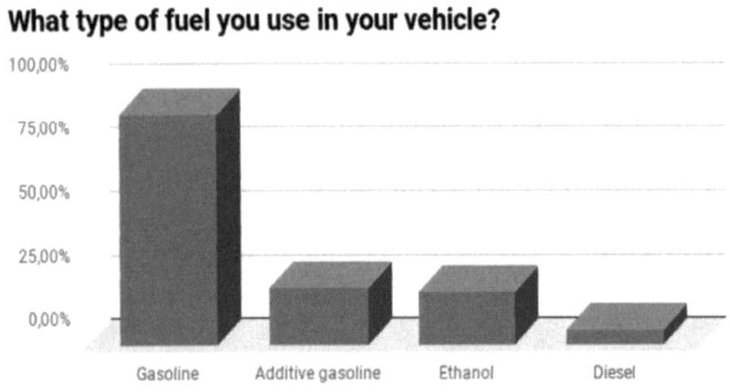

Figure 6. What type of fuel do you use in your vehicle?

Figure 7 presents the answers to the question: Do you fill up your vehicle at filling stations: on the way home, to work, school or place that you regularly go to? As shown in Figure 7, 36.5% answered that they fill up when they are on the way home, 32.4% said when they are on the way to work, 24.3% said they fill up in other circumstances and 6.8% answered that they stop at the filling station on their way to school or college.

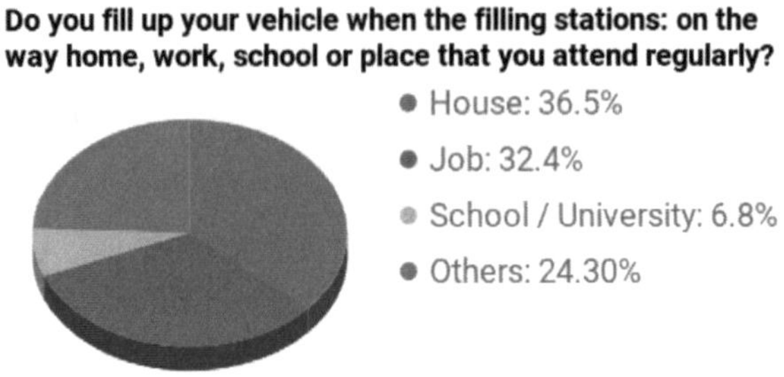

Figure 7. On the way home, to work, school or place that you go to regularly?

We considered the answers for adding a function to the app, so that users can see the location of the filling station registered using Google Maps and even request a route to reach the selected filling station. The screen with this function is represented in Figure 8.

Figure 8. App screen - Map

Figure 9 shows the list of application menus, used to access all the features of the application.

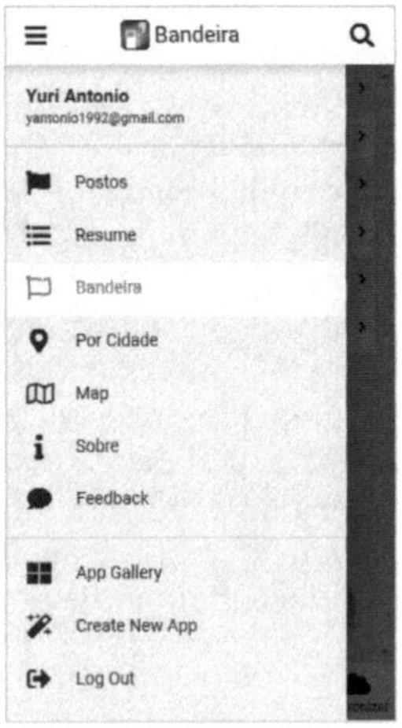

Figure 9. App screen - Menu.

Figure 10 shows the query screen for the filling station.

Figure 10. App screen - Fuel Station.

Figure 11 presents the Flag Menu (Fuel Distributors), meaning that the filling stations are grouped according to their distributors.

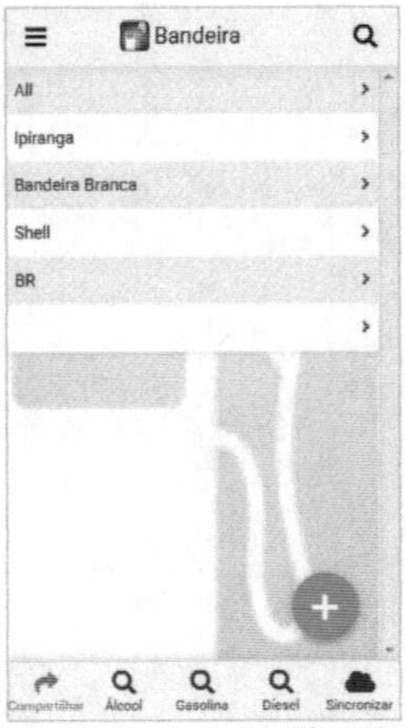

Figure 11. App screen – Flag Menu.

Figure 12 shows the screen for editing filling station information.

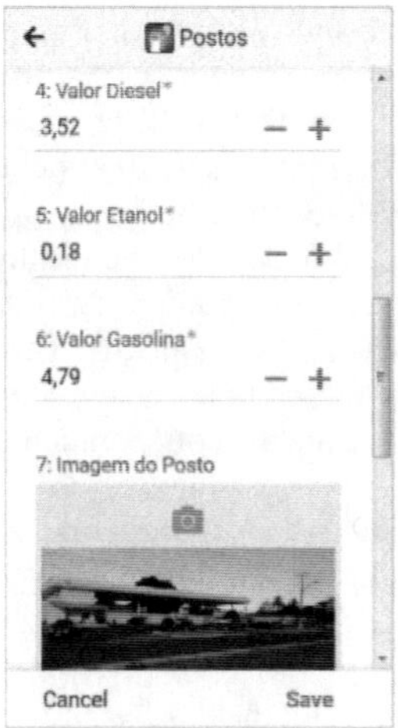

Figure 12. App screen - Editing Fuel Station.

In developing this application, our priority was to provide a user interface similar to the most commonly used applications. WhatsApp was chosen as the designer model, as represented in Figure 13.

Figure 14. Comparison Screen WhatsApp - Screen Gas-TO.

V. CONCLUSION AND FUTURE WORK

The methodology used illustrates the feasibility of developing solutions for society, enabling students from different areas of knowledge to create tools that can be used as facilitators for the daily life of their communities. This challenges the pervasive current thinking that only information technology professionals with a focus on programming can be providers/developers of technological solutions.

In addition, it is very important to emphasize that through the translational methodology used in this work, it was possible to traverse all the stages of project-based learning, starting from the acquisition of theoretical knowledge, passing through definition of the project, until the development and obtention of a solution.

Through the feasibility study, it was possible to verify that future users of the app believe that the application will contribute information that will provide input for their decision-making regarding where to refuel their vehicles

In view of this, because it is an application with a collaborative bias, the user is the centerpiece; in other words, without this collaboration, this solution becomes obsolete and unfeasible to maintain. This means that the major challenge is yet to come. That is, to put Gas-TO into production and stimulate the collaboration of users to ensure its viability.

As for implications for future work, although the Gas-TO application was developed in Palmas, Tocantins, and Brazil; this solution can also be distributed in other regions.

REFERENCES

[1] M. M. Lynch. The online educator: A guide to creating the virtual classroom. Routledge, 2002.

[2] T. R. Oliveira and F. M. R. Costa. Development of mobile reference application on vaccination in Brazil. Journal of Health Informatics, vol. 4, no. 1, 2012.

[3] R. Guimarães. Translational Research: an interpretation. Ciência & Saúde Coletiva 18 2013, pp. 1731-1744.

[4] N. Berbel N. A. Methodology of Problematization in Higher Education and its contribution to the plan of praxis. Semina. Londrina. vol.17, pp. 7-17, 1996.

[5] P. Letouze, J. I. M. de Souza Júnior, and V. M. Silva. Generating software engineers by developing web systems: a project-based learning case study. Software Engineering Education and Training (CSEET), IEEE 29th International Conference on IEEE, pp. 194-203, 2016.

[6] C. Ciurea. The development of a mobile application in a collaborative banking system. Informatica Economica, vol. 14, no. 3, p. 86, 2010.

[7] C. Cheong, V. Bruno, and F. Cheong. Designing a mobile-app-based collaborative learning system. Journal of Information Technology Education: Innovations in Practice, vol. 11, pp. 97-119, 2012.

[8] A. J. Quinn and B. Bederson. Appsheet: Efficient use of web workers to support decision making. University of Maryland, 2017.

[9] P. Samutrak and C. Kangvaravoot. Application to Calculate Potential Evapotranspiration. International Journal of Applied Computer Technology and Information Systems, vol. 7.1, 2017.

[10] V. Ojha. Facility Location and Development of Warehouse Management System for Cross Channel Business Model, 2017.

[11] P. G. Sylim and C. Cristina Santos-Acuin. Development of a Low-Cost Electronic Data Collection Tool for a Health Facility Survey: Lessons Learned in the Field. Journal of the International Society for Telemedicine and eHealth, vol. 27, 2016.

[12] M. Ludloff. AppSheet Named A Leader Among Mobile Low-Code Platforms for Business Developers by Independent Research Firm. 2018.

[13] L. A. Heidemann, A. M. M. de Oliveira, and E. A. Veit. Online tools in science education: a proposal with Google Docs. Física na escola. São Paulo. Vol. 11, n. 2, 2010, pp. 30-33 2010.

The Use of Augmented Reality as a Tool in Human Anatomy Classes

Michalany Turibio Glória, Fabrício Souza Nunes
Federal Institute of Education, Science and Technology (IFTO), Palmas, Brazil
e-mails: {michalany290, fabriciosnunes}@gmail.com

***Abstract*- Recently, there has been a major increase in the use of Augmented Reality (AR). Some hybrid teaching methodologies use different technological resources to improve teaching/learning programs. This research aims to assist such programs that involve human anatomy classes by providing an extended use of AR with the help of several tools, such as wireless networks, smartphones, computers, and other devices. Our goal is to simplify and further deepen the learning experience for human anatomy students in undergraduate health care courses. To achieve its goal, the research intends to produce a smartphone app and apply it to the target audience.**

Keywords- information technology; hybrid teaching; augmented reality; human anatomy; telematics.

I. Introduction

Teaching has always been fundamental to our culture as human beings. Because it has constantly evolved, constant improvement is also necessary.

Healthcare professionals are essential to society and thus well-trained professionals are vital for improving services provided to the population. This relevance has inspired us to contribute to their professional education.

In this context, virtual reality can be useful and Cardoso [9] affirms that virtual reality has the potential to provide an education as a process of exploration, discovery, observation and construction of a new vision of knowledge, offering the apprentice an opportunity to better understand the object of study.

The idea came after classes in the postgraduate course in Telematics offered at the Federal Institute of Education, Science and Technology - IFTO campus Palmas, located in the municipality of Palmas in the state of Tocantins, Brazil. This research aims to contribute to teaching and learning experiences with content related to human anatomy. The target audience are students from different institutions who are learning such content.

Tools such as computers, smartphones, and the Internet, are already used together for to purpose of teaching and learning. They are also used in anatomy classes, but generally at a high cost both for the educational institution and for the student, creating an economical obstacle to academic performance. Aiming to reduce such costs and offer a tool that accelerates and facilitates the process of teaching and learning, we intend to develop an app (application) for smartphones with human anatomy contents, presented in three-dimensional image format. In order to improve the users' experience and visualization of the images, our idea is to insert augmented reality technology to bring the user closer to the actual visualization of the object portrayed.

AR provides a view of reality by combining real-world elements with elements of the virtual world that are created in three dimensions in real time. The insertion of this technology applied to the teaching of anatomy can contribute to a more dynamic class and a more interesting presentation of the contents and so facilitate learning.

The app being developed was named Augmented Reality Applied to Medical Study - RAMED and is in production; it is currently in the prototyping phase and a first test has already been done in order to map the user experience. Resources from the LAB MATICA Tocantins laboratory and from the AppSheet were used to construct the RAMED prototype.

The rest of the document is structured as follows: Section II lists current examples of mobile apps applied to education; Section III explains the goals of this research and describes the materials used in construction of the app prototype; Section IV presents the results of the first customer survey; Section V presents the potential of this project and indicates its potential future uses.

II. Related Works

Google AppSheet tools are frequently used to facilitate database development and operation. In this paper, we are going to present some activities that have used this tool for facility development solution involving a database and cellular applications.

Mobile devices play a fundamental role in spreading information.

Manoel [2] affirms that cell phones and tablets are more common than television sets nowadays and that there are, on average, 4 mobile devices per person in a middle-class family.

Moreira [4] presents a solution to assist the mathematics teaching at the elementary school level by using a cellular app with augmented reality. According to the author, the use of this app in his classes, aided by the fact that all his students possess a cellular device, made the classes more attractive since everyone focused more on the exercises, knowing that the answers would be provided by cell phones and ranked as if in a game.

Magalhães et al. [1] also presented the use of a mobile app, created using an Open Source tool, to assist music teaching in high school classes. The authors demonstrably improved students' results using, in the classes, the application developed and with subjective evaluations provided by students. Additionally, Santos [5], shows that the use of a mobile app can help safeguard environmental preservation areas. For this purpose, they developed an app that generates a kind of social network where anyone can check whether there is any generating fact, spontaneous or caused by humans, that is compromising rivers, forests, etc. The app can take photos of the event and send them to the network in real time, including the location, so that public agents can reach the place.

Mobile apps have also been used to improve administrative procedures. Martins [3] proposed that, with a cell phone, teachers of the municipal school system of Palmas, in Tocantins can have access to the results of the national "Brazil Test", a objective test for measuring the knowledge of students in the elementary school.

The indicators provide important information for teachers to work with their students during the school year with methodological innovations. Without the use of the app in question, the access to this information was not agile, and was therefore irrelevant.

The use of AR can stimulate and help in the processes of knowledge and, according to Cardoso [9], both sides of the process can benefit; not only students, through the stimulus and ease of access, but also teachers by enabling different manners of teaching. Cardoso [10] affirms that use of AR stimulates and facilitates acquisition of knowledge by the student, helping teachers in their educational practices as well as providing various ways of teaching. The use of this methodology adapts very well to contents where the abstraction needed by the students becomes very complex.

Thus, in order to use mobile phones for helping to solve problems, this research presents a prototype of RAMED that aims to contribute to teaching human anatomy and that can be applied to different undergraduate courses that need it.

III. PROPOSAL

Society is increasingly looking for affordable and quality education.

The knowledge of human anatomy is fundamental for any courses that involve health and it has been one of the most complex and difficult subjects to learn. Even with the exhibition of anatomic parts in plastic and other tools, the students tend to be bored, since the content is very extensive. In this context, the possibility of an attractive and easy-to-read learning form, but one that maintains the quality of the classes, could prove useful.

In order to increase insertion of different technologies for teaching, AR with its many resources, if applied to the teaching of human anatomy can be an alternative to dynamize classes, making the visualization of the contents more interesting and contributing in this way to learning.

Anami [11] discusses AR immersion and navigation properties and the contribution each of them can make to the context of learning, mainly related to student involvement. She also talks about the interaction in AR environments, which provides links between student and content, students and teacher, and between students themselves. The benefits translate into better cognition, involvement, experimentation, collaboration, adaptation to rhythm and creation of appropriate environments.

Therefore, in order to use this technology for teaching human anatomy, the smartphone format was proposed, since it is considered to be a common and easily accessible tool for the majority of the population.

We provide a database of images of organs and systems, with visualization using AR technology.

It is assumed that a smartphone will provide greater learning effectiveness considering the ease of access and full availability of content. As a secondary benefit, it can dynamize classes by being a new instrument to aid teaching.

A. Materials

The construction of RAMED was a project conceived and carried by a group during the Mobile and Converged Networks course, a curricular component of the Graduate Program Course in Telematics at IFTO.

For construction of the prototype, the resources of the LAB MÁTICA physical laboratory of the Federal Institute of Education, Science and Technology - IFTO, Palmas - TO, were used. This lab has computers with an Intel Core processor I5-3330 with 8 GB of RAM and Ubuntu 16.04 LTS operating system. For the construction of the prototype the AppSheet [6] platform was used; this allows construction of group applications.

In August of 2018, the first test with the application prototype was carried out, with students of the Graduate Program in Telematics course as user. This audience of a total of 24 students, was chosen for the first design test because of the qualifications for evaluation and accessibility to the developers.

The main question focused on the usability of the application and the test with the prototype was able to provide answers. For access to the application, a link has been made available via WhatsApp [7].

IV. RESULTS

In order to learn about the evaluation of these first users, a questionnaire was produced using the Google Forms [8] tool and offered to users via a link released through WhatsApp [7]. The questionnaire was made available to 24 people and answered by a total of 8 people, who had access to the following questions shown in Table 1.

TABLE 1- DESCRIPTION OF THE QUESTIONS AND ANSWERS RELATED TO THE QUESTIONNAIRE USED IN THE USER SURVEY.

Question	Responses	Percentage
1- Do you know what Augmented Reality (RA) is?	Yes	100%
2 - How much RA can assist in learning anatomy in your opinion.	It helps a lot	62,5
3 - Just by accessing the application can you recognize its purpose?	I recognize	50%
4 - How much do you understand that this application can be a learning support tool?	Very useful	75%
5 - As for the use of the app you would evaluate how?	Little Easy Normal	37,5% 37,5%
6 - As for the layout of the application you would evaluate how?	Great	62,50%
7 - As for the fonts used in the application would you rate how?	Great	50%
8 - As for the Icons and colors used in the application would you rate how?	Great	62,50%
9 - Were you satisfied with the content of the application?	Excellent	37,50%
10 - Any additional comments about the sessions or the programming as a whole?	None	0%

All responses were answered after using the prototype for the purpose of demonstrating its action.

A. Data Analysis

The user experience, visualized through the answers to the questionnaire showed broad knowledge regarding Augmented Reality (Fig. 1), a fact that was expected considering that the audience surveyed has an affinity with the computing area.

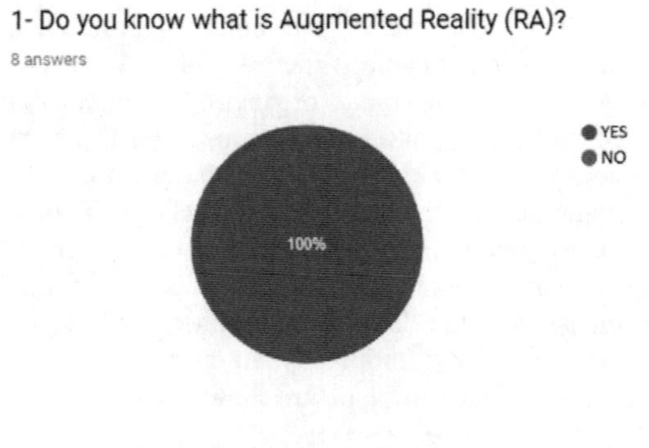

Figure 1 - Question 1 results.

Of this audience, 62.5% considered that Augmented Reality can contribute greatly learning anatomy, and 37.5% considered that it can contribute (Fig. 2). This demonstrates that Augmented Reality is already an established technology for aiding teaching and learning.

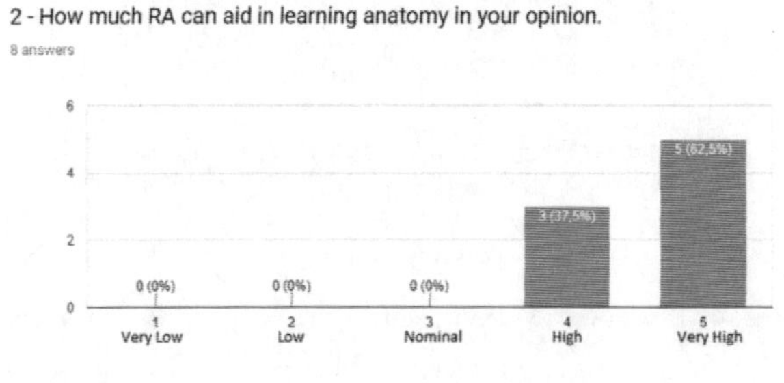

Figure 2 - Question 2 with the results on a sliding scale, where 1 is Very Low and 5 Very High.

Experience in using RAMED memory was reported by 12.5% of the surveyed public who reported that access to information was able to be fully realized. The others said they understood somewhat or understood very little (Fig. 3). This feedback demonstrates that the description of the purpose needs to be improved.

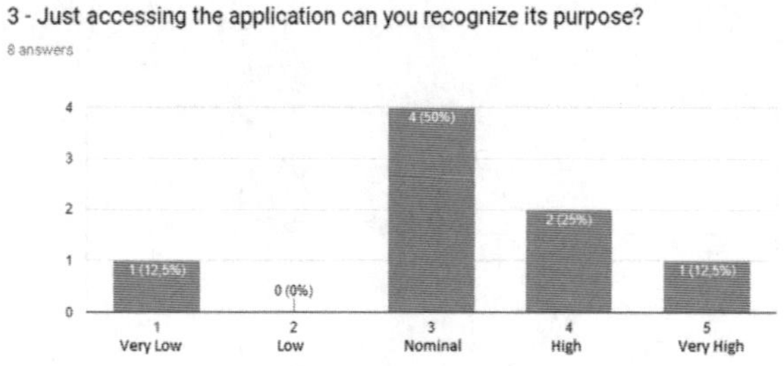

Figure 3 - Question 3 with the results on a sliding scale, where 1 means for I Very Low and 5 Very High.

In terms of the ability to develop a tool to support learning 75% said it had a great possibility of becoming the right type of tool, while 25% understood that there is some possibility (Fig. 4). This shows that although the goal may not have been well presented, the surveyed public understands that AR has the ability to be an educational tool.

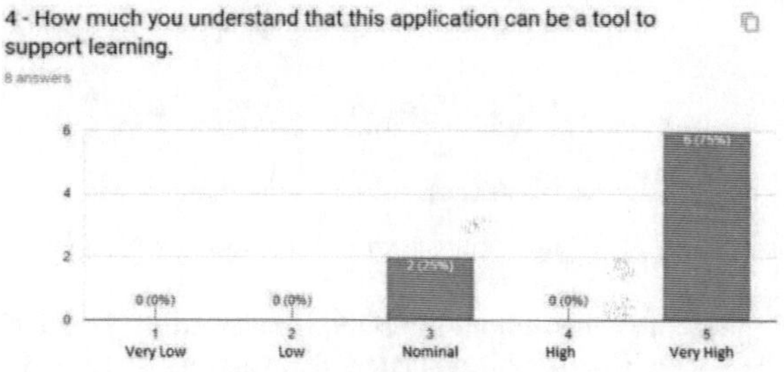

Figure 4 - Question 4 with the results on a sliding scale, where 1 is Very Low and 5 Very High.

The usability of the app was evaluated as very good by 25% of the public, good by 37.5% and fair by 37.5% (Fig. 5). As a result, we realize that improvements are needed.

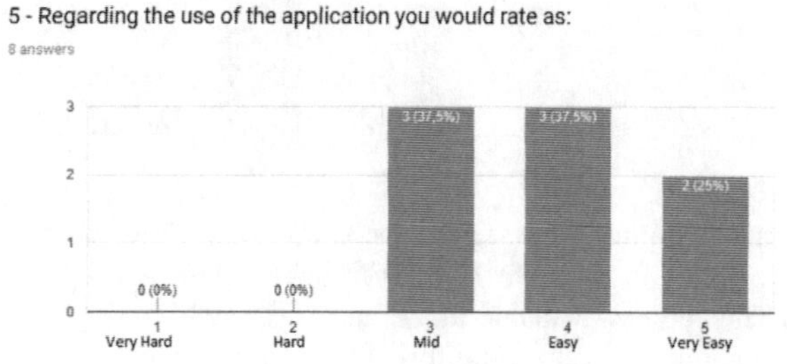

Figure 5 - Question 5 with the results on a sliding scale, where 1 is Very Hard and 5 is Very Easy.

The layout was positively evaluated with 62.5% rating it as good, 25% as fair and 12.5% as very good (Fig. 6). From this, it is observed that the current project is of good quality, but needs improvement.

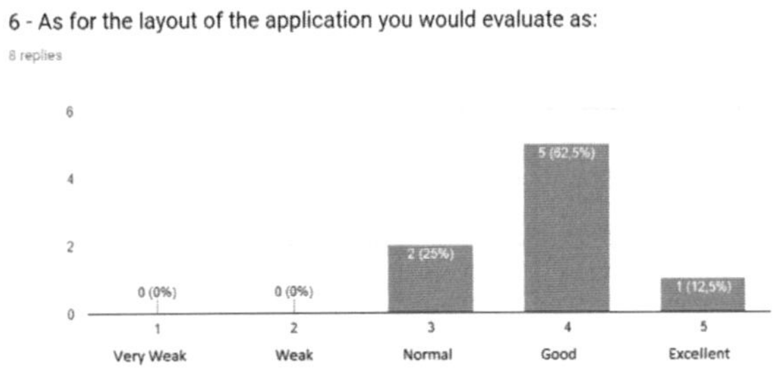

Figure 6 - Question 6 with the results on a sliding scale, where 1 is very weak and 5 is excellent.

The design was rated by 50% of the public as good, 25% as very good, 12.5% as fair and 12.5% as bad (Fig. 7). The fonts used in the words and images are subject to revisions, considering that they impact on the visual comfort and on comprehension of the screen and menus contents.

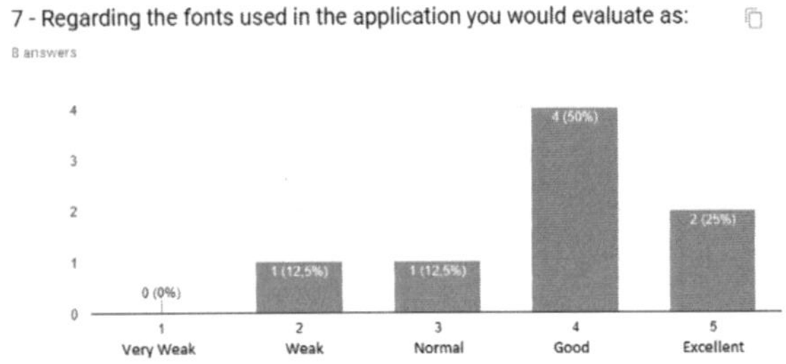

Figure 7 - Question 7 with the results on a sliding scale, where 1 is very weak and 5 is excellent.

The icons and colors presented received a positive evaluation when 62.5% evaluated them as good, 25% as very good and 12.5% as acceptable Fig 8.

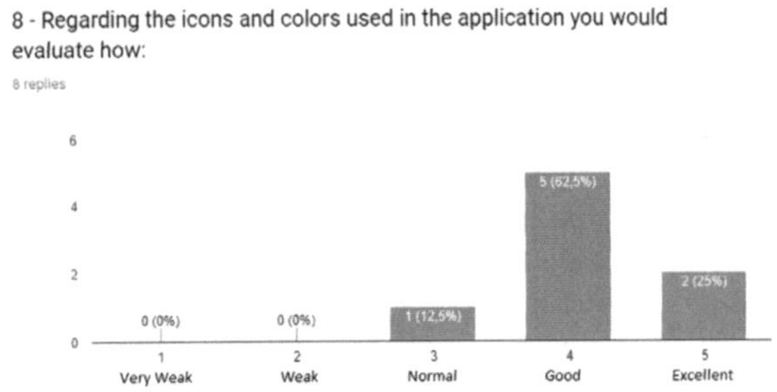

Figure 8 - Question 8 with the results on a sliding scale, where 1 is very weak and 5 is excellent.

The content available in the app was rated by 37.5% of the audience as very good, by 50% as good or acceptable, and by 12.5% as poor Fig. 9. The current content was inserted in the app for testing purposes; in the future it is intended for the teacher to insert the contents to be worked on in the classes.

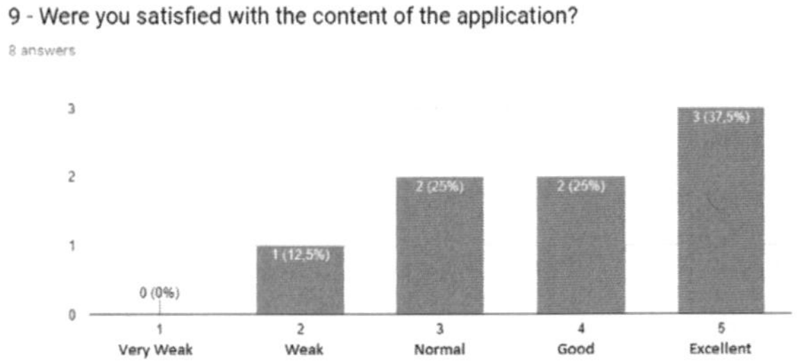

Figure 9 - Question 9 with the results on a sliding scale, where 1 is very weak and 5 is excellent.

Participants were asked for feedback and in this regard, and they pointed out failures in the operation of the buttons, suggestions as to the exchange and insertion of buttons on some screens and highlights for titles and images. Suggestions will be considered for future improvements in the app.

B. Description of the Prototype

The RAMED prototype, after four months in production, already has some functionalities ready such as: visualization of images of human organs in 2D, interaction by means of zoom, the possibility of consulting the menu for the course and downloading it and the possibility of giving feedback on use directly in the app. However, there are still other functions to be implemented such as Augmented Reality technology, the availability of high definition images and the definition of student and teacher users and their different operations within the app.

Some screens for the prototype are shown below.

Figure 10 - Demonstration screens: initial with logo and shortcut for menu.

Figure 10 is a Home Screen. This is the presentation of the application where the drawings of human organs are placed, and the name of the application highlighted. On the same screen, there is also a description of the application and a link to the course content.

Figure 11 - Demonstration screens: About and suggestion and complaint screen.

Figure 11 is the screen for "Suggestions and Complaints" where the user can report their experience and suggest any changes. The goal is to better understand the user experience by enabling future improvements in the usability of the application.

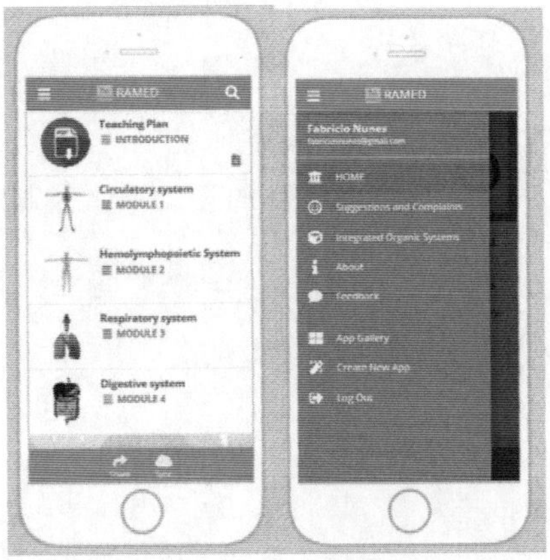

Figure 12 - Demonstration screens: side menu and suggestion and complaint screen and users choose the modules that divide the content.

In Figure 12 is the side menu with the application screen options. Each menu item directs the user to their needs. Note that the About, Feedback, App Gallery, Create New App, and Logout buttons will not be used for this app; the App Sheet platform [6] automatically inserts them. The available and functional buttons are Home, Suggestions and Complaints and Integrated Organ Systems.

The colors used are suggestive for the health area. There is also the screen with the application modules, where the contents are divided by a system with an illustrative figure on the side.

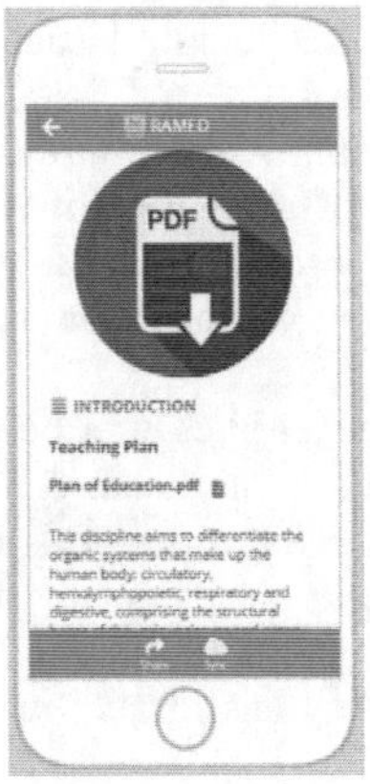

Figure 13 - Demonstration screens: Introduction screens.

Figure 13 is the "Introduction" screen, in which the content of each topic appears in summary form to facilitate the user's choice.

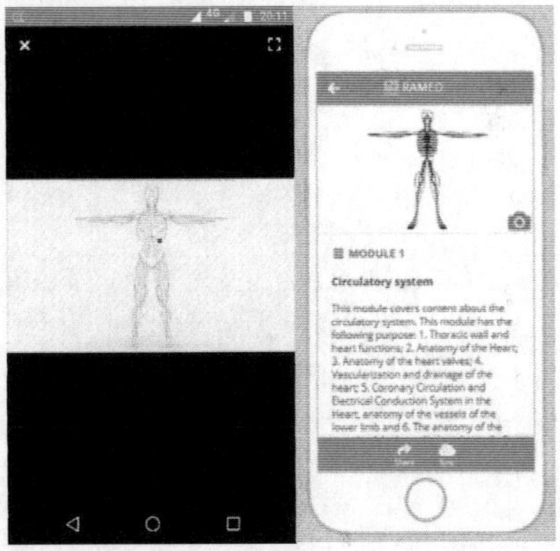

Figure 14 - Demonstration screens: Screen of the module with description of the content, and below the options of images and screen after choosing the image.

Figure 14 is the screen with module 1 which highlights the module number and the name. Below is a summary of the contents of the module. At the top is the figure representing the module. In the future the drawing in camera format will be the button to activate the AR attribute. On the right screen is the full screen image where the user can view the human tissues with resources for rotation, zoom and AR.

V. Conclusion And Future Work

We can verify that the use of AR provides an important learning tool for healthcare students in that it invigorates the applied content, presenting a new way of interaction between students and the anatomical structures presented. This important new resource allows the teacher to explore a new universe where virtual reality guides the students in approaching the objects of their studies.

Despite the fact that the project is still at an early development stage, it already presents practical uses by providing the students with a database of images accessible on the mobile device, facilitating visualization and study of the anatomical structures.

Even though the app is based on the resources provided by AR, at this stage of the project it is limited to the tool used for testing the prototype. The implementation of this important resource is planned for the next phases of development of the project.

In the near future, research will be conducted with the target audience in order to ascertain the effectiveness of the tool among students. Field tests will be carried out with undergraduate students in human anatomy, such as medicine, nursing, physical education and physiotherapy at higher education institutions located in the city of Palmas, Tocantins, Brazil.

Improvements will be made to the format with a focus on usability, utility, and content reliability. Teachers will also be consulted to give their opinion on the format.

The augmented reality feature will be implemented and access to it will be on the image preview screen, specifically through a button in camera format, as shown on the prototype screen in image 14. Titles will be inserted on each screen in order to improve the notion of location for the user.

REFERENCES

[1] W. M. Magalhães et al, "M-learning as a Motivational Method in Music Education", The Fourth International Conference on Human and Social Analytics - HUSO, 2018. in press.

[2] A. J. Manoel, "The technology revolution", Magazine Sitio Novo, Católica do Tocantins, Palmas, 2017. in press.

[3] B. Martins et al, "Mobile Technology to Support Didactic", Strategies, The Fourth International Conference on Human and Social Analytics - HUSO, 2018. in press.

[4] C. Moreira, "The math can be good", EDUCOMP. Rio Grande do Norte, 2018. in press.

[5] M. Santos, et al, "Mobile Technology and Conservation Areas: A Case Study", The Fourteenth International Conference on Wireless and Mobile Communications - ICWMC, 2018. in press.

[6] Appsheet, Available from: <https://www.appsheet.com/>, Accessed: 2018.10.02.

[7] Whatsapp, Available from: <https://www.whatsapp.com/>, Accessed: 2018.10.02.

[8] Google Forms, Available from: <https://www.google.com/forms/about/>, Accessed: 2018.10.02.

[9] A. Cardoso, et al, "Technologies and tools for the development of virtual and augmented reality systems", Editora Universitária UFPE (2007): 1-19.

[10] R. G. S. Cardoso et al, "Use of augmented reality in aid to education", Annals do Computer on the Beach, p. 330-339, 2014.

[11] B. M. Anami, "Good practices of augmented reality applied to education", Course Completion Work (College in Computer Science), State University of Londrina, v. 49, 2013.

FitoQuilombo - An App for the Cultural Maintenance of Medicinal Plants in *Quilombola* Communities

Gezivaldo Araujo Dias, José Valter Amaral de Freitas, Lucas Nunes Rodrigues, Sheyla Cristina de Castro, Walena de Almeida Marçal Magalhães

Federal Institute of Education, Science and Technology of Tocantins, Palmas, Brazil

E-mail: {gezivaldoa, josewalteraf, lucasbob19,

sheyla.cris}@gmail.com, walena@ifto.edu.br

Abstract—Quilombolas **are Brazilian traditional people who are descendants of black slaves from Africa. The present article discusses how technological tools can be used to help in maintaining their use of medicinal plants, in a cultural vision, to keep alive the history and culture experienced in two *Quilombola* Communities in the Northern portion of Brazil. It also treats environmental values as part of the history and cultural heritage of these people and discusses the contributions that knowledge of telematics can provide towards turning a regional culture into a source for ubiquitous knowledge. In this context, the importance of preserving and valuing the knowledge of these communities becomes urgent in the context of safeguarding the cultural diversity existing in the world.**

Keywords-Telematics; Culture; Quilombolas; Medicinal Plants; Ubiquitous Knowledge.

I. INTRODUCTION

Quilombola Communities are inserted in the concept of "Traditional People and Communities" - TPC - according to Quirino [1], and involve identity, historical, social and cultural peculiarities. In Brazil, since passing of the Law 6040/2017 [2] that deals with a National Policy for the Sustainable Development of People and Traditional Communities, conceptualization of the term TPC involves a legal framework. The third article of this Law defines traditional communities as culturally differentiated. Furthermore, it presents the forms of their social organization. In addition, *Quilombola* as a TPC use territories and natural resources as a means for cultural, social, religious, ancestral and economic perpetuation through practices produced and transmitted via tradition. This provides a guarantee of environmental conservation of their customs and institutions as fundamental rights defined by national and international legal systems. The legal instruments established in the country for the purpose of guaranteeing the cultural protection of *quilombola* communities also guarantee rights such as access to land, productive inclusion, infrastructure, citizenship and quality of life.

According to Vieira and Monteiro [3] estimates from 2004 indicated that Brazil had around 3000 Quilombola Communities distributed throughout the entire Brazilian territory, with less than half being catalogued [4]. Officially, the Brazilian National Secretariat of Policies for the Promotion of Racial Equality states that, by l 2013, the Palmares Cultural Foundation (PFC) had certified 2040 *quilombola* communities [5], present in the five regions of the country.

To be certified as a TPC it is necessary to request the beginning of a territory recognition process, which involves a Technical Report for Identification and Delimitation (RTID), analysis and rulings on appeals related to the RTID, recognition, decree and referral, removal of illegal occupants and titling. According to more recent data released for 2018 provided by PCF [6] Brazil has identified 3.051 remaining Communities of *Quilombos*, and has so far issued 2.547 certificates of recognition.

The state of Tocantins is one of the 27 federative units of Brazil, (NEDES) [7] located in the southeastern portion of the North region, occupying an area of 277,620 km². The state has 139 municipalities and its capital is the planned city of Palmas. The traditional communities are dispersed from north to south in the state of Tocantins. In Tocantins, 45 communities have been identified, of which 38 have a certificate of recognition as a TPC.

Initially, this research focuses on two of these Communities: Malhadinha Quilombola Community, located in the central region of the state, in the municipality of Brejinho de Nazaré, 90 kilometers from Palmas, the capital of the state; and São José Quilombola Community, in Chapada da Natividade, 210 kilometers from the capital.

The research intends to demonstrate how technology can help to maintain the culture of these communities, as a part of environmental knowledge.

This paper is organized into the following parts: After the Introduction, Section II presents relevant related works;

Section III presents the research proposal, showing the interdisciplinary relation between technology and cultural contents and materials and methods; and finally, Sections IV and V present the results, conclusions and suggestions for future work, highlighting how technology tools can help the communities in other areas, such as agricultural control.

II. RELATED WORK

Technology is ubiquitously used nowadays and can serve to turn local traditional knowledge into global knowledge, since it can provide solutions that offer information to the most diverse areas and problems. The use of mobile devices can be an example of that, playing a fundamental role in this dissemination process.

Pereira *et al.* [8] argue that technology can be complex to some people and that sometimes it is necessary to use easier tools, such as applications.

Magalhães *et al.* [9] also presented the use of a mobile App, created using an OpenSource tool, called AppSheet, that is an easier tool for use by people without specialized computing skills.

According to Santos *et al.* [10] mobile applications have already been used for environmental problems. They demonstrate the use of a mobile application for environmental preservation.

Regarding *Quilombola* Communities, Tesk [11] states that although globalization tries to bring cultural homogeneity, those *Quilombolas* resist through their culture, although they sometimes re-signify it.

Regarding TCP and healing practices, Auger *et al.* [12] say that it is important to have and provide access to traditional health care practices.

Thus, in order to continue pointing towards the use of mobile applications for social problem-solving in the path of mobility, this work presents a cultural catalog of medicinal plants, used as an alternative treatment for diseases, through the use of an App called FitoQuilombo.

III. PROPOSAL

The objective of this research is to solve a social problem in the environmental/cultural area, using technology as a support to aid in maintaining local tradition, by creating an application that can connect people and record *Quilombola* medicinal plants in a collaborative catalog. It presents two *Quilombola* Communities, both in the state of Tocantins, and the way they use medicinal plants, as an alternative method for treating diseases.

This research is based on two *Quilombola* Communities chosen by preliminary information and access provided by two researchers of this group who are themselves *Quilombolas.*

To solve the problem, the research group created an App that provides cultural information about use of medicinal plants by *Quilombolas*. The main challenges in doing this is that the communities do not have the appropriate access to technology, besides the fact that most young people, who are probably better at dealing with new technology, leave the community at an early age to study.

To identify how the tradition of using medicinal plants for disease treatments is culturally passed on, the authors need to register some plants, their therapeutic purposes, the best form of use and how *Quilombolas* prescribe them through a prior data collection with the members of Malhadinha and São João communities.

Because of the growing number of people with interest in medicinal plants, the App will be available to all people, providing anyone from anywhere in the world access the cultural catalog, which can facilitate the interaction of the public interested in obtaining the necessary information on medicinal plants, and sharing this cultural legacy.

This shows that telematics tools can directly help to maintain cultural knowledge, providing an evolution in aiding human social relations, and helping part of this process.

A. Materials

As mentioned before, one of the products from this research is an App called FitoQuilombo, developed using AppSheet [13], a free platform. The tool includes a catalog with *Quilombola* information, photos, and videos of medicinal plants, demonstrating how those people traditionally prepare and use them, with a brief presentation of each community (Figure 1).

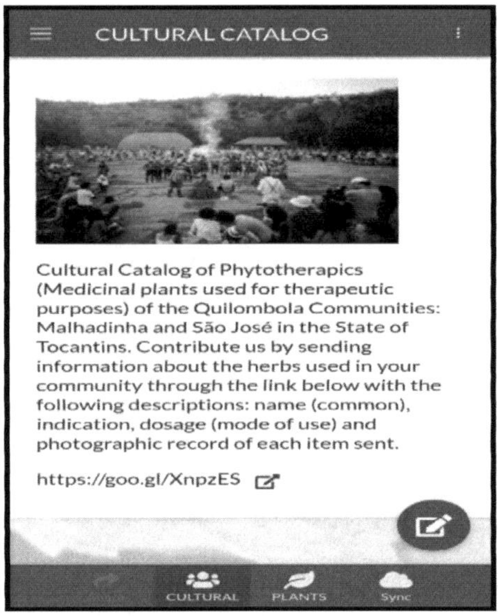

Figure 1. Presentation of communities.

The research was initially developed through meetings in the computer lab of the Federal Institute of Education, Science and Technology of Tocantins, Palmas Campus, using computers with Internet access, to carry out research on the project with the support of a tutor, who shared configuration techniques for creating a file with the commands and procedures to transform a machine with the Linux operating system into an access point.

Other tools were used for interaction between the research group and the tutor, enabling support from instant messaging Apps such as WhatsApp [14], and platform tools such as Google Family [15]: Classroom [16], Gmail [17], Forms [18], Drive [19], Doc's [20], Presentations [21], YouTube [22], and Screencasting [23].

To explore the possibility of using the Linux [24] operating system tools, the authors used the command terminal to develop a container docker, thinking of information from the project that will be stored. Work was done to configure a container docker and to install tools that provide a solution for the work, which was defined by the group. Still using the resources of the Linux command terminal, a draft of the solution proposed for the problem presented in the classroom was implemented by the tutor; he executed commands to access the server, change the password and access one of the machines in the laboratory, creating a subnet docker and a container connected to this subnet by installing net-tools.

B. Methods

This is a work in progress, using Problem Based Learning – PBL – as an initial method, where a problem is given and solutions are sought.

During the bibliographical research of related work, it was possible to identify a range of solutions, which apply to the problem that was identified. In this way, an application was designed that contains a catalog of medicinal plants, with an indication of use of these plants, in a collaborative context with the two communities, to offer information on the most diverse medicinal plants and indications for treating diseases.

A preliminary survey was carried out in Malhadinha Quilombola Community, with 64 families and 476 people. The research identified that in this community it is possible to have access to Internet, via mobile data, with a stable signal and some specific points in the community receiving a more stable signal. The community people have 16 smartphones used by the *Quilombos*.

The researchers investigated the empirical knowledge of medicinal plants available in the community, to learn what medicinal plants are in fact used for therapeutic treatment. Of the 64 families in the community, 22 were interviewed to identify which medicinal plants are used; the researchers identified 46 medicinal plants: *Mastruz, Babosa, Quebra Pedra, Tipi, Gengibre, Açafrão, Arnica, Arruda, Alecrim, Boldo, Cagaita, Hortelã, Inhame, Urucu, Unha de Gato, Manjericão, Arnica, Capim de Cheiro, Erva Cidreira, Laranja da Terra, Mulatinha, Alfavaca, Vinagreira, Açoita-cavalo, Cajá, Jatobá do campo, Pequi, Mangabeira, Mangaba, Cansanção, Fedegoso, Tamarindo, Inharé, São Caetano, Abacate, Negramina, Aroeira, Sucupira, Algodão, Assa Peixe, Amora, Cabelo de Milho, Jaborandi, Língua de Vaca, Noni* and *Quina*.

The FitoQuilombo App was developed on the AppSheet platform, with the help of spreadsheets created in Google Docs, which are formatted according to their use on App screens. Within the platform itself, there is a support area, where documentation is found to aid in setting up and adjusting the application. This documentation is presented in the form of text and video tutorials.

In the process of structuring the application it has a catalog of plants and herbs, which helps the user to know which plants and their parts to use for treating diseases and to perform tests and surveys with potential users of the application.

In addition to the configuration and development part, we use research to support this applied methodology. These searches are primarily done in other sites, and within the AppSheet development program itself, which has a library with documentation help as well as tutorials that demonstrate the development of the proposed functionalities, enhancing the application so that it performs the functions as desired.

Research was also carried out, with the help of a form created in Google Forms, where questions related to the use and application of herbal medicines contained in the application were made. The objective of this research was to evaluate the design of the system and also the relevance of creating this type of application, which is to inform the end users about the importance of preserving both the culture and the plants used in the preparation of these herbal products. This will be part of the FitoQuilombo virtual catalog. Given the results obtained with the research done through this online questionnaire, it is already possible to establish the need to design software of this nature, as the respondents desire.

Through analysis of the data obtained with these surveys, the need to make the interface of the application as intuitive and straightforward as possible was verified, since the users who will enter data to compose the catalog of plants of the system may be individuals who do not have much familiarity with mobile network technologies (smartphones and tablets), and may experience some difficulty in adding more items to the system.

This impediment can easily be remedied through guidelines on how to use the system, along with users who are part of the communities that will supply the application library with the registration of therapeutically valuable plants found in the communities that are part of this analysis.

IV. RESULTS

This paper had the intention of providing contributions as to how technology can serve as a s tool to maintain cultural identity in *Quilombola* Communities, focusing on registering their cultural use of medicinal plants through an App called FitoQuilombo.

Its purpose was to help transmit, teach and preserve *Quilombola* culture on a daily basis, creating alternatives that optimize the process of maintaining the local culture. It may be possible to adapt it for use by other traditional peoples around the world.

The registration of medicinal plants in FitoQuilombo App is described only culturally. These partial results were collected by bibliographical researches, previous visits to the communities, interface usability test of the App, information and application navigation, which allowed for improvements in the organization of the application structure.

The researchers tested the FitoQuilombo App with pharmacists and natural product users, and applied a heuristic usability assessment, presenting some considerations about the usability of the App prototype, using heuristics as basis for the decision, generating an order of analysis of the 10 Nielsen heuristics [25], on interface design, information, and navigation. Together with the navigation designer, they then analyzed the visibility of the application system with the argument that the application does not have information on where the user is browsing, meaning what screen the user is on. In possession of these considerations, we realized that one must insert titles in each screen in order to identify the screen on which the user is; in this case, the project will make changes to their screens, including the titles.

In analyzing the application, specifically in heuristic 10 concerning the help and documentation presented by the application, it was reported that: "The application does not have a 7- help menu or tutorial on how to use, or how it should work for a collaborator to send or register an alert". Based on this analysis, we emphasize what the group was already trying to put into practice, which is the provision of a tutorial to assist in user navigation, explaining the main steps, how to register an herbal medicine and how to send opinions to the designers of the application.

Mobile devices have a fundamental role in this process of information dissemination, enabling interaction with the world. The goal of FitoQuilombo is to allow the user to have a satisfactory experience when opening the application. He or she should be able, when using his catalog of herbs and medicinal plants, to carry out research for indicating a treatment for a particular disease and to be sure that this operation was done with confidence and responsibility in the information. Also, that the application is made available on hosting platforms, for users to download, and that the application fulfills its role without presenting technical problems that should have been solved during its development.

The FitoQuilombo project, presents an interface design, menus with two levels of depth to make usability accessible and direct, in interaction with clear and objective information in order to facilitate user navigation. A fault has been identified, which is the lack of title in each screen, as can be seen in the figure below:

The home screen of the application provides the menu of the home screen itself and the "medicinal plants" menu, allowing access to the catalog of medicinal plants. In the upper right-hand corner, there is the option of retrieving information contained within the application (Figure 2).

Figure 2. Application Home Screen.

The system contains submenus in which there is lateralized right-hand drop-down menu, with the following functions: "indication", "*Quilombola* Communities", "videos", "contact", "quilombola", "about" (Figure 3).

Figure 3. The layout of the menus.

The screen of the application provides images of the plants followed by their popular and scientific names; when accessing the image, it is possible to visualize and register the medicinal plants in the communities surveyed, providing information regarding indications, and mode of use by *Quilombos* (Figure 4).

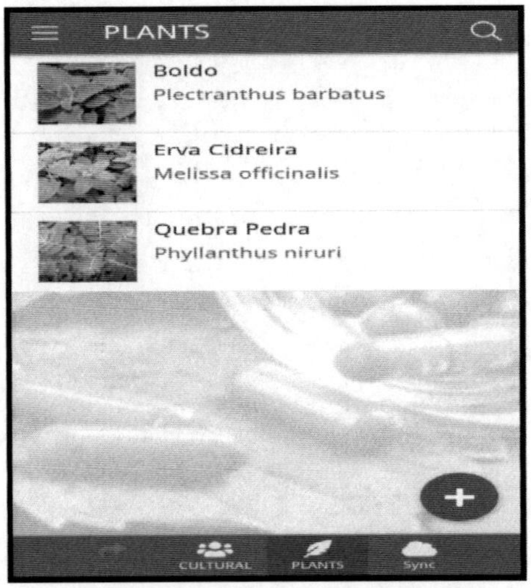

Figure 4. Catalog of medicinal plants.

The data obtained through the field research, for the development of the application, was used to produce a catalog of herbs and medicinal plants surveyed together with the Quilombola Communities; having this data, opens options for other works. Due to the unavailability of scientific research and the time needed to complete this project, scientific research of herbs and medicinal plants is recommended for future work, in search of validation of accessible knowledge, providing technical support to the communities involved.

V. CONCLUSION AND FUTURE WORK

Most activities for treating illness in the *Quilombola* Communities of Malhadinha and São José da Natividade in the state of Tocantins, can employ apps such as the one developed in this work as a viable alternative form of support for keeping the *Quilombola* culture alive in terms of its use of medicinal plants, along with technological growth among the people. A technology was sought to work collaboratively with the empirical knowledge of *Quilombos*, who are seeking alternative treatment for diseases.

At present, there is a growing number of people who seek herbal treatment, so an application has been designed that presents the recommendations, administration, and use of medicinal plants that are culturally used as an alternative treatment in the Communities. The conclusion is that technology is an excellent ally in disseminating information that contributes to society and that the empirical knowledge of *Quilombos* regarding medicinal plants can contribute to society.

Only some of the stated objectives we had proposed for this project were achieved. Due to the lack of communication via Internet it was not possible to test the application in the Communities described in order for them to use and feed this instrument.

This work is very relevant to environmental and cultural research in relation to the globalization of cultures, which depends on the technology that is the means for connecting us even at long distances. This issue needs to be deepened, because it allows a better understanding of this unification process. The culture experienced in *Quilombola* Communities is a local culture with its own identities, and we have been enabled to better understand their use of medicinal plants and to develop research, selection, organization, and information communication skills obtained with each *Quilombola* community.

This phase of the research deals with the partial survey of the results obtained with the study carried out on the need to catalog and keep alive the *Quilombola* culture, with its knowledge of medicinal plants that is passed on between generations by the members of the community and the form in which the authors presented their proposal for cataloguing and disseminating these teachings.

Future work could be done by testing the results of the App use by the Quilombolas communities, and also with further investigation of technology that can help organic production, as well as with automation of the irrigation of medicinal herbal gardens, avoiding the excess and waste of human and natural resources.

REFERENCES

[1] F. B. Quirino, "Diagnosis of Violations of Rights and Situation of Sovereignty and Food and Nutrition Security in Brejo dos Crioulos, Brasília, DF, FIAN Brazil 2017. [Online]. Available from: <http://fianbrasil.org.br/download-diagnostico-de-violacoes-de-direitos-brejo-dos-crioulos-mg/> Accessed: 2018.07.18.

[2] Brazil, "Decree n. 6040/2017 of February 7, 2007. National Policy for the Sustainable Development of Peoples and Traditional Communities". [Online]. Available from: <http://www.planalto.gov.br/ccivil_03/_Ato2007-2010/2007/Decreto/D6040.htm>. Accessed: 2018.07.20.

[3] A. B. D.Vieira ; P. S. Monteiro, "Quilombola community: analysis of the persistent problem in health attention under the focus of the Intervention Bioethics".[Online]. Available from:<http://www.scielo.br/pdf/sdeb/v37n99/a08v37n99.pdf> . Accessed: 2018.11.07.

[4] Brazil. Presidency of the Republic. Secretariat of Policies for the Promotion of Racial Equality. Foundation University of Brasília. Profile of the quilombola communities: Alcântara, Ivaporunduva and Kalunga. Brasília: SEPPIR; FUB, 2004a.

[5] ________. Presidency of the Republic. Secretariat of Policies for the Promotion of Racial Equality. Quilombola Communities. [Online]. Available from:<http://www.seppir.gov.br/comunidades-tradicionais/programa-brasil-quilombola> Accessed: 2018.11.09.

[6] ________. Presidency of the Republic. Ministry of Culture. "Palmares Cultural Foundation" [Online]. Available from: <http://http://www.palmares.gov.br/wp-content/uploads/2018/01/QUADRO-GERAL-29-01-2018.pdf.> Accessed: 2018.08.10.

[7] ________. Presidency of the Republic. Secretariat for Economic Development, Science, Technology, Tourism and Culture, [Online]. Available from: <https://seden.to.gov.br/desenvolvimento-da-cultura/>. Accessed: 2018.10.12.

[8] A. G. Pereira *et al.,* "Comparative study of tools to facilitate the development of mobile applications ". IX South Brazilian Congress of Computing - SULCOMP, UNESC, 2018. Santa Catarina. [Online]. Available from: <http://sulcomp.unesc.net/arquivos/comunicacao_oral.pdf>. Accessed: 2018.04.10

[9] W. Magalhães *et al.*, "M-learning as a Motivational Method in Music Education". The Fourth International Conference on Human and Social Analytics - HUSO, 2018.

[10] M. Santos *et al.*, "Mobile Technology and Conservation Areas: A Case Study". The Fourteenth International Conference on Wireless and Mobile Communications - ICWMC, 2018.

[11] W. Tesk, The Wheel of São Gonçalo: a process case study folk comunicacional. 4th edition. Goiânia: Kelps. 2018.

[12] M. Auger *et al.*, "Moving toward holistic wellness, empowerment and self-determination for Indigenous peoples in Canada: Can traditional Indigenous health care practices increase ownership over health and health care decisions?". Can J Public Health, [S.l.], v. 107, n. 4-5, p. e393-e398, dec. 2016. ISSN 1920-7476. Available at: <http://journal.cpha.ca/index.php/cjph/article/view/5366/3477>. Accessed: 2018.11.06

[13] Google Sheets, [Online]. Available from: <https://www.google.com/sheets/about/>. Accessed: 2018.04.18.

[14] Whatsapp, [Online]. Available from: <https://web.whatsapp.com/>. Accessed: 2018.04.03

[15] Google Searches, [Online]. Available from: <https://www.google.com.br/>. Accessed: 2018.04.03.

[16] Google Classroom, [Online]. Available from: <https://classroom.google.com>. Accessed: 2018.04.03.

[17] Google Gmail, [Online]. Available from: <https://www.google.com/gmail/>. Accessed: 2018.04.08.

[18] Google Forms, [Online]. Available from: <https://www.google.com/forms/about/>. Accessed: 2018.04.09.

[19] Google Drive, [Online]. Available from: <https://www.google.com/drive/>. Accessed: 2018.06.09.

[20] Google Docs, [Online]. Available from: <https://www.google.com/docs/about/>. Accessed: 2018.04.04.

[21] Google Presentations, [Online]. Available from: <https://docs.google.com/presentation/d/1-uiNPN7AYESC2XxM_LHZJmAUWrWGWmXJRpg23ljBZzs/edit#slide=id.p>. Accessed: 2018. 05.18.

[22] Youtube., IFTO Post Telematics - Mobile and Converged Networks - Lecture 06 [Online]. Available from: <https://www.youtube.com/watch?v=d-IzKcXYo28&t=7780s>. Accessed: 2018.06.26.

[23] Screencastify The #1 screen recorder for Chrome, [Online]. Available from: <https://https://www.screencastify.com/>. Accessed: 2018. 06.07.

[24] Operating system Linux, [Online]. Available from: <https://www.ubuntu.com/>. Accessed: 2018.04.05.

[25] N. Jakob, Nielsen's Ten Heuristics. [Online]. Available from: <https://nptel.ac.in/courses/106103115/Handouts/M4L4.pdf> 2018.09.13.

Augmented Reality as a Technological Solution in the Teaching/Learning Process in Civil Engineering Course Classes: a Case Study

David Araujo and Luiz Philipe
Federal Institute of Education, Science and Technology
Palmas, Brazil
E-mails: {iftodavidpereira, lpadias}@gmail.com

Abstract - **This paper is about the use of Augmented Reality (AR) in civil engineering classes at Federal Institute of Education, Science and Technology, Palmas, Brazil. It considers that AR is an expanding technology that is already used in some areas and can also be applied to education. AR can provide support for the teaching/learning process provided to the student through visualization and manipulation since learning improves when one sees what is being explained in a dynamic image. This kind of technology adds information and improves the current educational environment. This article proposes a solution with an application to assist teachers, more specifically concerning an undergraduate course in civil engineering.**

Keywords-Technology; Telematics; Augmented Reality; Civil Engineering; Education.

I. INTRODUCTION

Traditional methods are still used for teaching students in most universities, colleges and schools around the world. However, those methods have proved to be insufficient, considered in terms of their efficiency [1]. Students want a more dynamic approach in the classroom and this is possible with the use of technology. Augmented reality can be used to bring a new approach to a class, making it a more an exciting experience.

This research focuses on the challenge of developing an application with the use of AR as a contribution to expanding the concept of learning from theoretical to practical experiences. The purpose of the application developed is to serve as a teaching material resource for teachers to assist them in their classes and allow the students to empirically explore some key concepts of the Basic Sanitation I and II classes, which are undergraduate courses in civil engineering and as a proof of concept regarding the efficiency of augmented reality use in the teaching/learning process.

In this work we present an easy way for developing augmented reality solutions, without the need to know computer programing. We then introduce the AppSheet tool as the means for doing that.

II. RELATED WORKS

We will present in this section, some works that use the Google Appsheet as an easy way for developing solutions involving database and cellular applications, in order to demonstrate the real importance of the Google AppSheet tools for facility the development and database operation. Currently, technology is being used to offer ubiquitous information solutions for all areas and problems. Mobile devices provide a fundamental contribution in this process of disseminating information. Magalhaes et al. [2] also presented the use of a mobile application, created using an Open Source tool, to complement the teaching of music in second-year high school classes. The authors have demonstrated the improvement in student results, through implementing classes with the use of this tool and with subjective evaluations provided by students.

In this regard, Manoel [3] claims that cell phones and tablets are more common than TV sets nowadays, and there are, on average, four mobile devices per person in a middle-class family.Santos et al. [4], on the other hand, show that mobile applications can be applied in environmental preservation areas. To this end, the authors developed an application that generates a kind of social network where anyone can check to see if there is some triggering event, spontaneous or caused by human activity, which is compromising rivers, forests, etc. The application can take photos of the event and send them to the network in real time and with the exact location, public agents can act.

Based on these numbers, Moreira [5] presents a solution to complement the teaching of mathematics at the elementary school level, with the use of a mobile application. According to the author, the use of this application in mathematics classes, aided by the fact that all the students have a mobile device, has made school more attractive for students, since all of them focus more on exercises, knowing that the answers will be provided by cell phones and ranked as if in a game.

Mobile applications are also being used to streamline administrative procedures. This was proposed in Martins et al. [6], where with the help of a mobile phone, teachers in the city of Palmas, Tocantins, can have quick access to the result of a national student ranking test, called "Provinha Brasil", that shows indicators of use of learning in Portuguese Language and Mathematics courses. These indicators provide important information so that teachers may respond within the same school year, using methodological innovations to help students make up their deficiencies.

Therefore, in order to continue to encourage the use of mobile applications for resolving problems with the help of mobility, this research presents the construction of a mobile application that uses AR as a tool for assisting teachers in their classes.

III. PROPOSAL

According to Brighenti et al., even if students study for a long time, this may not be enough for them to adequately understand the topics presented by the teacher/professor. That happens because many students do not interact with the teacher in the classroom. Because of that, interaction with a teacher is probably the best way to encourage students for effective participation in or out of the classroom. The application of technology for improving availability of data content in the classroom can be a step towards improvement over the traditional methodologies.

Given that technology is currently present in various areas and that advances in information technology are changing the lives of everyone, it is necessary to include IT in educational processes. It is possible, with the use of AR, to improve some methods or methodologies in the teaching-learning process used in the classrooms.

Civil engineering is an area that requires considerable work from teachers and students. Technological resources may bring more interaction in the classroom and may make the classes more attractive. The possibility of viewing objects in 3D and interacting with them, can provide teachers and students with a new experience in the learning/teaching process.

This paper proposes the development of a solution to assist undergraduate course teachers in improving the reality of the teaching/learning process and its objective is to assist the education professionals involved in teaching in the state of Tocantins with this technology tool. The case study proposes to support teachers in the civil engineering course with a case study in Basic Sanitation classes. This solution can aid professors of any area, through the use of technological resources that enable collaboration that can help students to shorten the distance between theory and practice in the classroom through information technology.

Below is an image that graphically explains the flowchart of the solution. Figure1.

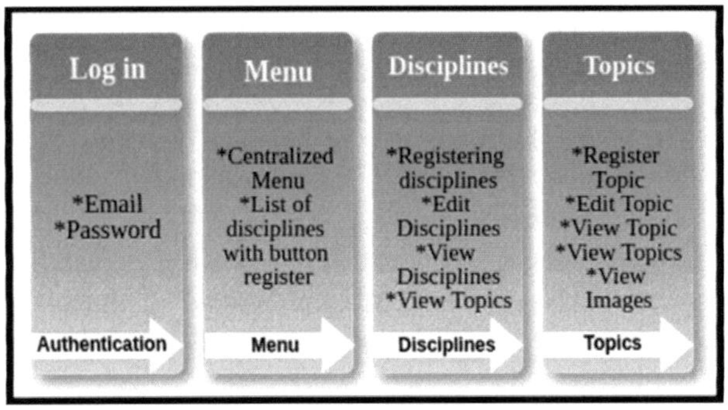

Figure 1. Solution Flowchart.

As seen in Figure 1 above, the screens are being presented, i.e. the modules of the proposed solution. The Minimum Viable Product (MVP) has a login screen, a course menu, and a menu of topics. Users will be able to access these screens with a few clicks and thus access the content provided by the teachers. The application has two levels of access: Administrator level for teachers to manage content and Default level for users accessing digital files via mobile device.

A. Materials

The materials used to develop the MVP, the prototype called AR applied in civil engineering (S.C.A.T.) used the AppSheet [6] tool of Google [7] that is simply software in a Web platform that enables the development of mobile device-independent devices in a simple and dynamic way.

Not only does the AppSheet stand out due to its practicality and agility in the development of mobile applications, but another striking quality in this software is it's the integration with the free Google tools, notably Google Drive [8] used for storing data and application information. In this scenario, Google Sheets [9] were used as a database to store application settings and data during development and testing.

During the construction of the MVP the laboratory of the graduate course in Telematics of the Federal Institute of Tocantins was used, where the implementation of the tasks proposed by the group and the use of the tools cited above were also done. Computers (desktops) in the Telematics laboratory were used during the classes as well as personal smartphones of the researchers with IOS and Android operating systems. All those tools guaranteed that the content produced during the work was safe and available at any time, in the cloud. Below is the list of materials used in this research:

- Desktop computer with Linux operating system Ubuntu version 16.04 LTS.
- Personal email accounts, Gmail [10] email provider, from survey participants.
- For the construction of application usability validation forms, Google Forms [11] was used, due to its practicality in sharing with respondents.
- To produce the application flowchart, the software was used on a web platform called Cacoo [12].
- To test the prototype, the personal smartphones of the researchers were used, these being: a 5s from Apple with operating system version 11.2.6 and J5 of Samsung with operating system version 6.0.1.
- For dissemination and sharing of the link to forms, social networks were used: Facebook [13], Instagram [14], Twitter [15] and WhatsApp [16], with the aim of involving a larger number of respondents.

B. Methods

This Section will present the methodology used in the solution proposed in this article. The research was developed in the Graduate course in Telematics. The work of the research group consisted of meetings in the Computer Science Laboratory of the Federal Institute Palmas campus, alternating with some virtual meetings. According to Magalhaes et al. "since the course uses Problem-Based Learning (PBL) methodology, the first part of each meeting was dedicated to solving problems that were presented to the research group by a tutor. The second part of the meetings was dedicated to the search for solutions."

For virtual meetings the research group used tools such as YouTube [17], WhatsApp, Gmail, Hangouts [18], Docs [19], Sheets, Slides [20], Forms, and Overleaf [21]. In order to provide students and teachers with technological tools to support the process in the classes using information technology, much of the research was dedicated to creating an application as a solution capable of providing content such as high-quality images, related to civil engineering in digital formats available in the cloud and accessible through mobile devices such as smartphones, regardless of the operating system of the device.

A review of the literature was first carried out to assemble the necessary requirements for development of the Augmented Reality in Civil Engineering (RAEC) application, with an emphasis on learning and assimilation of content.An MVP was created, which is simply a version of the application with the minimum possible features, but that maintains the essence and all the features proposed for the application. During application development the research group was guided by a tutor in the process of developing the initial and other test versions.

To develop the application with the AppSheet tool, three electronic spreadsheets were used that contained data to model, create the tables and serve as a database for the application. During construction of the project Programming Object Orientation (POO) techniques were applied to create the tables of courses, topics and menus, since the configuration of the AppSheet tool for the display of contents was inherited from the experience of researchers in the area of programming and software development.

After creating the application database through the worksheets created by the research group, these were imported into the AppSheet tool, assuming that the tool allows creation of an application in three ways, namely: building an application from examples set by the tool itself, from a blank template or from existing data in spreadsheets. The research group chose the third option. After choosing which option to follow, it was necessary to inform the name of the tool and the application category. The initial functions of the application are: Add, edit and delete.

Soon afterwards, the authors began working on the flow that users would use to have access to the content that the application would provide. To create the flow the authors used the Cacoo tool mentioned in the previous section. After discussing and drawing the flow of application functionality and navigability, the research group began the application design improvements, that is, the authors began to insert pertinent to the civil engineering course; the researchers also put in buttons and icons, changed the standard fonts of the texts and customized Application default messages.

For the testing phase of the application, when implementing the functionality of the application, in order to make all the necessary configurations in the tool for the perfect functioning of the prototype the researchers had to enter the App Stores of survey participants' smartphones and install the AppSheet application to have access to the project developed. Fictitious data were thus removed and then data such as the course name were added to the main screen of the application, along with the courses and all the information in the fields created in modeling the tables. These courses served as the case study.

Tests of the application were carried out by all the students and the faculty of the Graduate course in Telematics and participating friends of the researchers; the tests were necessary for the prototype to obtain contributions of opinions, suggestions and criticisms so that the Group could have the chance to analyze possible improvements and functionality of flow and design in the application. The application was tested by more than 40 people who contributed to the advancement of the proposed solution.

IV. Results

A public opinion survey was carried out with the students in the graduate course on usability improvements and navigability of the prototype for the proposed solution with the research presented in this article and the results obtained through the preparation of five questions with an emphasis on usability and navigability, with each issue containing ten alternatives, on a scale of one to ten. With this research, it was possible to create an MVP version of the proposed application and this version went through several tests to analyze inconsistencies in the project, including tests on multiple platforms.

With this research the research group attempted to extract information that would add value to the design of the application as well as enable the navigation flow so that people could conclude an activity in a few steps and thus have rapid access to the contents available in the application. Below is the graph with results obtained from applying the questionnaire. The questions applied were: Did you encounter any difficulty in navigating between the screens? Regarding usability of the application, can you easily identify what screen it is on? Has the application adapted to the screen size of your Smartphone or Tablet? Can you identify what kind of application this is?

For the first question, according to Figure 2 we obtained a percentage of 77.8% replying "yes," while 22.2% replied "no."

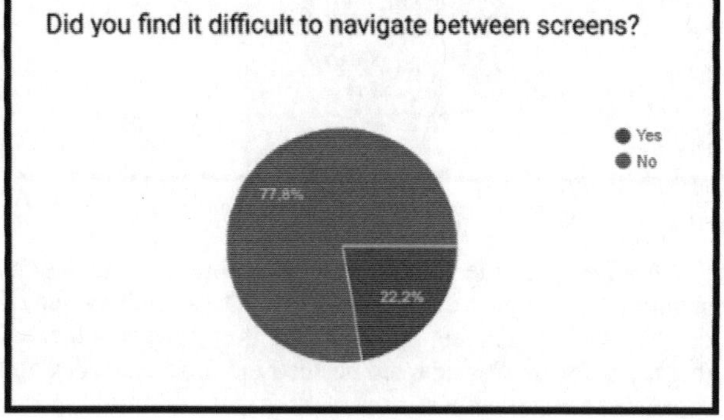

Figure 2. Graph with the answers tothe first question in the form.

The graph in Figure 2 presents the result of the answers obtained from the first question applied in the design evaluation questionnaire for the RAEC application to measure the navigability of the prototype on the different screens of the application This result was considered satisfactory by the researchers, because the App is still in the early stages.

For the second question, according to Figure 3 the results were that 90% answered "yes" to question two, while 10% of the answers obtained in question two were "no."

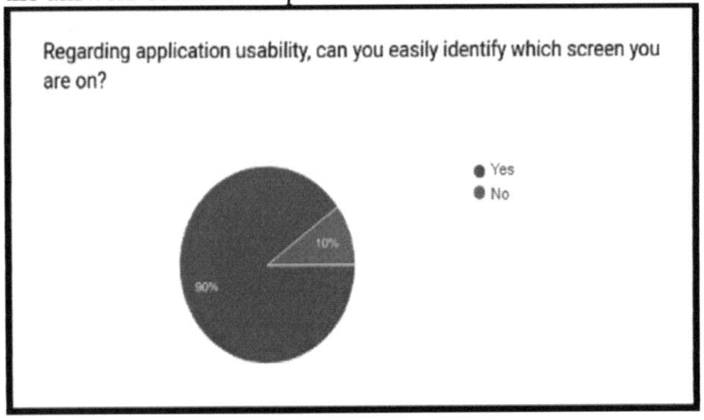

Figure 3. Graph answers to question two.

Figure 3 shows the percentage of responses obtained through application of questionnaire, question 2, to evaluate the usability design of the application; the results were satisfactory for the researchers because 90% of the people who answered the questionnaire said they were able to easily identify which screen they were on.

In question 3, the goal was to analyze the application's adaptation across multiple smartphones and platforms. According to Figure 4, the results were that 100% of the people who tested the application said that it adapted as expected.

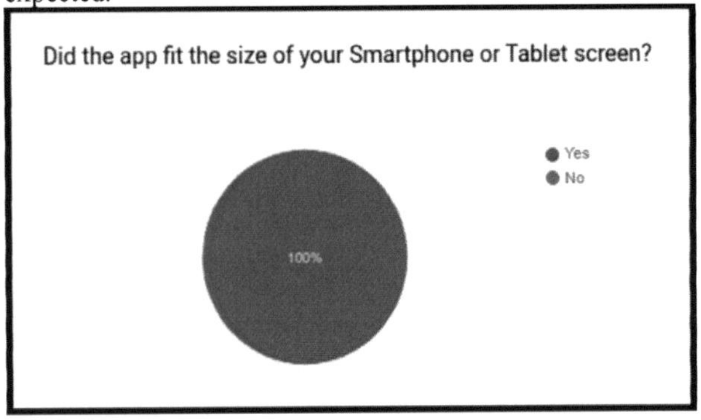

Figure 4. Graph with the answers to question 3.

In Figure 4, the graph is used to present the results acquired by applying the questionnaire. Question 3 evaluated the behavior of the application, and the answers indicated that the software was adapted perfectly in different types and screens of mobile devices.

For the fourth question, according to Figure 5 a total of 77.2% answered "yes" to question 4 and 22.2%, replied "no." This is a positive point for motivating researchers to follow up on the research. That is because the App is still at an early stage. Nonetheless, 77.8% of the people who answered the questionnaire affirmed that they were able to identify the application.

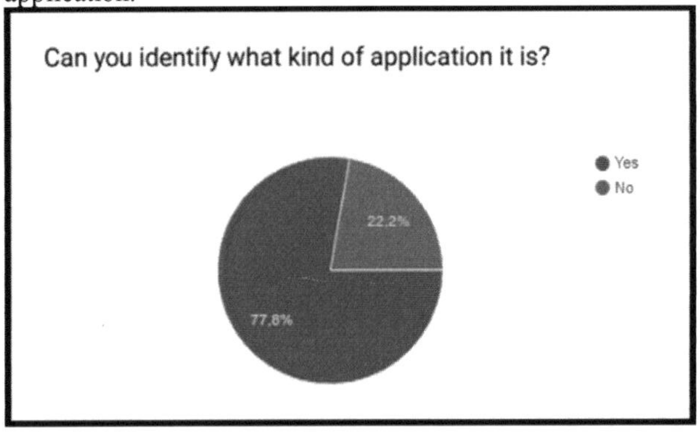

Figure 5. Graph Graph with the answers to question 4.

The graph presented in accordance with Figure 5 shows the result of question 4 used to evaluate whether the people who tested the prototype were able to identify what type of application was being used, and once again the result was satisfactory for researchers.

For the fifth question, according to Figure 6 we obtained a total of 90% "yes" answers to question 5, while 10% replied "no."

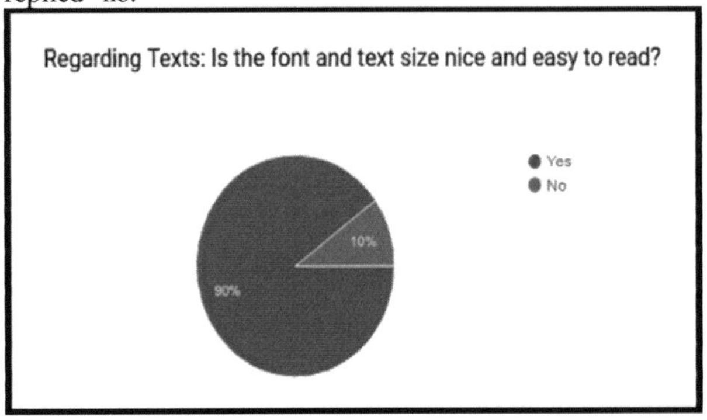

Figure 6. Graph with the answers to question 5.

According to Figure 6, the graph presented above shows the result of question 5, which elicited information as to whether the texts: fonts and sizes of the texts had a pleasing appearance and were easy to read by users who tested and responded to the Questionnaire. The graph shows that 90% of people answered positively.

A. Expected Results

The MVP developed by researchers provides all the features proposed for the final version of the application that will be used by teachers of Basic Sanitation I and II of the civil engineering course, except that the use of augmented reality increased the presentation to an hour, with static images presenting the topics to be addressed by these project courses.

For better contextualization of the features proposed by the application developed by this research group follows the screenshots of the main application screens.

Figure 7. Home screen and screen listing courses.

According to Figure 7, the prototype has several screens: the first image of Figure 7 is the main screen, that is, the home screen for the app. When any user of the app is accessing it, the software will start on this screen. The second picture in Figure 7 is the course menu screen after the user has passed the main screen and selected the course to be consulted. On this screen the user can choose which course to access and verify the details of the chosen course; the user can also edit or add a new course.

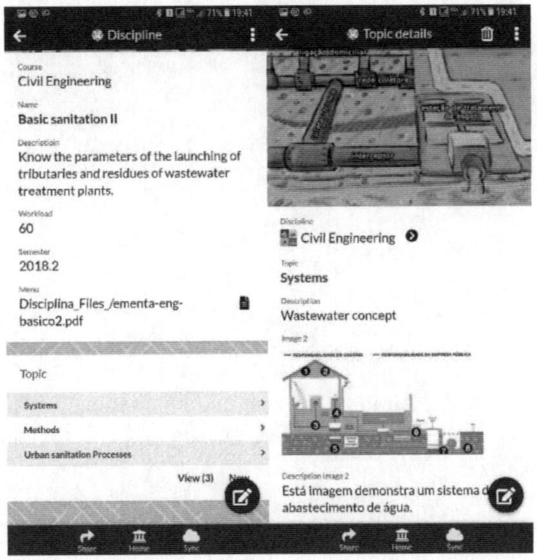

Figure 8. Screen details of the courses and screen listing topics.

When accessing a specific course, the user will have access to the details of the course, in addition to adding a new topic and accessing any of the topics covered by the course, according to the first image of Figure 8. When selecting a topic, the user can view the information that is available for this topic and also edit it.

The expectation of the research group is that the final version of the application will have all the functionalities presented in the above figures, along with the implementation of a new functionality that will utilize augmented reality technology. That functionality is added in the second image of Figure 8, and with this new functionality users can point the camera from their mobile devices to a bookmark that will display virtual images on their device that can be manipulated by users.

V. Conclusion and Future Work

The authors believe that information technology can continue to make major contributions to education; this has been demonstrated over time with the use of multimedia resources used in the classroom. Newer technologies, such as microcomputers, smartphones, and tablets must also be used in the classroom. It is in this sense that the research reports presented in this article show that the authors believe that technology can change the teaching-learning scenario. Based on the research, the authors believe that with the use of technology in the classroom it is possible to more quickly identify the weaknesses of each class or even of each student in using technological resources.

This prototype mobile application focuses on being a tool towards a solution for educational problems than can assist the teacher and the students in the classroom in a more intuitive, faster and effective way. It is worth pointing out, therefore, that there is a need to invest in education technology. In light of that, the expectation of the researchers is that this prototype can be tested in the educational environment and provide contributions to professionals for possible improvements and thus become a useful tool with more updated versions.

However, some obstacles still exist: the lack of financial investments in Brazilian schools for research and implementation; difficulties in access to new technology by the students; and of course, integration of AR as proposed in our research. To that end, further research will be needed on the subject and new implementations will remain to be dealt with in future work, so that they can provide the expected results being empirically tested in the classroom.

References

[1] J. Brighenti, V. Biavatti, T. Souza, "Methods of teaching-learning approach in the perception of students" GUAL Magazine. 2018, pp. 2-22.

[2] W. Magalhaes, D. Magalhaes, J. Carvalho, J. Monteiro, and C. Monteiro, "M-learning as a Motivational Method in Music Education," The Fourth International Conference on Human and Social Analytics - HUSO, 2018, pp. 2–8.

[3] J. Manoel, "The technology revolution, "New Place Magazine. Catholic of Tocantins, 2017, pp. 10–16.

[4] M. Santos, E. Martins, J. Scarton, J. Edmundo, W. Oliveira, and C. Monteiro, "Mobile Technology and Conservation Areas: A Case

Study," The Fourteenth International Conference on Wireless and Mobile Communications - ICWMC, 2018, pp. 20–16.
[5] C. Moreira, "Math can be good," EDUCOMP, 2018, pp. 21–27.
[6] B. Martins, G. Quixabeira, L. Barros, and C. Monteiro, "Mobile Technology to Support Didactic Strategies, "The Fourth International Conference on Human and Social Analytics - HUSO, 2018, pp. 2–6.
[7] "AppSheet," 2018, Available from: https://www.appsheet.com/ [accessed: 09-18].
[8] "Google," 2018, Available from: https://www.google.com/ [accessed: 09-18].
[9] "Google Drive," 2018, Available from:https://www.google.com/drive/ [accessed: 10-18].
[10] "Google Sheets," 2018, Available from: https://www.google.com/sheets/about/ [accessed: 09-18].
[11] "Google Gmail," 2018, Available from: https://www.google.com/gmail/ [accessed: 10-18].
[12] "Google Forms," 2018, Available from: https://www.google.com/forms/about/ [accessed: 09-18].
[13] "Cacoo," 2018, Available from: https://cacoo.com/ [accessed: 10-18].
[14] "Facebook," 2018, Available from: https://www.facebook.com/ [accessed: 09-18].
[15] "Instagram," 2018, Available from: https://www.instagram.com/ [accessed: 09-18].
[16] "Twitter," 2018, Available from: https://twitter.com/ [accessed: 09-18].
[17] "WhatsApp," 2018, Available from: https://www.whatsapp.com/ [accessed: 10-18].
[18] "Youtube," 2018, Available from: https://youtube.com/ [accessed: 10-18].
[19] "Hangouts," 2018, Available from: https://hangouts.google.com/ [accessed: 09-18].
[20] "Google Docs," 2018, Available from: https://www.google.com/docs/about/ [accessed: 10-18].
[21] "Google Slides," 2018, Available from: https://www.google.com/slides/about/ [accessed: 09-18].
[22] "Overleaf," 2018, Available from: https://www.overleaf.com/ [accessed: 10-18].